D0996858

Get Happy

ALSO BY GERALD CLARKE

Capote: A Biography

GERALD CLARKE

GET HAPPY

The Life of Judy Garland

LITTLE, BROWN AND COMPANY

A *Little, Brown* Book

First published in US by Random House in 2000
First published in Great Britain in 2000
by Little, Brown and Company

Copyright © Gerald Clarke 2000

The moral right of the author has been asserted.

All rights reserved.
No part of this publication may be reproduced, stored in a
retrieval system, or transmitted, in any form or by any
means, without the prior permission in writing of the
publisher, nor be otherwise circulated in any form of
binding or cover other than that in which it is published
and without a similar condition including this condition
being imposed on the subsequent purchaser.

A CIP catalogue record for this book
is available from the British Library.

ISBN 0 316 85595 2

Printed and bound in Great Britain by
Clays Ltd, St Ives plc

Little, Brown and Company (UK)
Brettenham House
Lancaster Place
London WC2E 7EN

TO L. A. S.

once again, for faith and fortitude

Forget your troubles and just Get Happy

You better chase all your cares away

Sing Hallelujah, come on, Get Happy

Get ready for the judgment day.

from "Get Happy,"
a song often sung by Judy Garland

Contents

Get Happy

Frank and Ethel Gumm in their vaudeville costumes

Ethel and Frank

He came from a little town in the South, and his smile was as spacious as summer's sun. She came from an even smaller town in the far North, and her eyes, so dark that they were almost black, were as sharp as winter's wind. But for both of them, the home of the heart was neither north nor south, nor in any other direction the compass pointed. It was a simple wooden platform, and it could be anywhere, any size, any shape: no stage was ever too mean or insignificant for Frank and Ethel Gumm.

They had grown up to the sound of applause, and they met, in late 1911 or at the beginning of 1912, at the Orpheum Theater— a "picture house," as such places were then called—in Superior, Wisconsin, a rowdy, lively port at the western end of Lake Superior. The city, which still retained much of its frontier exuberance, boasted many such establishments, and the creaky wooden sidewalks of its main street, Tower Avenue, were crowded with people just like them, all eager to break into the big-time world of vaudeville.

Ethel pounded out the background music for the films that

flickered on the Orpheum's screen. Frank sang the songs of the day while the reels were being changed. Far from his home in Tennessee, he rented a room from her parents, John and Eva Milne, and romance blossomed. It died when he suddenly upped and left, then unexpectedly sprang to life again when he returned many months later, in the late summer or the fall of 1913. He took a job at the Parlor Theater, she played the piano at the Lyric, which was across Tower Avenue, and they picked up where they had left off.

This time Frank did not bolt, and on December 31, 1913, they were issued a marriage license by the Douglas County clerk. There was apparently still some reluctance to take the final step, however, and Frank carried that weighty document around in his pocket for more than three weeks. But at five o'clock on the afternoon of Thursday, January 22, 1914, their roller-coaster courtship ended at last. Standing before a newly ordained Episcopalian priest, they exchanged vows in the parlor of the Milnes' house on Banks Avenue. Ethel wore a gown of ivory silk and carried a bouquet of roses. Her younger sister, Mary, was her maid of honor, while Alfred Street, Jr., who was often seen at the Superior theaters, stood up as best man for Frank.

After the bridal dinner, the little wedding party bundled up against biting winds and temperatures that hovered just a few degrees above zero—winter is a serious affair in that part of the world—and crossed the St. Louis River to the neighboring city of Duluth, Minnesota. There the festivities continued in a box Ethel's father had reserved at Duluth's leading vaudeville house. Topping the bill that night was one of the era's most popular singers, Ernest R. Ball, whose best-known song might have been written for the occasion—"Love Me and the World Is Mine," it was titled. With its sweet lyrics still humming in their ears, the young couple—she was twenty and he was twenty-seven—said their good-byes and boarded a train for their honeymoon in Minneapolis and Chicago.

The motion-picture era was just starting, but one scenario was already a screen standard: boy meets girl, boy and girl part, boy and girl are reunited for a happy ending. And that familiar script, observed the *Superior Evening Telegram,* was the one that had been followed so faithfully by the happy bride and groom. Their romance, said the paper, had rivaled some of the melodramas shown in the theaters in which they worked: fate, which is the "arch enemy of the god of love," had separated them; but they had found their way back to each other, allowing Cupid to triumph in the end, "as he always does in good moving picture plots." But good moving picture plots never tell everything. So it was with the sentimental scenario the newspaper had sketched for Frank and Ethel: their story, then and later, was not what it appeared to be.

|||

After leaving Tennessee, sometime between the end of 1910 and the first part of 1911, Frank had traveled through several states before arriving, in the fall of 1911, at the Head of the Lakes, as the Duluth-Superior area was called by its boosters. He was to travel through many more states before he returned in 1913. Ethel, by contrast, had never ventured far from the often turbulent waters of Lake Superior, the largest of all the Great Lakes, near which she had been born, had grown up, and now had married.

Her parents were Canadian. Her father, John Milne (Milne was pronounced with one syllable and rhymed with "kiln"), was the son of Scottish immigrants. Born in Hamilton, Ontario, in 1865, he was a railroadman, as his father had been, and he had crossed the border in 1888 to take a job with the Duluth, South Shore & Atlantic Railway, whose trains ran along the south shore of Lake Superior. Ethel's mother, Eva Fitzpatrick Milne, most likely had also been born in Ontario, in the town of Cornwall in 1864. But her family—her father was a shoemaker—apparently moved to Massena, New York, across the St. Lawrence River, when she was a child. It was most likely in Marquette, Michigan, a busy lake port like Superior, that John and Eva met. It was there that they married in 1890, and it was also there that Ethel, the first of their eight children, was born on November 17, 1893.

John Milne remained with the South Shore line for many years, advancing from fireman to engineer, from a job that had him shoveling coal into the locomotive boiler to one that had him actually driving the train. The Milnes lived in several towns in Marquette County, but it was Michigamme, where they lived from 1903 or 1904 until the late summer of 1910, that Ethel knew best. With no more than six hundred inhabitants, Michigamme provided few obvious amenities. Sanitation meant backyard outhouses—even the school relied on such uncouth facilities—and winters were so bitter that money was made by hacking ice, sometimes as much as two and a half feet thick, from Lake Michigamme and shipping it to cities that lacked such natural refrigeration.

Yet if life in Michigamme could be harsh and forbidding, it also could be remarkably congenial. Amusements were all homemade. People in Michigamme did not pay to be entertained; they made their own fun. Most nights during the winter there was a dance, a basketball game, or a meeting of one club or another. When the snow melted in the spring, doors burst open and the residents rushed outside, like prisoners released from jail. On Independence Day the South Shore Line lowered its fares, and people from all over the county converged on Michigamme, which was famous for the enthusiasm with which it celebrated the nation's birthday.

Energetic and outgoing, the Milnes had a prominent role in the life of the town, particularly its musical life. Both John and Eva sang and played instruments—he, the violin; she, the piano—and in the early years of their marriage, they occasionally toured those northern precincts with their own medicine show, drawing the curious with their music, then coaxing them to buy an evil-tasting laxative that was derived from the bark of the cascara tree.

Some parents impart to their children a love of reading or of sports, and their offspring become writers or athletes. John and Eva taught a love of music, and their sons and daughters became singers and pianists. Performing was like breathing, and almost as soon as they began walking and talking the Milne children were singing, dancing or practicing on a keyboard. There was scarcely a waking hour when a chord was not sounded or a note was not struck in their house on Railroad Street. They may have lived in the backwoods, far from opera, symphony or vaudeville, but no family anywhere was more eager to please an audience than the Milnes of Michigamme.

The first to follow in their parents' footsteps were Ethel and her younger brother, Jack. Teaming up to play, sing and dance at school parties, they left such a vivid impression that they rated a special mention in the town's centennial book, which was written more than sixty years after they had left. Ethel was not the most gifted of the musical Milnes—Jack, Mary and Norma vied for that honor—but she was the most versatile. She could sing, play the piano, dance, even write songs; indeed, when it came to music, she could do almost anything passably well.

In an age of faith and piety, John Milne was a proud and vocal agnostic. He went so far as to name his third son after Robert Ingersoll, the late-nineteenth-century thinker who toured the country lecturing against orthodox religion. Just as Ingersoll delighted in making it hot for "the dear old stupid theologians," as he once phrased it, so John, who was perhaps too fond of the bottle, seemed to enjoy making it hot for his dear old Episcopalian wife. Possessed of an equally strong will, Eva matched him insult for insult. Their bickering never stopped, and despite all the music, there was not much harmony in the Milne house.

Ethel had inherited her parents' strength and obstinacy, as well as their love of music. Tirelessly energetic, unconquerable in spirit, she relentlessly pursued what she wanted, keeping to the chase no matter how long it took. None of the other children had anything like her force, and her relationship with her parents, Eva most particularly, was never easy. She and her mother argued and fought, yet were closer, paradoxically, than more compatible pairings, constitutionally incapable, it seemed, of being apart for very long. If he did not know it then, Frank was soon to discover that he was not just marrying one of the Milne daughters, he was marrying the entire clan.

"Pretty Miss Milne," the Superior newspaper had called Ethel. But that was the flattery accorded all young women on the day of their wedding. Neither pretty nor ugly, she belonged to the great majority, the plain. Her face was unremarkable except for her eyes, which were not only unusually dark, but also slightly crossed. She was short, no more than five feet tall, and somewhat stout, like all the other Milne women. At twenty she already had a matronly figure. All in all, her marital prospects had appeared so dim that Maude Ayres, a soprano who also worked at the Orpheum, was amazed when she announced her marriage to Frank, who was considered something of a catch.

Ethel was lucky to get him, was Ayres's opinion, and who would have disputed her? Everyone who knew Frank in those days said that he was good-looking—some thought him handsome. A little above average in height, about five feet nine inches tall, he had dark hair, blue eyes and a round, open, pleasant face. What most people recalled, however, was not his looks, but his captivating manner. He could bring more cheer to a gloomy afternoon than the best Tennessee bourbon. Decades after he had left the South, people there could still picture, as vividly as if he were standing there before them, the young man with the songs and the smiles. "Always happy, laughing" was how one woman remembered him, adding that "when Frank dropped around, the music began." One fact can be stated at the beginning: no one ever disliked Frank Gumm.

|||

His Tennessee roots ran strong and deep. Both the Gumms and the Baughs, his mother's family, had lived there since the beginning of the nineteenth century, when it was still pioneer country. That was when John and Mary Baugh were born, and they were already middle-aged—Mary was in her early forties and John was over fifty—when Frank's mother, Clemmie, was born in 1857. Clemmie was the last of the Baughs' six children, and the fact that Mary Baugh was past the ordinary time for childbearing may have contributed to her daughter's lifelong infirmity: Clemmie was an invalid from infancy.

By contrast, John and Martha Gum—some, even some in the same family, spelled the name with one "m"—were young when Frank's father, William Techumseh Gumm, the first of their seven children, was born in 1854. Will married Clemmie in 1877, but instead of taking her away to a home of their own, as most husbands do, he moved into the Baughs' large and handsome house in Murfreesboro, on East Main Street, the address of most of the town's gentlefolk. Built in the Federal style, with thick brick walls, a fourteen-foot-wide central hall, and ceilings twelve feet high, the house had enough room for Clemmie and her new husband, as well as for the three boarders Mary Baugh was forced to take in after John Baugh died in 1870.

During the years to come, it was also to be home to the five Gumm children. Invalid though she was, Clemmie gave birth once every three years. Mary, the only girl, came first in 1880; then Robert in 1883; Frank in 1886 (March 20, to be exact); William in 1889; and finally Allie in 1892. Although money was scarce, life on East Main Street seems to have been pleasant enough. The five children were apparently close, and one relative remembered a parlor that reverberated with song. Like the Milnes, the Gumms were devoted to music.

Situated in the geographic heart of Tennessee, astride a vital rail line, Murfreesboro had been a strategic, much contested prize during the Civil War. Though it never regained the wealth it had enjoyed before the cyclone of war whirled through, it was, when Frank was growing up, a pleasant place to live nonetheless. With a population of only five thousand, half of which was black, it was small enough to retain a village flavor—pigs and cows wandered freely through the streets—yet large enough to offer such urban pleasures as a theater.

Many traced their ancestry back to Virginia, and they liked to think that they also retained the refined manners of the Old Dominion. Conversation was the common currency, and by universal custom, houses were built close to the street so that residents, sitting on their porches, could gossip with passersby. Everyone knew who was up, who was down, and whose husband was sneaking off for some illicit pleasure in Mink Slide, the red light district. People were allowed few secrets in Murfreesboro.

Money was admired but not venerated, and the Gumms remained people of respectable standing even as their financial situation descended from bad to desperate. Two years after Mary Baugh's death in 1892, her big house was sold, and Will and Clemmie had to move their brood into a cramped brick cottage nearby, one of three or four dwellings Clemmie had been left by her mother. Worse followed. Clemmie herself died in October 1895, when she was only thirty-eight. Then, three months later, fire partially destroyed the overcrowded brick cottage. With no home, no money and no prospects, Will asked the Rutherford County Chancery Court to give him permission to use most of his children's slim inheritance to buy a larger and more comfortable house four blocks away on Maney's Avenue.

This was only one of several trips Will made to the court, which officially pronounced him insolvent. His children's sole support was the tiny income that Clemmie's properties brought in. Court records make no mention of an illness or handicap that would explain Will's inability to hold a job—he testified only that he could not find one—and it seems likely that he had been dependent on his wife's family from the day they were married. Whatever the reason for his fecklessness, it caused hardship for his children. He did not have money to educate them beyond public school, and after using up most of their legacy to give them more space in the new house, he was forced to crowd them together again to make room for a paying boarder, a young doctor from Mississippi.

|||

For Frank, rescue came, as if by divine intervention, from the richest man in town, George M. Darrow. Darrow and his wife, Tempe, lived in the town's finest house, Oak Manor, a graceful Italianate villa in which they entertained with lavish seven-course dinners. Tempe, whose family owned plantations in Alabama and Mississippi, had always been rich; it was her money that had bought Oak Manor and that paid for all those fancy dinners. But George had grown up poor in Nebraska, and he liked helping young people who were in the position he himself had been in.

Armed with Tempe's money and his own determination, Darrow, whose nickname was "the Boss," always got what he went after. When he could not find American workmen who could restore Oak Manor the way he wanted, he imported craftsmen from Europe. When he could not find a church of his own Episcopalian faith in Murfreesboro, he proceeded to establish one. Its modest frame building on South Spring Street looked downright puny by comparison with the stately structures of the long-dominant Baptists, Methodists and Presbyterians, but St. Paul's had something the others could envy: it had Frank Gumm, whose voice had so captivated the Boss that he had recruited him to sing in his choir. Darrow's church could not match the attendance numbers of its bigger rivals; but with Frank singing solo, his boy's soprano as pure and sweet as childhood itself, it surpassed them all in its musical devotions.

Just two years younger than Will Gumm, Darrow became Frank's godfather, a role he fulfilled, as he did all others, with unrestrained vigor. In June 1899, three months after Frank's thirteenth birthday, Darrow plucked him out of poor Will's beleaguered household and sent him off to an Episcopalian boys' school, the junior adjunct of the University of the South, or Sewanee, as it was usually called. Frank's voice had been his deliverance, and Darrow had procured him a scholarship to sing in the Sewanee choir. "I am sure neither you, or any of those interested will ever have cause to regret helping this bright boy along," Darrow wrote the school's head, Lawton Wiggins. "He knows that he is taken for *his services in the choir,* and that he must be ever anxious to render service to his benefactors." On the morning of June 13, a few days before the start of the summer term, godfather and godson journeyed by train to Sewanee, which was about sixty miles southeast of Murfreesboro. Darrow personally presented his young charge to his new benefactors, thus beginning what Frank was later to call "six of the happiest, the most beautiful years of my life."

Not much known outside the South in those years, Sewanee inspired the fanatical devotion of all those associated with it. Set high on the Cumberland Plateau, about eighteen hundred feet above sea level and often referred to simply as "the Mountain," it was an academic aerie that had little to do with the troubles of the world below. It was set "in the middle of woods, on top of a bastion of mountains crenelated with blue coves," wrote Frank's friend and schoolmate William Alexander Percy, in his richly brocaded autobiography, *Lanterns on the Levee.* "It is so beautiful that people who have once been there always, one way or another, come back. For such as can detect apple green in an evening sky, it is Arcadia."

Along with a rigorous dose of the classics, Sewanee taught manners and style, how a gentleman behaves. Small and friendly, it was, as Percy noted, "a place to be hopelessly sentimental about and to unfit one for anything except the good life." It suited Frank exactly, and he suited it exactly, doing what Darrow had promised he would do—he filled the chapel with glorious song, in a voice that eventually matured into a brilliant tenor. Writing of the Easter services of 1900, the student newspaper, the *Purple,* said that such beautiful music had never before been heard at Sewanee, and it singled out Frank's solo for its purity of tone.

|||

"Hurrah! Hurrah! Sewanee boys are we" went the words to the college song. "Away with melancholy and let care and trouble flee, while we are at Sewanee." But at the end of 1904, his second year in college, Frank's carefree youth ended abruptly. With two years left to go before graduation, he ended his academic career and returned to Murfreesboro, probably to help support his impoverished family. Will Gumm died in 1906, and for the next four years Frank worked as a stenographer and court reporter by day and at night performed at a theater owned by an uncle, Walter D. Fox.

In 1909 he left those familiar surroundings for the town of Tullahoma, a resort and health spa about forty miles to the southeast. His uncle Walter, who was the state secretary of a fraternal organization called the Knights of Pythias, was building a home there for the widows and orphans of deceased Knights. Ovoca, he named it, and he took Frank along as his secretary. Joining Frank in Tullahoma were his sister Mary, who was still unmarried at twenty-nine, and his sixteen-year-old brother Allie. All three lived in a small frame house on East Lincoln Street, half a block from St. Barnabas's Episcopal Church. In this new setting Frank's voice once again opened doors. He sang in the church choir, he joined a quartet that was much in demand for parties and weddings, and before long he was associating, as one prominent Tullahomian said, "with our best people." Universally admired, he seemed to have as bright a future as any young man in Tennessee. But by the end of 1910, or possibly the first part of 1911, he was gone—gone from Tullahoma, gone from Tennessee, gone from the South itself.

In those days most American towns had at least one theater that offered live entertainment. In all probability Frank traveled from stage to stage, along a third-string vaudeville circuit. By September 1911, the date of his next documented appearance, he knew the business well enough, in any event, to buy his own small theaters. In the most unlikely of spots, the logging town of Cloquet, Minnesota, he became a show-business entrepreneur, purchasing both the Bijou and the Diamond. "Mr. Gumm impresses one as a very capable young man in his line of endeavor and most desirous of pleasing the theatre-going public of Cloquet," said the *Cloquet Pine Knot.* Yet weeks after he had taken them over, this very capable young man inexplicably handed over his Cloquet theaters to his older brother, Bob, and moved twenty miles east—to Superior, the Orpheum Theater and Ethel Milne.

|||

Frank and Ethel first approached the altar in 1912, not long after they had met. Ethel was so certain that they were getting married that she boldly—and rashly—invited Frank's singing partner, Maude Ayres, to a between-shows engagement supper on the Orpheum stage. Ethel had an enviable knack for making a little seem like a lot, and she transformed a card table into a festive board, covering it with a crisp white tablecloth on which she placed fried chicken, salad, rolls, glasses of champagne, even a wedding cake. With no other company than the rows of empty seats staring at them from the darkness below, the three of them toasted their friendship and peered happily into the future. But Ethel had celebrated too soon. Before they could make their vows official, Frank had skidded off, leaving Superior as abruptly as he had left Tullahoma and Cloquet.

By his own count, Frank visited twenty-eight states during the months that followed, once again, it seems likely, traveling the vaudeville circuit and performing in out-of-the-way towns like Cloquet and in theaters like the Bijou and the Diamond. Eventually he landed in Portland, Oregon, where, for a year or more, he managed the Crystal on Killingsworth Avenue. But Portland, which was then a bustling, rambunctious port city much like Superior, did not keep him, either. By the autumn of 1913 he was back in Superior, singing at the Parlor on Tower Avenue and resuming his romance with Ethel, whose determination to marry him apparently had never wavered during the many months he had been away.

Since leaving Tennessee, Frank had moved around the country at a dizzying pace, like a bullet that had missed its mark and now ricocheted aimlessly. At times his behavior—his sudden departure from Cloquet, for example, which was followed by an equally hasty exit from Superior—

seemed bizarrely erratic. But Frank was not crazy, and actions that appeared irrational were in fact eminently sane. For Frank had a secret that explained everything: he was basically homosexual, and his advances to young men and teenage boys sometimes made him unwelcome in the towns in which he took up residence. Cloquet was one of the places he had been forced to leave. "He was accused of being a pervert and he had to skip town and get out fast," said Ayres.

When the news reached Superior, he found it expedient to leave there as well. "Everybody in Superior was talking about it," said Ayres. "I was shocked because I had had no idea that there was anything like that going on." What Ethel thought, no one can know, but when Frank returned at last in the fall of 1913, she was ready to say yes to his proposal. Their wedding on that cold afternoon in January was indeed a victory for the god of love, just as the Superior newspaper had said it was. What the paper did not say—what it did not know—was just how impressive little Cupid's triumph had been.

|||

Frank's days of frantic zigzagging were over, and for a decade and more he and Ethel seemed likely to conclude their story with a happy ending. As if adhering to the newspaper's hopeful script, they left Superior soon after their honeymoon for one of those star-spangled, all-American towns that movie studios would later go to elaborate efforts to reproduce on Hollywood back lots. There, in Grand Rapids, Minnesota, surrounded by lakes and forests and all the bounty of a generous nature, they made their home. And there they begat three daughters who followed them onto the stage as soon as they were out of diapers. All three had talent. One, the youngest, possessed genius.

This new life began on March 5, 1914, when the newlyweds were hired to run the New Grand, one of Grand Rapids' two theaters. Frank was the manager and singer; Ethel was the piano player, providing sound effects for the silent pictures, as she had done in Superior. The team of Gumm & Gumm was an instant success—"Frank Gumm continues to please his audiences by that rich Southern brogue," the *Grand Rapids Herald-Review* was soon to say—and their arrival quickly spelled the doom of the New Grand's only competitor, the Gem. Frank and Ethel had found their niche in show business, small though it was.

At the beginning they probably did not think of Grand Rapids, which was just eighty miles northwest of Superior, as much more than a temporary stop, a way station at the start of a long journey. Like all other young performers, they nursed ambitions to play on bigger stages in bigger cities: Minneapolis, St. Louis, Chicago, someday perhaps even New York. During their months together, they had worked up an act, and they were eager to try it out on the circuit. Jack and Virginia Lee, Sweet Southern Singers, they called themselves. "Gumm" was not a name that danced across theater marquees.

Jack and Virginia may have sung sweetly, but Frank and Ethel did not want to give up the security of steady jobs in Grand Rapids on the mere hope of success. They therefore asked the New Grand's owners, James Barlow and Fred Bentz, to let them go for the winter, then come back in the spring. Bending the truth to suit the need, they said that they wanted to spend the winter in Florida with Frank's parents, both of whom were permanent residents of a cemetery in Murfreesboro. To make it easier for the owners to say yes, they recruited two of Ethel's siblings, Jack and Mary Milne, to fill in for them while they were gone. Barlow and Bentz agreed, and in the middle of December 1914, Frank and Ethel set out to make it in vaudeville.

Their first stop, which was not so far away, was Cloquet, where Frank's indiscretion of three years before was overlooked, if not forgotten. Their second was Superior. Florida may indeed have been their eventual destination, but both their trip and their dream ended in Chicago, where Ethel came down with such a severe case of the flu—it bordered on pneumonia—that she could not rise from her bed for three weeks, and then only to exchange it for another one in her parents' house in Superior. On February 20, 1915, two months after they had left, the Gumms were back in Minnesota, their visions of bright lights reduced to just one, the solitary lamp that hung over Grand Rapids' main intersection, the only streetlight in the entire village. Yet Ethel's illness may have been a blessing. Talented as they were, their act had more spirit than polish, by all accounts, and Jack and Virginia Lee almost certainly would not have risen to the top, or anywhere near it. A case of the flu had probably saved them from years of futile struggle and a succession of dreary, third-rate hotels.

If they felt defeated at being back in Grand Rapids—and so soon—they did not admit it. Whatever disappointment they experienced was lightened, in any event, by the record crowd that greeted them their first night at the New Grand. He had seen a large number of towns, Frank told the *Herald-Review,* but "not one of them looked any better to him than Grand Rapids and that the chances are that he will hereafter be content to remain here."

And so for many years he was. Pokegama Avenue may not have been as glamorous as Broadway, or even Tower Avenue in Superior, but audiences clapped just as loudly at the New Grand as they did at any of the other theaters in which Jack and Virginia Lee had hoped to appear. Grand Rapids, moreover, had at least one advantage over the perilous vaudeville trail: it was a good place to raise a family. Suddenly that was a matter of concern, for Ethel was pregnant, and probably had been even when they were in Chicago. Perhaps luck, which seemed to have conspired against them then, had been on their side all along.

|||

Their future decided at last, the Gumms did not waste time settling down, and in mid-March, three weeks after their return, Frank purchased a half-ownership in the New Grand. No longer were he and Ethel show-business gypsies, and on September 1, 1915, after nearly twenty months of living in hotels and rooms, they rented a house on Kindred Avenue. They had scarcely unpacked when Ethel gave birth to an eight-and-a-half-pound girl. Born on September 24, she was named Mary Jane.

As far as outsiders' eyes and ears could tell, the next few years were happy, almost halcyon ones for Frank and Ethel. Since both had grown up in small towns, they had no trouble adjusting to Grand Rapids, which had a population of no more than three thousand, not counting wayward deer, wolves and bears. For those who did not mind the Siberian winters, it was a spot of natural enchantment. Adorning the landscape in every direction were dozens of lakes—not oversized ponds pretending to be lakes, but real lakes, sparkling sheets of sapphire blue, four within the village itself. As if they did not provide enough of a watery vista, flowing through the middle of town was the Mississippi River, which began its long journey not far to the west, in the chilly depths of Lake Itasca.

Timber gave Grand Rapids its start, and although the dense pine forests that had once covered Itasca County had largely disappeared by the time the Gumms arrived, the manufacture of wood products was still the major local industry. Business was generally good. If few in Grand Rapids were rich, few were poor, either. Just about everybody could afford the ten or fifteen cents it cost to get into the New Grand, which, under Frank's direction, was not just a place of entertainment but a social center. "The public likes Mr. Gumm because he not only insists upon an entertaining but also a clean performance," said the *Herald-Review,* and the theater's Thursday afternoon matinees became a childhood ritual in Grand Rapids.

Though they had banished their hopes of becoming vaudeville stars, Frank and Ethel had not given up the stage. Jack and Virginia Lee were never to play the big cities, but they did play Bigfork, Bemidji, Hibbing, Taconite, Warba, Floodwood, Coleraine and Deer River. As if working at the New Grand and touring with Frank were not enough, the indefatigable Ethel also directed amateur musicals and joined a jazz quartet. "Just one busy lady," was how one frequent visitor described her, always noisily rushing up or down the stairs, singing at the top of her lungs.

Frank moved at a slower, Southern pace, but he was no less active. Half-ownership of the New Grand had not made him rich, and to supplement his income, he took a part-time job as a reporter for the *Itasca County Independent.* Most of his information he gathered walking around town and stopping off, as he did most mornings, for a dish of ice cream and a song at the confectionery store. "We had a piano in the store," said Mabel MacAdam, who was the manager. "He'd come in early to get the news and sometimes we'd play the piano and sing for half an hour or so." Seen here, there and everywhere, Frank and Ethel were as well-liked as any couple in town—an ideal pair, as far as outsiders could judge.

So life progressed for the Gumms, in a steady, unsurprising way. They rented several different houses before at last buying a simple frame house at the corner of Hoffman Avenue and West Fourth Street, a short walk from the New Grand. They often visited Ethel's relatives in Superior and in Duluth, and they were visited even more often by the Milnes, who joined them in their favorite pastime, singing and playing: a grand piano sat in the living room, and atop the piano sat a violin. The Southern Gumms, Frank's sister, Mary, and his brothers Bob and Will, dropped in for a week or two, and twice Frank drove his own family down South. "I always liked his little wife," said one of his aunts. "But, you know, she was a Northern girl."

On July 4, 1917, Ethel gave birth to a second daughter, Virginia, and both girls eventually made their debuts, singing and dancing, on the stage of the New Grand. As far as Ethel was concerned, two children were enough, however, and when she became pregnant again in the fall of 1921, she did everything she could to induce a miscarriage, swallowing strong doses of castor oil and sitting through stomach-churning car rides over bumpy roads. Nothing worked, and in November Frank drove to Minneapolis to ask the assistance of a young friend, Marcus Rabinowitz, a second-year medical student at the University of Minnesota whose father ran a theater much like Frank's in a little town northeast of Grand Rapids.

"Marc, I'm in trouble," Frank told Rabinowitz. "I've got to talk to you. You know, we don't have much money and we're just getting along decently. We've got the two little girls and Ethel's pregnant. We cannot have another baby." Could Rabinowitz help with an abortion? The answer was a loud and emphatic no. "Frank, it can cost Ethel her life," replied Rabinowitz. "You can't do this. I will not permit you to. It's impossible. I want you to go back and tell Ethel that I personally guarantee that she will think that it was the luckiest day of her life when she didn't do it, and that she will have the happiest baby in the world."

Convinced or not, Ethel now had no choice in the matter. Preparations were made, friends were told—"the Gumms are expecting another stick," went the joke—and a name, Frank Junior, was selected: after two girls, a boy was expected. Nature had other plans, and on June 10, 1922, Ethel gave birth to her third child, a seven-pound girl. Not giving up entirely, the disappointed parents gave her the first name of Frances. For her second name they chose Ethel. Thus, in name as well as body, she was a combination of both of them: Frances Ethel. But she was rarely called that. As she was the youngest, she was known as Baby, and Baby was the name to which she answered.

||

"The beginning of my life was terribly happy," she was later to say, and in the years to come the woman who had been Baby Gumm looked upon Grand Rapids as her own lost Eden, a place of peace and serenity hidden amid the lakes and forests of that northern latitude. The prism of memory transformed an ordinary Midwestern community into "a magnificent-looking town" and exalted a plain house, whose only visible attraction was a purple honeysuckle bush next to the front door, into "everything that represents family: clean, old-fashioned, beautiful, not frightening, and a gay, good house." What she really remembered— and what made a homely house beautiful—was the contentment she had known there, a contentment shared, so she thought, by everyone around her. "That's the only time I ever saw my mother and father happy," she said, "in that wonderful town."

That wonderful town provided the kinds of innocent pleasures that can be recalled today only with a twinge of nostalgia. In the summer there were family excursions to nearby lakes, secret forays to steal cherries from a farmer's orchard, walks to the blacksmith's shop to watch the sparks shooting from his anvil, and tearful burials of the unfortunate birds that ended their lives in the Gumm backyard. Parked across the street was the candy wagon, a never-ending delight for a little girl with a sweet tooth. A cheerful contraption with a bright red body and yellow wheels, it sold everything good: popcorn, chocolate, caramel apples and ice cream.

Winter meant the snow that was to symbolize the unsullied simplicity of those years. Highlight of the season was Christmas Eve, when Frank left work early to help his daughters make angels in the snow. Falling backward into that thick blanket, they waved their arms and legs, then jumped up, leaving behind the impressions of angels, complete with wings and gowns. All four then rushed inside to marvel at their handiwork from an upstairs window and to warm themselves with the cups of hot malted milk Ethel had waiting in the kitchen. Almost every night, winter and summer, Frank brought home a treasure from the box office, a sack of pennies for their trips to the candy wagon.

The only dark spot on that agreeable picture—the only blotch that Baby saw, anyway—was illness. Frequent ear infections required her to endure painful lancings, followed by hours in which her ears were covered by socks filled with hot salt. More serious was a stomach ailment, most probably acute acidosis, that threatened her life in September 1925. Frank and Ethel rushed her to a specialist in Duluth, where she was hospitalized for nearly a week. Neither of her sisters had suffered such afflictions, and Baby was all but smothered with attention, as sickly children often are. As much as she had been unwanted in the fall of 1921, so was she wanted—spoiled, pampered and petted—in subsequent years.

No one could have accused Ethel, who made Baby's dresses, filled the socks with hot salt and sat by her bed in the hospital, of being an inattentive mother. But Frank was more than attentive. He worshipped her, and Baby reciprocated with all the ardor of a small but passionate heart. "At night before he went to the theater," she said, "I used to crawl up into his lap in a white flannelette night suit while he sang 'Danny Boy' and 'Nobody Knows de Trouble I've Seen' for me. It was a bedtime ritual in our house for Daddy to get me ready for sleep, and it was one I loved." The older girls spent their days in classrooms, while Baby sat beside her father as he drove around town. No princess on her throne could have looked prouder than did the little girl on the front seat of Frank's Ford.

By 1924 Mary Jane and Virginia—Jimmie was her nickname—were appearing regularly at the New Grand. No one asked whether Baby would join them; everyone knew that she would. The only question was when. The hint of an answer came in August. Ethel was in Duluth for a goiter operation, and to cheer them up, Frank took his daughters to see the newest act at the New Grand, the Blue Sisters, three girls who ranged in age from five to eleven. Baby, who was only two months past her second birthday, was all but uncontrollable with excitement, humming when the sisters sang, bouncing up and down when they danced. When the youngest sang a solo, she suddenly became quiet, as if transfixed. Only at the end did she break her silence. "Can I do that, Daddy?" she asked.

She had seen her future and she liked it, in the following weeks badgering both parents for permission to go onstage with her own sisters. "Later, not yet, honey," they said. "Wait a bit." Finally, toward the end of the year, Ethel started rehearsing her for her debut. Eva Milne made plans to come from Superior, and a date—December 26, the night after Christmas—was announced in the *Independent:* "Added attraction for Friday evening: The three Gumm girls will entertain in songs and dances featuring Baby Frances, two years old, Virginia seven and Mary Jane 9. The little girls will appear between the shows at 9 o'clock."

There are several versions of what happened between nine and nine-twenty that night, but Jimmie's version is probably the most reliable. As Jimmie told the story, the curtains opened to reveal the two older sisters. They were midway through their newest song, "When My Sugar Walks Down the Street," when a third voice was heard and they made room for a tiny figure with huge dark eyes who had been hidden behind them. After two more numbers, Baby was left alone to sing "Jingle Bells," which she punctuated by jingling a real dinner bell. Laughter filled the theater, and Baby was so thrilled that instead of bowing off at the end, she sang all the verses again—and again and again. As delighted as everyone else in the audience, Frank at last motioned to Eva, who emerged from the wings and carried her granddaughter off. If she cried at such an undignified exit, Baby's tears soon gave way to the rapture of for the first time hearing applause meant only for her, the most beautiful music in the world, she was later to say. Not only had she seen the future, she had heard it: she was, at the age of two and a half, an entertainer.

From that time on the Gumm sisters were a trio—the Gumdrops, they were sometimes called. It cannot be said that Baby immediately outshone her older sisters. But her talent grew as she did, and gradually it became clear that she was indeed the star. No one knew it better than her mother. When they visited the Milne relatives, Ethel carried in the car a small portable stage, a folding table with short legs. Out it would come at some point during the stay, and Baby would be told to jump up and do a couple of tap dances. She had been performing constantly since the age of two, she later said, and in no way was she exaggerating: her mother had packed a stage next to her dresses and dolls.

|||

Sunlit years they had seemed, but it is doubtful that the marriage of Frank and Ethel was ever as blissful as it had appeared. If they were never heard to argue, it was because Frank always did what he was told. Theirs was not a relationship of equals. "A Northern girl," Frank's aunt from Murfreesboro had called Ethel, which may have been a Southerner's way of saying that she was pushy. But Northerners, her own relatives included, also found Ethel bossy and overbearing. "We referred to her as Gabby," recalled her nephew, James Milne. " 'Be quiet! I'm talking!' she would say."

Love can be expressed in many ways, but one thing is constant: people in love long to be together. That could never have been said of Frank and Ethel. Early on, at a time when most brides can scarcely be torn from their husbands, Ethel had formed the habit of spending several weeks each year with her relatives in Superior and Duluth. Frank and Ethel, it became clear, were as happy apart as together. Yet even when they were together, they seemed to be uncomfortable without the company of other adults. The bonds that joined them, ties of affection and common interest, were genuine enough, but they were those of performing partners rather than husband and wife. Theirs was a singular, decidedly odd marriage. For a long time it seemed to suit both of them, however. Frank did not complain about constant visits by Ethel's family, and Ethel did not object to her arid sex life—she later talked to Marc Rabinowitz's wife about Frank's failures in bed. What she doubtless did object to, however, was his behavior in other beds. After seven apparently tranquil years, Frank was behaving recklessly again.

He was no longer the slim, good-looking young man who had turned heads in Murfreesboro—those daily stops at the confectionery shop had rounded his face and added several inches to his waistline—but Frank still had the magician's gift for making those around him feel good, for transforming frowns into smiles. If, during the first few years of his marriage, he had engaged in homosexual activity of the kind that had sent him scurrying from Cloquet, he had been discreet about it. That he delighted in the company of younger men was obvious, but not something that worried anyone. But all that changed in the early twenties.

For many months in 1923 and 1924 the chief object of his esteem was the high school basketball star, with whom he often journeyed to other towns, sometimes with Ethel and the boy's parents, sometimes alone. On at least one occasion Frank and his athletic companion spent a night by themselves in Minneapolis. Apparently nobody, including the boy's parents, thought there was anything odd about such a curious friendship, but as the months passed, Frank became increasingly care-less, as if he wanted to set off alarm bells. When two of the New Grand's ushers reported that he had made sexual advances to them, the bells did ring. Frank's actions could no longer be ignored. Measures had to be taken. Though nobody in Grand Rapids wanted to hurt ami-able Frank, much less his family, with a public fuss, those in charge made it clear to him that he was no longer welcome. The Gumms would have to find a home elsewhere.

|||

Forced to move, Frank and Ethel, like thousands of other Midwestern-ers in that decade after World War I, looked west, to Southern Califor-nia. Marc Rabinowitz—Marc Rabwin, he now called himself—was a doctor at Los Angeles County Hospital, and he suggested that they consider California: they would love it, he assured them. They took his advice, and on June 8, 1926, two days before Baby's fourth birthday, the five Gumms boarded a train and began their journey to the Pacific.

In no hurry to get there, they followed a roundabout northern route, defraying some of their expenses by entertaining in such colorful spots as Devils Lake, North Dakota, and Whitefish, Montana. In Los Ange-les, where Marc Rabwin's parents opened their house to them, they picnicked on the beach, attended a concert at the Hollywood Bowl and toured no fewer than four movie studios. To get into one of the biggest, Metro-Goldwyn-Mayer, Frank boldly stood in front of the entrance and stopped a convertible driven by Fred Thomson, the studio's cow-boy hero. "My kids have been dying to meet you!" he shouted, to which Thomson responded by escorting them inside.

Their inspection trip had been a success, and the Gumms returned to Grand Rapids on July 18 only to pack. A buyer was found for the New Grand, and in October, as the trees glowed with the dazzling reds and yellows of a Minnesota autumn, their friends gave the Gumms a series of good-bye parties. Most of the valedictions were for Ethel. The farewells to Frank, who had done so much for Grand Rapids for so many years, seemed muted, scarcely even perfunctory. By the end of the month the Gumms were gone, and a new family had moved into the house on Hoffman Avenue.

||

When they thought of California, Frank and Ethel were thinking of the Los Angeles they had visited in July, a place of sandy beaches, Holly-wood glamour and perpetual spring, where the sting of winter and the sullen weight of summer were equally unknown. What disappoint-ment, then, they and their children must have experienced when their California turned out to be not that Camelot by the Pacific, but a dull and dusty, decidedly unglamorous town in the Mojave Desert—hot in the summer, cold in the winter, and windy all year round.

Frank had hoped to buy a theater in or near Los Angeles, and for sev-eral months the Gumms lived in West Hollywood while he searched. No theater could be found, however—none at a price he could afford, anyway—and Marc Rabwin persuaded him to take a look at Lancaster, a little desert community he had discovered on his medical rounds. About forty-five miles northeast of downtown Los Angeles, a two- to two-and-a-half-hour drive across the San Gabriel Mountains, it not only had a theater but had the only one for miles around, the only one in the entire Antelope Valley. As luck had it, the owner was eager to be freed of his obligation, and at the end of May 1927 Frank became pro-prietor of a five-hundred-seat theater, so new—it had been open only since Christmas—that its upholstered leather seats were as smooth and shiny as the day they were unpacked.

Thus it was that the Gumms, who had come from a land of blue waters and green forests, found themselves surrounded, except where man had intervened, by an endless dun-colored expanse shaded only by sagebrush, greasewood and an occasional yucca tree. Movie cowboys galloped through Red Rock Canyon—the area was a favorite location for Hollywood westerns—and real cowboys still came into town for supplies and a good time, tying their horses to the hitching posts along Antelope Avenue, where Frank's new theater was located.

Situated in what was called the high desert—it was 2,350 feet above sea level—Lancaster never got quite as hot as towns in the low desert to the south. Nor was it entirely barren. After a wet winter, flame-red poppies would suddenly burst forth in March or April—miles and miles of them, dancing in the wind and setting the hills ablaze with their fragrant fire. Given enough water, the Antelope Valley could grow almost anything, and well water had, in fact, transformed hundreds of acres of sunbaked earth, hard as pottery, into fertile and productive soil: fields of alfalfa, wheat and barley; orchards of pears, peaches, apples and apricots. A rapidly expanding Los Angeles had an insatiable appetite for such produce, and the twenties were boom years for Lancaster, whose population almost quadrupled, from four hundred in 1920 to more than fifteen hundred in 1930.

"It Pleases Us to Please You," which had been the motto of the New Grand, became Frank's slogan in Lancaster as well, and he worked hard to ingratiate himself with his new neighbors, lowering prices for children and installing the town's first neon sign atop the entrance. Red and blue and fifteen feet high, it lit up that drab and colorless downtown like a fireworks display on the Fourth of July.

The Valley Theater's biggest draw was something brighter than that flashy sign, however. It was Frank's own family, which he wasted no time in introducing to the plainspoken people of the desert. He signed his lease on Saturday, May 21, and on May 22 and 23 he was onstage with Ethel and the girls. They were an instant hit. "Gumm Family Wins Lancaster Approval" read the headline in the next edition of the *Antelope Valley Ledger-Gazette*. "Mr. and Mrs. Gumm are accomplished musicians and gave two very pleasing songs," said the paper, "while the little daughters completely won the hearts of the audience with their songs and dances." Separately and together, the Gumms were soon performing throughout the Valley, at everything from Kiwanis Club meetings to teachers' conventions; no major gathering could be called a success, it seemed, without a Gumm in attendance.

Rarely has a family had such an immediate impact on a town as the Gumms had on Lancaster. By the end of 1927, seven months after their arrival, they had become an indispensable part of life in the Valley. "One of the finest assets of the community" was how the *Ledger-Gazette* characterized Frank's theater. Entertainment is not usually put on the list of civic resources, but a town without joy might as well be bankrupt. The Gumms had given Lancaster something it did not even know it was missing: they had put a smile on its weather-beaten face.

|||

During their first year the Gumms lived on the outskirts of town, east of the railroad tracks. In May 1928 they relocated nearer the center, to a large house on Cedar Avenue, in what was considered one of the best parts of town; Bankers Row, it was sometimes called. Three years later they moved to the even larger house next door, on the southwest corner of Twelfth Street, directly across from the grammar school. Both houses were so central—and Lancaster was so small—that Frank had only to stand outside and whistle when he wanted his daughters. Wherever they were, they could hear him.

Like the land around them, the denizens of the desert were capable of pleasant surprises. Beneath their sometimes gruff exteriors they were naturally friendly, and it was not long before all five Gumms had settled in. Frank and Ethel joined what passed for the fast set, meaning those who played cards and gave parties, and their girls quickly made friends of their own. For the most part, however, Baby, or Babe as she was known in Lancaster, spent her time with just one friend, an athletic tomboy who was two years older but ideally matched in size and temperament. Ina Mary Ming was her name—Ming was Scotch, not Chinese—but nobody ever called her anything but Muggsey.

During summer vacation, the girls could be found every afternoon at the high school's outdoor swimming pool, the only cool place in town. Frank often visited for a few minutes, causing a scramble of up-turned bottoms when he threw a handful of the theater's pennies into the water. When they were not in the water, Babe and Muggsey were usually on their bikes, endlessly cruising those dusty streets or riding a mile out past Marble's Dairy for a picnic lunch in the grudging shade of a sagebrush.

They also made frequent stops at the Jazz Candy Shop, a few doors from the Valley Theater. Babe always seemed to be eating—"she was forever with a candy bar in her hand," recalled Muggsey's brother Wilber—but never seemed to gain weight. Most people remembered her as downright skinny, with a tiny body connected to long, outsized arms and legs. As far as anyone in Lancaster could see, Babe had a conventional, normal childhood, unremarkable in every respect but one. That single exception made all the difference. She may have been an ordinary girl, but her voice had been touched by magic.

|||

Patrons of the New Grand had been the first witnesses to that magic, small and embryonic as it then had been, and now the citizens of Lancaster saw it as well. Despite the fact that she was so much younger than her sisters, everyone knew that Babe was the chief attraction of the Valley Theater. "All three of them were talented," said Henry Ivan Dorsett, the young man who distributed the theater's handbills. "But little Frances was beginning to shine like a star. She had a voice that just boomed over the others. That tiny gal opened her mouth and, boy, her voice carried all over that theater." So brightly did she shine and so far did that voice carry that her parents worried that the older girls would suffer from the comparison. "We didn't want this to happen," Frank told Dorsett. "Baby is getting all the attention."

The girls performed at nine o'clock, before the second show. When they finished, they rushed to their father, who was waiting on a couch in the empty lobby. Mary Jane and Jimmie anxiously sought his approval. "Well, Daddy, did I do all right? Was I okay?" they would ask. Always careful to give equal praise, Frank hugged all three and invariably exclaimed: "Good show! It was great again!" But the only way he could have made them equal onstage was to have put a gag over Babe's mouth. Settling down on her father's lap, Babe alone neither showed any anxiety nor inquired how she had done. "She knew that she had done well—and that was it," said Dorsett. "Every word and every action seemed to say, 'I know it was good. It had to be good because I did it.' "

Her mother, who played the piano for those performances, also knew that she was good. Ethel began to look beyond the Valley Theater, to Los Angeles and its schools of song and dance, its big variety houses and, ultimately, its movie studios. Most people in the Antelope Valley journeyed across the San Gabriel Mountains to Los Angeles perhaps two or three times a year. "Down Below," they called it. But if those squat and ugly hills had been the High Sierras, they would not have deterred Ethel, who careered through the twists and turns of the Mint Canyon Highway with brake-burning speed. "The girls and I used to say that it was like a roller coaster," said Dorothy Walsh, a next-door neighbor who sometimes went along for the ride. "We had to hold on to something in the backseat. But Ethel was fast in everything she did. She wanted action, action, action!"

Action was what Ethel got, and her shrewd dark eyes searched restlessly for an opening through which she could propel her daughters into show business. Never too proud or too shy, she pushed every door, hoping to find one unlocked. In August 1928, she finally succeeded. Learning that Los Angeles radio station KFI was planning to hold auditions for its Wednesday afternoon children's show, *The Kiddies Hour,* she promptly presented her daughters to Big Brother Ken, the show's host. That was the moment she had prepared them for, and they did so well that Ken gave them a regular spot. Once a week she drove them to the station, and every Wednesday afternoon at five the voices of the Gumm sisters could be heard all over Southern California.

|||

Shortly after her arrival in California, Ethel had become friendly with another indefatigable Ethel, Ethel Meglin, who ran a well-known children's dance school. Months later, Ethel Gumm enrolled her daughters in her friend's school; early every Saturday morning, she would drive them to Hollywood for Saturday and Sunday classes, all four spending Saturday night at a nearby hotel. At four o'clock Sunday afternoon, she

Kute, Klever and Kunning: Mary Jane, Jimmie and Judy

would start up the Gumm Buick again and put them back on the roller coaster to Lancaster.

"A compact woman with glistening eyes" was the way Shirley Temple, one of Meglin's pupils, was later to describe Ethel Meglin, and Meglin's astute training and promotion made her students—Meglin Kiddies, they were called—much sought after by both the movie studios and vaudeville houses. At Christmastime the Loew's State Theater in downtown Los Angeles usually booked the entire troupe for a week. "One Hundred Meglin Wonder Kiddies . . . Kute . . . Klever and Kunning!" read the theater's ad in 1928, the year the Gumm sisters joined the contingent. Among the wonderful one hundred who appeared on the Loew's stage that year, only one stood out, however—the skinny six-year-old with the booming voice. "I'll Get By," Babe sang, with a voice that, in the words of one listener, "cut straight through to your heart. The audience went crazy. She had many, many encores."

Together with other Meglin Kiddies, the Gumm girls did at last break into the movies, in a one-reel short, *The Big Revue,* that was filmed during the summer of 1929. Set in a glossy nightclub, it has a chorus line of not-so-buxom nine-year-olds, an all-boy orchestra, and the three Gumms—the only ones given their own spot—who sing a song called "In the Sunny South." Mary Jane and Jimmie look nervous, their eyes wandering up and down, left and right, everywhere, in fact, but straight ahead. Babe alone has stage—or, in this case, camera— presence. She not only looks into the camera; she pierces it, transfixes it with her eyes. The camera, that most human of all mechanical in- struments, is, in turn, so mesmerized that she might as well be by her- self, because she is the only one it seems to notice.

Some managers have a clear plan for their clients' careers, turning down those jobs that fall outside their guidelines. Incapable of distin- guishing between the big and the small, the important and the unim- portant, Ethel, by contrast, had no plan at all. As a result, her girls frantically juggled performances in Lancaster with trips to Los Angeles and other, more distant spots like San Diego and Santa Barbara. A big night at the Loew's State or the Wilshire-Ebell might be followed, for instance, by an appearance before the Eastern Star Lodge in little Tehachapi, an hour or so north of Lancaster. At one tiny theater outside Los Angeles, rowdy teenagers caused a nauseating stench on stage by squashing garlic on the hot footlights, then hurled a half-eaten salami sandwich at Mary Jane. That was too much even for Ethel. "We're going home," she declared and promptly drove her brood back to Lan- caster.

|||

More and more, bookers and managers were asking not for three Gumms, but just one—the youngest. "Without Babe, the act would

have been very mediocre," said Maurice Kusell, who produced the
"Stars of Tomorrow" variety shows for the Wilshire-Ebell. "Babe was
the whole thing, really, even as a young kid of eight years old." As she
grew older, Babe's voice leaped ahead of her body, developing remarkable timbre, resonance and richness. She thought, acted and looked like
a small girl, but she sounded, increasingly and ever more astonishingly,
like a woman. In the winter and spring of 1932, she was twice invited to
sing at perhaps the last place a chanteuse of nine might have been
expected—the Cocoanut Grove, one of the movie colony's favorite
hangouts.

The songs that Hollywood applauded also drew audiences to the
Valley Theater, which, like most other businesses, needed all the help it
could get in the Depression years of the thirties. "Baby Gumm will feature popular numbers between shows," announced one of the theater's
ads. No longer could Frank, or anyone else, maintain the fiction that all
three sisters were equal.

The reaction of Mary Jane and Jimmie was not what might have
been anticipated, however, and neither showed a glimmer of envy.
"Mary Jane and Jimmie were sick of the whole show-business thing,"
said Dorothy Walsh. "They worked under protest most of the time.
They thought: if Babe can do it, wonderful! They wanted to quit." The
sisters would continue to perform as a trio, but from now on the main
burden would be on Babe. In the cheers and applause for her, Mary
Jane and Jimmie heard their salvation, as the fury of their mother's ambition was turned on the youngest, smallest and most vulnerable, the
child she had not even wanted.

Judy and Ethel on a visit to
Grand Rapids in 1938

A Meager Stream— and a Love Like Niagara

W hen I was a child," Babe was later to say, "more than anything else I wanted to be loved by my parents." But she was really speaking of just one parent, her mother. She did not have to seek her father's love. He gave it without being asked, in a torrent, a soaking, drenching waterfall of care and devotion. Those same warm waters also showered Mary Jane and Jimmie—of Frank's affection there was never a shortage—but his feelings for Babe had a singular intensity. "Boy, did he adore her!" exclaimed Glen Settle, a young Lancastrian who listened again and again to Frank's recitation of her accomplishments. "Adore," indeed, was the word everyone used to describe the bond between father and daughter. "She adored her father, absolutely adored him!" said Dorothy Walsh. "And he adored her. *There* was a love affair."

A long list of other words, a whole dictionary of them, could have been used to describe the far more complicated relationship she had with her mother. Her own Milne relations had thought Ethel a nag, and where her daughters were concerned, nothing that could be seen by the eye or heard by the ear escaped her notice and possible correction. "She was somehow just too fussy with those girls," said Grace Pickus, who worked in the Valley Theater box office. "She was always combing their hair, or straightening their collars, as if she couldn't wait to get them just right so that she could take them off somewhere." Yet as much as she fussed with Mary Jane and Jimmie, she fussed that much more with Babe.

There are many stories of her vigilance, but one is enough to illustrate the sharpness of her eye, the tightness of her grip. Behind the Gilmore house on Twelfth Street, there was a sloping stretch of ground on which Muggsey's brother Wilber had set up a rope slide. With ingenuity Tom Sawyer would have admired, Wilber and a friend had tied one end of a rope to a cottonwood tree at the top of the slope, the other end to a tree at the bottom, a hundred feet away. Holding on to a sling attached to a pulley, the boys would then launch themselves from the high end and slide down the rope, flying between the two trees like Tarzan through the jungle. Since their descent never actually took them more than ten feet off the ground, the chance of injury was slight, and girls also took rides on Wilber's rope.

Babe was not to be one of them. Visiting the Gilmores with her mother, she wandered out to play and, with Wilber's help, eagerly prepared to take her first flight. She was climbing a ladder to reach the sling when Ethel burst out of the Gilmore house, crying hysterically—a sight that no one in Lancaster had ever seen or had ever expected to see. "No! No! No! No! No! Don't take a chance!" she screamed. "Babe wanted to be a regular kid" was Irma Story's sad commentary, "but her mother didn't give her a chance. She didn't really have a free kid's life like the rest of us."

Ethel also tried, with less success, to curb some of the kids who were free—Irma, Muggsey and just about everyone else who came into contact with her daughter. If they included Babe in their Halloween plans, for instance, her friends knew that they would have to abide by her mother's rules, which meant spending the evening safely inside the Gumm house rather than walking the streets, knocking on doors and making minor mischief, as they preferred. If they failed to include Babe and went their own way, on the other hand, they knew that Ethel would call their parents the next day and inquire why, then invite them to a party that would make them all feel guilty.

Such tactics usually backfired, and Babe, the unwitting victim of her mother's clumsy machinations, was frequently excluded from group activities. Ignorant of her friends' feelings, she was later to express her resentment, claiming that there had been a bias against her in Lancaster because she had come from a show-business family. What she did not know was that her friends were only doing what she herself could not or would not do: they were rebelling against Ethel. "Everybody wanted to be Babe's friend," said Story. "But we didn't want to be bossed by her mother. I wouldn't say that I disliked Mrs. Gumm. But I was glad she wasn't my mother."

Many others felt the same way. Despite her care, her concern and her watchfulness—despite all the things she did—an essential ingredient was missing from Ethel's notion of motherhood. Perhaps it was something as simple as tenderness. Not once in all the years the Gumms lived in Lancaster did Babe's young companions see Ethel open her arms to hold or to hug her, as Frank so often did. Not once did they witness an open display of affection. If Frank's love was like Niagara, unending and unstoppable, Ethel's could be compared to the flow that comes out of a faucet: a meager stream that she could turn on, and turn off.

Was it, in fact, love Ethel felt? Babe herself was uncertain, but some of her Lancaster friends believed that they knew the answer. To their skeptical and unblinking eyes, Ethel seemed to regard Babe as an asset to be exploited, rather than as a child to be cherished. This was a harsh but probably accurate judgment. The fact of the matter was that Ethel did seem to look at Babe with chilling detachment, more like a manager studying a promising talent than a mother looking at her own flesh and blood.

"Drive, drive, drive! That's the way Ethel was," said Dorothy Walsh, and Ethel drove Babe not only beyond reason, but beyond need, which was worse. For Babe did not have to be prodded to perform, any more than she had to be prodded to eat or sleep. To her ears applause was a sound made by angels, as soothing as a lullaby, yet as exhilarating as a bugle call. To sing was to be loved: it was as simple as that. Walking onto a stage was like stepping into a warm embrace. What did she want to be when she grew up? people in Lancaster asked her. "I'm going to be a movie star," she said. No one laughed, because no one doubted that she would be.

|||

Much as she enjoyed performing before an audience, so, to an equal degree, did Babe detest singing before unresponsive movie executives. Her ordeal, which is what the trips to the studios were for her, began each Friday afternoon when the last school bell rang. That was a signal for her friends, the regular kids, to throw down their books and run off to the baseball diamond or the Jazz Candy Shop. For Babe it was a summons to go home to have her hair put up in curlers for a Saturday morning audition. But before she went into the house, she sat down with Muggsey and cried, so much did she dread the twenty-four hours to follow. "She hated going, just hated it," said Ming, who often went along to keep her company.

Nearly every Saturday, when dew was on the grass and the morning air was sharp with the smell of alfalfa, the Gumms' dark blue Buick backed out of the driveway on Cedar Avenue. Because Ethel, who was in a hurry even at that early hour, refused to give the engine time to warm up, it was seldom a smooth getaway. Sputtering in shocked protest, the Buick jumped down the block like a jackrabbit—*chug, chug, chug, chug, chug*—until the motor caught. Huddling together in the backseat as Ethel speeded down the Mint Canyon Highway, Babe and Muggsey sang, talked and occasionally dabbed at coloring books with their crayons—anything to keep boredom at bay.

For Babe, the long drive might have been less onerous if she had known that at the end of the journey there would be a reward—a clapping of hands, some amiable words, perhaps a hint of a smile. But enthusiasm seemed to be a precious commodity in Hollywood. "She would knock herself out," said Ming, "and those studio people would sit there so stern-faced, never cracking a smile, never saying whether she was good or whether she wasn't. Just blank faces. I used to feel real bad because they were so mean."

Silence and sour expressions were not the worst of it for Babe. What made those sessions so unnerving was her belief that when her own audition was over, her mother's began. Babe was convinced that, in hopes of furthering her career, Ethel would then have sex with one or more of those blank-faced men. "That's the main reason Babe hated going down there," said Ming. "That's why she always wanted me to go along, so she wouldn't be alone." What proof Babe had, what conversations she had overheard or what incidents she had witnessed, Muggsey never knew. Muggsey knew only that when Babe had finished singing, Ethel would order the two of them outside to play, while she remained inside, sometimes for an hour or more. Whether Ethel, who was still several years shy of forty, was, in fact, trading sex for favors is impossible to say. What can be said is that Babe and Muggsey believed that she was. Yet even if they were wrong, they were right in thinking that there was virtually nothing that Ethel would not do, or make Babe do, to see the Gumm name at the bottom of a studio contract.

Indeed, Babe had proof that that was the case, evidence she could hold in the palm of her hand. When Babe's energies flagged, as they often did, Ethel did what she had done with her two older daughters: she gave her pep pills. Then, when the pep pills started keeping her awake at night, Ethel counteracted them with sleeping tablets. "I've got to keep these girls going!" was her bright, cheery comment whenever Dorothy Walsh suggested that she was pushing too hard. Thus, even before she had reached her tenth birthday, did Babe become acquainted with the drugs that were to be her companions evermore. And her mother, her guardian, her defender, her shield against the world, had made the introductions.

|||

The question is not why Ethel did what she did to Babe, but why Frank allowed her to do it. Babe herself thought she had the answer. "She defeated him, you know. And he was a very strong man, my father! Very strong. There was nothing weak about him at all." But she was only half right. If the occasion warranted, Frank could, in fact, be tough; movie distributors could attest to that. But he was tough only with outsiders.

When he came up against his wife, he might just as well have been made of rubber, so easily did he bend and stretch to her will. Ethel did, indeed, defeat him, but only because Frank let her.

It was a measure of his love that where the welfare of his girls were concerned, he actually did try to stand up to her. "Slow down! Slow down!" he would shout. "Stop pushing them. Stop wearing them out." These arguments usually occurred late at night, and Ethel often concluded them by rushing into Babe's room and pulling her out of bed. "We're leaving Daddy," she would announce. When Babe objected that she did not want to leave her father, Ethel would say simply, "Then you don't love me," a comment that left Babe feeling both guilty and helpless. Sleepy and confused, she would then be bundled into the backseat of the Buick and, for the rest of the night, without a word of explanation about where they were going or when they would return, Ethel would drive at high speeds across empty desert roads. Dawn would usually find the Buick pulling into the driveway on Cedar Street, but sometimes Ethel drove all the way to Los Angeles, where she and Babe would stay three or four days in a hotel.

Ethel never physically abused Babe, never even spanked her, but her brand of discipline left scars nonetheless. If Babe did something wrong during one of their trips, her mother would pack her bags and walk out of their hotel room, slamming the door behind her. Babe never knew when, or if, she would return, but until she did, anywhere from one to five hours later, Babe would sit silently in a chair, afraid that if she cried or made even the smallest sound, she would never see her mother again. Her panic, she said, was beyond description. Only when the door opened again did she allow herself to cry, telling Ethel that she was the most wonderful mother in the world. "Well, you're just lucky I came back at all this time," Ethel would reply, "because the next time I won't."

Yet Ethel could be kind as well as cruel, doing little things—cooking special meals, for instance—to make her youngest daughter happy. Nor was she always heartless. One year she had arranged for Babe to work on Christmas Day, but felt guilty herself as just the two of them were sharing a lonely Christmas dinner at a drugstore across from the theater, eating hot enchiladas rather than turkey and the trimmings. "You should be home with your family having a beautiful Christmas dinner," Ethel suddenly cried, and there was nothing Babe, who was quite happy with her enchilada, could say to console her. Such moments made Babe love Ethel, but she always knew that even then, even "in the middle of great kindness or loud laughter, she was capable of saying something or doing something that would scare me to death." For Babe, love for her mother was always mixed with fear.

|||

At home, on Cedar Street, her parents had all but declared war, and from her vantage point next door, Dorothy Walsh could hear them battling, angry words occasionally punctuated by the crash of a hurled pan. Inside the house, where the clanging pans reverberated like thunder, Babe would put in an emergency call to Muggsey. "Would you come over?" she would ask. Faithful Muggsey always did, arriving to find Babe crying under a tree on the front lawn. Tears produced more tears, and soon they were both bawling, not stopping even when the shouting ceased and Frank sat down at the piano to sing a love song, the signal that a cease-fire had been signed. On the lawn outside, that was an occasion for still more weeping. "His songs were always so sad," said Muggsey.

Nothing in the world is more frightening to a child, Babe would later say, than the sound of parents squabbling. It was frightening to her, in any event, and the disturbances at home, combined with pressure from an overbearing mother, doubtless contributed to her obvious anxiety. Her hands sometimes shook and she suffered from insomnia, sleeping well only when she stayed all night with Muggsey. "She seemed to relax just getting away, even if it was only a couple of blocks," said Ming. Listening to the sounds of combat as she sat on that tiny lawn, that beleaguered spot of green in a khaki-colored town, Babe must have thought that the verdant Eden of Grand Rapids was as distant as the mountains of the moon.

It must have seemed equally faraway to Frank and Ethel, who were more and more at odds. The arrangement that had kept them together in Minnesota had broken down, irretrievably and beyond repair. Both were to blame. Undeterred by the scandal that had caused them to

leave Grand Rapids, Frank continued to lust after teenage boys, while
Ethel, for her part, had taken a lover.

|||

Will Gilmore was Ethel's lover's name, and he and his wife, Laura,
were the Gumms' best friends in Lancaster. The two couples spent
much of their free time together, at bridge games and picnics and on
trips to the ocean and scenic spots in the desert. Wherever the Gumms
were, the Gilmores were also likely to be. Their offspring were friends
as well, the Gilmores' daughter, Ruth, often joining Babe and Muggsey
on their excursions around town. Bill, one of the two Gilmore boys,
was a close friend of Muggsey's brother, Wilber.

A salesman of the water pumps that were so vital in that thirsty re-
gion, Gilmore was tall and broad-shouldered, with sharp, aquiline features, dark hair and a forceful, if dour personality. On the hottest days,
when most other businessmen surrendered to the heat, loosening their
ties and rolling up their shirtsleeves, he defied the thermometer, keeping his coat on, his high-collared shirt buttoned and his tie firmly knot-
ted. Though he was a few years younger than Frank, his stern and
unbending demeanor made him seem older, at least to those of Babe's
generation. "He was a sour old man," said Wilber. "I was scared of
him."

So, apparently, were many other people, and Gilmore had a mean
streak to match his violent temper. He once planted the teeth of a rake
in the back of a dog that tried to break into his chicken pen, then gave
chase to the terror-stricken animal, which was painfully dragging the
rake behind it as it tried to escape. When he caught up with the dog and
extracted his rake in front of the Ming house, Sam Ming, Muggsey's
father, stepped out to tell him what he thought of such cruelty. "He was
a peculiar bastard," Sam Ming said of Gilmore. "I never had any use for
him." Neither did Babe. "A terrifying man," she later wrote. "I loathed
him. He had very white teeth, very bad clothes, a miserable haircut, and
he was a petty, weak man, narrow-minded and unkind."

A man more unlike the genial Frank could not have been born, but
that may have been Gilmore's chief attraction for Ethel. When Frank

was away, Ethel often took her girls to dinner at the Gilmore house, where Gilmore himself seemed to take as much delight in torturing Babe as he had the unfortunate dog. He criticized Babe's eating habits, her table manners—everything she did, in fact. To make her empty a glass of milk, he once shook the dinner table so violently that he overturned an entire pitcher of milk, all but coating her in white. "Each meal was a horror," she said, "and the anticipation was worse." Worse still was watching her mother stand idly by, sometimes, indeed, even joining in, the two of them laughing at her as she walked to a miserable bed.

Though probably few in Lancaster objected to Ethel's affair with Gilmore—there were many such couplings in that frontier town—they did feel sorry for poor Laura Gilmore, who was confined to a wheelchair by a stroke. "We thought it was pretty stinky of Mrs. G. to be 'playing bridge' with Will Gilmore while Laura was unable to get around" was the way Dorothy Walsh summed up the prevailing sentiment. If it had not been for a game of hide-and-seek, Babe herself probably would have remained ignorant of her mother's adultery.

Searching for a hiding place from the Gilmore children one afternoon, she and Muggsey ran into an abandoned pump house on the Gilmore property, scampering up its creaky wooden stairs to find refuge in an empty storage room on the second floor. It is not hard to imagine Babe's astonishment when she burst through the door to discover that instead of being empty, the room was occupied by Gilmore and her mother. The lovers were as astonished as she was, and by the time Muggsey arrived a few seconds later, an angry Gilmore was already at the door. He pushed them both out. Babe never revealed what she had seen, but as she walked down the stairs, Ming recalled, she looked stunned, as if someone had struck her across the face.

|||

Many people resented Ethel's obvious desire to say good-bye to Lancaster, to move Down Below where the action was. Frank, by contrast, was admired as much in Lancaster as he had been everywhere else. Always most at home in small towns, he settled down to a comfortable routine: a morning shave at John Perkins's barbershop, lunch at the

Jazz Candy Shop, dinner at home, then a walk to the theater to give a big hello to incoming patrons. Sunday mornings were reserved for services at St. Paul's Episcopal Church, where he sang in the choir. A booster by nature, Frank soon became one of the town's movers and shakers, a vice president of the Kiwanis Club and a prominent figure at many important gatherings. Even in his forties he retained his youthful zest and exuberance, the essence of which was captured in a snapshot from May 1930. Taken on a golf course, it shows a slightly pudgy, unremarkable-looking man who is memorable for one reason alone: a huge, all-embracing grin that seems to say, "Isn't life grand?"

But there was also another Frank, and for that man life was not so grand. This second Frank was a lonely, middle-aged man who constantly humiliated himself, as he had done with such disastrous results in Grand Rapids, by panting after teenage boys and young, good-looking men. It was this Frank who sometimes patted their rear ends when they walked into the Valley Theater. "Boy, those look nice!" he might exclaim when he saw one of them wearing a pair of tight-fitting trousers. It was this Frank who invited them to sit beside him in the Valley Theater's dark back row for mutual masturbation. "Don't you want to sit back here, boys?" he would say beguilingly. "I've got some popcorn." And it was this Frank who also made advances to his young employees. To fend off such overtures, one of his projectionists, John Carter, often asked Irma Story's brother Tom to keep him company in the projection booth.

In the high school locker room, two of the school's top athletes, Steve Castle and Lyle Hatley, bragged about the pleasure Frank was giving them with oral sex, not neglecting a description of how they made him beg. Since they were doing the same thing with the track coach, no one doubted that they were telling the truth. If further evidence had been needed, it could have been found at the Valley Theater, where Castle and Hatley strolled through the doors without paying while their friends were lining up at the box office outside. "Hi, Frankie," the cocky Hatley would yell as he sauntered through the lobby.

Still, what was common knowledge among the town's teenage boys remained a secret from their parents. None of the boys wanted to make trouble for likable Frank. "I don't see any harm in talking to those boys back there," Frank himself explained to Henry Dorsett. "Once in a while I get a little lonesome." Though Babe later heard rumors of her father's activities, she refused to believe them, angrily denouncing them as a "ghastly dirty lie" spread by that "horrible man"—the hated Will Gilmore.

|||

Almost from the day she arrived, Ethel had been trying to escape Lancaster. Her first attempt had come in March 1929, when, misled perhaps by the girls' early successes into thinking that stardom was near, she had gone so far as to rent an apartment in Los Angeles. She and her daughters would return to Cedar Avenue only on weekends, she had told the Lancaster newspaper. But the breakthrough never came, the apartment was given up and once again she and her girls became reluctant commuters on the Mint Canyon Highway.

Ethel sometimes admitted setbacks, but defeat never, and every month that followed made her more eager to pack her bags and to find a home Down Below. Not only were the Saturday morning trips becoming harder and harder on Babe, but the Gilmores had already made the move, which meant that Ethel and Will could meet less often. She had every reason to want to leave Lancaster, in short, and only one reason to stay—money. The girls often spent more traveling to their performances than they were paid, and except for the small sums Ethel herself earned teaching piano, the box office of the Valley Theater remained the primary source of family income.

To Ethel, it must have seemed like a miracle, therefore, when she was offered a job in Los Angeles by Maurice Kusell, the stylish young impresario who had spotlighted the Gumm sisters in his 1931 "Stars of Tomorrow" show at the Wilshire-Ebell. Impressed as much by the girls' mother as he had been by the girls themselves—"she was a hell of a woman, and I liked her immensely"—he had hired Ethel to lead the show's eight-piece orchestra, then, at the end of 1932, asked her to also teach popular singing at his school of song and dance. Ethel brought her mother and sister, Eva and Norma Milne, from Minnesota to take care of the girls for the rest of the school year, and at the beginning of 1933 she finally settled Down Below.

Although Frank stayed behind to manage his theater, the girls began saying their own good-byes to Lancaster after Mary Jane's graduation from high school, and on July 30 they joined Ethel in a house she had rented near downtown Los Angeles, in the Silver Lake district, not far from Kusell's studio. They did not have long to make themselves at home, however. Twenty-four hours after leaving Lancaster, Ethel put them on a ship bound for San Francisco and a week's run at the Golden Gate Theater, which was quickly followed by three big jobs in Southern California—in Long Beach, Hollywood and downtown Los Angeles.

|||

For Babe, the youngest and most vulnerable member of the family, the long separation from her father was particularly difficult. But Ethel had been right to jump at Kusell's offer. It was time, and past time, for the Gumms to leave the desert: a family whose chief interest was show business had always been out of place in a town whose biggest excitement was the annual Alfalfa Festival. In Los Angeles, by contrast, where a good part of the population worked for the movie studios, or wanted to, the Gumms found many others just like themselves. They were not only among friends; they were among colleagues.

Babe discovered that on her first day at the Lawlor School for Professional Children, or Ma Lawlor's as it was nicknamed. Located on Hollywood Boulevard, right next to the offices of Central Casting, the school taught the usual academic subjects, but on an unusual schedule. Classes were held only in the mornings, leaving afternoons free for auditions and rehearsals, and no fuss was made when a child missed school to take an out-of-town job. Providing an education was not the primary reason for the school's existence—*Variety* received more attention than Shakespeare—and one sometime student, Mickey Rooney, was undoubtedly right when he said that "if the truth be known, Ma Lawlor's school was a dodge, a way of pacifying the LA Board of Education."

Mary Jane and Jimmie had attended the school briefly in 1926 and 1927, during the months when Frank was searching for a theater. Now Jimmie, who was sixteen, returned with her younger sister. A plain girl whose dress was a little too long: that was how Babe looked on that first day to a girl who had been known to moviegoers of the twenties as Baby Peggy. When Mrs. Lawlor asked Babe to introduce herself to her classmates with a song, Baby Peggy thought it a cruel humiliation. She changed her mind the instant she heard Babe's "incredibly rich voice," which, she said, already possessed the emotional power of a mature woman's. The song Babe sang was "Blue Moon," and when the last note sank into silence, that sophisticated audience of show-business kids was clapping and cheering.

Admired and appreciated—an enthusiastic Lawlor claque crowded into the front row whenever the Gumm sisters appeared nearby—Babe was all high spirits at Lawlor's, with "more bounce to the ounce than everyone else in the school put together," in Rooney's words. But Rooney, who was two years older, bounced just as high himself. "Well, I met Mickey Rooney," Babe said when she came home that first afternoon. "He's just the funniest. . . . He clowns around every second!" With another Lawlor student, Frankie Darro, who was dating Jimmie, Rooney drove out to the desert whenever the girls did a show at the ailing Valley Theater, both boys sometimes jumping onto the stage to join in, an unexpected bonus for Frank's customers.

The Kusell studio fell victim to the Depression early in 1934, leaving Ethel, suddenly out of a job, with nothing to do but push her girls. Their schedule became more hectic than ever, and thanks to the Lawlor school's tolerant attitude toward absences, she was able to take them on their first extended trips, beginning, in mid-February, with a month's tour of the Northwest and Northern California. Frank, who always tried to see his daughters at least once wherever they performed, drove more than twelve hundred miles to meet them in Seattle. "When they were on stage, he would stand, whistle and clap," said Muggsey Ming. "He would get so emotional that tears would run down his cheeks. Then when they were through, Babe would jump into his arms and he would give her a big hug and tell her how good she was."

Perhaps in response to a bad review on their previous trip to San Francisco—one critic had accused Babe of shouting her numbers—Ethel had revised the act. Now when the curtain opened, Babe was seen sitting atop a piano, only her face visible in the spotlight, her head and body hidden under a dark shawl. She sang "Bill," the lovely, melancholy torch song Helen Morgan had sung in Jerome Kern and Oscar Hammerstein II's *Show Boat,* and not until the applause had begun did she jump down from the piano to reveal that that rich, womanly voice had come from a girl—and a small girl at that. "Of course the house then went crazy because you did not know that it was a child!" recalled a witness to one of those performances. "It was a marvelous presentation." The reaction was so encouraging, indeed, that when the Gumms returned from the Northwest in mid-March, Ethel made a bold announcement: she and her girls would soon be venturing even farther, all the way to Chicago and New York. "She was sure," said Dorothy Walsh, "that the trip would be the making of the Gumm sisters."

Though New York was dropped from the itinerary, Frank opposed the expedition anyway, strenuously arguing that it was too dangerous for four unescorted females to drive more than halfway across the country. He lost the argument, of course, and on the afternoon of Sunday, June 17, 1934, several family friends, Will and Laura Gilmore among them, came to Silver Lake to say good-bye to Ethel and her adventurous daughters. Ethel had saved up money of her own, but Frank also gave her about three hundred dollars in traveler's checks, a considerable sum for a man who was even then several months behind in his rent for the Valley Theater. Frank's checks were meant only for an emergency, however, and when they started driving east on Monday, June 18, just a week after Babe's twelfth birthday, the Gumm women were thinking of triumph, not trouble.

|||

Their first stop was Denver, where the "trio unusual," as the girls awkwardly described themselves, had two jobs, the first at the Tabor Grand Theater, the second at a gambling club that was temporarily without gambling because the police had confiscated its equipment. Colorado Springs was next; then, in mid-July, they reached Chicago, where the World's Fair, "A Century of Progress," was in its second year. Ethel had arranged a booking on the fairgrounds, at a nightclub whose other acts included a fan dancer, a society dance team and a comic mule—or at least a woman masquerading as a mule. But the club, the Old Mexico, was so far from the center of things that "it didn't draw flies," in Jimmie's words, much less customers. After advancing thirty-five dollars of the girls' salary, the club gave excuses instead of cash, leaving them without so much as a cold tamale when it shut its doors three weeks later. Ethel would be well advised, the managers said in ominous tones, not to press for the money they owed her. She took the hint. The Gumms then moved from the St. Lawrence, which was a first-class hotel, to a less expensive apartment hotel on the North Side.

While they were at the Old Mexico, Ethel had sought other bookings from the William Morris Agency, the city's chief talent broker. But the agency, which was besieged by hungry entertainers who had come to Chicago for the fair, refused even an audition. Try the Belmont Theater, Ethel was told; every Friday night it offered its stage to acts that were willing to work for free, and a scout from William Morris was always there, looking for fresh faces. The Gumm sisters dutifully performed at the Belmont, and they were so good, as Jimmie remembered it anyway, that they stopped the show. But that Friday no one from the agency had in fact been present: they had stopped the show for nothing. Misery breeds misery. One morning the Gumms awoke to discover that Ethel's money had run out, that they had nothing to eat but one egg and half a loaf of moldy bread. This was the emergency Frank had anticipated. Ethel cashed one of his traveler's checks, and she and her girls went out for a big breakfast.

Another, somewhat older trio of sisters—Laverne, Maxene and Patty Andrews—was already staying at the apartment hotel and glowered when they saw competition walking through the door. To prevent the newcomers from using the hotel's tiny rehearsal space, Maxene got up very early every morning and locked herself inside, then waited for her sisters. Hearing them practicing one day, Babe meekly inquired if she could come in to listen. After they did a couple of numbers, Patty politely asked her to return the favor by singing for them. Like the students at Lawlor's, the three sisters probably expected only embarrassment from such an ungainly girl. But after a few notes of "Bill," Maxene found herself in tears, unprepared for the warmth and feeling that poured from that small and unlikely vessel.

After that the Andrews sisters and the youngest Gumm were friends who sometimes met on those hot summer evenings to sit by the big console radio in the hotel's roof garden. Babe was already there one night when the sisters arrived, downcast after having been fired by one of Chicago's top vaudeville houses, the Oriental Theater. Did they know of another girls' trio? George Jessel, the master of ceremonies, had inquired. Out of loyalty to Babe, they had mentioned the Gumm girls, and that night on the roof Maxene told Babe to get over to the Oriental first thing in the morning. By coincidence, Jack Cathcart, the young trumpet player from the Old Mexico, was just then phoning Ethel with the same recommendation. Rush over to the Oriental, he said.

Jessel was unimpressed by Mary Jane and Jimmie, but, like everyone else, he saw something unique in Babe: she sang, he later said, "like a woman carrying a torch for Valentino." He had only one problem with the Gumm sisters. When he introduced them, he noticed that their name, which rhymed with words like "bum," "crumb," "dumb" and "scum," made the audience snicker. "These kids should have a new name!" he told Ethel. "I think so too," she replied, and happily accepted his alternative: Garland, after Jessel's friend Robert Garland, the drama critic of the *New York World-Telegram*. Though Ethel used "Gumm" a few more times—a typographical error found one theater advertising the Glum Sisters—the Garland Sisters they now were, and the Garland Sisters they remained.

Babe evoked the usual gasps of excitement with her rendition of "Bill," and the newly christened Garland Sisters saw their star ascend the same day they were hired—Friday, August 17, 1934. After that their mother no longer had difficulty finding jobs for them. Following their week at the Oriental, they went into another Chicago theater, the Marbro, then drove to Detroit for a stint at the Michigan Theater. Finally heading home in mid-September, they stopped off on the way for three more engagements—in Milwaukee and in St. Joseph and Kansas City, Missouri. They reached Los Angeles in mid-October, almost four months to the day after they had left. Though it was three o'clock in the morning when they arrived, Frank, who had been alerted that they were near, was waiting outside. When she jumped into his arms, Babe said, she cried—cried out of happiness. "It's hard to explain, but all the times I had to leave him, I pretended he wasn't there; because if I'd thought about him being there, I'd have been too full of longing."

|||

Although she did not believe in the magic of names, Ethel was later to say, she could not help observing that after Gumm was changed to Garland, the bookings never stopped. In fact, the girls scarcely had time to unpack before they were in the spotlight at the Beverly-Wilshire Hotel, with Grauman's Chinese Theater and the Orpheum in downtown Los Angeles coming soon after. Writing about their appearance at Grauman's Chinese, the *Variety* critic said that as a trio they were nothing; but when Babe was featured, they became class entertainment—"she has never failed to stop the show."

In December the girls were back at the Wilshire-Ebell Theater. It was there that Babe received the kind of notice entertainers carry with them ever after, like a good-luck charm, for warmth and comfort in dark moments. Her singing, wrote W. E. Oliver, the drama critic for the *Los Angeles Evening Herald and Express,* produced sensations the Wilshire-Ebell audience had not experienced in years. "Not your smart, adult-aping prodigy is this girl," continued Oliver, "but a youngster who has the divine instinct to be herself on the stage along with a talent for singing, a trick of rocking the spectator with rhythms and a capacity of putting emotion into her performance that suggests what Bernhardt must have been at her age."

|||

As Babe's fortunes rose, so did Frank's fall. When his family moved Down Below, he stayed in Lancaster to manage the Valley Theater, forsaking the house on Cedar Avenue for a cheap, one-room apartment off Antelope Avenue, the best he could afford after Ethel and the girls had been taken care of. "Boy, those were miserable days and nights for me," he later wrote, and he was telling no more than the truth. He ate his meals in restaurants, and his rented room—his shack, he termed it— was so cold in the winter that, to keep from freezing, he had to sleep in his bathrobe and wool-lined shoes.

Though he and his girls exchanged visits, whatever pleasure those meetings brought was soon drowned in the tears of parting. When it came time for Babe to say good-bye, father and daughter both gave way to wrenching sobs. "She missed him," said Muggsey Ming, "and he was just so lonely." To Babe, Frank's mean, uncomfortable little room must have been a tangible symbol of the sorry state to which he had been reduced. What she did not know was that he was largely responsible for his unhappy condition and that for many months the tawdry drama of Grand Rapids had been repeated in Lancaster, act by act, scene by scene.

His family had acted as a shield against rumor: who could have believed that Frank, a man with three lively daughters and a go-getting wife, was chasing after teenage boys? When Babe and her sisters left for Los Angeles in the summer of 1933, they not only removed the shield, but they also stimulated the activity. Lonesome and depressed, Frank became more reckless in his pursuits, just as he had been during the last years in Minnesota. The games he played with boys in the back row of the Valley Theater had not got him into trouble, curiously enough, and he had been safe fooling around with Steve Castle and Lyle Hatley, who were so wild and unruly that nobody watched, or much cared, what they were doing. But when Castle and Hatley graduated and went their own ways, Frank entered into what seems to have been a more intense, more visible and far more dangerous dalliance with another high school student.

Often seen at the Valley Theater, the boy, tall and slim, became a figure of derision in the school's hallways. "Frankie's lover boy," he was called behind his back. This time word spread to the town's adults, who suddenly remembered things that had escaped their notice before, things they had seen but to which they had paid no attention, such as the number of teenagers who went in and out of the theater during the daytime, when no films were on the screen. All at once Frank's entire life in Lancaster, past as well as present, came under scrutiny. "When the dominoes started to fall, there was a bunch of them that fell over," said Ronald Carter, whose father, Whit Carter, owned the building in which the Valley Theater was housed.

"Frank would walk down the street and people would say, 'Oh, that's that Frank Gumm, the pansy,' " recalled W. M. Redman, one of Frank's friends. "The rumor killed him in the community. People kept mouthing about it and mouthing about it, and it just ruined his career here. You get somebody on your back in a small town, and you'd better get your fanny out, because he'll kill you." Though they did not give their real reason, many parents now refused to let their children go to the movies by themselves, and Frank fell further and further behind in his rent: even as his daughters were receiving ovations at the Oriental Theater in Chicago, Whit Carter was presenting him with an eviction notice.

If money had been the sole problem, Frank might have muddled through. He was not the only businessman behind in his rent during those Depression years, and Carter was usually lenient with tardy tenants. But toward the end, anyway, he was not lenient with Frank. Gone were the days when Frank had been invited to sing at nearly every club meeting, funeral and wedding. Forgotten was a full-page newspaper advertisement his fellow businessmen had bought to express their appreciation for his contributions to civic life. Now their message was different. No records exist, but it is almost certain that a small group, probably led by Doc Savage, the physician who had charge of the moral as well as the physical well-being of the citizenry, approached him and made it clear, as it had been made clear in Cloquet, Grand Rapids and perhaps other places as well, that he was no longer a welcome member of the community.

This time Frank did not rush to get his fanny out of town. Only after months of delay did he agree, at the end of 1934, to surrender his lease on the Valley Theater. Though he was given three months to vacate, he still seemed unreconciled to what was happening, and on January 3, 1935, a few days after the agreement, he ran a long, extraordinary advertisement in the *Ledger-Gazette,* every sentence of which shouted his rage and resentment. "The New Year finds me still sole owner and operator of the Valley Theater," he said defiantly, then proceeded to lay down a list of rules for anyone who wished to enter his domain. From then on, patrons would not be allowed to sit through the same show twice, there would be a strict limit on charity benefits, and "let's have a definite understanding about the FREE LIST. There is None." No longer would his movie house be the relaxed establishment of previous years; no longer would he be the generous, easygoing Frank who had stood by the door to make everyone welcome.

His bitter tone must have sounded all the more startling because it was so out of character. As his deadline approached in the spring, he obstinately clung to the fiction that, no matter what anyone said or did, he would remain. "I regret that my lease expires April 1 and the building has been leased to an outside party," he told the readers of the *Ledger-Gazette* at the end of March. "Unless I can obtain this lease I will be forced out of business temporarily but expect to open a new show as soon as possible." He scarcely sounded rational. He knew, of course, that he could not obtain the lease—a front-page story in the same issue reported the names of the men who had bought it—and he could not have had any expectation of opening a rival theater. His farewell statement was really his way of having the last word with his former friends and neighbors. He was not being run out of town, Frank seemed to be saying: he was leaving merely because his lease had expired. But leave he did, finally joining Ethel and the girls in Los Angeles.

That he had been hurt by his expulsion from Lancaster no one could doubt. When his old barber, John Perkins, sent a card announcing the birth of a daughter a few months later, Frank replied with almost pathetic gratitude. Two or three times, he had been about to write, he told Perkins and his wife, but each time he had stopped because he did not know if his letter would be welcome. "It makes me happy," he said, "to feel that someone up in that old burg does think of me once in awhile."

|||

"I'm going to be a movie star," Babe had told people in Lancaster, but despite an avalanche of raves, she seemed no nearer that goal in 1935, the year she entered her teens, than she had been when she had started auditioning in the late twenties. To the surprise of those who had cheered her stage performances, all the major studios had turned her down. Even *Variety*, which supposedly knew the ins and outs of the motion-picture business, confessed its bewilderment. "Little Frances

Garland seems to have been mysteriously overlooked by local talent scouts," said one of its reviewers, "because this remarkable youngster has an amazing amount of talent for both stage & pix shows."

But there was no mystery: remarkable as Babe was, no one could think of a role for her. Hollywood had parts for the cute and cuddly— Shirley Temple, the box-office princess, was proof of that—and it had always been able to find spots for teenage beauties. But it had no roles at all for a somewhat awkward, ordinary-looking girl of thirteen, even if her singing did thrill everybody who heard her. "What can we do with a little Huckleberry Finn?" demanded an executive at Columbia Pictures. It was a good question, but an answer was soon to come. Perhaps it was the result of the years of hard work. Perhaps it was luck. In any event, just as a rush of theatrical bookings had followed a new last name in 1934, so was a movie contract to follow a new first name in 1935.

Babe had never liked either her given name, Frances, or her nickname, Babe, or—worse still, Baby. "That's a rough rap," she was later to say, and in the summer of 1935 she renamed herself Judy, after a Hoagy Carmichael and Sammy Lerner song about a girl with a voice as fresh as spring. From then on she stubbornly refused to respond to "Babe" or "Frances," however loudly they were shouted. "Judy" was the only name she answered to, and it was for Judy—Judy Garland— that Hollywood finally opened its doors.

|||

For years Ethel had dragged her youngest daughter to every film company in town, unsuccessfully searching for at least one person who would take more than a passing interest in her. Suddenly, without her prodding or plotting, there appeared, as if by magic, not one such person, but three: Al Rosen, a movie agent; Ida Koverman, the chief assistant to Metro-Goldwyn-Mayer's Louis B. Mayer; and Roger Edens, a rising star in M-G-M's music department.

Beginning in August or September, Rosen started ushering Judy through the studios yet again. Though the biggest of them all, M-G-M, or Metro as it was sometimes called, had rejected her at least twice, her third visit found a receptive and influential listener in Koverman. In early September, Koverman dispatched Edens, who had once been

Ethel Merman's pianist, to listen to Judy in the offices of a music publishing house that happened to be owned by M-G-M. Edens arrived to find Ethel providing accompaniment, as she always did. Unimpressed by her playing, he took her place at the keyboard and turned to her daughter. What did she plan to sing? " 'Zing! Went the Strings of My Heart,' " replied Judy. Then, with the innocent audacity of the very young, she posed a question of her own: "Can you change keys?" She might just as well have asked a professor of mathematics whether he could do long division. Edens shot back a cool "Yes, can you?"

After that slightly barbed exchange, it was love at first hearing. Listening to Judy, Edens later said, was like discovering gold where none had been expected. "Mrs. Koverman, Mr. Mayer must hear this girl," he insisted when he returned, and Koverman immediately set up an audition at the studio. Judy's summons, which came on Friday, September 13, caught the Gumms by surprise. Ethel was playing the piano at the Pasadena Community Playhouse, and Frank answered the phone. Could Judy come to Metro that very day? the caller inquired. So eager was he to be there on time that Frank rushed her into the car just as she was, in her casual play clothes—slacks, a blouse and sandals. It did not matter. Judy had been summoned because of her voice, not her looks.

One of Judy's standards, as happy chance would have it, was a Jewish religious song she had learned in her days of performing before B'nai B'rith groups: "Eyli, Eyli" (My God, My God), which she sang in its original Yiddish. Its dirgelike notes invariably made Mayer's eyes glisten, and when Koverman was certain Judy could sing it, she called the great man. She had a new singer he should hear, Koverman said. Koverman's strategy worked, and on Monday, September 16, a memo was sent to M-G-M's legal office: "Please prepare contract covering the services of JUDY GARLAND as an actress."

The contract, signed on September 27, was to begin October 1 and to run for seven years, with Judy making a hundred dollars a week at the start and ten times that much, a thousand dollars a week, at the end. To eyes accustomed to thirties poverty, that final figure must have looked like a staggering sum; even a hundred dollars a week was a boon to the financially beleaguered Gumms. As far as M-G-M was concerned, there was nothing unusual about Judy's contract—the studio wrote dozens just like it every year—but to Ethel it was more than a typical legal document: it was the Holy Grail she had been seeking all those long years. Her search was over. She had what she wanted.

|||

For the Gumms—or the Garlands, as now even Frank called himself and his family—life had settled down to a conventional routine. Their household had been diminished by one in August, when Mary Jane, who had taken the name Suzanne, had married a musician, Lee Kahn. Another defection seemed likely; Jimmie, now eighteen, was engaged to Frankie Darro, her boyfriend of many months.

Judy, too, Frank told John Perkins, was starting to give the boys the "once over," although M-G-M gave her scant time for romancing. She spent every day at the studio, where she took academic classes in the morning and was coached by Edens and others in the afternoon. Already her name was being mentioned in connection with two or three upcoming movies. Eager to put her before the public, M-G-M twice procured her a guest spot on NBC radio's *Shell Chateau Hour,* which was broadcast throughout the country. "We have a girl here who I think is going to be the sensation of pictures," said the show's host, Wallace Beery, when she first appeared on October 26. "I take great pleasure in presenting to you Judy Garland. Wait until you hear her!"

The family had moved from the hills of Silver Lake to a more conveniently located two-story house at 842 North Mariposa Avenue, in a pleasant, if nondescript, neighborhood south of Hollywood. No longer scurrying from stage door to stage door with her daughters, Ethel kept busy nonetheless, working at the Pasadena Community Playhouse and teaching singing to private pupils. Also busy was Frank, who had found another small theater in Lomita, a tiny suburb near the harbor of San Pedro, about twenty miles south of Los Angeles.

Although Frank and Ethel had exchanged frequent visits, they had not lived together full-time for more than two years, a separation that may have prolonged an otherwise doomed marriage. On Mariposa Avenue it was evident, as it had been on Cedar Avenue in Lancaster, that they were unalterably unhappy together. Fighting resumed—it probably had never really stopped—and Ethel was almost certainly still deeply involved with Will Gilmore. That, anyway, is what the girls believed. Many nights, while Frank was in Lomita, their mother would say she was going off to play bridge with the Gilmores, but anybody who saw Laura, whose entire left side was now paralyzed by a stroke, knew she was an unlikely bridge partner. "Awfully pitiful" was how Frank described her.

|||

Uplifted by good news, undampened by bad, Frank's high spirits had returned—Frank without a smile was not Frank at all. But a trace of nostalgia, a touch of autumnal melancholy, had crept into his voice. Ethel was to turn forty-two on November 17, he himself was six months shy of his fiftieth birthday, and he was, he said, feeling old. He could envision the day when all three daughters would be gone, and he and Ethel would be left alone with little Phooey, their Pekingese. Even the Grand Rapids newspaper conspired to turn his mind to the past. One day that fall he picked up a copy and was startled to read the announcement of the birth of Mary Jane, the new Mrs. Lee Kahn, in the "Twenty-Years-Ago" column. "Gosh just think of it," he said, indicating that he himself had thought much about it, of the roads he had taken—and had not taken.

Despite his money worries, Frank was dealing with the Depression as well as most and better than many. Although he had often had to fend off bill collectors—he had departed Lancaster owing more than two thousand dollars in back rent for the Valley Theater—somehow he had always been able to give his wife and daughters a comfortable house in a good area, as well as many luxuries. In an era when many middle-class people could not afford a car, the Gumms had not one, but two, one of which was a brand-new 1935 Ford. His creditors may have had reason to complain; his family did not. No one could have accused him of being anything less than a good provider.

A life cannot be measured in dollars, however, and by most other standards Frank's life had been a gnawing disappointment. Three times his indiscretions with teenage boys had brought ruin to his reputation; three times they had forced him to leave the place in which he had made his home and living. For a decade, moreover, he had watched impotently as, ignoring him altogether, his wife robbed his daughters of their happy childhoods. Yet his submission had not made her respect him, and Frank probably knew that, bad as it was, his marriage would not outlive poor Laura Gilmore. No wonder that he remembered his years at Sewanee, that honeysuckle Shangri-la, as the happiest he had known. No wonder that, in the fall of 1935, he concentrated his hopes and dreams on the one signal success of his nearly fifty years—his golden-voiced Judy.

The acclaim she received thrilled him perhaps even more than it did Ethel. Dorothy Walsh recalled his childlike excitement when he first spotted her name on a theater marquee, then rushed pell-mell for his camera to make a photograph of the historic sight. The M-G-M contract had brought an end to Ethel's hustling. With Judy no longer being dragged away from him, Frank saw more of her than he had since she was a small child. Now he drove her to the studio nearly every morning, often walking her to Metro's one-room schoolhouse. "Judy's mother was a fighter, but Judy and her father were gentler, more poetic people," said Mary MacDonald, who taught Judy and seven or eight other underage actors. "He had a kind of spiritual quality, just as Judy did, and he was very concerned about her. The last time I saw him he said to me, 'Will you take good care of Judy, Miss MacDonald?' "

|||

It was, as it turned out, a particularly poignant question. On Friday, November 15, not long after he had made that request, he left his Lomita theater early, complaining of an earache. For years he had suffered from recurrent ear infections, as Judy had when she was little. "Oh, it's that ear again!" he would exclaim when anyone wondered why he looked so troubled. On this occasion the pain was worse than usual, and it became more severe as the night progressed. Marc Rabwin was called, and on his orders the semiconscious Frank was admitted to Cedars of Lebanon Hospital at one-forty Saturday afternoon. He had spinal meningitis and the prognosis could not have been grimmer: death was all but inevitable.

Unaware how desperate her father's condition was, Judy kept a date to perform on the radio that night, her second appearance on the *Shell*

Chateau Hour in less than a month. "Zing! Went the Strings of My Heart" was the song she had chosen. Before she went on the air, Rabwin telephoned to say that he had placed a radio beside Frank's bed. Sing for him, Rabwin said, and the urgency in the doctor's voice told her that Frank was dying. Knowing that her father would never hear her again, Judy sang her heart out for him, as she herself phrased it, embracing those pedestrian lyrics—a recording of her performance still exists—with a warmth they had probably never known before.

> *Your eyes made skies seem blue again,*
> *What else could I do again,*
> *But keep repeating through and through,*
> *"I love you, love you!"*

It is doubtful that Frank, who was falling deeper and deeper into a coma, actually heard those tender words. He died at three o'clock the next afternoon, Sunday, November 17—Ethel's birthday. The conjunction of death and birthday was an unfortunate coincidence, made more unfortunate still by the fact that, unbeknownst even to the girls, Frank had planned a surprise party for his wife. Laden with presents, guests arrived all afternoon, cheerfully shouting "Happy birthday!" as they walked through the door, then backing out in embarrassment when they learned the bad news.

Other than showing exhaustion from two sleepless nights and many trips to the hospital, Ethel seemed remarkably unaffected by Frank's death. Not once, then or later, was she seen to cry or otherwise to display real emotion. Indeed, that very night, a few hours after their father had died, she left her daughters alone in their grief, allowing Dorothy Walsh and Frankie Darro to supply whatever comfort they could. Nor, incredibly enough, did she stay with them the following two evenings either. Too upset to cook, the girls sent Darro out for hamburgers all three nights. Ethel offered no explanation and no one asked where she was going: everyone assumed that she was meeting Will Gilmore.

Frank's funeral was held Wednesday morning, November 20, in Glendale, at Forest Lawn's Little Church of the Flowers, which had been constructed, stone by stone, to resemble an English village church. Boyd Parker, the rector of St. Paul's in Lancaster, conducted the Episcopalian services, and many of Frank's former friends also traveled over the mountains—forgiving, now that he was dead, behavior they could not accept while he was living. It was Judy's first funeral, and, unfamiliar with the customs, she watched with indignation as the mourners stopped at the open coffin to pay their respects. "Oh, Dottie! Don't let them do that!" she said to Walsh, who had been assigned by Ethel to shepherd her through the ordeal. "Don't let them come up and stare at my daddy like that! I don't like it. It's just not right. Tell them to go away!"

The casket was closed soon enough, and Frank's story came to its conclusion. Judy was later to say that his death, so sudden and so shocking, was the most terrible event in her life, and with that statement there can be no arguing. Within less than two months she had gained everything she had wanted and worked for, but had lost what she treasured most, her devoted father. Weak and flawed though he was, Frank had loved her as no one else ever had or was ever to do again. "Now," she thought bleakly, "there is no one on my side."

Aspirants to a royal family:
Judy and Deanna Durbin

CHAPTER 3

A Princess in the Realm
of Make-Believe

ith Frank gone, Judy's home, the place where she spent most of her time and energy, was no longer the address on Mariposa Avenue, or any of the other houses she was to share with her mother. Her real home was several miles to the west in Culver City—in that tiny principality, that singular realm of imagination and make-believe, known as Metro-Goldwyn-Mayer.

A more unlikely spot for a fantasy factory could scarcely have been found. Although it was only four miles from the surging Pacific, Culver City, which had a population of about six thousand, had a decidedly provincial, Middle Western flavor. Sitting at the foot of the Baldwin Hills—brown hillocks, really, with a sprinkling of oil derricks in place of vegetation—it even looked like a town in the Middle West, with a slow-paced main street, blocks of small but well-kept houses and acres and acres of empty fields, some of which were still used for farming. One resident kept a couple of cows, whose milk he delivered in a horse-drawn cart, and much of the town was suffused with the homey aroma of baking bread, a gift of one of its biggest employers, Helms Bakeries. Had it not been for the indisputable fact that it was almost entirely surrounded by the fifth largest municipality in the United States, little Culver City could have been situated in the wheat fields of Nebraska, the birthplace of its founder, the go-getting Harry Culver.

Yet fate had endowed it with four movie studios, and to that homely town came, every day but Sunday, dozens of the most glamorous people on the globe, stars whose faces were more familiar to the earth's multitudes than those of presidents and popes, generals and kings. They, and the hundreds who worked with them, were the spinners of cinema magic. Appearances aside, Culver City was one of the most extraordinary cities in the world: it manufactured dreams the way Detroit made cars and Pittsburgh produced steel. "The Heart of Screenland" were the words emblazoned on the city's official seal.

The entrance to Metro-Goldwyn-Mayer, by far the largest of the four film factories, was proclaimed by the Corinthian columns lining Washington Boulevard—mute symbols of the studio's grandeur. Inside the gates was yet another city. With a weekday population of more than four thousand, M-G-M had its own police force, fire department, hospital and telephone exchange. Metro even had its own transit system, cheerful-looking open-sided jitneys that constantly plied the ten miles of roads that lay within the six-lot complex.

The heart of that vast establishment was Lot 1, which occupied forty-five of the studio's one hundred and eighty acres. There, jumbled together in no discernible order, were soundstages, offices, rehearsal halls, dressing rooms, wardrobes, laboratories, film vaults, warehouses and shops for all the craftsmen, from electricians to tinsmiths, who labored behind the scenes. On the five outlying lots—the back lots, they were called—were such necessary appurtenances as the studio's zoo and stables and the permanent outdoor sets that, with a few artful changes, looked different each time they were seen on screen.

For westerns there was Billy the Kid Street, lined with dusty-looking adobe buildings. Verona Square, with its ornate fountains and statuary, was constructed with Renaissance Italy in mind, but it also doubled for towns in Spain and France—even twentieth-century Cuba. Copperfield Street represented Old England, Brownstone Street stood for New York, and Fifth Avenue, which was wider and a little more modern, could give a good imitation of New York, London or Chicago. On the back lots, too, were the water tanks and ponds that could simulate oceans and rivers, the turbulent Atlantic or Tom Sawyer's swimming hole. There was nothing in nature, nor any work of man, that could not be duplicated in Culver City.

The M-G-M Judy joined can only be described in superlatives. It had the most of everything required for the production of motion pictures. It had the most stars—"more stars than there are in heaven," the studio liked to boast—and the greatest success in creating still more stars. But it also had the most feature players; the most producers, directors and writers; the biggest budgets; the most advanced film laboratory; the largest accumulation of art, furniture and antiques; and the best research library. Its hoard of original musical manuscripts, for example, dated back to the dawn of history, to Sumerian hymns written in cuneiform in the eighth century B.C. Without leaving the lot, M-G-M's researchers could provide the appropriate sound, as well as the right look, for any picture, however ancient or foreign its setting. The other big studios— Paramount, Warner Bros., 20th Century–Fox and Universal—also had their own stars, talented technicians and collections of art, of course. But whatever they had, Metro had more.

There had never been, nor probably ever will be again, such a splendid moviemaking machine. Nothing was allowed to stand in its way. No problem was too large to take on, or too small to notice; an obsessive attention to detail was built into the system. At other studios, good was often good enough. At M-G-M, it could invariably be better. As Mary Astor, who was one of its chief feature players, recalled, a painting never hung crooked in a Metro production, a door never squeaked and stocking seams were always straight. "Retake Valley," Culver City was nicknamed, so frequently were casts and crews reassembled to reshoot flawed or troubled scenes. Irving Thalberg, Metro's creative genius, set the standard when he said, "Films are not made, they're remade."

Even when everyone at the studio was satisfied, a feature was not considered finished until at least one test audience had announced its approval at one of Metro's most sacred rituals, the secret preview. On the designated night all those concerned would board a chartered Pacific Electric trolley car—in those days Southern California was crisscrossed by electric trolleys—and depart for someplace like Pomona or Santa Ana, a farming or working-class community supposedly untainted by the worldly attitudes of Hollywood. There, in a small theater much like the ones Frank Gumm had run, they would strain to hear the laughs and sighs of the first paying customers. If the test crowd's verdict was favorable, the picture would be left alone; if not, yet more changes would be made.

Such a rigorous structure of checks and balances caught most big errors, and M-G-M's highly centralized apparatus guaranteed a quality no other studio could consistently match. The worst Metro movie usually had a sheen and polish that declared that no corner had been cut, no effort had been spared. But if it turned out few truly bad movies, Metro also turned out few truly great ones, particularly after Thalberg's death in 1936. Greatness thrives in an environment of independence and innovation, and both were viewed with profound suspicion at M-G-M. Talent was prized only as long as it worked within the tight framework of a team; anyone who attempted anything radically new was deemed a malcontent.

With several conspicuous exceptions, therefore, Metro's films were conservative in both form and content. M-G-M would not have countenanced a pioneering work like *Citizen Kane,* a dark, pessimistic drama like *The Informer,* or a ribald and suggestive Mae West comedy like *I'm No Angel.* The last major studio to enter the era of sound, it was also slow to accept color, and it all but ignored the profound political and economic crises of the thirties. Universal was best known for horror films; Paramount, for sophisticated comedies; Warner Bros., for gangsters and crime. But Metro was identified with glossy entertainments: drawing-room comedies like *Dinner at Eight,* elegant romances like *Camille,* and lavish costume dramas like *Marie Antoinette* and *Mutiny on the Bounty.* When they bought a ticket to an M-G-M picture, moviegoers knew, they could escape their troubles and spend a couple of hours with dazzling people in dazzling settings. From Metro they could count on glamour.

Glossy entertainments, expensively packaged in Culver City, were what the audiences of the thirties seemed to want, and M-G-M's big budgets brought big returns. The studio's annual balance sheet was proof, if proof were needed, that the rich do indeed get richer. While other powerful studios were humbled by bankruptcy or teetered close to it, Metro remained relatively untouched by the hard times. When Judy was hired in 1935, M-G-M's profits were greater than the combined total of its seven ranking competitors; for the entire decade nearly three-quarters of the industry's profits poured into Culver City. No wonder that a grateful Loew's, Inc., M-G-M's parent company, paid Louis B. Mayer, the man in charge, $1.3 million in 1937 and gave him the distinct honor then, and for nearly a decade to follow, of earning the highest salary in the United States. And why not? He ran the largest and most prosperous studio in the world, the yardstick by which all the others were measured.

|||

Almost invariably dressed in dark three-piece suits and wearing round glasses that gave him a somewhat owlish appearance, Mayer looked like a model executive, the chairman of a New York or Philadelphia bank perhaps. But he behaved more like a patriarch out of the Old Testament, Culver City's Father Abraham. Every Metro employee was a member of his family, he thought, and from those who worked for him, whether they were monarchs of the box office like Clark Gable or mere aspirants like Judy, he demanded both love and loyalty.

For the most part he was a benevolent papa, and no other studio inspired such fervent devotion. "It had the climate of Eden" was the fond memory of character actor Richard Ney, and many agreed that amid those unpromising fields and bungalows Mayer had created his own land of milk and honey. To those who agreed to abide by his rules, Mayer offered broad smiles, lifetime jobs—"I keep everybody on who behaves," he bragged—and the best working conditions in Hollywood. He could be stingy with salaries, but from air-conditioned rehearsal halls, a rarity in the thirties, to lavish dinners for crews on location, Mayer always provided an atmosphere of luxury unknown at the other film factories. "There seemed to be that little air of something special at

M-G-M," recalled stuntman Gil Perkins. "You went first cabin everywhere."

For stars, Metro seemed at first glance like a cloudless paradise. Doctors and nurses came running if their heads ached or their throats were sore, limousines stood outside the soundstages to ferry them around the lot, and fully furnished personal trailers, equipped with toilets and telephones, provided many of the comforts of home while they were resting between takes. Did they require a lawyer? A cook or a maid? No need to look. One would be located. M-G-M stars were not to be bothered by the quotidian concerns of ordinary mortals. Did they plan to travel? Tickets would be ordered—the cost would be deducted from their salaries, of course—hotel reservations would be made and someone would roll out the red carpet when they arrived at their destination. "Your problems were taken care of," said Katharine Hepburn. "It was a wonderful sensation."

Did they have trouble with the law? Metro could help there, too. If a drunken actress smashed into a tree on Sunset Boulevard, the police would be persuaded to say that her car's brakes had failed. If an actor, the hypermasculine hero who always walked away with the girl at the end, was arrested for having sex with a sailor in Long Beach, an invisible hand would reach into the police station to erase the incriminating records. Between them, Howard Strickling, the head of the publicity department, and Whitey Hendry, the studio's police chief, could grease enough important palms to fix almost anything. No less a figure than Los Angeles's top prosecutor, District Attorney Buron Fitts himself, was on the take. Metro was, or so it seemed, omnipotent.

|||

Living in paradise had its price. Like the original inhabitants of Eden, M-G-M's stars paid for all this pampering with the loss of freedom and individuality. If no other film company gave its players such twenty-four-hour-a-day coddling, neither did any other company expect them to submit to such smothering, twenty-four-hour-a-day supervision. When he signed his actors and actresses to a contract, Mayer maintained, he bought them: they were his, body and soul. "It's not your life," he once informed Mickey Rooney. "Not as long as you're working for me. M-G-M has made your life." Ava Gardner liked to joke that Metro's stars were the only kind of merchandise allowed to leave the store at night; but, she added, it was not really a very funny situation.

It was, in fact, a deadly serious one. Most of the stars, particularly the women, might just as well have worn a sign saying "Property of M-G-M." Having sex with the female help was regarded as a perk of power, and few women escaped the demands of Mayer and his underlings. Even the mother of little Shirley Temple was pawed and propositioned by Mayer, who, according to Judy, was one of the worst of the sexual predators. Between the ages of sixteen and twenty, Judy herself was to be approached for sex—and approached again and again. "Don't think they all didn't try," she said. Top on the list was Mayer himself. Whenever he complimented her on her voice—she sang from the heart, he said—Mayer would invariably place his hand on her left breast to show just where her heart was. "I often thought I was lucky," observed Judy, "that I didn't sing with another part of my anatomy."

That scenario, a compliment followed by a grope, was repeated many times until, grown up at last, Judy put a stop to it. "Mr. Mayer, don't you ever, ever do that again," she finally had the courage to say. "I just will not stand for it. If you want to show where I sing from—just point!" To her surprise, Mayer reacted not with anger, but with tears, sitting down, putting his head in his hands and crying. "How can you say that to me, to me who loves you?" he asked, looking so miserable that Judy found herself consoling him. "It's amazing how these big men, who had been around so many sophisticated women all their lives, could act like idiots," she was later to write.

Some of the propositions those big men made borrowed more from screwball comedy than scenes of seduction. When she was seventeen, Judy and a girlfriend spent a weekend in Arrowhead Springs, a resort east of Los Angeles. There, in the hotel lobby, they encountered Benny Thau, one of Mayer's chief lieutenants, and three or four other Metro executives. Thau had a reputation for dour silence—"when he laughs, dust comes out of his nose," as one actor put it—and at a cocktail party that night Judy was flattered to be singled out for his paternal attention. The next day he was less fatherly, however. As he was leaving the swimming pool, Thau called her off the nearby tennis court, then met her on the slippery incline between the court and the path to the hotel. As she leaned down to hear what he wanted, he grabbed her, then, as he tried to plant a kiss on her mouth, lost his footing and started to slide down the hill. Once again she came to the aid of one of Metro's lascivious moguls, holding him up against what might have been a nasty fall.

Not all such attempts were so comical. Another executive—Judy did not identify him—summoned her to his office, as he had summoned so many other, more glamorous Metro stars. Eschewing any pretense of small talk, he demanded that she, too, have sex with him. "Yes or no, right now—that was his style," Judy recalled. When she refused—"No, sir, I'm sorry," she said—he began screaming. "Listen you—before you go, I want to tell you something. I'll ruin you and I can do it. I'll break you if it's the last thing I do. You'll be out of here before I'm finished with you." As Judy later told the story, she simply smiled and quietly replied, "Oh, no, you'll be gone before I will." And she was right. A few months later he was out, accused by Mayer of scheming to take his own job.

|||

No aspect of its players' lives escaped Metro's scrutiny. Stars were told not only how they should look, but how they should dress and how they should behave, whom they should date and whom they should marry. Women were even advised when they should and should not have children. Many did not mind such gross interference and manipulation. Others, who found the atmosphere stifling, came to regard themselves as little more than indentured servants. From Mayer's gaze there was no hiding. Like his friend and hero, J. Edgar Hoover, whose photograph was on prominent display in his office, he insisted on knowing everything about everybody. "Young girls don't need locks if they have nothing to be ashamed of," Mayer said when his two daughters asked for locks on their bedroom doors, and he might well have said the same thing to his many foster children in Culver City.

He granted them, in any event, no privacy at all, and Metro's network of informants, both inside and outside the lot, reported their every movement. "Mr. Mayer had spies everywhere, eyes in the back of his head," said Ann Rutherford, who played Rooney's girlfriend in the

Andy Hardy films. "We never knew quite who the culprits were, but whatever we did, the word got back." Hanging over everyone's head was the morals clause in the studio contract, which, among many other things, cautioned against doing anything that would "tend to shock, insult or offend the community." The wording of the clause was so vague, yet so all-embracing, that almost any action that irritated the front office was grounds for suspension.

The existence of spies was common knowledge. What few realized was just how much further Metro's intelligence service would go to keep them in line. At the end of every day, for example, Mayer's chief henchman, Eddie Mannix, was handed copies of all the telegrams, personal as well as official, that had passed through Western Union's M-G-M branch. Since telegrams were then used for all kinds of communications, the way long-distance telephone calls and e-mail messages are today, Mannix and Mayer were aware of who was cheating on a spouse, who was in financial or legal trouble, and who was worrying about a sick friend or relative. They missed nothing.

Like all dictators, Mayer had an unshakable belief in his own rectitude. Whatever he did, he was convinced, was for the benefit of the studio in particular and the movie industry in general. "His relationship with God was intimate and confidential," the playwright S. N. Behrman observed with a touch of amusement. "He spoke for Him as well as for himself; they thought along the same lines." Unable to admit error, Mayer found it impossible to respect an opposing view. Those who held one, or who otherwise rebelled, learned that while their boss could be excessively indulgent to those who obeyed, he could also be mean-spirited and vengeful to those who did not. "I hate disloyalty!" he exclaimed. And he expanded the word's meaning to include disagreement of any kind.

When Lena Horne aroused his ire by refusing a role, Joan Crawford offered her the counsel of a battle-wise veteran. "You're perfectly right in what you feel," Crawford told her, "but you can't get away with being proud. You must go and cry and beg Mr. Mayer to forgive you. I've done it. I've had to. They were going to can me a couple of times." With children to feed, Horne wearily agreed, and her tears sent tears cascading down Mayer's cheeks as well. "I always knew that you were the humble good girl that you seemed at the beginning," he said. "You've been a bad girl, but we'll forgive you."

Men who defied him quickly discovered that Mayer's anger could be as terrible as Jehovah's. "A man of temperament" was how he euphemistically described himself, but he sometimes behaved more like a disturbed adolescent, striking out with his fists the way he had when, as a boy in Canada, he was up against the Jew-baiting bullies of St. John, New Brunswick, the fishing port where he grew up. The list of those he assaulted, actually sent sprawling, included important producers and box-office stars—Charlie Chaplin was one. Sensing the menace in his small but muscular physique, the British director Michael Powell likened him to a raging bull. But a lion, like the commanding beast that roared three times at the beginning of every Metro movie, would have made a better comparison. Short in stature, Mayer was big in every other way: he talked big, he thought big, he acted big. In his own mind, and in the minds of everyone who knew him, he was big.

He was a man of almost infinite contradictions: the kind father and the ruthless tyrant; the generous boss and the small-minded bully; the indefatigable moralizer and the greedy libertine. Yet after everything else has been said about him, after all of his faults have been enumerated, it must also be said that he was one of the twentieth century's supreme showmen. Few loved the movies, the movie business or M-G-M with as large a passion. He had not only given his last name to the corporate title: he *was* Metro-Goldwyn-Mayer. And it was to this man, this congeries of opposites, that Judy looked for support and approval at the end of 1935, and for many years thereafter. "When Dad died," she later said, "M-G-M took over as my father. In our house the word of Louis B. Mayer, who ran the studio, became the law. When Mother wanted to discipline me, all she had to say was, 'I'll tell Mr. Mayer.' "

|||

When he first heard Judy sing, Mayer had sat stony-faced, walking out without a word after she had finished: to have shown enthusiasm, after all, might have raised her price. Once he had signed her to a contract, however, he wanted all Hollywood to know about his discovery. "We have just signed a baby Nora Bayes," he exclaimed, which in 1935 was praise of the highest order: endowed with a voice that soared past the second balcony, Bayes had been one of vaudeville's biggest draws.

Given their cue by the boss, Metro's starmakers immediately went to work on Judy. Thenceforth she belonged to the studio, which controlled nearly her every waking hour. Her weekday mornings were spent in Miss MacDonald's schoolhouse—California law mandated a minimum of three hours of study a day for child actors—but her afternoons were the studio's. Not only did she attend the usual beginners' classes, but she also spent two hours a day with Roger Edens, who had displaced Ethel as her vocal coach. Their sessions achieved a modest renown within the studio walls. Dependable as a clock, a small audience gathered around Edens's office windows every afternoon to hear the results of their collaboration. On a lot crowded with famous faces, Judy had quickly managed to make a distinct impression, and as her reputation spread, she was recruited to entertain at the homes of Metro's top stars and executives. Everyone at M-G-M had heard about the Garland girl.

Her first champion, Ida Koverman—or Kay, as she preferred to be called—remained her most ardent promoter. Celebrated for her austere and forbidding demeanor, Koverman seemed to enjoy the unfamiliar role of fairy godmother. A childless, white-haired widow, she kept track of Judy at the studio and watched over her outside as well, often inviting her to dinner parties at her house in Beverly Hills. "Make no mistake about it: Kay was a tough lady," said Rita Maxwell, whose parents were Koverman's close friends. "But as much as she could care about anybody, Kay Koverman cared about Judy."

With all Metro delighting in her voice, how could Judy fail? Left with almost nothing when Frank died—$256 in cash and a stock certificate worth $150—Ethel felt sufficiently confident to move from Mariposa to a more expensive address closer to Culver City. The new house, on McCadden Place, even boasted a swimming pool, one of the most obvious badges of success in the movie world. "It looked as though Judy was going to be doing something," said Dorothy Walsh, "so Ethel thought she'd step up a little."

III

There was every reason, in fact, to believe that Judy soon would be doing something: she had tentatively been cast in at least one film, with others in the offing. But in the offing is where they remained; the pictures were either postponed or not made at all. Not once was Judy actually given lines to say, a role to fill. Too young to be considered sexy, too old to be thought cute, she was exactly where she had been before M-G-M hired her: in limbo. As she herself ruefully remarked, "They didn't know what to do with me because they wanted you either five years old or eighteen, with nothing in between. Well, I was in between."

As the weeks slipped aimlessly by, optimism gave way to anxiety. Always ahead of her, blinking ominously, like an amber light at a dangerous intersection, was her contract's option clause: she was bound to M-G-M for seven years, but M-G-M was not bound to her. At the end of every six months, the studio had the right to let her go, as it had so many other promising newcomers. Although she passed her first six-month test in March 1936, it was far from certain that she would be as lucky in September. If Metro could find nothing better for her to do than entertain at studio parties—a demeaning chore she did not much relish, in any event—she, too, would eventually be pushed out the gate. To Walsh, Judy plaintively kept saying, "I want to *do* something. Why don't they give me something to do?"

Causing still more alarm was the sudden appearance, at the end of 1935, of a pretty rival, a budding opera singer by the name of Deanna Durbin. For the new girl, who was just six months older than Judy, Metro did have a part. She was to play the young Ernestine Schumann-Heink, a much-loved opera singer whom Metro had just signed to a contract. Not long before shooting was to begin, Schumann-Heink fell ill, however. The movie was canceled and M-G-M suddenly found itself with not one, but two teenage singers for whom it had no parts, no plans and no prospects.

For Judy, the suspense was interrupted in June 1936, when she was sent to New York City for appearances on Metro's radio affiliate WHN. Accompanied by her mother, the "youthful chanter," as *Variety* dubbed her, was to remain in New York indefinitely, singing on WHN every

Thursday night until she was notified to return to California to make a film. " 'Baby Nora Bayes' Sings on WHN Awaiting Pix" was how *Variety* described her uncertain situation. Judy's first visit to the big city did not give her much time to spend gazing up at skyscrapers, however; scarcely had she arrived when Metro ordered her home.

Once more the studio was to disappoint her. The picture she was needed for was not a picture at all, but a short, one of those snippets of film the studios turned out, along with newsreels and cartoons, to fill up the time between features. *Every Sunday* it was titled, and she was paired with Durbin, who sang opera while Judy sang swing. Though it eventually did find its way into the theaters, *Every Sunday* was, in essence, a screen test to help Metro executives decide which of their gifted teenagers they wanted.

Though Judy won the contest, she, too, found herself fighting tears, almost as upset as Durbin was. "If they don't want Deanna," she wailed, "I'm sure they don't want me either." She was probably right, or nearly right. Metro did not want to lose her, yet it could not bring itself to use her, a stalemate that could not last forever and that seemed destined to end as unhappily for her as it had for Durbin.

It doubtless came as a great relief to everyone, therefore, when not one, but two other studios asked to borrow her. Her first suitor was Universal, where producer Joe Pasternak was looking for a girl with "indefinable charm," as he termed it, for his romantic comedy *Three Smart Girls*. A long search had led nowhere, and Pasternak was about to give up and change his title to *Three Smart Boys* when he saw Judy in the screen test with Durbin. "That's the girl!" he shouted, persuaded that she not only had that indefinable charm, but also "sang in a way to win your heart." Her second suitor was 20th Century–Fox, which was planning a spoof on college football—*Pigskin Parade* was to be its name—and which needed a younger sister for its touchdown hero. Only one of her admirers could have her, and Metro picked Fox. After making some changes in his script, a disappointed Pasternak settled for the other girl in that screen test, Deanna Durbin.

By the end of the summer of 1936 both Judy and Durbin were doing what they had so long dreamed of doing: making movies. But neither was doing it for the studio that had discovered them. They had the comfort and satisfaction of at last being wanted, but not by Louis B. Mayer's starmaking enterprise in Culver City—glittery, glamorous M-G-M.

|||

Although it was made later, *Pigskin Parade* beat *Every Sunday* to the theaters. Thus, through an accident of timing, Judy's introduction to movie audiences was not as the ordinary-looking, ordinary-sounding teenager she had been in the Metro short, but as the barefoot, mushmouthed hillbilly she was in the Fox comedy. "Y'all stop for melons?" were her first words. "I'm Sairy Dodd and I can sing—you want to hear me?" she goes on to ask. The songs will have to wait. The visitors to the family farm are more interested in her brother, who can throw a melon the length of a football field and who is just the man, they think, to help their Podunk college beat snooty Yale on the gridiron.

There are several twists to the story before Yale receives its comeuppance, but *Pigskin Parade* is not about football. It is about jokes, songs and pretty girls, and it is nothing but an amiable and predictable B-picture until, nearly halfway through, Judy appears to give it a jolt of high voltage. She sings only three mediocre songs, all of which would probably slip by unnoticed if they came from any mouth but hers: as she sings them, they are incitements to riot. She poured so much power into one of them, which she sang on the playing field of the Los Angeles Coliseum, that it could be heard all the way out to Figueroa Street. "The voice!" exclaimed June Levant, who was a bit player sitting in the bleachers. "The voice! I can hear it now, it was so remarkable."

Released in mid-October, *Pigskin Parade* received surprisingly good reviews. "Daffy and delightful," declared the *New York Herald Tribune*'s Howard Barnes. "One of the season's most entertaining contributions," added Frank S. Nugent of *The New York Times*. Judy, who was ranked ninth on the cast list, was mentioned in passing, if at all. One of the few who singled her out was Robert Garland, the very man whose name George Jessel had bestowed upon her two years earlier. "Judy Garland is a girl to keep an eye and ear on," Garland wrote in the *New York American*.

The one who was keeping the closest eye was Judy, who was horrified and dismayed by the unattractive, clumsy-looking girl she saw in

Pigskin Parade. A "fat little frightening pig with pigtails," was how she described herself. No one else saw such an apparition; but it was undeniably true that she was overweight—not really fat, but too pudgy, by Hollywood standards anyway, to be thought of as anything but slightly comic. Gone was the skinny child of the Lancaster years, who had eaten and eaten but who had never gained an ounce. In her place was a teenager who was beginning to show the unfortunate proportions she was to have as an adult. Small—she was just under five feet in 1936— she had a disappearing neck, a big chest, a very short waist and long, long legs. Even a few excess pounds, which might have been invisible on a more conventional figure, were, and were to be, cruelly apparent on hers. To make matters worse, in *Pigskin Parade,* Fox actually accentuated her weight, dressing her, in her opening shots, in a tattered, shapeless bag of a dress. She was supposed to be a figure of fun—and so she was. Squirming in her seat as the film unrolled, Judy was convinced that her first movie would also be her last.

|||

Even talk of a part in a new picture, *Broadway Melody of 1937,* did little to brighten her return to M-G-M. She had heard similar promises before, and once again she spent her mornings in Miss MacDonald's schoolroom, her afternoons with Roger Edens. "What I like to do is sing—good and loud," she was to say; but Metro still let her do that only at parties. The M-G-M machine, which had worked so hard on her behalf a year earlier, was now all but silent. Although Ida Koverman was still pushing her, Mayer was not, his excitement in 1935 having turned to indifference in 1936. "The Boss has lost interest in Judy," Koverman told screenwriter Frances Marion. "Whenever I suggest her name for a small part in a musical all he says is, 'Stop bleating! I'm running this studio, not you!' " Yet she would not be intimidated, Koverman insisted. Judy had become her cause. "I'll never give up! Somehow I'll manage to get his interest back to Judy again."

If Deanna Durbin's experience was any indication, it was better to be fired than hired by M-G-M. The loser in the Metro sweepstakes, Durbin was the clear and almost instant winner in the bigger contest to become a star. After her tearful exit from Metro, she became a regular on Eddie Cantor's show, perhaps the highest-rated program on all radio, and a darling of Universal, her new studio. "Universal's New Discovery," the studio called her. "Universal's Savior" would have been equally appropriate. Released in December 1936, *Three Smart Girls* was such a big hit that, all by itself, it rescued the company from bankruptcy and transformed its dimpled lead into a genuine star. "When am I going to get my chance!" Judy demanded after seeing it at a preview. "I can't wait!"

If the success of Durbin's picture was unsettling to her, it was positively galling to Mayer and his men, who belatedly realized their mistake in letting their little soprano go. How could they have chosen chubby Judy over the slim and pretty Durbin? How could those famous starmakers have passed up such an obvious star? "Mayer let Tiffany go and held on to Woolworth," went one widely repeated wisecrack. After reading Durbin's ecstatic reviews, Judy may have been saying the same thing to herself, crying so much that a worried Ethel took her to see Koverman. Throwing herself into Koverman's lap, Judy started sobbing all over again. "I've been in show business ten years and Deanna's a star and I'm nothing!" she told Koverman.

"You just wait," replied the determined Koverman. "You're going to get your chance, you'll be starred, and you're going to have your footprints in Grauman's Chinese—you'll see."

|||

A chance of sorts did, in fact, come a few weeks later. On February 2, 1937, Judy was scheduled to appear on a radio variety show run by Ben Bernie, otherwise known as the "Ole Maestro." She was longing to sing a hot love song, "Drums in My Heart," that Edens had arranged and played for Ethel Merman. After working with Judy for more than a year, however, Edens had concluded that the torch songs that had caused such a stir in her vaudeville days were now hindering, not helping her career. Audiences were indeed amazed to discover a woman's voice coming from a child's body, but it was a phenomenon that, at the same time, made them vaguely uneasy. It seemed almost indecent to hear sexy lyrics sung by a girl who had barely reached puberty. Judy would do better, Edens reasoned, with songs more appropriate to her age.

Confident in his analysis, he informed her that she was too young for "Drums in My Heart." It was a song for a woman, he said, not a girl. That was the last thing Judy wanted to be told, and after an angry exchange she stalked out of his office. When she later returned—she could not remain mad at Edens very long—he made a deal with her. He had an idea for a number he thought she would like. Give it a try, he said, and if he was wrong, she could sing Merman's song.

It was a gamble Edens was not in much danger of losing. What he had come up with was all but irresistible: a torch song with a funny twist. His notion was to present her as a moonstruck fan who falls for Bernie's voice on the radio. She writes him a musical love letter that soon turns into "You Made Me Love You," a romantic ballad of such ancient vintage that Frank and Ethel might have sung it on the stage of the New Grand before Judy was born. Since the cigar-chomping Old Maestro was perhaps the last man in Hollywood who would inspire such a love song, Edens figured that Bernie's listeners would get the joke. So long as nobody took it seriously, Judy could sing a torch song.

At that point Koverman stepped in, as she so often had at crucial moments in Judy's career. The day before Judy was to appear on Bernie's show, Mayer was planning a surprise birthday party for his leading male star, Clark Gable. Realizing that the party provided her with the long-awaited opportunity to bring attention back to Judy, Koverman put in a call to Edens: she wanted Judy to sing. The audience would be small, but it would be select; all of Metro's top executives were expected to pay tribute to Gable, "the King," as he was known in Culver City. With no time to work up a new number, Edens changed "Dear Mr. Bernie" to "Dear Mr. Gable." Judy had her song.

So it was that on the afternoon of February 1 a festive group surrounded Gable on the set of his latest movie, *Parnell*. After the birthday cake had been cut and the gifts opened, piano notes were heard and a spotlight illuminated a dark corner, where Judy was sitting nervously atop Edens's piano. It was, she later said, her first experience of stage fright. "Dear Mister Gable," she began. "I am writing this to you, and I hope that you will read it so you'll know." Explaining that every time she saw one of his movies her heart went bang, bang, bang and she was so giddy she could hardly speak, she decided to let him know how she felt in a letter:

You made me love you
I didn't wanna do it. . . .

When she ended by telling him that he had the brand of kisses she would die for, Gable went over and really did kiss her, causing Judy to burst into tears ("maybe," as Mickey Rooney impishly suggested, "because Gable had such terrible halitosis"). Flustered as she was, wrote Rooney, Judy was not so overcome that she lost her senses, however. "Out of the corner of one eye, she spied Mr. Mayer, beaming with his arms held out to her. She left Gable's side, went over, and climbed into Mr. Mayer's lap. At that, everyone just about went nuts."

By coincidence, Judy was scheduled to entertain that night at a charity benefit at the Café Trocadero, along with such big names as Sophie Tucker, Eddie Cantor and her old mentor, George Jessel. It was an ideal opportunity to test her love letter to Gable before another kind of crowd. Would the Trocadero's sophisticated show-business audience have the same visceral reaction as Gable's friends and colleagues? If the answer was yes, Metro's assembled executives realized that in Judy and her new song they had a guaranteed moneymaker. That night's applause told the story. Judy, wrote columnist Sidney Skolsky, was the sensation of the evening, overshadowing everyone else on that illustrious bill.

Three more times that winter and spring an audience heard Judy sing "Dear Mr. Gable." The third occasion, Metro's annual show for theater owners and exhibitors, brought the loudest roar of all. "I have never seen such enthusiasm from an audience," said Ann Rutherford. "They banged the tables!" By that point nobody at Metro needed convincing that the Garland girl had a future in the movies. *Broadway Melody of 1937* was at last under way—so late that it was retitled *Broadway Melody of 1938*—and both Judy and her new song, "Dear Mr. Gable," were in it. Never again was she heard to complain that M-G-M was not giving her enough to do.

III

So at last, after a year and a half of false starts and disappointments, Judy's movie career really began. The M-G-M machine sprang to life, then began whistling and whirring on her behalf. Now, instead of looking for excuses to keep her out of pictures, Metro searched for reasons to put her in, inserting songs into stories that otherwise would have had none at all. Its ingenuity in finding films was such that she was kept almost constantly busy: from the spring of 1937 through the summer of 1938 she made no fewer than five movies, an average of one every three months. *Broadway Melody of 1938* was followed by *Thoroughbreds Don't Cry* and *Everybody Sing;* they, in turn, were succeeded by *Love Finds Andy Hardy* and *Listen, Darling.*

Her smallest, but perhaps most noticeable part was in *Broadway Melody.* In a film that included Eleanor Powell's knockout tap dancing and the brassy voice of Sophie Tucker, Judy more than held her own. As Metro had anticipated, just about the whole country responded to her love letter to Clark Gable, which one critic described as "heart-rending." Many reviewers also agreed with the *New York Daily Mirror,* which said that Tucker and "small Miss Garland" walked off with the show. So visible had she become that Judy was considered for the role of one of Scarlett O'Hara's younger sisters in the most talked-about movie of the decade, *Gone With the Wind.* (That part eventually went to a somewhat older Metro player, Ann Rutherford.)

If she walked off with *Broadway Melody,* Judy ran away with her four other pictures. Without her, they would scarcely be worth looking at today. Though all have fine casts, the usual M-G-M polish, and an undeniable congeniality, they are, like so many other Metro products of the post-Thalberg era, deeply mired in Mayer's gluey sentimentality. *Thoroughbreds Don't Cry* is, of course, a racetrack yarn. Mickey Rooney plays a smart-aleck jockey, and Judy, whose aunt runs a boardinghouse for riders, teaches him humility, a lesson she was to repeat many times in the eight other movies they made together. A screwball comedy with music, *Everybody Sing* is pleasant entertainment, but it does not make the grade as either a comedy or a musical. What it does is give Judy, who plays the youngest member of a scatty theatrical family, a chance to show the wide range of her talent: with equal aplomb, she sings, bounces comic lines off that old vaudevillian Fanny Brice, and sheds a small bucket of tears in her first crying scene.

In *Love Finds Andy Hardy,* she is smitten with the irrepressible Andy, who is played by the equally irrepressible Rooney. Although Andy considers her too young to be anything more than a pal, he is glad to accept her aid in straightening out his tangled romantic life, which is always the chief concern of this long-running series. In *Listen, Darling,* Judy is Cupid again. Aided by Freddie Bartholomew, who, until recently, had been the studio's most important child star, she prevents her widowed mother (Mary Astor) from marrying the stodgy town banker, then leads her to happiness with a more exciting younger man (Walter Pidgeon).

Already, M-G-M has established the persona that will remain with Judy almost to the end of her screen career. She is the wholesome girl next door, the sensitive soul mate boys like but do not lust after, the understanding friend to whom they confide their troubles with prettier, sexier girls. Metro, in short, was asking her to play a girl much like Judy Garland, and its writers had an uncanny knack of providing her characters with lines she herself might have spoken. "I'll never be able to get a man, much less hold him," one of them, Betsy Booth, laments in *Love Finds Andy Hardy.* "No glamour. No glamour at all. No glamour. That's my trouble." To anyone who would listen, Judy herself was making identical complaints in almost identical words.

Even when they are cast to type, as most stars were in the Hollywood of the thirties, actors usually go through an apprenticeship, a period in which they sometimes stumble and fall as they learn their peculiar craft. Judy was not one of them. She was that rarity, a natural performer who was born, as Joe Pasternak observed, "with what might be called perfect theatrical pitch." Although her talent matured as she herself grew older, never, except possibly in *Pigskin Parade,* did she appear to be speaking someone else's words, silly as they sometimes were. "There are moments with other actresses, even the greatest ones, when you think—'She's acting,' " said Lillian Sidney, drama coach to two generations of Metro players. "Never Judy." Watching her progress, those in charge in Culver City seemed to take it for granted that she would be a star, and with each succeeding movie they moved her a rung or two higher on the cast list. Placed near the bottom of the credits when *Broadway Melody* reached the theaters in September 1937, Judy was first, nudging out Freddie Bartholomew, when *Listen, Darling* was released in October 1938.

The studio's favorite, she could not have been held in higher regard had Leo the Lion, the regal symbol of M-G-M, licked her hand, nuzzled her cheek and given her a ride on his tawny back. Everybody liked Judy, just as everybody had liked Frank Gumm. She was "a kid, a real kid," observed Mary Astor, and her natural effervescence, combined with her keen, impish sense of humor, caused even Mayer, who possessed neither, to smile indulgently when he was around her. "Judy, none of your tricks on me now!" he said, wagging his finger in her face. "I'm on to you!" Added to her father's appeal was an attribute a practiced charmer like Frank did not have: a becoming diffidence, an appealing vulnerability that warmed the coldest heart. "There was always something childlike and shy about Judy," said songwriter Ralph Blane. "You wanted to pet her."

Yet that endearing, childlike quality, which was one of her greatest assets, was also to prove one of her most serious liabilities at M-G-M. She was, then and later, taken seriously as a performer, but not as a person; she was treated like a minor, an attitude of condescension that pursued her, like an unwelcome childhood nickname, well into adulthood. No one at M-G-M could ever forget that she had grown up on Lot 1; few could substitute the image of the woman for the girl with the giggles. Even after she had reached her majority—and was a certifiable star at that—Mayer still referred to her as "that poor little girl, Judy Garland." Small wonder, then, that as long as she remained at Metro, Judy also thought of herself as a poor little girl. Small wonder, too, that however high her salary rose, she always felt that in Culver City she was looked upon as a poor relation.

|||

If M-G-M intruded into the personal affairs of its grown-up players, it virtually ran the lives of its adolescents. For them, Mayer's plush patriarchy was a luxurious reform school, the studio often guaranteeing around-the-clock obedience by putting their mothers on the payroll. Ethel was one such mother-employee, assigned the single task of making sure that Judy did as she was told when she was told. Praised when they were good, Metro's underage offspring were scolded and all but spanked when they were bad—"bad" being a word that the studio could define any way it wanted. In the case of Judy, who was cheerful on the set, who learned her lines with phenomenal ease and who caused no disturbances in the world outside, it meant only one thing: she ate too much; she was too heavy.

In the months when it had nothing for her to do, Metro did not much care whether she was thin or fat. Once she actually started making movies and her box-office appeal became apparent—"They love the kid!" exclaimed songwriter Arthur Freed when *Broadway Melody* came out—Judy was subjected to closer and far more critical examination. The camera is sadistically cruel to the overweight, and a fat star was a former star. For Judy, all that was at issue was a few unnecessary inches around the middle; but that bulge at her waist might just as well have been the Maginot Line, so large did it loom in the imaginations of those who controlled her destiny. "My little hunchback," Mayer himself began to call her. Trying to turn humiliation into a joke, Judy would repeat the line herself. "I am Mr. Mayer's little hunchback," she would say with a laugh.

Other pudgy girls of fourteen or fifteen are spared such intense scrutiny and usually slim down as they grow up. A movie star in the making—"plump Judy Garland," as the *New York Post* called her in its review of *Thoroughbreds Don't Cry*—was to be granted no such luxury. Her body now belonged to M-G-M, not to her. Every time she picked up a french fry or dipped a spoon into a bowl of ice cream she was damaging a valuable corporate asset. "From the time I was thirteen," she said, "there was a constant struggle between M-G-M and me—whether or not to eat, how much to eat, what to eat. I remember this more vividly than anything else about my childhood."

An attempt was made to shame the pounds off her. Stood in front of a mirror, she was told to compare herself with the clothes dummy standing next to her—the figure of a fat woman. "Now look at yourself," she was instructed. "Do you want to look like that dummy or do you want to be a star?" As any first-year psychology student could have predicted, such rough tactics inevitably backfired. By undermining her confidence, Metro made her only more eager to find solace in old friends, sweet, fattening treats being among the oldest. The girl who had grown up with a candy bar in her hand found it devilishly hard to live without sweets. "My idea of a good time," she confessed, "was a caramel sundae at Wil Wright's ice-cream parlor in Hollywood—oodles of sauce and whipped cream. Whenever I could, I used to slip off and gorge myself."

Increasingly frustrated, the studio also took more direct steps to bring down her weight: as long as she was on the lot, she was to be starved into slimness. No matter what she asked for when she sat down for lunch in the studio commissary, waitresses were told to serve her nothing but chicken soup. It was good chicken soup, filled with light, fluffy matzoh balls made according to a recipe from Mayer's own beloved mother; but it was still chicken soup. Metro was not playing games; to prevent cheating, she was discouraged from eating at the teenagers' table, where one of her friends might have sneaked her a for-bidden morsel, a bite of hamburger or a piece of cake. If she ignored all the hints and sat there anyway, Roger Edens was quickly dispatched to join her and prevent transgressions. Though Judy later joked about what she termed her "prisoner's menu," there was always an angry edge to her humor. Mayer's chicken soup, she said, had been well salted— with her tears.

All the spies on the lot and the one at home—which is to say, Ethel— could not watch her twenty-four hours a day. Despite all the eyes fas-tened on her, she still managed to escape to Wil Wright's and to find hiding places in her studio dressing room for cookies, chocolates and candies. In desperation, the studio finally brought out a new weapon to curb those renegade desires. Ethel had been giving her pills, pills to wake her up and pills to put her to sleep, since the Lancaster days. Now, Metro added diet pills, combinations of Benzedrine and phenobarbital, to that already potent mixture. The studio had found the ultimate weapon.

To a later generation, which can count the victims of prescription drugs, the dangers of such a course are obvious. They were less so in the Hollywood of the thirties and the forties, when amphetamine-based stimulants like Benzedrine and, later, more sophisticated off-shoots like Dexedrine and Dexamyl, were nearly as common as aspirin. To many, they seemed like miracles of science. Some used them for dieting, as Judy was forced to do; others, for energy and concentration. The day after trying his first Benzedrine, Joseph Mankiewicz, who was then a rising young writer at Metro, was back demanding more. "Give me a roomful of them! I never wrote so much and so well in my life. I want them!" So did many others, and at most of the big studios there was a doctor who carried a bag stuffed with variously colored pills, each formulated to have a different effect on the mind or body.

Not far off was a time when everyone—Mayer, Ethel and, most poignantly, Judy—would regret Metro's drastic solution to her weight problem. For the moment it seemed to work. The pounds began to disappear. But her fight to stay slim was unrelenting and remorseless, coloring her whole existence from the moment she woke in the morning until the instant she fell asleep at night. Indeed, if the truth could be known, the battle probably continued, more fiercely and ferociously still, in the privacy of her dreams. For Judy, it was a war without end, or hope of end.

|||

At the beginning of 1938 Metro placed an ad in *Variety:* "It's a little early to predict but here's a prophecy for 1938! JUDY GARLAND STARDOM!" Not counting on fate to decide the matter, it soon put Judy on a train to Miami, the first stop of a two-month publicity tour to promote *Everybody Sing* and, of course, herself. The last time the studio had sent her east, in the spring of 1936, she had been a contract player with an uncertain future, and her mother had been her only company. This time, thanks to her new stature in Culver City, she was accompanied by an entourage. Ethel went along, but so did Roger Edens, her older sister Suzanne, and her tutor, who, in obedience to California state law, would be teaching her the three R's until she turned eighteen.

Arranged with all the care given a presidential campaign, Judy's tour actually began in Houston, where her Miami-bound train stopped for half an hour on its way from Los Angeles. At the station to meet her were the mayor and a high school guard of honor, twenty-five girls. Six younger girls, each dressed in a copy of one of her *Everybody Sing* costumes, presented her with a box of pralines. Even more elaborate was her reception in Florida, where she traveled in a motorcade to her hotel on Miami Beach and where searchlights lit up the night for the movie's world premiere. Accustomed to visitors from Hollywood, New York City, next on the itinerary, gave her a cordial but more restrained welcome. Several papers sent interviewers to her hotel suite; all came away impressed by the confident and unassuming demeanor of a girl who was soon to top the bill at the giant Loew's State Theater in Times Square. "M-G-M's Sensational Singing Star," as the ads were calling her, was assured but far from brash, said one admiring reporter.

Judy could have used some of that assurance a few hours later. Stepping out in front of her first New York audience on February 10, she suffered a potentially disastrous case of stage fright, so anxious that she lost control of her voice and all but shouted her first song. Nonplussed, the house responded with an epidemic of nervous coughs. Awakened, or perhaps frightened by her earsplitting volume, a baby howled, and the coughs suddenly turned into chilly laughter. Halting in mid-song, Judy also started laughing. Her giggles, which proved that M-G-M's Sensational Singing Star was, after all, just a girl, broke the tension and brought on a second round of laughter, warm and friendly this time around. The unhappy baby had saved her. Nervous no longer, Judy started all over, not stopping again until, twenty-four minutes and two encores later, she had made what *Variety* called an undeniable smash. "Kid has an unspoiled, bashful manner that is irresistibly appealing," said the *Variety* critic.

It was her singing, not her manner, that audiences found the most appealing, however. When she reached Pittsburgh at the end of February, another *Variety* critic described her effect on them. "Lassie has the mob tearing up the seats, swinging her slight, lithe frame in syncopated jig-time, and dusting off the rafters with her rhythmic bleatings." What that meant, translated into English, was that, in addition to the usual menu of ballads, Judy was also delivering songs with a relatively new sound—the sound of swing.

|||

An offshoot of jazz, swing dominated American popular music for about ten years, from the mid-thirties to the mid-forties. Pioneered by black musicians, then made commercial by the big bands of white leaders like Benny Goodman, Glenn Miller and Artie Shaw, it was the creation of performers, not composers. The "swing" was all in the performer's timing, inflection and energy, not in anything the songwriter had put on paper. The same tune could swing or not swing, depending entirely on who played or sang it; given a swing rendition, the most familiar music could be transformed into something almost unrecognizably new—even Bach was made to jump and jive. To young audiences, swing was not only joyful, but liberating, with a kinetic vitality that was catching. Under its spell, fingers began to snap, feet started to tap and youthful bodies automatically moved toward a dance floor.

It was a style that Judy, with her congenital bounce, had taken to immediately. The first songs she recorded, in fact, were swing—"Stompin' at the Savoy" and "Swing, Mr. Charlie," both done with the Bob Crosby orchestra on her earlier trip to New York. With Edens as her guide, she had not merely sung those stomping, swinging lyrics; she had invested them with so much of her own energy that they seemed to have a life of their own, almost leaping off the phonograph record. Capitalizing on her natural bent, Metro made her affinity for swing one of the plotlines of *Everybody Sing:* her character is expelled from a stuffy private school for supposedly corrupting her classmates with its subversive rhythms. "But I can't help it, Miss Colvin," she says apologetically. "Honestly I can't. I don't know why, but when I hear music, it does something to me."

Now, on her second trip to Manhattan, Judy alternated between swing and what she called sweet—the old-fashioned ballads she sang so well. Sometimes she sang the same song in two tempos, one swing, one sweet. One such song, "Bei Mir Bist Du Schön," was probably familiar to everyone in her audience. No one, including Sammy Cahn and Saul Chaplin, who had adapted it from its original Yiddish, had heard it sung the way she sang it at the Loew's State, however. The girl who had so often sung in Yiddish at B'nai B'riths began leisurely, almost chanting the words, as a cantor would. Then, without a moment's pause, she pushed them into high velocity—swing. "It was the most incredible arrangement of that song I had ever heard," said Chaplin, who returned again and again to hear it. "There was nothing like it. The way she did it was fantastic!"

|||

After New York Judy journeyed on to engagements in Pittsburgh, Detroit, Chicago, Minneapolis and Columbus, Ohio. In Pittsburgh the "Metro moppet," as *Variety* dubbed her, was the biggest box-office surprise in years, breaking all records at the Stanley. Attendance would have been even higher, indeed, if many who had come to the first show had not liked her so much that they had refused to leave, clinging to their seats for the second, third and fourth shows. Hoping to cash in on the excitement she had aroused, a rival theater, the Alvin, dug up an old print of *Every Sunday,* and ran it along with its first-run feature, giving the short, which lasted no more than ten minutes, top billing in its ads.

Helped along, no doubt, by Howard Strickling's publicity department, Judy's fame had preceded her to Columbus, where Ohio State University's Sigma Chi fraternity named her its official sweetheart. Declaring that she had "personality plus," the brothers escorted her from the stage of the Ohio Theater to their frat house, where they entertained her with dinner, toasted her success with glasses of milk and bent over—all in fun, of course—so that their swinging sweetheart could whack them with a ceremonial paddle.

She had triumphed in every city she had visited, but it is probably safe to say that nowhere was Judy happier with her reception than she was on the final stop on her schedule—Grand Rapids. Choosing to forget that they had almost run her family out of town, people there had followed her career with a jealous, proprietary interest. "Local Girl Starred in Movie Coming Here," read the headline in the *Itasca County Independent* when *Pigskin Parade* was making its rounds.

On the morning of March 31, a delegation of leading citizens met Judy's train at Aitkin, a town to the south, and several cars plowed through a dangerous storm of snow and sleet—the passage of time had not shortened the interminable Minnesota winters—to carry her back to Grand Rapids in time for a gala luncheon at the Pokegama Hotel. After lunch, she was taken sight-seeing. She went back to the house she had last seen when she was four years old, and she visited the schools she would have attended had she remained. That week's issue of *Life* magazine featured a lavish five-page spread on her frolic at the Ohio State fraternity house—"*Life* Goes to a Party with Judy Garland," the article was titled—and when she walked into the high school auditorium, the school band greeted her with its brassy version of that old favorite of barbershop quartets, "The Sweetheart of Sigma Chi."

After making an appearance at the Rialto Theater, the successor to Frank's New Grand, Judy was driven to a nightspot outside of town, where several teenagers threw a spur-of-the-moment party in her honor. Defying the blizzard outside—"It was a murderous night, a real corker," recalled one—they drank sodas and danced to a jukebox. One boy, Bill Binet, who had played with Judy when they were both small, gave her his military-school pin, in return for which he received her warm and grateful kiss in the coatroom. Attaching it to her coat a few weeks later, Judy wore it when she was shooting *Love Finds Andy Hardy*. Captured on film, Binet's pin, two shiny crossed rifles, can be seen still, a cherished memento of that snowy night.

The next day, April 1, she was on her way back to the warmth and sunshine of California. Summing up her stay, the *Itasca County Independent* seemed mildly surprised to find itself full of her praises, reporting that Grand Rapids' most famous daughter was "a sweet, wholesome young person, unspoiled by the success she has made in her chosen work and by the way people have made much over her wherever she has appeared."

Despite the cheerless weather, Judy was perhaps even more pleased with Grand Rapids than Grand Rapids was with her. In her twenty-four hours there, she had seen only smiles, heard only kind and flattering words. She believed it was always like that in that "gracious little town, full of trees and porches and people who know how to live in simple goodness." During bleak moments, she would occasionally wonder what her own life would have been like had she never left. In a scene that might have been lifted from an Andy Hardy movie, she pictured herself carrying her schoolbooks in a strap, sighing over the milkman's son and passing her days in perfect safety and security. Her roots, she thought, would have been as deep and solid as those of the rugged snow-covered pines that guarded Grand Rapids on every side. For her, that frosty utopia was not a real place but a symbol. Her imaginary life there was a movie she sometimes ran in her mind, a sentimental M-G-M production with a guaranteed happy ending.

Judy with a Tin Man,
a Scarecrow and a Cowardly Lion—
Jack Haley, Ray Bolger
and Bert Lahr

CHAPTER 4

Production No. 1060—
The Wizard of Oz

udy was in Pittsburgh, midway through her tour, when she heard surprising news from California. "Metro has acquired the screen rights for 'The Wizard of Oz' from Samuel Goldwyn and has assigned Judy Garland to the role of Dorothy," *Daily Variety* reported on February 24. "Mervyn LeRoy will produce the Frank Baum childhood fantasy." Much beyond that a tight-lipped M-G-M did not go, and the absence of the hoopla that accompanied most new Hollywood projects, the trumpet fanfares and the excited chatter of typewriters, was, in retrospect, almost startling. For the film announced that day—Production No. 1060—was not to be just another product of the Culver City machine: it was destined to become the most popular motion picture in the history of the cinema.

Metro probably said so little because it knew so little. Inspired by the unexpected success of another children's story, Walt Disney's *Snow White and the Seven Dwarfs*, which had been filling the theaters since December, M-G-M had indeed acquired screen rights to *The Wizard of Oz*. Judy was to portray Dorothy Gale, the orphan who is transported by a cyclone from the arid plains of Kansas to the magical land of Oz, and Mervyn LeRoy was to produce. The production department had even prepared a budget: to build an imaginary world, create the necessary special effects and deploy a huge cast would cost in excess of $2 million—an enormous sum to spend on a picture in 1938.

The star, the producer and the budget: that much the studio knew; but that was about all it knew. Probably never before had it committed so much money to a project about which it still had so many basic questions. Would its *Oz* be funny or serious? Metro did not know. What kind of music would be sung? Opera, swing or Broadway-style ballads? Metro did not know that either. Having paid $75,000 for the film rights, M-G-M could make of *The Wizard of Oz* exactly what it wanted. The trouble was that it was not sure what it wanted, and in the absence of guidelines, almost all options were open, bad as well as good.

Chance played a larger part in these decisions than the studio would likely have admitted. More than once, circumstances forced it to settle for its second or third choice and steer a different course from the one it had intended. Mayer's boss in New York, Nicholas Schenck, president of Loew's, had, in fact, suggested that the lead go not to Judy, but to Shirley Temple, the nation's box-office queen for three years running. But Temple could not sing—"her vocal limitations are insurmountable," Roger Edens gleefully reported—and, in any event, 20th Century–Fox would probably not have loaned her out.

Time and again, luck—or some guardian angel—thus saved *Oz* from its handlers and prevented such mistakes. Perhaps the biggest wonder of a movie whose theme is the wonderful is that though M-G-M often went astray, sometimes far astray, it invariably returned to what can now be seen as the one true path. The final choice—whether it was first, second or third—was always the right one. It was by fits and starts, by trial and error, that the film progressed, slowly but persistently overcoming all obstacles to arrive at last at its destination. Unlikely as it would have seemed to those mired in the day-to-day confusions, *Oz*, like all genuine works of art, was to emerge from its long gestation with the unblemished appearance of inevitability. Who can imagine the Mona Lisa without her smile? *A Christmas Carol* without Tiny Tim? And *The Wizard of Oz* in any way different from what it is?

Initial thoughts had been to make a musical comedy, with either Ed Wynn or W. C. Fields, two of the top comics of the era, playing the Wizard, and either Fanny Brice or Beatrice Lillie, their female counterparts, playing Glinda, the Good Witch. All four dropped out, however, and those key roles went instead to two character actors, Frank Morgan and Billie Burke, both of whom specialized in what might be termed kindly befuddlement. It was despite Metro, then, that the film became not a broad slapstick comedy, which the studio appeared to want, but a drama with strong comic overtones. Then and later, *Oz* seemed to have a life, a will and a future of its own, beyond the control of anyone in Culver City.

As crucial as casting was the selection of the kind of music that would be sung and played in Oz, a choice that LeRoy left up to his associate producer, Arthur Freed. An accomplished songwriter—he had written the lyrics of such songs as "Singin' in the Rain" and "You Were Meant for Me"—Freed had once hoped to produce *Oz* all by himself, consenting to the subordinate position only at the urging of his friend Louis B. Mayer. If he learned the producing ropes from the experienced LeRoy, Mayer had told him, Metro would then give him a picture of his own. With that inducement, Freed had dutifully agreed, and LeRoy, for his part, had entrusted him with responsibility for everything musical.

Opera, swing or popular ballads? That was still the basic question, and the choice was not as obvious in the early weeks of 1938 as it might seem now. Both Metro and Universal had enjoyed great success with their operatic musicals, Jeanette MacDonald singing the arias for M-G-M, Deanna Durbin for Universal. Perhaps, went one idea, Metro could combine opera and swing, much as it had done in *Every Sunday*.

Only after weeks of vacillation did Freed conclude that he wanted neither opera nor swing, nor any combination of the two, but more conventional, down-to-earth melodies—the kind he and his partners turned out. Many of his old friends were eager to write them, but Freed decided that Harold Arlen and E. Y. Harburg, who had written the songs for Broadway's *Hooray for What?*, had precisely the quality of naïveté and sincerity he desired. When he signed them to a contract, the last piece of the puzzle fell into place, and the outline of the picture became clear: *Oz* was to be a musical drama rather than a musical comedy, and it was to have traditional songs in traditional styles.

III

Looking toward a Christmas release, Metro had hoped to begin shooting April 19, 1938. Such an optimistic schedule soon surrendered, however, to a sobering truth: if it were done right, *The Wizard of Oz* demanded long, careful preparation; it could not be rushed before the cameras. Even if all the outstanding questions about the script and music had been answered, several months would still have been required to create its fanciful world, which eventually was to occupy six soundstages, to design and make its extravagantly odd costumes, and to figure out how to create what were, in those days, spectacular special effects. How could monkeys, witches and even houses be sent flying through the air? How could a cyclone be reproduced on a soundstage? No one knew for sure. A challenge to the studio's writers and producers, *Oz* was a still greater challenge to its technical experts.

To sharpen the distinction between fantasy and reality, the realistic Kansas scenes were to be filmed in black-and-white, and the scenes in Oz—four-fifths of the picture—were to be shot in Technicolor. The cyclone was to carry Dorothy not only from Kansas to Oz, but also from drab, dry actuality to a rich and colorful world of the imagination, a place that, in the words of the film's theme song, was "somewhere over the rainbow." The difficulty, for the technical staff anyway, was that Technicolor was a new and still primitive technology—*The Wizard of Oz* was to be one of just eight color features released in 1939—that capriciously favored some hues over others. It turned most yellows into green, for instance, forcing the art department to spend nearly a week searching for the right yellow for the Yellow Brick Road that was to lead Dorothy to the Wizard. Pushed back once, the starting date was pushed back again, and again after that.

Casting was not completed until the fall. Judy, of course, was Dorothy, Frank Morgan was the Wizard, and Billie Burke and Margaret

Hamilton were the Good and Wicked Witches. Joining Dorothy on her journey down the Yellow Brick Road were three old-timers from vaudeville: Ray Bolger as the Scarecrow, Buddy Ebsen as the Tin Man and Bert Lahr as the Cowardly Lion. All were paid more, and sometimes many times more, than Judy, who got $500 a week. Only the Cairn terrier that played Dorothy's dog, Toto, received less—a measly $125 a week.

On Thursday, October 13, 1938, Production No. 1060 finally got under way. "LeRoy Starts 'Wizard,' " said the headline in *Daily Variety,* with what sounded like a note of relief. But LeRoy started only to stop, and scarcely a week had gone by before he abruptly called a halt. The aluminum powder used to give the Tin Man his metallic look had coated Ebsen's lungs, causing him to suffer an almost lethal allergic reaction. As Ebsen rested in an oxygen tent, LeRoy had time to carefully scrutinize the footage that had already been shot. He did not like it, and on October 24 he fired the director, Richard Thorpe. Like most of Metro's directors—"efficient traffic cops" is how one studio biography describes them—Thorpe was competent but uninspired. "He just didn't quite understand the story," the producer explained. "He just didn't have . . . the warmth or the feeling. To make a fairy story, you have to think like a kid."

While a new director was being sought, George Cukor stood in. One of the few Metro directors who was more than a traffic cop, Cukor had put his mark on some of the studio's most distinguished pictures, including *Dinner at Eight, David Copperfield* and *Camille.* As dismayed by Thorpe's work as LeRoy had been, Cukor instantly saw where Thorpe had gone wrong: his *Oz* was not believable. He had invested so much effort in making Judy look pretty, for example, that she looked not like a simple farm girl from Kansas, but like a Hollywood starlet masquerading as a simple farm girl, with heavy makeup and long blond hair. Even her acting seemed artificial to Cukor, as if she had been instructed to be cute, to act, as he described it, in "a fairy-tale way."

To be convincing, Judy could not be cute. The film would work, Cukor realized, only if she were transparently sincere. Her eyes had to be the eyes of the audience. She had to be like a tourist in an exotic country, aware that the inhabitants of Oz were a little unusual—by

Kansas standards, anyway—but just as real as the folks walking down the street in Wichita, Topeka or Garden City. There could be no hints, by her or anyone else, that the cyclone had set her down in a fantasy land. If she did not unhesitatingly accept the strange creatures she was to meet—a scarecrow that dances, a lumberjack made of tin, and a lion that talks—neither would the audience.

Although Cukor's involvement lasted no more than a week, his contribution was key: he put the picture on the right track. At his command, most of Judy's makeup was washed off. Off, too, came her elaborate blond wig, to be replaced by girlish pigtails in her natural reddish brown. When Cukor was through with her, Judy not only looked but acted the part. Taking to heart his advice not to be "fancy-schmancy," she thereafter played Dorothy naturally, without a trace of artifice.

No one had to tell Victor Fleming, the director who followed Cukor, to avoid the fancy-schmancy. Rough, tough and gruff—and sometimes sadistic, particularly toward women—Fleming was a he-man's he-man. He could, and did, use his fists, pilot a plane, ride a motorcycle and shoot a gun. Still slim and handsome at fifty-five, he was adored by women as much as he was imitated by men. Some, in fact, thought that Clark Gable modeled his virile screen persona on Fleming, who was both his friend and the director of several of his pictures. "There was more of Fleming in Gable at the end than there was Gable in Gable," said director Henry Hathaway, who knew them both.

At first glance, such an eccentric tough guy, best known for directing adventure stories like *Treasure Island* and steamy romances like *Red Dust,* was a peculiar choice for a fantasy like *Oz.* Hidden behind that fearsome façade, however, lay the sensibility of an artist. Like Cukor, Fleming stood apart from Metro's house directors. He was, in any case, precisely what *Oz* needed after so many months of indecision and second-guessing—a disciplinarian, a general with a heart. On a Fleming set there was never a moment of hesitation: he knew exactly what he wanted. On November 4, after a new Tin Man, Jack Haley, had been hired to take the place of the ailing Ebsen, Fleming ordered the cameras to roll again.

||||

"Obstacles make for a better picture!" Fleming liked to say, and if he was right, *The Wizard of Oz* was many times blessed. Some of the difficulties were expected, the result of Metro's decision to use real people in its fantasy rather than animation—as Walt Disney had done so successfully in *Snow White*. Animated characters could do their own stunts; they never got tired or sick; they never fell victim to faulty makeup, as Buddy Ebsen had done; and they never suffered accidents, as several of the actors in *Oz* were to do. Real people, Metro discovered, meant real problems.

Every morning, Bolger, Haley and Lahr—the Scarecrow, Tin Man and Cowardly Lion—had to get up before dawn, for instance, to undergo two unhappy hours in the makeup department. The rest of the day they spent encased in costumes so heavy and hot—Technicolor required lights of blazing intensity—that they sometimes felt as if they were suffocating. Even Judy, burdened with nothing but her simple gingham dress, was in some discomfort: beneath her blouse her grown-up breasts were tightly bound and corseted, all in an effort to make her look like a young girl rather than the blossoming teenager she was.

In the middle of November came a major complication, or, to be precise, more than 120 small complications. Converging on Culver City from all over the country was an army of Lilliputians, the midgets who were to play the little people—the Munchkins—who greet Dorothy on her arrival in Oz. Stories of miniature orgies and giant binges soon began to circulate on the set. To collect all the little people for shooting, Judy later joked, the studio had to send security guards out with butterfly nets. After one of the male midgets fell into a toilet bowl, Metro assigned big people the delicate task of helping the tiny folk perform their natural functions. "We had a hell of a time with those little guys," recalled LeRoy.

Far more serious disasters befell some of the full-sized performers. The first, Ebsen's aluminum poisoning, had knocked him out of the picture altogether. The second nearly did the same to Margaret Hamilton. After threatening Dorothy and Toto—"I'll get you, my pretty, and your little dog, too!"—the Wicked Witch was supposed to vanish in what the script described as a "burst of smoke and fire and a clap of thunder." That impressive disappearing act was achieved with the help of a hidden elevator, which pulled Hamilton below the stage before flames actually shot up where she had been standing. All went well on the first several takes, but on the sixth or seventh, the flames erupted too soon, setting fire to Hamilton's huge hat and witch's broom. In agony because of serious burns to her face and right hand, she could not work for six weeks. When Hamilton adamantly refused to do any more scenes with fire, her stunt double rode the Wicked Witch's smoky broomstick, until, on the third take, it exploded, putting the double, too, out of commission. Also a casualty was the terrier that played Toto, whose paw was squashed by one of the Wicked Witch's heavy-footed guards. Until the injured paw healed, Dorothy had to make do with a look-alike pooch.

Although she had more scenes than anybody else, Judy escaped the catastrophes around her, receiving only a minor injury to her pride at the hands—or hand—of the new director. Her seemingly uncontrollable attacks of the giggles had ruined take after take of *Listen, Darling,* her previous picture. "There goes Judy!" people around her had shouted, resigning themselves to a long wait while she recovered her composure. Those disruptive giggles followed her onto the set of *Oz,* where, instead of angrily boxing the nose of the Cowardly Lion, as the script demanded, she did just the opposite, loudly laughing at his antics.

Unwilling to waste any more time on such behavior, Fleming stepped in and stopped her in the only way he seemed to know—with a hard slap on the face. "All right now," he sternly ordered her, "go back to your dressing room." Brutal though his method may have been, it worked. When she returned, Judy did the scene in one take, without laughter. Fleming could not claim total victory, however. A smile, so quickly suppressed that it is almost spectral, can still be seen mischievously tugging at her face when Lahr whimpers: "Ya didn't have to go and hit me, did ya? Is my nose bleedin'?"

|||

Once shooting began, most Metro pictures were completed in no more than a couple of months. Some were finished in as little as four or five weeks. Filming of *The Wizard of Oz* took more than five months, and, with the exception of the midgets, who were bedazzled by the business of show business, few remembered anything but hard, slogging work. For Bolger, Haley and Lahr, who suffered most from the hot lights, one of the high points of the day was the appearance of Judy's tutor. "School time!" someone would yell, and the lights would be turned off, giving everybody but Judy a chance to relax. "We used to long for that sound," said Lahr. "It meant we had an hour's rest."

Even the disciplined Fleming made mistakes that contributed to the production's tardy pace. Haley was before the cameras for three days, for example, before anyone realized that his Tin Man, who was supposed to have been standing outside for months, should have looked dirty and weather-beaten, rather than shiny clean as if he had just emerged from the tinsmith's shop. It was an expensive oversight. The cost of reshooting the scenes with a rusty Tin Man was a cool $60,000. As the budget rose well past projections, Metro's headquarters in New York, which had been dubious about the picture from the start, became more and more nervous. What was going on in Culver City?

To find out for himself, and perhaps in the process to embarrass Mayer, his often uppity subordinate, Nick Schenck traveled all the way from Manhattan and asked the question directly. Rarely involving himself in the details of production, Mayer, who did not have a ready reply, did what all good bureaucrats do in such situations: he called a meeting. Unfortunately, Mervyn LeRoy, the one man who could have supplied a satisfactory response, was either out of town or playing hooky, and it soon became clear that nobody else could really respond. Schenck, who liked to be addressed as "General," though the only uniform he had ever worn was a pinstripe, was not slow to emphasize what seemed to be the obvious. "Louie," he said to Mayer, "you don't seem to be in control here." But Mayer was in control. *The Wizard of Oz* was running over estimates not because of wastefulness, or good times on the set, but because it was one of the most difficult and most ambitious films Metro had ever made. By the time Schenck got around to asking the question, however, the answer was beside the point: the picture had already cost too much to stop. Like it or not, the unsmiling General had no choice but to let Judy and her companions continue down the Yellow Brick Road.

They finished their journey with a different escort. In mid-February Fleming was yanked away to replace George Cukor as director of David O. Selznick's *Gone With the Wind,* in which Metro had a substantial financial interest. Though Fleming had already shot about 80 percent of *Oz* before he departed, the remaining 20 percent, which included the beginning, the end and all the Kansas scenes, comprised perhaps the most crucial footage of all. But luck once again smiled on Production 1060. Fleming had not left at the wrong time; he had left at exactly the right time. The consummate director of action stories, he had been just the man to oversee Dorothy's adventures in Oz. But a he-man's he-man, even one with an artistic side, was not the best choice to direct the Kansas segments, which dealt mainly with the tender emotions of a frustrated adolescent. For those scenes, a more subtle, feeling touch was needed.

Enter a man who plainly had that touch; although he was on the set a little less than a month, King Vidor was an essential part of the *Oz* equation. One of Hollywood's most innovative filmmakers, Vidor, the director of such elegant heart-tuggers as *The Big Parade* and *Stella Dallas,* had the emotional equipment Fleming lacked, together with a singular ability, acquired in the silent days, to tell a story in simple visual images: he made words almost superfluous. Most other directors would have planted Judy in one spot to sing "Over the Rainbow," for example, keeping her there from first note to last. Not Vidor. Borrowing from the vocabulary of the silents, he moved her around the barnyard, underlining the longing that lay behind Harburg's plaintive lyrics by leaning her wistfully against a haystack one minute, a harvester the next. "I wanted to keep the movement going," he said, "just as we had in silent pictures."

When shooting ended on Thursday, March 16, 1939, it was Vidor who turned the lights off at last on *The Wizard of Oz.* By the time post-production work was completed that summer, the budget for Baum's gentle children's fantasy had risen to what was then the enormous sum of $2,777,000. Small wonder that Schenck was worried. For M-G-M, *Oz* had become a costly gamble. For those most prominently involved, Judy included, the stakes were higher still: their reputations, perhaps even their futures, hung on its success.

|||

The first previews of *The Wizard of Oz* were held in mid-June, in such bellwether towns as Pomona, San Bernardino and San Luis Obispo. Nearly two hours long, it had to be shortened by fifteen minutes or more to meet the accepted standards of the day, when most movies were no longer than an hour and forty-five minutes. Several minutes were eliminated by the accumulation of numerous small cuts, a few seconds here, a few seconds there. A few scenes had to be dropped totally, resulting in small inconsistencies that film students always delight in pointing out. Trimmed as well were at least a dozen of the Wicked Witch's most alarming lines—"I'm here for vengeance" was one—that had proved unexpectedly terrifying to many children. (Even so, some still found her too scary. In England, the London Board of Film Censors ruled that children could see the picture only in the company of an adult.)

After one screening, several of Metro's men in dark suits suggested yet another deletion—"Over the Rainbow" and the entire scene that surrounded it. Overlooking the fact that "Rainbow" was not just a pretty song, but the key to everything to follow, "those ignorant jerks," as Harburg called them, deemed it inappropriate for an M-G-M star to be photographed singing in a barnyard, her only props being pigs, chickens and rusty farm equipment. Ignorant or not, the naysayers held positions of power, and their recommendation posed a real and potentially fatal threat to the movie: without "Rainbow," *Oz* would scarcely have made sense. But once again, and for the very last time, that watchful guardian angel flew to the rescue. Mayer himself was prevailed upon to stop the attempted vandalism, and Judy was allowed to continue singing of a land she had heard of once in a lullaby. Pared to an hour and forty-one minutes, *The Wizard of Oz* was as short as it was ever to be.

As the August release date approached, Metro mounted the kind of advertising and marketing campaign it reserved for its biggest pictures. With assistance from Culver City, many theaters sponsored *Oz* contests, teenagers formed *Oz* clubs, and manufacturers produced a wide and sometimes odd array of *Oz* paraphernalia, everything from Judy

Garland dresses to writing paper, soap and coat hangers emblazoned with *Oz* decals. In addition to Metro's own lavish advertising, the studio's publicity department persuaded more than thirty magazines and newspapers to run feature stories that read like ads; Howard Strickling could not have written more flattering copy. Typical was the two-page color spread that appeared in *Life* magazine. "Dazzling Brilliance Marks M-G-M's Color Version of *The Wizard of Oz,*" proclaimed the headline.

Ever since filming of *Oz* had stopped in mid-March, Metro had kept Judy in almost constant motion. After a five-week publicity tour of the East in late March and April, she had been hurried back to California to begin work on the film adaptation of Rodgers and Hart's Broadway hit *Babes in Arms.* Shot on a tight, demanding schedule, that film finished production in early July and was to open in September, just a few weeks after *Oz.* When Judy traveled east in early August, she was thus promoting not just one, but two pictures. Rooney, her *Babes in Arms* costar, went with her, and rousing ovations greeted them on their first stops, in Washington, D.C., and three cities in Connecticut—Hartford, Bridgeport and New Haven. Nothing could have prepared them for the pandemonium of Manhattan, however, and not even Metro could have gathered the delirious crowd of ten thousand that defied the August heat to scream their names in Grand Central Station. At five-thirty on the morning of August 17, many of those same fans, quieter but no less enthusiastic, were standing in front of the Loew's Capitol Theater on Broadway, where, that very morning, Judy and Mickey were to share the bill with the New York premiere of *The Wizard of Oz.* IN PERSON NOW, said the marquee, ROONEY-GARLAND.

By nine-ten every one of the Capitol's five thousand seats was occupied, and perhaps ten thousand more people were waiting outside, in a line that stretched all around the block. Prepared for a long stay, some had brought books and knitting; many carried their lunches. "Mickey, Judy, 'Oz' Tie Up Broadway," said the *Hollywood Reporter* the next day. So many people demanded seats that the manager of the Capitol hastily tacked on an extra performance, raising the first day's attendance to 37,000. At noontime, those two often warring partners, Louis B. Mayer and Nick Schenck, arrived to watch the excitement from nearby

Lindy's. Indulging in a rare moment of warm good-fellowship, they telegraphed Mervyn LeRoy in California. "We had the best lunch ever," they said. "Had the crowds for dessert."

From then on Mickey and Judy did five shows a day during the week and seven shows a day on weekends, seldom escaping the theater for anything other than promotional stunts, such as an appearance with Mayor Fiorello La Guardia at the New York World's Fair. Supplied with almost superhuman energy, Mickey, who was No. 1 at the box office that year, thrived on the unsparing pace: he sang, he danced, he pounded the drums and he did impersonations; he even conducted the orchestra when its leader fell ill. Judy was not so fortunate. She became so exhausted that she once collapsed in the wings, forcing Mickey to improvise until she recovered, four or five minutes later. But none of that weary strain was visible to New Yorkers, who saw only what the New York *Daily News* described as "the verve and rhythmic bounce of youth." Rooney and Garland were as big a hit as *Oz* itself. As tickets continued to sell, Metro extended their Capitol run through a second week, keeping Judy on for still a third week when a new Hardy picture took Mickey back to Hollywood.

Despite her hectic schedule, Judy was able to sneak out a few times before leaving New York in early September. One of her dates, improbably enough, was with a young French aristocrat, the magnificently titled Viscount Lawrence d'Yago de la Vernier. After interviewing her for a Paris youth newspaper, the eighteen-year-old viscount pursued her with flowers and telegrams until she finally agreed to dinner—then a second dinner after that. Only later did she learn that her ardent swain had acquired his charming accent at a high school in the Bronx; on the Grand Concourse the baby viscount was better known as Lawrence Yago, dentist's assistant.

|||

"*Oz* should find a ready-made audience practically everywhere," *Film Bulletin* had predicted, and so it did. The winding queues in New York were repeated all over the country: big cities and small, East and West, nearly everybody loved *The Wizard of Oz*. Popularity does not always translate into profits, however, particularly in the motion-picture business, and *Oz* was not the financial bonanza it appeared to be. This was due, in part, to the youthful makeup of the audience. Since children, who constituted at least a third of those standing outside the theaters, were charged much less than adults—an average of ten cents a ticket, compared with twenty-five cents for adults—a full house did not necessarily mean full receipts.

The picture would have been a solid moneymaker, nonetheless, had it not been for the big production budget Schenck had complained about. To the $2.777 million cost of making the movie, Metro had to add almost a million dollars for distribution, advertising and promotion. Real costs, money the studio actually spent, thus approached $4 million dollars. That meant that although the picture's box-office gross ($3.017 million) was among the year's highest, M-G-M still lost something like $750,000. Not until it was released a second time in the late forties did *Oz* begin to turn a profit; only after it was shown on television—in 1956, and nearly every year thereafter—did it start to reap large sums on its investment.

Judged by its reception rather than its financial returns, the film was a smash, however, recognized by most reviewers as something out of the ordinary. "Just sit and look back in wide-mouthed astonishment and admiration," advised Clark Rodenbach in the *Chicago Daily News*. "You can see it again and again and never tire of its marvels," declared Harrison Carroll in the *Los Angeles Herald-Express*. Similar comments could be read in most other publications as well, the picture's few pans coming almost entirely from supposedly highbrow magazine critics. With the untiring aptitude intellectuals sometimes display for seeing everything but the point, the *New Yorker*'s Russel Maloney, for example, dismissed it as "a stinkeroo."

|||

Like Fords out of Willow Run, the movies rolled off the California assembly lines in 1939, 365 in all, an average of one a day. As in any other year, most were forgotten the minute their names left the marquees. Who today recalls *King of the Turf, Undercover Doctor* or *The Kid from Kokomo*? *Those Glamour Girls, Boy Slaves* or *Beasts of Berlin*? But perhaps two dozen of the 365 are not only remembered, but enjoyed, talked about and studied still: *Stagecoach. Wuthering Heights. Mr. Smith Goes to Washington. Love Affair. The Roaring Twenties. Dark Victory. Young Mr. Lincoln. Juarez. Gunga Din. Jesse James. Only Angels Have Wings. Union Pacific. Of Mice and Men. The Rains Came. The Story of Alexander Graham Bell. Idiot's Delight. Ninotchka. Intermezzo. The Women. Goodbye, Mr. Chips. Destry Rides Again. The Hunchback of Notre Dame. Drums Along the Mohawk. Gone With the Wind.* Those were some of the titles of what is now regarded as the greatest single year in film history, a prolonged and precious moment in which the Hollywood studio system, whose sole purpose was to make money, produced an astonishing and unexpected harvest—popular art of high and lasting merit.

The result, on Oscar night, February 29, 1940, was a parade of excellence such as Hollywood had never seen before. To most of the public, however, as well as to most of those who picked the winners, one picture, David O. Selznick's *Gone With the Wind,* stood out even in that stellar grouping. Other movies, *Oz* among them, had struck bright sparks; *Gone With the Wind*—the longest, most expensive and most eagerly awaited picture of the decade—had shot giant bolts of lightning. When the victors were announced at a gala dinner at the Cocoanut Grove, the outcome thus seemed foreordained. "What a wonderful thing, this benefit for David Selznick," quipped Bob Hope, the master of ceremonies. The second time Selznick was called to the podium to pick up an award, Hope added the obvious: "David, you should have brought roller skates."

When the night was over, *Gone With the Wind* had appropriated ten of the seventeen major awards, including one for Victor Fleming's direction. Judy herself received a minor honor. For everything she had done in 1939, which meant *Babes in Arms* as well as *The Wizard of Oz,* she was named the best juvenile performer. Her old pal Mickey, who had shared the award with Deanna Durbin the year before, presented her with a miniature version of the Oscar statuette—"the Munchkin Award," she was jokingly to call it.

Surrounded by so many other more glamorous pictures, *The Wizard of Oz* seemed to shrink into shy invisibility, winning only two fairly predictable awards, one for the best original music score, another for the best song. "Over the Rainbow," the song that almost wasn't, at least not in *The Wizard of Oz,* had received the ultimate vindication. By the usual measurements, *Oz* had probably been justly rewarded. Almost any of the year's other major movies had far greater star power, for instance. Among the many sitting in the Cocoanut Grove, who could have imagined that of all the memorable films of 1939, that grand and glorious assembly, the one that eventually would have the widest and most enduring appeal—that would be seen, indeed, by more people than any other movie ever made—would be Metro's gentle children's fantasy?

The answer is no one, because no one was able, at such close range, to see *The Wizard of Oz* for what it really is. And what it really is is not just a movie, but a Technicolor retelling of a story more ancient than antiquity. M-G-M, which liked to think of itself as the world's chief purveyor of slick, commercial, escapist entertainment, had produced a movie that touched emotions deep and true, unwittingly creating the first myth for the age of moving pictures. Dorothy is not merely walking down that Yellow Brick Road; she is treading in the footsteps of heroes, of Odysseus fighting the hostility of gods and men to return home to Ithaca, of Galahad venturing into dark and sunless forests in search of the Holy Grail, and of many another figure of legend and literature who has braved injury or death in some lonely quest.

In mythology, such quests through field and forest were metaphors for psychological journeys, and every monster that lay waiting in the fog had its counterpart in the murky depths of the subconscious. Like those heroes of old, young Dorothy is on a journey of self-discovery: she is making a spiritual passage from adolescence to adulthood, immaturity to maturity. Dependent on her aunt and uncle, on the Wizard and the Good Witch—even on her ruby slippers—she must find herself; she must establish her own identity. Her pilgrimage ends when the movie ends, when she realizes that she does not need protection: she can take care of herself. Her destiny is hers to determine—no one else can do it for her. That is what she means when she says: "If I ever go looking for my heart's desire again, I won't look any further than my own backyard."

Caught up in the suspense, children—and adults, too, for that matter—who see *The Wizard of Oz* do not think about meanings, any more than did those who sat around Attic fires, eager to learn the fate of Odysseus. They do not need to; if they did, the movie would be a failure. *Oz* speaks to their feelings, not their intellects, and they instinctively understand its message. That message, which they find both comforting and inspiring, is that if a poor little girl from Kansas can walk down a perilous path, slay wicked witches and stand up to mighty wizards, so, too, can they confront the threats, real and imagined, to their own emerging futures. If Dorothy can survive the hazards of growing up, in other words, so can they. In former times, it took centuries for a story to acquire the potency of myth, to lodge itself so firmly in mind and memory that the mention of a familiar line could be an open sesame to a vault of buried emotions. Thanks to television, *The Wizard of Oz* needed mere decades to be granted such incantatory powers. Embraced with natural and spontaneous affection by each succeeding generation, it is now a universal reference point, beyond language and national identity.

|||

Without Judy, it seems safe to say, *The Wizard of Oz* would have had no such echoes or reverberations. If Nick Schenck had got his wish and Shirley Temple had played Dorothy, *Oz* might still have been a good movie. But with Temple in the part, or with any actress other than Judy, it almost certainly would have been just a movie, not the call to the heart and soul that Judy makes it. It is she who gives it its special poignancy. It is she who, through an act of conjuration, persuades the audience to look at all the fantastic goings-on through her wide and trusting eyes. She makes the unbelievable believable, the unreal real. Writers can write words and directors can describe how they want them spoken; thereafter, they belong to the actors, who, if they have any talent, bring them to life in original and sometimes surprising ways. That is what Judy does with Dorothy. She makes her the quiet center about which the movie turns; she puts her imprint not only on her own role, but on everyone else's as well.

She has help, of course, most notably from the soulful sounds of "Over the Rainbow," which, like the soft and suggestive words of a hypnotist, assist her in building a mood of wonder and trust. "Our sweetest songs are those that tell of saddest thought," wrote Shelley, and Judy's sweetest songs, the ones that she sang with the most feeling and effect, were always tinged, as "Over the Rainbow" is, with a tender, companionable melancholy. In their bittersweet ballad of frustrated hopes and inexhaustible yearnings Arlen and Harburg had found the perfect musical expression of her own turbulent emotions.

Rarely have song and singer been so ideally matched. Many other singers have had a signature song, but none has been so closely identified with a single number as Judy was to be with "Over the Rainbow." In the decades to come she was to joke about almost everything and everybody. But she never joked, nor allowed anyone around her to joke, about "Over the Rainbow." That was her anthem, her sacred text, and it was safe from even *her* humor. " 'Rainbow' has always been my song," she was to say. "I get emotional—one way or the other—about every song I sing. But maybe I get more emotional about 'Rainbow.' I never shed any phoney tears about it. Everybody has songs that make them cry. That's my sad song."

About the making of *The Wizard of Oz* she would tell funny stories. But *Oz,* too, she regarded with an almost religious reverence. When she began filming it in the fall of 1938, she had a bright but still uncertain future. A year later, because of *Oz,* she was a bankable, certifiable star. If anyone had any doubts, Metro, which never acted hastily in such matters, made her rank official by placing her name on its glittering roster of stars. There she resided, right next to Gable and Garbo, the grandest, most regal figures on the lot. *Oz* had given her a kind of rebirth, she said, and "the people at M-G-M stopped referring to me as the kid they were stuck with when they'd let Deanna Durbin go."

Oz had done more than make her a star, however: it had touched her with its own peculiar but potent magic. Whether Judy liked it or not, the girl who had traveled that Yellow Brick Road had become her doppelgänger, a companion she could never shake. To audiences around the world, little Dorothy was not just a character in a movie, and the girl who had played her was not just an actress repeating lines from a script. One and the same, actress and character, Judy and Dorothy, they were a symbol of grit and pluck, a personification of faith and fortitude in the face of adversity. When audiences clutched Dorothy to their hearts, they grasped Judy along with her.

|||

"I'm going to be a movie star," Babe Gumm had told people in Lancaster. Now, transformed into Judy Garland, she had achieved that extravagant ambition, sooner and more spectacularly than perhaps even she could have conceived. By the fall of 1939, just four years after coming to Culver City, she had become one of M-G-M's hottest properties, the crown princess, if not the queen, of the lot. Audiences were still lining up to see the *The Wizard of Oz* when *Babes in Arms* opened to yet bigger crowds, surpassing *Oz* and all of Metro's other big-budget pictures to end up as the studio's biggest grosser of the year. Judy had made only two movies in 1939, but both ranked among the year's top ten at the box office. Radio, a medium she had helped pioneer back in 1928, magnified her fame still further; beginning September 26, she became a regular on Bob Hope's *Chesterfield Radio Hour*, which was heard by millions every Tuesday night.

In 1936, when Deanna Durbin had rocketed past her, Ida Koverman had comforted a tearful Judy with the promise that her day would also come: her footprints, too, would adorn the pavement in front of Grauman's Chinese Theater, the closest thing Hollywood had to a hall of fame. On October 10, the night of *Babes in Arms'* West Coast premiere, Koverman's prediction came to pass. Dressed in a gown by Adrian, Metro's chief costume designer—"I wanted to look glamorous that night," she said, "as I had never wanted to before, or since"—Judy reenacted one of the oddest rituals in a town that venerated the odd and peculiar. With Mickey Rooney helping on her right side, her mother on her left, she pressed her feet and hands into a slab of wet cement, so that, like the image of some girl of Pompeii, immortalized by a belch from Vesuvius, her lithic impression would remain long after she herself was gone. "For Mr. Grauman, All Happiness," she scrawled. "Judy Garland, 10-10-39." She had arrived: she was a star, really and truly.

A movie star needs a movie star's house, and in 1939 Judy moved into hers. In a landscape dotted with theaters in the shape of Oriental pagodas and Egyptian temples, restaurants that resembled men's hats, coffee shops that masqueraded as giant hot dogs, and gasoline stations that were topped by flying horses, the stars felt free to indulge their own most opulent fantasies. Some chose Spanish haciendas and the tinkling fountains of Seville; others preferred the half-timbered wainscoting of Elizabethan England, the pointed turrets of medieval Normandy, or one of a dozen other styles they might have gleaned from the *National Geographic*—Old World whimsy with New World plumbing.

Judy's fantasy was just the opposite, but, in its own way, just as whimsical. Since leaving Lancaster, she had changed addresses ten times or more; she had no place she could call her own, no tree she had watched grow from a sapling, no memorabilia-stuffed attic she had explored on rainy days. "We're going to move again!" her mother, who disliked staying very long in one place, would gaily announce, and once more they would begin packing. Now, with her career firmly established, Judy yearned for roots, for a sense of belonging. Her idea of a house was not something strange or exotic, mock Tudor, pseudo-Spanish or bastardized Chinese; she wanted a house that spelled home, the kind of all-American home she had had, or liked to think she had had, in Grand Rapids.

She got what she asked for at 1231 Stone Canyon Road in Bel Air, a section of Los Angeles that was as exclusive as nearby Beverly Hills, but quieter and more countrified, with pungent eucalyptus scenting the air and pesky deer descending from the hills to graze on lawns and hedges. An idealized vision of New England, her house had a brick exterior, a covered front porch, rustic shingles and a white picket fence. "Friendly" was the adjective one reporter attached to it. Suggesting hot cider and a cozy fire on a cold and blustery day, it was Connecticut as the M-G-M art department might have imagined it, which is to say that it was more Connecticut than Connecticut. Not grand enough to be described as a mansion, the house was roomy enough, nonetheless, for an ever-changing cast: Ethel; Ethel's mother, Eva Milne; and Judy's sister Sue, who was now divorced from her musician husband. Judy's other sister, Jimmie, who had also married a musician—her engagement to Frankie Darro had not resulted in a wedding—often came by with her husband and baby daughter, Judalein. Judy herself had a suite upstairs, with a private bath, a mirrored dressing room and a large bed-room, complete with a fireplace and sofas, in which she could enter-tain.

What Judy was really seeking in her Christmas-card house was, of course, a Christmas-card atmosphere, those sentimental things carolers sing about once a year—a welcoming hearth, cheery company and the security that can be found in a loving family. But Frank, who had sup-plied all that and more with just a smile, was dead, and warmth and in-timacy were perhaps the only things the capable Ethel was incapable of providing. In their absence, the rosy, rutilant glow of Stone Canyon Road was rendered bogus and counterfeit. Like the period houses that lined the stage streets on Metro's Lot 3, Judy's dream house was little more than a set, a beautiful façade, with nothing, nothing at all, be-hind it.

|||

Hoping to make some money when she was living in Lancaster, Ethel had written a song about a parent's love for a daughter—"Deep, Deep in My Heart," she had titled it. "Did I hear you sigh little girl?" began her lachrymose lyrics. "Life's too short to cry little girl. Let those eyes of blue just keep smilin' thru' and, remember I love you." But it was just a song; she harbored no such sentiments deep in her own heart, or, if she did, she neglected to let her own girls see them. Much as she tried to believe that her mother loved her, Judy could never be certain. Al-though publicity photographs from the time show them in happy, smil-ing embrace ("Mother and I—we're almost one person," Judy told a fan magazine), off-camera the embraces were infrequent and the opposite of what might have been expected: Judy would hug her mother, but her mother was never seen to hug her. "Ethel didn't love Judy the way Judy's dad did," was the sad observation of Dorothy Walsh, who had known the family since Lancaster days. "But then Ethel was not affec-tionate to anyone. Hugging wasn't her way of doing things."

The nature of a relationship is sometimes best delineated not by dra-matic, landmark events but by seemingly trivial moments, candid snap-shots that catch their subjects unawares and record the give-and-take of an ordinary day. So it was that a small incident during the making of

The Wizard of Oz offered a glimpse of unrehearsed life with Ethel. There was a little party in Judy's dressing room, the end of which found Judy sitting on the floor at her mother's feet, her arms wrapped fondly around her mother's legs. Then, thinking perhaps of similar occasions when her father was alive, she startled everybody with a flood of tears. "Why can't it be like the good old days in Grand Rapids?" she cried. "Why can't it be like the olden days?" Embarrassed, and not knowing what to say, her friends waited expectantly for her mother to reach down, hold her tightly and blanket her with words of comfort and reassurance—to do what their own mothers would have done. But the words and gestures that come so naturally to most mothers were altogether alien to Ethel: she made not a move, said nothing.

All children want and need affection from their mothers and fathers. For adolescent stars like Judy the concern was more urgent. They were dependent on their parents, as all children are; but, in a reversal of the usual order of things, their parents were even more dependent on them—the children were the family breadwinners. Without them, there would have been no house, no car and no new clothes, and Mommy and Daddy would have been scratching, as most Americans were in the thirties, merely to survive and put food on the table. The young stars knew all that—they were told often enough—and, like it or not, they had to ask themselves some unsettling questions. Did their parents take such good care of them because they loved them? Or because they brought in a paycheck every week? Where Frank was concerned, Judy had never had any doubts. Above her mother, however, hung a permanent question mark.

What seemed like incontrovertible evidence of the stoniness of Ethel's heart came in November 1939. On her forty-sixth birthday the Widow Gumm—or Mrs. Garland, as she was now known—traveled to Yuma, Arizona, just over the California line, to stand before a justice of the peace. There, in his office, she exchanged vows with Will Gilmore, a widower himself after the death of the long-suffering Laura. Ethel's old paramour had been her frequent escort, and the marriage should have caught nobody by surprise. Yet surprise it did, and the reaction of Ethel's daughters, all of whom detested their mother's sour-faced lover, was disbelief followed by anger. "They were absolutely dumbfounded," recalled Dorothy Walsh. "The general feeling was, 'Oh, no, not Will!' " But Will it was.

It is not uncommon for children to disapprove of second marriages, and Ethel, well into middle age, could scarcely be faulted for ignoring their unhappy faces and making her own choice, bad as it may have been. What Ethel could be faulted for—what was dumbfounding—was not her decision to marry Gilmore, but her choice of a wedding date. November 17 was not only her birthday; it was also the anniversary of Frank's death. If she had spat on his grave, Ethel could not have shown greater contempt for her children's father and all their years together. "That was the most awful thing that ever happened," Judy was to say. "My mother marrying that awful man the same day that my daddy died."

Making separate arrangements for his own children, two of whom were old enough to be on their own, the bridegroom soon exchanged his address in Santa Paula, a town north of Los Angeles, for the one on Stone Canyon Road. There, in a photograph taken a few weeks after the wedding, Gilmore, caught in a rare smile, can be seen taking part in the traditional gathering around a tinsel-draped Christmas tree.

But the smiles soon faded, and Ethel's cynical daughters may have been right in suspecting that Gilmore had married their mother for the money made by Judy—Judy, whom he had so delighted in mocking and disparaging and belittling. He gave the impression that he was after her money, anyway, when, his bags barely unpacked, he made a bold grab for control of his new family's finances. "From here on in," he declared, "I intend to take over all the handling of business in this family." To which Ethel quite predictably replied: "Like hell you will! Judy's money? Never!"

The temperature on Stone Canyon Road plummeted from there, and Gilmore may soon have wondered whether he had made a mistake in going to Yuma. Judy fumed at the thought that her hard-earned dollars were helping to support Will and his children—Ethel bought one of the Gilmore boys a car—and she did her best to avoid him. Ethel's Milne relations were not much more cordial. "He was a fast-talker, a slicker, a used-car salesman who reeked of insincerity," said her nephew James Milne. "I didn't want anything to do with him." As lovers living apart, Ethel and her Will might have continued for many years; as husband and wife, they could not go on. Marriage had doomed their relationship—not because they were too dissimilar, but because they were too much alike, impatient, bossy and controlling. They were both bulldozers, accustomed to pushing aside anybody, spouses and children included, who had the misfortune to stand in their way.

The only surprise is that they lived together as long as they did, three and a half years. They finally confessed failure and separated on March 17, 1943, receiving their official divorce papers on August 2, 1945. To Judy the damage had been done several years earlier, however; it had been done, indeed, on that terrible day in November 1939. In betraying her father's memory, she felt, her mother had betrayed her as well, and it would be hard to say that she was wrong. The wound never healed. Many years later, when her girlhood friend Muggsey Ming started to give her an update on the Gilmore children, Judy's reaction was almost violent. "Don't even mention their name to me!" she shouted. "I don't want to know anything about them. Nothing!"

CHAPTER 5

The Men of Her Dreams

s the new decade, the decade of the forties, began, Judy was an audience favorite. But it was a teenager with wide, searching eyes and a tentative, beseeching smile whom people paid to see. Would they line up at the box office for a grown-up Judy Garland? For Judy Garland the woman, not the girl?

That was a question M-G-M did not want to ask, or even contemplate asking. The careers of most child stars ended with adolescence; once they had lost their heart-tugging, playful-puppy innocence, a fickle public quickly became bored with them. Jackie Coogan and Baby Peggy, darlings of the twenties, had long since been shown the door; Jackie Cooper and Freddie Bartholomew, darlings of the thirties, were soon to follow. Even Shirley Temple, whose popularity had seemed as durable as Gibraltar, was beginning to lose her race with time. No one in Culver City wanted Judy to suffer the same fate. Audiences knew her only as a girl in her mid-teens, and if a nervous Metro had had its way, she would have remained that age forever.

The studio did its best, certainly, to stop the clock, continuing to give her the sexless young-teenager parts her fans were accustomed to. In her first picture after *Babes in Arms*—*Andy Hardy Meets Debutante*, it was awkwardly titled—she again played Mickey Rooney's lovestruck sidekick, Betsy Booth. Next, starting in April 1940, came filming of *Strike Up the Band*, which, the songs aside, was almost a copy of *Babes in Arms*, a sequel in all but name. Once more poor Judy was Mickey's junior partner; once more her loving glances went unnoticed as his busy eyes fastened on other, prettier girls. "You're as important to me as a brass section" was as amorous as the scriptwriters allowed him to get. For the moment, romance was not to be hers—not on-screen, anyway. A perpetual adolescent, with as much sex appeal as a tuba or a trombone, was just the image Metro wanted Judy to have.

The portrait painted by Metro's artful propagandists was not entirely false: in some ways Judy was an ordinary, all-American girl. She met her friends, mostly other show-business brats, for malteds at the drugstore. She spent hours listening to the latest records. She invited the gang over on Saturday nights to dance and play charades. Handsome, energetic and fun-loving, her friends looked as if they had stepped straight out of Hardy country, which was just what many of them had done. Mickey, Andy Hardy himself, was a regular at Stone Canyon Road. So, too, were a dozen or more other familiar faces from thirties films, a collection that included Leonard Sues and Sidney Miller, both of whom had landed small roles in *Babes in Arms;* Bonita Granville, the lead in the Nancy Drew girl-detective series; Buddy Pepper, who appeared in *Seventeen* with Jackie Cooper; and Frankie Darro. A more attractive snapshot of young America, refulgent in its well-scrubbed wholesomeness, could not have been taken in Grand Rapids, or in any one of the thousands of other small towns that sententious commentators liked to say represented the real United States.

Yet if the studio's portrait of Judy was not entirely false, it was not entirely accurate either. She was not sixteen when the new decade began, as Metro was still claiming; she was almost eighteen. Nor was she the sexual innocent the studio presented, and persuaded her to present, to the public. "Nobody thinks less about boys than I do," she assured one fan magazine. "I don't want to get married till I'm 24. Why 24? Well, that sounds like a good long while away."

Even M-G-M could not repeal the biological mandate, however, and the truth was the exact opposite. Not only did boys dominate her thoughts, not only did she dote on their rude and boisterous company, but she had been enjoying sex with them for many months. Marriage? She did not plan to wait until she was twenty-four, twenty, or even eighteen. She wanted—she was desperate, in fact—to say her vows immediately; she would have done so that very afternoon if it could have been arranged. She had the man of her dreams already picked out. He loved her, or so she thought, and there was just one barrier to a quick trip down the aisle: he had not yet asked her to marry him.

Celebrating Judy's seventeenth birthday at Louis B. Mayer's beach house, with Mickey receiving a helpful push from his Hardy series costar Ann Rutherford

III

In her attitudes toward love and romance, as in so many other aspects of her life, Judy was more representative of American youth of the thirties than the bland and antiseptic teenagers M-G-M was foisting on the world. She probably got her first kiss in her father's theater in Lancaster; the boy, Galen Reed, was ten and frequently joined her onstage to sing duets, for which Frank Gumm rewarded him with a silver dollar. Also making a claim on her affections was another Lancaster boy, bucktoothed Charles Murphy. When her mother carried her away at last to Los Angeles, Judy cried for hours at the prospect of losing him. "I had a feeling I wouldn't see you for a long time and here it is going on 4 yrs.," she later wrote him. "But don't think there has been a day I haven't thought of you."

At thirteen or fourteen, she was holding hands with Freddie Bartholomew at screenings in Louis B. Mayer's darkened living room—"Judy and I were very much in love," Bartholomew recalled— and sneaking kisses with Jackie Cooper on the beach. She dropped both of them for the older, manlier Billy Halop. The leader of the "Dead End Kids," six boys who had come from New York to play tough street kids in such pictures as *Dead End* and *Crime School,* Halop warmly returned her tender feelings. Judy, he rather fetchingly confessed to one reporter, was his "weak moment."

Who finally introduced her to the pleasures of sex, and where and when, is a question without an answer: what is certain is that Judy had lost her virginity by the age of fifteen. One who went to bed with her then was Buddy Pepper, her senior by just seven weeks, who had several trysts with her in his apartment. Another, most likely, was Frankie Darro. Nor were they her only partners during that period. Where sex was concerned, Judy was a free spirit, unencumbered by guilt or inhibitions. On occasion, indeed, she was almost breathtakingly bold and aggressive.

No one would have been surprised to hear that Lana Turner—the "Kissing Bug from the Andy Hardy film," as Metro billed her—had engaged in sex at an early age. Nor would anyone have been astonished to learn that Mickey, who visited prostitutes, who fondled girls' breasts in the car that drove him to the commissary for lunch, and who said that Turner had "the nicest knockers" he had ever seen, claimed to have made her pregnant—an assertion Turner stoutly denied. But many, it seems safe to say, would have been shocked to discover that Judy was probably just as active as Turner, and probably just as early.

In fact, Judy's sexual history was likely not much different from that of many other girls, and no different at all from that of most of her own girlfriends—the boys usually started earlier. In Hollywood, sex was not just sex. It was a commodity, an article of merchandise that was put on constant, conspicuous display, like a high-powered car or a diamond bracelet. Is it any wonder that in the movie world, as in all others, the young emulated their elders? Or that Judy, Mickey and all those other fresh-faced teenagers who came to Stone Canyon Road did what comes naturally?

|||

Most teenagers go through periods in which they fall in and out of love with almost comic frequency. Judy differed from the norm only in degree: her crushes, most of which went unrequited, came and went with unvarying regularity. A deep-dyed romantic, she was the kind of girl whose heart pounded when she listened to the sweeping strains of a Rachmaninov concerto and whose eyes watered when she read the pensive verse of A. E. Housman. She was an enthusiastic, if not very inspired or polished, poet herself, and she undressed her emotions in several compositions, which, with disarming naïveté, she proudly had bound and sent to her closest friends. Laden with rue, as Housman's were, as well as with clichés, as Housman's were not, her poems speak of "forbidden treasures," "trembling lips" and "racking desires." Love, as the young Judy viewed it, almost always ended in distress and desolation.

Romantics are as fond of shadow as sunshine—"hail divinest melancholy," proclaimed Milton—and Judy's gloom-shrouded poesy cannot be read as a direct rendering of her state of mind, like a progress chart hanging from the end of a hospital bed. Still, it is a critical clue, which, combined with all the other clues, offers an insight into her psyche, disclosing what her close friends already knew: her feelings, her highs as well as her lows, were always exaggerated. At the start of a romance she was happier than most other girls; at the end she was more miserable. "She laughed more than anybody else, and she cried more than anybody else," said Buddy Pepper.

The result was a series of heartbreaks. Jimmie's boyfriend, the blond and amiable Bobby Sherwood, was one of those who inadvertently caused unhappiness. Judy had a secret crush on him, and when she learned that he was to marry Jimmie, she could not stop her tears— "because I'm so happy for you," she lamely explained to her suspicious sister. For Judy, the teen years were an emotional roller coaster— thrilling, dizzying ascents quickly followed by wrenching, harrowing descents. "People like me don't grow up easily," she was later to explain. "They bounce. One day they're adults with a head full of wisdom, and the next day they're stubborn children who have to be led by the hand." That was the Judy who was taking title to her womanhood at the beginning of the forties, a wise adult and an obstinate, mercurial child.

|||

The years spent rushing from stage to stage, job to job, had deprived Judy of that period in which, as Mickey was to observe, "kids learn to cope with life's problems, test their equipment, learn what works and what doesn't." With her contemporaries, as a consequence, especially those outside of show business, she was often shy and uncertain, like a child in a new school who has not yet learned the local do's and don'ts. She desperately wanted to be accepted by the group, to go to football games and high school proms, to enjoy, in short, all the ordinary things she had been denied; but that part of America, the part experienced by most middle-class Americans, she knew mostly from the movies. Without a script, she did not know how she should behave; without Metro's costume department to guide her, she did not even know how she should dress.

No one, for instance, had told her what real college girls wore. When one boy arrived to take her to his fraternity pledge party at USC, she greeted him in a slinky split skirt, with a white-fox stole draped around her neck—the kind of outfit a sexy starlet would wear to a premiere. Fearing hoots of laughter from his fraternity brothers, the boy feigned a sudden headache and fled in horror, only to be sent back by his angry father; he had made a date, his father informed him, and he would have to keep it. The second time he knocked, Judy had changed costumes, putting on a quieter, if duller, party dress: she had learned her lesson.

The years in which kids spend their time mostly with other kids Judy had spent with adults. She was, therefore, perfectly at home with her elders, gliding so easily through the grown-up world, even when she was fourteen and fifteen, that most people soon forgot that she was not, in fact, grown-up. By seventeen, she was an adult—in her own eyes and the eyes of everybody but the executives in Culver City—and males her own age no longer caught her fancy. She was interested only in mature men, men of a particular type, musicians mostly, and of a particular talent. Good looks were not mandatory; keen intelligence and a sharp, jabbing humor were.

To that potent mixture add the adjective "neurotic," and a picture of one of her major crushes begins to emerge. The "wit's wit," as one critic dubbed him, Oscar Levant was a concert pianist and composer; the lovely, bittersweet ballad "Blame It on My Youth" was his most memorable song. Until 1938, when his humor found him a home on the radio, he was known chiefly for his friendships with the famous, George Gershwin most notably, and for his devastating one-liners. When a date upbraided him for yawning in a nightclub, for example— "I hope I'm not keeping you up," she said sarcastically—Levant retorted: "I wish you were."

Thirty-two when he met Judy in New York in the summer of 1939, Levant, who had the sad eyes and droopy face of an aging basset hound, had divorced one beautiful woman, a Broadway chorus girl, and was courting another, a 20th Century–Fox starlet named June Gale, a "demure Jean Harlow," was how he described her. Neither his age nor the fact that he had already proposed to another woman stopped Judy from making a play for him herself.

"What do you think of me?" she demanded shortly after they met.

"You're enchanting," he answered.

"Don't give me that. What do you really think of me?"

"You're like a Mozart symphony," he said, a reply that so pleased her that she went out to buy recordings of all Mozart's many works—

symphonies, piano concertos, chamber music and operas. This time, however, one of Levant's one-liners had missed its target. Judy was nothing at all like a Mozart symphony—cool, classical and finely balanced—and after listening to all her new records, she angrily told him so. "She couldn't make contact with the purity of Mozart's music" was all Levant would say. Still, she was not angry enough to stop pursuing him, or to put an end to an avalanche of phone calls, letters and copies of her poems. Though their relationship remained platonic, his choice apparently, not hers, the attraction was mutual. Despite the wide, almost cavernous age gap, he was captivated, Levant confessed, by such a "throbbingly emotional girl."

Judy's tireless pursuit did at last bring Levant to the altar, but not with her: she was the catalyst that made June Gale, the woman Levant really loved, say yes at last. "I had been taking Oscar too much for granted," remembered the ultimate Mrs. Levant. "And Judy came on very strong about men. She didn't give up." Gale finally accepted Levant's proposal, a date was set and on December 1, 1939, the wit's wit had a new wife on whom to practice his craft. It was just as well that Judy got no further with him than she did. Suffering from too many of the same problems, with addiction to prescription drugs heading the list, they undoubtedly would have made a quarrelsome and unhappy couple. "If we had married," Levant later joked, "she would have given birth to a sleeping pill."

|||

If Judy was not distraught at Levant's marriage—and she did not seem to be—it was because she had fallen for someone else. And not just any someone, but the man who seemed to have captured every female heart in Hollywood, Artie Shaw. "Oh, my God . . . what a beautiful man!" Ava Gardner said to herself when she first met him. Along with the usual attributes of a lady-killer—he was, of course, tall, dark and handsome—Shaw possessed one that was not so usual: he could make musical magic with a clarinet. Benny Goodman's rival for the title "King of Swing," he was, in the words of jazz historian Gunther Schuller, "an uncompromising searcher for the lofty and the expressive," a musician who was virtually incomparable in the beauty of his tone.

Shaw had found fame in the summer of 1938, when his sweet and satiny recording of Cole Porter's "Begin the Beguine" had the whole nation dancing. From then on, he was, in his own words, a "sort of weird, jazz-band-leading, clarinet-tooting, jitterbug-surrounded Symbol of American Youth." His newfound celebrity, combined with the edgy, almost dangerous quality in his personality—no one could guess what he would say or do next—made Shaw a headline writer's delight. He carried with him a sense of drama. Attracting more attention than most movie stars, he could scarcely make a move without causing a commotion.

A poor Jewish boy—Arthur Arshawsky was his real name—who had grown up in the shadow of Yale's privileged towers, Shaw was to spend his long life in pursuit of an education. He never stopped reading, and he never stopped talking about his reading, lecturing one bewildered beauty after another on the merits of Nietzsche, Schopenhauer, Kierkegaard, Freud, Thomas Mann and numerous other umlaut-sprinkling Middle Europeans. Whatever the cause, Shaw was all but irresistible to Judy and any number of other stars and starlets. "I got Ava Gardner, I got Lana Turner, I got whoever was around," he recalled, running down the list like a sport fisherman showing off his prize-winning trophies. "With their cooperation. I didn't 'get' them: they came after me. It's true." It was indeed true, and Judy, who was not one of the most beautiful women of Hollywood, was yet the one who went after him the most aggressively and tenaciously of all.

|||

They had met when Shaw was playing in New York, probably on Judy's second visit in the winter of 1938, a few months before his "Begin the Beguine" was bouncing off the top of the charts. Excited by his innovative style—"she flipped out over what I was doing"—Judy introduced herself and handed him a bright bouquet of praise, one musician complimenting another. Though he was flattered by the attention and impressed by her precocious musical sophistication, Shaw was conquered by her high spirits and zest for living. "Judy was marvelous!" he said. "Bubbly, laughing, full of joy, just starting life. I was enchanted by her, crazy about her. I 'dug' her. That's better than 'loved' or 'cared for.' "

So began a friendship that sprouted and flourished despite the fact that when it began, Judy was only fifteen, little more than half Shaw's age. Even so, she was a livelier, more sympathetic companion than the grown women he dated. "I felt that she was the best friend I had had in a long, long time," said Shaw, who saw himself in desperate need of such companionship. Supremely confident in the eyes of most of the world, he was, in fact, plagued by doubt and self-loathing, so scarred by childhood encounters with anti-Semitism, among other things, that he was ashamed of being a Jew, ashamed of being himself. Judy, who was afflicted with different but equally corrosive insecurities, could understand such feelings better than anyone else. To Shaw, she was like a sister: they were born of the same anxieties.

But Judy did not regard Shaw as a brother. He was, indeed, the very definition of everything she desired in a man. Despite Ethel's furious objections to such a renowned womanizer—a man who had been twice divorced before the age of thirty, moreover—Judy was not in a mood to obey. Still smarting from her mother's marriage to Will Gilmore, she engaged in an elaborate ruse to throw her off the scent, recruiting Jackie Cooper to pick her up for a date, then deliver her to Shaw. When Cooper tired of the game, Jimmie provided cover, telling Ethel that Judy was with her rather than the man Judy now considered her lover.

In fact, Ethel's fears were groundless. Though they were often together, Shaw was not Judy's lover, not even her boyfriend. According to him—and it is hard not to believe him—they never so much as approached the bedroom. "She was the closest thing to a little sister I ever had," he said, "and sex with her would have felt incestuous. It would have been utterly impossible." Besides, he admitted, Judy was not the kind of woman he invited into his bed, not the "all-American, long-legged beauty" he favored.

But as Levant had discovered, when Judy cared about a man, she was relentless. Blind to both the competition and common sense, she did all she could to arouse her clarinet-tooting hero. Every time Shaw leaned down to give her a brotherly good-bye kiss, she greeted him with her lips instead of her forehead. When they came close together, she would rub her body against his. "Cut it out!" he would command. "Now watch that, kid!" he would say. But Judy regarded such comments as come-ons, not rebukes. Disregarding all the evidence, she had convinced herself that Shaw was not only in love with her, but wanted to marry her. Soon, she told herself, she would be the third Mrs. Artie Shaw.

|||

That much-contested title was won by someone else, however. On February 8, 1940, Shaw was making a recording on the Metro lot. Together with a friend, the comedian Phil Silvers, he paid a visit to the set of *Two Girls on Broadway,* where, Silvers had said, one of the two girls, Lana Turner, wanted to see him. "And zoom! Like a bee making for the honey," to use Silvers's words, Turner rushed over. She made a date with Shaw for that very night. Shaw talked, as he usually did, about Nietzsche and Schopenhauer, but he was more interested in Turner's flawless face than in philosophical verities. "It really was The American Dream," he said, with something approaching reverence. "Unbelievably beautiful." Before the night was half over, Paul Mantz, the "Honeymoon Pilot," was flying them to Las Vegas, where, roused from his sleep, a justice of the peace united them in holy matrimony.

Like everybody else in Hollywood, Judy learned about their marriage from a newspaper headline the next morning. Her mother, who had brought her the paper on a breakfast tray, heard a shriek from her bedroom and ran back to find her sobbing uncontrollably, staring at the horrifying news. "Well, so what?" responded Ethel, who had been taken in by her deceptions. "But I love him!" wailed Judy, who was so completely shattered that Ethel telephoned Shaw to complain. "You've broken her heart!" she screamed. Shaw was astonished. Wrapped up in himself, unable to look beyond his German philosophers and his Hollywood starlets, he had not realized until then that his best friend, his little sister, also wanted to be his wife. When he later tried to make amends, he only made matters worse: "Lana is a whole different thing, Judy. Lana is a woman I'll have sex with. . . . I never thought of you in that way and I didn't think you thought of me in that way."

Not since her father's death had Judy been so distraught. She had been betrayed, she believed, both by Shaw and by Turner, in whom she had confided her feelings. Shortly after their flight to Las Vegas, she went to the NBC radio studios for an appearance on Bob Hope's show. Walking into the dressing room of a fellow singer, Margaret Whiting, she threw herself into Whiting's arms, then, so complete was her despair, lurched away and started banging her head against the wall. "He said he wanted to marry me," Judy cried. "I'm going to die. I'm going to kill myself." Grabbing her, Whiting thrust her into a chair; then, with the help of David Rose, another guest on the show, she did her best to calm her down. "Never," said Whiting, "have I seen anybody so devastated as Judy was that night."

Desolate though she was, Judy once again was lucky that one of her crushes had not ended in wedding bells. Describing her marriage as hell, the third Mrs. Shaw walked away from it after only four months. Before he finished making trips to the altar, Shaw could count eight wives, two more than Henry VIII. "I made an unholy botch of every last one of them," Shaw said, which seems to be about the truth of it. His friendship with Judy was, in fact, more enduring than any of his marriages. Putting on a smiling front, Judy visited the newlyweds a few times, prompting Shaw to inquire why she did not come around more often. Her answer, made without any apparent malice, was as lethal, yet as accurate, as any of Oscar Levant's cracks. "Lana's nice," she said, "but talking to her is like talking to a beautiful vase."

|||

A beautiful vase, lovely to gaze at but tiring to talk to—that was Lana Turner. Yet if a sorcerer, brewing potions in some damp Malibu grotto, had told Judy he had a concoction that would enable her to trade places with Turner, she would have gulped it down in a second. "Who would you like to look like?" a friend asked her. Judy's reply was instantaneous: "Lana Turner. *That* is beauty."

The sultry young woman whom Walter Winchell, the reigning gossip columnist of the day, dubbed "America's Sweater Sweetheart" had everything Judy longed for: looks, glamour, sex appeal and the ability to land any man she wanted, including the only man Judy wanted. "I liked the boys," Turner recalled with relish, "and the boys liked me." Blond buccaneer that she was, Turner liked them still more if she knew somebody else had her eye on them, and she may have gone after Artie Shaw because Judy had told her of her infatuation: she was to make a mischievous habit of stealing Judy's heartthrobs. "Every boyfriend I get, Lana comes and takes him away from me," complained Judy. "I have a date with a guy, I mention him to Lana, and the first thing I know, she's moved right in."

Most other women would have reacted with hurt and anger to Turner's gleeful plundering. Judy's response was more revealing. She was always hurt and angry, of course. But after the initial shock and despair, she also sounded resigned, as if, deep down, she expected a sex goddess like Turner—a "queen of soft desire," to use Homer's happy phrase—to get the better of a mere mortal, particularly one as plain as Judy believed herself to be. Star though she now was, Judy was convinced that she was fat, homely and unattractive to men.

Her feeling of inferiority seemed to peak, perversely enough, in the very year, 1940, in which the rest of the world was starting to say, with genuine but delighted surprise, that the Garland girl had finally lost her baby fat—she was actually pretty, "dangerously near being glamorous," in the words of one reporter. After a summer preview of *Strike Up the Band,* several comment cards were returned with remarks like "Judy is getting prettier all the time." One enthusiastic member of the test audience went so far as to make a special plea for more movies featuring the "lovely Judy Garland," underlining the word "lovely" so that nobody at Metro would miss the point.

What people were, in fact, noticing was not that Judy had lost some weight—though that was the case—but that she had sloughed off the cocoon of a difficult, lumpy adolescence: she was a woman. On June 10, she turned eighteen, an occasion honored by the presence of Mayer, the paterfamilias himself, who helped her cut her birthday cake. Two weeks later, on June 26, came a ceremony of equal significance. Wearing a blue organdy dress and clutching two pink roses, she received a diploma from Los Angeles's University High School, her official school of record even while she was being tutored at M-G-M. No longer would shooting be interrupted so she could study grammar and geography, biology and American history. Childhood really was over.

Despite her unflattering assessment of herself, many men were beginning to take something more than a friendly interest. Shaw and

Oscar Levant may have resisted her advances, but there were dozens of others who found her captivating—a princess, if not a queen, of soft desire. "She had a great face, beautiful eyes and such a great personality," said Sidney Miller, one of the gang that so often came to Stone Canyon Road. "I wanted to make it with her—Oh, God!—but to her I was just friend Sidney. 'Hi, sweetie!' she'd say, or, 'Hi, doll!' "

Perhaps the most besotted of her admirers—alarmingly so, as it happened—was nineteen-year-old Robert Wilson. Smitten with the Judy he had seen dancing across movie screens in his hometown, snowy Buffalo, New York, he traveled all the way across the country to grab her and whisk her away to some cozy hideaway in the mountains. JUDY GARLAND KIDNAP PLOT LAID TO "LOVE," declared the March 9 edition of the *Los Angeles Examiner.* Fortunately for Judy, the amorous Wilson, who had apparently staked out her house, succumbed to cold feet and disclosed his intentions to the Culver City police. Sounding as moonstruck as Miller, he told them why he was so irresistibly attracted to her. "Every time she wiggles that cute little pug nose of hers, I fall more in love with her," he said. "She is my dream girl."

Leery of love after the Shaw debacle, Judy herself was not irresistibly attracted to anyone, without a crush for perhaps the first time in years. As a result, she went out with not just one man, but several, a diverse list that included a handsome young actor, Robert Stack; a struggling comedian, Peter Lind Hayes; and a fledgling movie agent, Baron Polan. No less notable a Hollywood figure than Spencer Tracy, who was, at forty, more than twice her age, and married to boot, was seen holding her arm at one or another nightspot.

Escorted by such a changing cast of men, Judy hit the nightclubs almost as often as Turner, who had her own table at Ciro's. Though Judy, along with nearly everyone else in the industry, was also a Ciro's regular—"everybody that's *anybody* will be at Ciro's to-night," boasted the club's ad—she continued to patronize old standbys like the Cocoanut Grove and the Trocadero and adopted new favorites like the Victor Hugo and La Conga. For an insomniac like Judy, the evening did not end when the nightclubs closed. Very often she went on to one of the after-hours places that had a sleek, homosexual sheen: amusing spots like the Café Gala that guaranteed good, offbeat entertainment and offered an urbane, liberated atmosphere. "It was kind of 'in' to go to gay clubs," said one young actress, who often saw her in such places. "A lot of us did that. It was considered sophisticated."

"Sophisticated" was not a word Metro wanted attached to Judy, and her nocturnal wanderings soon set off alarms in Culver City. It was all right for Turner to be labeled as a party girl; that only added to her on-screen allure. But it was not all right for Judy, whose girl-next-door image had become an important asset to the studio. Though Metro's publicists, one of whom was stationed in every major club every night, made sure that its stars were never photographed smoking, drinking or doing anything else that their fans might consider naughty, they could not stop the columnists from reporting who was where—and with whom. Worried that too many such sightings might tarnish her innocent reputation, studio caretakers privately urged Judy to stay home more often. When their warnings were ignored, at the end of July they asked an authentic Hollywood dragon to help out by blowing a little smoke and fire in her direction. Glad to oblige, the dragon—Louella Parsons, whose widely syndicated movie column could make or break a career—wrote that "Judy Garland's boss, who knows what's best for the lively Judy, has requested that she curtail her night club activities."

Even that public reprimand was not enough to stop the lively Judy. If Lana Turner could club-hop every night, why couldn't she? She was tired of being regarded as the kind of girl a boy might safely take home to the family, a "nice, old-fashioned girl," as Andy Hardy's mother called her in *Andy Hardy Meets Debutante.* Nor did she want to be admired for her cute little pug nose, as if she were a child to be patted on the head or chucked under the chin. What she wanted was to be a seductress, a temptress who could look into a man's eyes and cause him to reel with lust and longing, abandoning everything for just one delirious night with her. She wanted to smile at an Artie Shaw, as Turner had done, and cause him to tootle to her tune and her tune alone. She wanted, in short, to be Lana Turner.

Millions of others, including a few of Judy's friends in Culver City, indulged in similar fantasies. That was one of the main reasons M-G-M movies were so popular. For an hour and forty-five minutes, ordinary people could forget their troubles, pretend that they were the gorgeous leading lady or the virile leading man, and watch their daydreams un-roll in front of them. But when the lights went back on, most of those once-a-week fantasists blinked their eyes, returned to reality and appeared content to be who they were. Judy was not so content: the movie star had become a prisoner of movie myth. More fervently than any Woolworth's salesgirl, she believed that beauty was the ticket to romance and that if she only looked like Turner, she, too, could have any man she desired. Unable to accept the fact that she herself was merely pretty, Judy viewed Turner's physical perfection, and the perfection of Metro's other dazzling divinities, as a personal rebuke, a painful reminder of all she was not.

|||

When Judy arrived in 1935, Culver City was the beauty capital of the world, and Metro's lots were awash with several dozen of the most gorgeous females on the face of the globe. Greta Garbo. Jean Harlow. Joan Crawford. Myrna Loy. Norma Shearer. The list stretched on and on. From all over the world they came, actresses, dancers and contract players, many of whose names were known only to the casting department. At the end of the thirties came a second wave of ostentatious pulchritude—Hedy Lamarr; Greer Garson; Esther Williams; Lana Turner, of course—and another catalogue of anonymous lovelies. Wowed by the glamour parade in *Ziegfeld Girl,* the fourth picture Judy was to make in 1940, *Time* magazine allowed that beings so sensational did not need to act—undulating would be sufficient.

Glorious as they were—blond, brunette or redheaded—Metro's glamour queens were all of a certain type, however. Wherever they came from, the United States, Canada or Europe, they all looked the way Louis B. Mayer, a Jew born in Russia and reared in Canada, imagined American women should look: fair-cheeked and vaguely Anglo-Saxon, with roots that seemed to extend all the way back to the *Mayflower.* Excluded from Mayer's platonic conception was anyone who appeared at all "ethnic," which in those days meant southern European or Jewish. A studio that was run almost entirely by Jews, as most of the Hollywood studios were, was thus, incongruously enough, perhaps the world's most artful and successful purveyor of the myth that only Gentiles could be beautiful. Even more incongruous was the fact that, no matter how handsome they might have been, none of the women in Louis B. Mayer's own family could have been employed as a leading lady in a studio he controlled.

Sitting in their offices on the third floor of the Thalberg Building, Mayer and his myrmidons were convinced that they were Hollywood's beauty experts. They had no doubt that they could grade a woman's attractiveness as accurately as a jeweler could grade gems, or a metallurgist gold. They were at least partly right: the women who passed the third floor's test were undeniably lovely, each and every one. Yet there was, it must also be said, an equally undeniable sameness, a perceptible blandness, to the group overall. Just as all gems of a like size and quality look much the same, so, too, did most of M-G-M's standardized, homogenized beauties share a kissing-cousin resemblance.

The reason was obvious: M-G-M was suspicious, as always, of unruly individuality. It made no allowance for the charming deviation, such as the dimple embedded in Ava Gardner's chin, that made a face not merely beautiful, but memorable. If Gardner, that spunky North Carolina cracker, had not threatened rebellion, Metro would happily have erased one of her most distinctive characteristics, thereby beautifying her into a nonentity.

The other studios also burned incense at the altar of beauty, of course, but none defined the word as narrowly as did Metro. Most of Metro's competitors also recognized that, through the electricity of her personality, a woman who was not commonly considered a looker—a Bette Davis, for example, or a Barbara Stanwyck—could sometimes be more exciting, more glamorous even, than one who was. At M-G-M, a concession like that would have been branded as heresy, as subversive to the established order as an anarchist's bomb. Let other studios have the Davises and the Stanwycks, Metro seemed to say—stars who looked like everyone else. Mighty M-G-M would continue to make movies—and profits—with stars who looked the way everyone else wanted to look.

Small wonder that, growing up in a place with such smug and unbending rules, a chunky teenager with a hard-to-fit body would have been awed and intimidated, made to feel more awkward than she actually was. Judy had been at Metro only a short time, in fact, when she confided to a sympathetic Joan Crawford that she felt like a polliwog—a polliwog on its way to becoming a frog. "Until M-G-M I had enjoyed being myself," she was later to explain. "I had been judged by my talent, but in the movies beauty was the standard of judgment—and definitely I didn't have it. And so I began to dislike the me I saw reflected in my mirror, especially when I compared myself with the real beauties on the lot, like Lana Turner, for instance."

In her early years in Culver City, some tactful handling by the people in charge might have saved Metro, as well as Judy herself, untold amounts of future pain. But the studio that thought of its stars as high-paid serfs was not known for its tact. Week by week, month by month, in large ways and small, without any malicious intent and against its own best interests, it confirmed Judy's opinion that she was an eyesore in an otherwise flawless landscape. From the start Metro simply assumed, and assumed that Judy assumed, that audiences would take one look at her and agree that she was the kind of girl no one would care to look at twice. Billie Burke's line in *Everybody Sing*—"Poor little ugly duckling! Well, well, Mother loves you anyway"—summed up the tone of genial disparagement.

"Mr. Mayer calling her 'my little hunchback'!" exclaimed an indignant Irene Sharaff, the inspiration behind some of Metro's most brilliant costume designs. "Do you know what that did to a girl who was basically shy? A girl who was competing with the glamour pusses? It was torture." To have been the silent recipient of such ridicule must have been torture indeed. For the advancement of her career, a Mayer-run M-G-M was the ideal studio for Judy; for her psychological and spiritual well-being, it was the worst. Metro made her a star, but it also destroyed, or helped to destroy, her self-confidence. She believed what she had been taught to believe: that she was, in truth, a poor little ugly duckling—an ugly duckling surrounded by swans.

|||

A strong ego, built on a sturdy foundation of parental love, probably could have enabled even a shy girl to withstand Metro's bombardment of slights and insults. Judy, however, did not have a strong ego. Missing from her makeup, to the astonishment of those who marveled at her gifts, was a sense of her own merit. From the age of two she had been instructed that her identity was her performance, that the offstage Judy was a mere shadow of the one singing on stage: she was only as good as the folks out front said she was. If they liked her, her value as a person, as well as an entertainer, was ratified; if they did not like her, she had no worth at all. How hard, then, it must have been for her at M-G-M, where hands never clapped and voices were rarely raised in praise. Suddenly she was exposed, alone and vulnerable. "What is Judy so worried about?" someone scribbled on a comment card when *Babes in Arms* was previewed in Inglewood, a town just south of Culver City. "There is terror in her eyes." So, to anyone who cared to look closely, there was.

Plain and unappealing was what Judy thought she was, in any event. As she blossomed into womanhood, she was persuaded that what she had feared most had come to pass—that the polliwog had finally turned into a frog. A hapless witness to her misery was Metro's drama coach, Lillian Sidney, who in the autumn of 1940 helped prepare her for a difficult scene in *Ziegfeld Girl,* a musical melodrama in which Judy topped the bill with Lana Turner and Hedy Lamarr. Once again the script called for Judy to play a good girl, the cheery, dutiful and all but sexless daughter who is trying to help her father make a comeback in vaudeville. Turner and Lamarr were counted on for sex appeal—they were the ones men were expected to drool over. For a woman as uncertain as Judy was, the script was bad enough. Worse still, as she lamented to Sidney, was the attitude of the stagehands, who seemed to drool over everybody but her.

"Judy, dear, what's wrong? What's wrong?" Sidney asked anxiously when Judy, shrouded in gloom, walked into her office.

"I don't like myself" was Judy's short but devastating answer.

"Judy, hate yourself, but love your talent!" remonstrated Sidney. "You're loaded!"

"Yes," replied Judy. "But when Lana walks onto the set, all the guys whistle until she gets across. When Hedy walks on, there's a sigh of I don't know what. And when I walk on, they say, 'Hi, Judy!' " To anyone who could not see, as Sidney did, the anguish in her face, such dialogue would have sounded more like farce than tragedy. It was not funny to Judy, however, and not all of Sidney's heartfelt praise could boost her anemic spirits—she listened, but did not hear. Deaf to all those who were now calling her pretty, blind to the evidence of her own eyes, Judy peered into the mirror and saw reflected back not the attractive young woman everyone else saw, but the comical hillbilly of *Pigskin Parade*. The silhouette of the pudgy girl she once had been was burned on her retina, and there it would remain. Completely coloring her existence, the ineradicable conviction that she was ugly affected virtually every thought she had, every move she made and every relationship she entered into.

|||

Like the savage rites of the Aztecs, M-G-M's religion of beauty demanded human sacrifice—an offering of spirit if not blood. Judy, who was its most devout believer, also sacrificed the most: she surrendered her self-regard. What she never was to realize was that her faith in the gospel according to Louis B. Mayer was woefully misplaced. The god that was celebrated in Culver City—that is, the moviegoing public—did smile on the beautiful. But it reserved its special blessing for a still rarer breed, those lucky few, who, beautiful or not, could keep it entertained. On them it did not merely smile; it positively beamed, grinning

Three Ziegfeld girls: Judy, Hedy Lamarr and Lana Turner

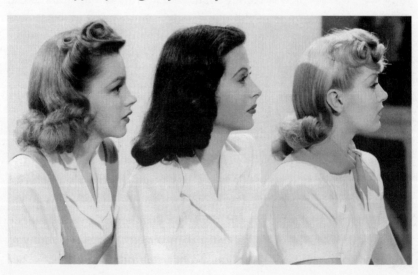

with the crazy enthusiasm of first love. Judy belonged to that small and select group. For her, more than for Lana Turner, Hedy Lamarr, or any of Metro's other glamour pusses, audiences were always to have a tender affection.

The proof of that simple proposition came at the end of 1940, when the *Motion Picture Herald,* a trade journal, published its annual list of the stars whose films had made the most money in the previous twelve months. Only two women were among the top ten, and neither was among the perfect specimens so much admired in Culver City. One was Warner Bros.' bug-eyed but electrifying Bette Davis—"Popeye the Magnificent," *Time* magazine had facetiously anointed her. The other was Mr. Mayer's little hunchback—Judy Garland.

Mayer, who had been counting the receipts all along, did not need the *Herald* to tell him how one of his stars was doing at the box office. Three months earlier, at the end of September, he had acknowledged Judy's popularity by tearing up her old seven-year contract, which still had two years to run, and giving her a new one. Her salary was quadrupled, jumping from $500 a week to $2,000. Another rise, to $2,500, was scheduled for 1943, and a third, to $3,000, for 1945. His ears attuned to the sound of ringing cash registers, Mayer had belatedly realized, even if Judy had not, that though the swan may be more pleasing to the eye, the nightingale has greater powers of enchantment.

III

"The success of the little Garland girl has been one of Hollywood's most interesting stories," wrote Louella Parsons, and for once the dragon was right. From the spring of 1939, when she began shooting *Babes in Arms,* through the spring of 1943, when she finished *Girl Crazy,* Judy made ten pictures, dashing breathlessly from project to project, sometimes starting work on one while still doing final scenes for another. As if that hectic pace were not enough, she also maintained a busy radio schedule, appearing on the Bob Hope show every Tuesday night in 1940 and accepting a variety of guest spots in 1941 and the years thereafter.

Although it usually took longer to make a musical than it did to make other kinds of films, such a crowded agenda was not uncommon in the

Hollywood of the thirties and forties. What was uncommon was that in six of the ten movies she made during that period, Judy had the same costar, Mickey Rooney. What was more unusual, extraordinary even, was that in six of the ten, she was also directed, in whole or in part, by the same man—Busby Berkeley. The first partnership brought her nothing but smiles and joy; the second, little more than anxiety and exhaustion.

Judy's collaboration with Mickey had actually started in 1937 with *Thoroughbreds Don't Cry,* then had continued with *Love Finds Andy Hardy* in 1938. Though the sparks they struck provided the single flicker of interest in either of those two otherwise unmemorable pictures, it was not until their third film, *Babes in Arms,* went into previews that Metro awoke to what a potent and profitable combination they might be at the box office. "After such a hit Judy and Mickey should never be parted," was the advice offered on one preview card. "Would appreciate Garland and Rooney again," said another.

After counting the picture's unexpectedly large grosses, M-G-M was quick to oblige: if the public wanted Garland and Rooney together, the public would get them together. Judy was written into the scripts of two more Hardys, *Andy Hardy Meets Debutante* in 1940 and *Life Begins for Andy Hardy* in 1941, and she was paired with Mickey in the second installment of what was to be, in everything but name, a four-part *Babes in Arms* series. "You Asked for *another* 'Babes in Arms,' " the studio said in its ads for the sequel, *Strike Up the Band.* "Here it is!" The popularity of *Strike Up the Band,* which was released in 1940, led, in turn, to *Babes on Broadway* in 1942, and the success of that resulted in *Girl Crazy* a year later.

Once it had a winning formula, as it had in the continuing Hardy saga, Metro repeated it again and again, and sometimes again and again after that. A genealogist might argue, in fact, that the *Babes in Arms* pictures were not really a new series, but an offshoot of the Hardys. Mickey is still the central character, concocting schemes, issuing orders and getting himself in and out of trouble. Judy is his right hand, his chief adviser and his conscience, the not-so-gentle voice that informs him when he is breaking Hardyland's strict code of honesty, integrity and small-town piety.

The only real difference between the Hardy series and its *Babes in Arms* offspring is the music. In each of the *Babes in Arms* installments, Mickey and Judy convince their stagestruck gang to put on a musical to raise money for some worthy cause. Obstacles arise and disaster looms, but ten or fifteen minutes before the film ends, they put on a show that Ziegfeld would have cheered. Judy sings, Mickey struts and dozens of dancers join them to demonstrate what a group of eager kids can do when they have a liberal budget, the most modern equipment and the support of the biggest studio in the world—no one ever claimed that a Metro musical had anything more than a passing acquaintance with reality.

|||

"We performed magic, the two of us, together, on film," said Mickey, and he was not exaggerating: something rare and remarkable did take place when he and Judy teamed up for the cameras. Those working on their sets were accustomed to their off-camera clowning, to hearing Mickey's jokes, then, from Judy, a glissando of laughter, as carefree and playful as a waterfall. Judy and Mickey were not two actors who had to pretend to be friends; they were friends. They were, indeed, each other's biggest fans.

At Metro, Mickey gave Judy what she called her "first real insight into acting." Though she had already made five movies, it was not until he pulled her aside on her first Hardy that she felt she was on her way to becoming a good actress. "Just before our first scene together," she recalled, "he took my hands and said, 'Honey, you gotta believe this, now. Make like you're singing it.' And all at once I knew what I had been doing wrong. Good singing is a form of good acting; at least it is if you want people to believe what you're singing. If you can make yourself *believe* what you're saying—and you have to say some pretty silly things in musicals—everything else falls into place. Your timing, your gestures, your coordination, all take care of themselves."

After that, they were a perfect match—sympathetic hearts and quicksilver minds. Blessed with photographic memories, both could glance at a script, then repeat it word for word when the director yelled "Action!" Confident, cocky even, they never stopped trying to shake each other with lines and movements of their own invention. "With other actresses, I had to play everything straight," said Mickey. "If I tried to clown around with a novice, fiddle with the timing, or ad-lib, I'd rattle her and ruin the scene. With Judy, it was the exact opposite. We actually tried to throw each other off track, tried to get the other one to mess up a scene."

Almost two years older, Mickey assumed the role of older brother to the girl he nicknamed "Jootes." Though the studio publicity machine tried to exploit their affection by hinting at romance, they were, to Judy's visible chagrin, never more than close friends. Like Betsy Booth in the Hardy movies, Judy obviously adored Mickey, her eyes jealously watching him watching the beauties who populated any Metro musical. "Mickey understood me," she was later to say. "And he must have known I was crazy about him." Mickey did know it, but the Hardy pictures had accurately reflected the nature of their relationship: he was as crazy about her as she was about him, but in a nonsexual, arm-around-the-shoulder kind of way. Like Andy Hardy, he was on the lookout for prettier, sexier girls. "I have always loved Judy without ever being *in* love with her" was how he characterized his feelings.

Romance or no romance, their relationship caught the public's fancy, and by 1943 the combination of Garland and Rooney meant a guaranteed hit for M-G-M. "One of the hottest box office announcements that any exhibitor could make these days," reported *Box Office Digest,* "is the simple listing of the names 'Mickey Rooney and Judy Garland' on his marquee—and not worry about the title of his picture." Since Mickey was the bigger and more established star, it is not surprising that Metro paid him more than it did her. What is surprising is that it gave him so much more, double or triple what Judy received: $23,400 versus her $8,833 for *Babes in Arms,* for example, and $68,167 versus her $28,667 for *Girl Crazy.* Money talks, and those loquacious figures say two things simultaneously: actresses were generally paid less than actors in Hollywood, and even under her new, more lucrative contract, Judy was grossly shortchanged by M-G-M.

The passage of time has made the inequity all the more glaring. Though Mickey was an actor of diverse and exceptional gifts, he often seemed overwhelmed by his own talent, and his uncontrolled mugging, which Metro unwisely encouraged, is now embarrassing to see. He could do everything, as *Time* magazine's critic tartly remarked, except behave himself. It is Judy alone who prevents his runaway ego from turning the *Babes in Arms* stories into portraits of Mickey. Despite the scripts, which spotlight him rather than her, she is the still center around whom the pictures rotate. What is clear today, as it was to some then as well, is that whenever they are together, Judy, without even trying, steals the scene from Hollywood's most shameless scene stealer.

|||

Busby Berkeley, Judy's other collaborator in the early forties, was also both uniquely gifted and conspicuously out of control. The driving force behind the Warner Bros. musicals of the early thirties, a landmark list that includes *42nd Street, Footlight Parade* and the *Gold Diggers* series, Berkeley was the master of the motion-picture extravaganza, the Cecil B. DeMille of the movie musical.

Berkeley had learned the craft of choreography, oddly enough, not on the stage, but on the parade grounds of France, where he drilled American troops during World War I; his innovative screen numbers owed more to West Point than they did to Hollywood, Broadway or the Ballets Russes. Interested less in individuals than in masses, Berkeley deployed scores, sometimes hundreds, of dancers in a myriad of different and arresting ways: his signature number was a giant kaleidoscope in which each dancer was but a tiny piece in an ever-changing, mesmerizing pattern. By 1939, Berkeley's reputation for cinematic derring-do had already made his name part of the American vernacular: in the *American Thesaurus of Slang*, a "Busby Berkeley" was defined as "a very spectacular, elaborate, and original number."

The trouble for Judy, who worked with him on *Ziegfeld Girl* and *For Me and My Gal,* as well as the four *Babes in Arms* pictures, was that the creation of a Busby Berkeley could be a wrenching, nerve-racking experience. Like most obsessives, Berkeley never knew when to stop. He always demanded too much—too much from the scenes he directed, too much from his actors, too much from his crews, too much even from himself. "There was fun and there certainly was excitement," he said, "but what I mostly remember is stress and strain and exhaustion."

Convinced that he was always on trial, that he always had to top himself, Berkeley rehearsed endlessly, oblivious to the clock. Once shooting began, he would think nothing of keeping his cameras rolling long after midnight, until one, two, three o'clock in the morning. On one picture, *Lady Be Good,* he forced poor Eleanor Powell to dance so long and so hard that she limped away covered with bruises, as if he had beaten her with his fists, which, in a sense, he had.

Judy's bruises were only emotional, but far more painful in the long run. At the end of each picture she, too, felt as if she had been beaten. An alcoholic with what Mickey called an "alcoholic's perfectionism," Berkeley had a mean and vigilant temper that turned the slightest misstep into an occasion for a public denunciation. "If you couldn't toe the line," said Mickey, "make it just so for Buzz, he'd go crazy." Always a quick study, Judy had never had much difficulty pleasing other directors. But she was unable to satisfy Berkeley, who seemed to take sadistic pleasure in berating and belittling her. Although he perceived, quite correctly, that her animated eyes were one of her best assets, she could never open them widely enough to make him happy. "Eyes! Eyes! I want to see your eyes," he would bellow, forcing her, in some shots, to push them out so ostentatiously that she appeared to be suffering from a thyroid condition. The effect was startling enough for one London critic to remark, in a review of *Girl Crazy,* on the "pop-eyed Garland charm."

The cruelty of Berkeley's tongue shocked even Hedda Hopper, Louella Parsons's chief rival in the Hollywood gossip trade and the possessor of a pretty cruel tongue herself. Visiting one set, Hopper noticed a wild gleam in his eyes, as, in take after take, he yelled and screamed at an increasingly nervous and agitated Judy. "She was close to hysteria," wrote Hopper. "I was ready to scream myself. But the order was repeated time and time again: 'Cut. Let's try it again, Judy. Come on, Judy! Move! Get the lead out.'" Conjuring up the image of Simon Legree standing over a cringing Eliza, Judy told Hopper that she felt as if he were lashing her with a big black bullwhip. "Sometimes I used to think I couldn't live through the day," she said. "Other times I'd have my driver take me round and round the block because I hated to go through the gates."

The stars and their bosses, Busby Berkeley and Louis B. Mayer

The torment of working with "that crazy old Busby Berkeley," as Esther Williams was to call him, began to take its toll. By the end of *Strike Up the Band*, Judy was so tired, emotionally as well as physically, that even her mother, the pusher and the prodder, became alarmed, brusquely informing the studio that thenceforth she would not let her daughter work more than eight hours a day. Metro's response was not recorded; but whatever it was, it was unfavorable. Mayer would not let Ethel, or anybody else, tell him how to run his studio, and it was probably then that he barred Ethel from the lot, not allowing her to return for several months, by which time she presumably had learned to mind her own business.

|||

At the end of January 1943, M-G-M finally called a halt to Berkeley's megalomania. The breaking point came three weeks into *Girl Crazy*. The first scene to be shot was a college rodeo for which Roger Edens wanted what he later described as a simple staging. But "simple" was not in Berkeley's vocabulary. He wanted a genuine Busby Berkeley, a rodeo such as the West had never seen, with guns blazing, cannons blasting, whips cracking and battalions of cowboys and cowgirls doing high steps through the sagebrush. Berkeley won the argument—his rootin'-tootin' rodeo eventually concluded the film—but lost the picture. His complicated staging added nearly $100,000 to the budget and so outraged Edens that Edens issued an ultimatum to Arthur Freed, who had, even as Mayer had promised, become a producer. If Berkeley stayed, Edens said, he would go.

Confronted with such a stark choice, Freed had no difficulty coming to a decision. Though no one was ever able to define precisely what Edens did on a Freed musical, everyone knew that his contribution was vital: he was involved in a production from script to staging, from conception to preview, advising, arranging and, when needed, writing both music and lyrics. A tall Texan who was kept from being handsome only by a droopy, teardrop nose, he exuded the movie cowboy's air of casual authority. Almost universally liked and admired, he had already proven himself, at thirty-seven, to be indispensable to both Freed and the Metro musical. Berkeley had not, and in the third week of January Freed fired him, replacing him with the uninspired but reliable Norman Taurog, who had directed Judy in *Little Nellie Kelly* three years earlier.

But inspiration was not what Metro wanted in the *Babes in Arms* series. "Don't try to make these films any better," Mayer had said about the Andy Hardy pictures, and his edict applied to their musical relations as well. Audiences had liked the first *Babes in Arms* just the way it was. Why risk failure by tampering with the sequels? Metro wanted the series to be good, but not very good. The result was planned mediocrity: tiresome plots, hackneyed scripts and smothering mountains of the corn the post-Thalberg M-G-M cultivated so enthusiastically. "If a story makes me cry, I know it's good," Mayer had once said, and Freed, who produced the entire series, made sure that the boss had plenty to cry about in those stories of good-hearted, all-American kids struggling to put on a show. If the scripts are mediocre, the music is not, however. Freed, the lyricist, knew the difference between good songs and bad, and, aided by Edens, he chose some of the best songs of some of America's best songwriters, an exalted company that included Richard Rodgers and Lorenz Hart, Harold Arlen and E. Y. Harburg, and George and Ira Gershwin.

Had they been ten times better, the *Babes in Arms* pictures would still not have been worth the price Judy paid for them. For her, the cost of working with Berkeley could be counted in frayed nerves, sleepless nights and further damage to her emotional stability. In some dim cavern, deep inside her mind, she was to continue, for long years to come, to see his dark brows furrowing and his hand tightly clutching a big black whip. There was a still-worse legacy of the Berkeley years, however: an increased dependence on prescription drugs. Small wonder that when she thought of Busby Berkeley, as she herself was to say, she recalled only gray, numbing fatigue and too many trips to the Benzedrine bottle.

|||

"I won't marry yet. Not for three or four more years." So a hurt and disillusioned Judy assured an interviewer after Artie Shaw, the man she had hoped to marry, had run off with Lana Turner. In the weeks after that collision with rude reality, Judy may actually have meant what she said, putting marriage, and all that went with it, off to a time when she would be an almost middle-aged woman of twenty-one or twenty-two. But if she did mean it, she did not mean it for long. Though she was, by the summer of 1940, no longer a girl, she was still acutely susceptible to girlish crushes, and anyone who knew her could have predicted that a new man would soon take Shaw's place in her heart. She could live without being loved, but Judy could not live without loving. In her romantic fantasies, as in every other aspect of her life, it was more important to please than to be pleased, to present herself to an audience, even an audience of one, and to beg for approval.

Several men passed in and out of her life in the months following Shaw's abrupt leave-taking, and Judy had an affair with at least one of them, the songwriter Johnny Mercer, whose face was round and homely, but whose huge gap-toothed grin, which looked as if it had been stolen from a Halloween jack-o'-lantern, spread cheer wherever he went. Only thirty-one when they were carrying on their affair, Mercer had already written the words for such durable favorites as "You Must Have Been a Beautiful Baby" and "Jeepers Creepers"; he was to go on to write many others—"Laura" and "Moon River," to name just two. That "bouncy butterball of a man from Georgia," as his friend and frequent collaborator Hoagy Carmichael called him, the irrepressible Mercer had followed Judy's career since she was a girl. By April 1940, when they recorded a duet of Cole Porter's "Friendship," their relationship had become considerably more than friendly, or was about to do so. As besotted with Judy as Judy had been with Shaw, Mercer wandered around in such a lovesick daze that a friend of the family finally pleaded with her to let him go. Judy did as she was asked—Mercer was not a serious crush—but Mercer continued to pine, paying her sly tribute a year or so later with an ode to impossible love, "That Old Black Magic." Though Judy was loath to admit it, even to herself, occasionally she, too, could play the siren, causing hearts to pound and heads to lose their reason.

Judy may have let Mercer go so willingly because, even while they were having their fling, she was finding her own black magic with another man. At first glance, the new object of her affections, David Rose—the same David Rose who had helped Margaret Whiting stop Judy's hysterics after the Shaw-Turner nuptials—looked like the last man who would interest a lively, fun-loving young woman. Short, with a pleasant pudding face and light, sandy hair, he had not a hint of Shaw's brooding good looks. Quiet and "painfully shy," according to one profile, he also had none of Oscar Levant's caustic Gotham wit or Mercer's hush-puppy charm. At parties he usually faded into the background, not opening his mouth for half an hour at a time; though he was only thirty, one fan magazine said that he sometimes seemed older, which was probably a polite way of saying that some people found him boring. Rose was, all in all, such a well-camouflaged suitor that for months the gossip columnists were blind to the romance blossoming right in front of their quick, ferrety eyes. "Little was thought of their 'going together,' " wrote one reporter, "until Hollywood suddenly became conscious that Judy Garland and David Rose, sitting there at a floor table at Ciro's, had been occupying that same table off and on for three months! Judy must be in love!"

So she was, and a closer examination disclosed that Rose, in fact, did possess a few of the features of her previous crushes. Like most of them, he was at least a decade older than she was; like most of them, he made beautiful music—and a talent for music had always been a potent aphrodisiac for the women in the Gumm family. Rose also had one characteristic her other crushes had not had: he was thoroughly nice, and Judy was in need of a little niceness. She saw some of his kind consideration on the day of her great upset. After helping Whiting calm her down, Rose left, then returned with a big slab of his mother's chocolate cake. "How did you know this was just what I needed!" she exclaimed.

More often than poets and songwriters like to acknowledge, love is the product of time and circumstance. A year earlier, and perhaps a year later, two such peculiarly matched people would probably have ignored each other. In 1940, time and circumstance merged, bringing them together at the exact moment in which they were feeling most vulnerable. Judy was in shock from the news about Artie Shaw; Rose was just emerging from a bad marriage to Martha Raye, the singer and comedienne. Unhappiness, and a bit more, they had in common, and after stopping and staring, they stayed together.

|||

"In-Between Music" was the label Rose gave his compositions, which meant that they were neither classical nor popular, but somewhere in the middle. Like such contemporaries as Morton Gould and André Kostelanetz, he gave symphonic treatment to simple themes. Lush and romantic, his style favored strings over brass and winds: his best-known work is aptly titled "Holiday for Strings." Though his music never appealed to purists, it was ideal for radio and the movies—and television, too, in later years. "The most appreciative listeners are always those who know nothing about music," he said. "But they invariably know what they like." And they obviously liked the music of David Rose, which, like its creator, was congenial and undemanding, if perhaps a bit bland.

Although he was wholeheartedly dedicated to his profession, Rose reserved his passion for his hobby—his own private railroad. "I got my first engine—a little stationary job—when I was seven years old," he said. "It was a birthday present, and I flipped over it. It's been that way ever since." Like his music, his trains were also in-between: they were too big to be called toys, but too small to pass as the real things. About one-eighth the size of the sleek streamliners that pulled in and out of Los Angeles's Union Station, they were propelled by coal-burning steam engines and were thus powerful enough, as well as big enough, to carry Rose and his friends around the nearly eight hundred feet of track he had laid around his house in the San Fernando Valley.

So enamored was Rose of the huff-puff of the engine and the clickety-clack of train over track that for a long time he could not make up his mind whether he wanted to be a musician or a train engineer. In the end he decided he could be both—and both he was. After a frantic day at the radio studio, he would go home, put on his engineer's cap and, happy as a boy on the first day of summer vacation, ride the rails, round and round, up and down, never going anywhere. "Dave Rose— Eccentric Genius, Odd Combination of Youth and 'Old Man' " was one magazine's short but accurate description of Judy's new heart-throb.

A night on the town for
Mr. and Mrs. David Rose

CHAPTER 6

A Ride to Nowhere
on the Gar-Rose Railway

I n the Hollywood of the forties, the matrimonial plans of a teenage star were scrutinized as carefully as those of an heir to the British throne. And for the same reason: the folks in charge did not want to offend the hoi polloi with an unpopular alliance. Judy had reaped the advantages of stardom— fame, money and the admiration of millions of her contemporaries. Now she was discovering one of the major disadvantages: if she valued her career, she needed the studio's blessing before saying yes to any proposal of marriage. But the studio had no intention of giving its blessing, not anytime soon at least. If her nightclubbing caused annoyance, the possibility of an imminent betrothal brought forth an angry roar from the Metro lion, which saw in any union nothing but trouble.

With the exception of *Little Nellie Kelly,* in which she had portrayed a wife and mother, Judy had never played an adult. Her role had always been that of a virginal teenager, from Dorothy in *The Wizard of Oz,* to Betsy Booth in the Andy Hardy series, to the bouncy, fresh-faced youngsters in the *Babes in Arms* quartet. Such parts had made her one of Metro's top money-earners, and such parts, Metro believed, would continue to provide surefire profits for two or three years to come. "That baby," Mayer called her, doing his best to ignore the fact that she was growing up—that, indeed, she had grown up. But all those grass-green parts, and possibly all those surefire profits, would disappear the minute she changed the title in front of her name from "Miss" to "Mrs."

According to conventional wisdom, audiences naively assumed that the star and the screen character were essentially the same, that Clark Gable really was the he-man of *Gone With the Wind* and *Boom Town,* that William Powell really was the urbane wit of the *Thin Man* series, and that Judy Garland really was the corn-fed kid from Hardyland, to whom a peck on the cheek was a daring sexual adventure. By that logic, an actress whose wedding would be covered by all the fan magazines could not very well thereafter pretend that she was an unworldly adolescent, ignorant about what men and women do when the bedroom doors are closed. What if the new Mrs. Rose became pregnant? What would that do to her image? The suggestion sent shivers of terror scurrying down half a dozen well-padded spines on the third floor of the Thalberg Building.

In Metro's opinion, Judy was not only rushing to the altar, but rushing with the wrong man, a man who was twelve years her senior, who was not good-looking and who was not even divorced—he would not be legally free of Martha Raye until March 1941. If Judy did marry him, she would not be the first, but the second Mrs. Rose. In an era in which many Americans still considered divorce a badge of dishonor, that was a serious and, from Metro's vantage point, a decisive objection. Lana Turner, to repeat a refrain that Judy was doubtless tired of hearing, could get away with such things. Judy could not. What would her fans say if she married a divorced man? The studio did not want to hear. Its resistance to any marriage was firm; its opposition to Rose, implacable.

Metro's scowling disapproval underlined Ethel's own heartfelt objections. She, too, was convinced that Judy was not old enough to settle down; she, too, was convinced that when she did marry, Judy should find a husband closer to her own age, someone who did not carry the burden of divorce. On the last point, she had good reason to worry. Ignoring her concerns, both her older daughters had married divorced men, and both had suffered as a result. Sue's marriage to Lee Kahn had long since dissolved, while Jimmie's marriage to Bobby Sherwood was showing signs of strain and would soon unravel altogether. Kahn and Sherwood were also musicians, which, to Ethel's way of thinking, put a cloud over any subsequent horn-tootler or piano-pounder who came calling. The hapless Rose had been convicted without a trial. "I wish you girls would find someone who digs a slide rule instead of a slide trombone," complained Ethel.

Judy's humor and high spirits had disguised the fact that, from earliest childhood, she had been remarkably docile and obedient, almost always doing what her mother and, later, M-G-M told her to do, rather than what she wanted to do. Now, with her marriage plans under attack, with her lover under siege, missiles peppering him from all sides, she was neither docile nor obedient: she was defiant. Not only did she continue to see Rose in public, but she also saw him in private, using a variety of subterfuges to keep her suspicious mother from knowing where she was going and what she was doing. Ethel eventually learned the truth, however, and when she did, her indignant shouts rumbled along Stone Canyon Road like an earthquake. Faced with such profound hostility, Rose, who had been a reluctant suitor from the beginning, suggested they wait. Since everybody but Judy opposed their union, Louella Parsons assured her readers that it would never take place. "If you ask me"—though of course no one had asked her—"and if it is any comfort to M-G-M, I don't think there is a chance of Judy and Dave marrying."

|||

What nobody—M-G-M, Ethel, Parsons or Rose himself—had reckoned with was Judy's unexpected and unyielding determination: she loved Rose and she intended to become his wife. Every morning, as they were being made up for their parts in *Ziegfeld Girl,* she asked poor Eve Arden to listen to the gushy love poem she had written the night before. "She seemed like such a baby to me," recalled the patient Arden, "and so vulnerable." A few weeks later she invited Rose to the Academy Awards ceremony, so that all Hollywood could behold what a happy pair they made.

Conveniently forgetting her earlier pronunciamento, even Parsons was starting to hear wedding bells ringing in the distance. "I am wondering what will happen when Dave Rose gets his final divorce decree in March!" she wrote. "Judy is frankly in love with him, and although they feel at M-G-M that it is just a young girl's infatuation, still Judy is a young woman now, and if she decides to marry Rose, I doubt if anyone can change her mind." No one could, and finally Ethel, too, accepted the inevitable. "If Judy has only a year's happiness, it would be worth it to me," she told a friend. "Because if I don't let her marry Dave, she'll always say, 'Well, if you had let me marry him, I might have had some happiness.' "

More concerned about satisfying their stockholders, the glum-looking men in Culver City refused to join the rosy epithalamium. Feeling an unaccustomed chill coming from "that cold storage plant they call the Thalberg Building," as Raymond Chandler once described it, an obviously worried Judy turned to Parsons for reassurance. "I don't see how a happy marriage could possibly hurt a career, do you?" she plaintively inquired. Aside from issuing veiled warnings, there was, in fact, nothing Metro could do to stop a woman who, made misty-eyed by love, seemed immune to its threats, and on May 28 the newspapers carried word of her betrothal. "I want a home wedding," said Judy, "with bridesmaids and all the trimmings. I don't believe in silly elopements and since I only expect to be married once, both Dave and I consider it a very solemn occasion and we want a minister to officiate."

A little more than two weeks later, on the afternoon of Sunday, June 15, her mother gave a combination engagement and birthday party—Judy had just turned nineteen, Rose, thirty-one. Tables and umbrellas were set up on the broad back lawn of the house on Stone Canyon Road, and perhaps as many as six hundred people watched the happy couple cut into their huge cake, which had been baked in the shape of hearts entwined. Much of Hollywood, from Joan Crawford, who was photographed admiring Judy's three-and-a-half-carat diamond engagement ring, to Lana Turner and Tony Martin, who gave her a set of huge cocktail mugs, drove up Stone Canyon Road on that flawless spring day. Nowhere to be seen, however, was Louis B. Mayer, who usually showed up at such occasions to honor favored stars with his thin-smiled benediction.

The wedding itself was tentatively scheduled for late summer, when both partners thought their work schedules would allow enough time for a honeymoon. But once having started down the road to matrimony, Judy was eager to reach the end, and on the evening of Sunday, July 27, over dinner at the Brown Derby in Beverly Hills, she and David decided to end the wait—they would say their vows that very night. A phone call brought Ethel and Will Gilmore hurrying to the restaurant, and all four were soon aboard a Western Air Lines flight bound for Las Vegas. There, at exactly one-twenty on Monday morning, in his office in the courthouse, Justice of the Peace Mahlon Brown said the words that made Judy and David husband and wife.

Expected later that morning in Culver City, where shooting on *Babes on Broadway* was about to go into its third week, Judy dispatched a hasty telegram to Arthur Freed, begging for a few days' honeymoon: DEAR MR. FREED. I AM SO VERY VERY HAPPY DAVE AND I WERE MARRIED THIS AM PLEASE GIVE ME A LITTLE TIME AND I WILL BE BACK AND FINISH THE PICTURE WITH ONE TAKE ON EACH SCENE. In no mood to indulge a star who had all but thumbed her nose at it, M-G-M answered with a deafening no: she must be back on the set that day, she was told. Thus it was that on Monday afternoon, July 28, less than twenty-four hours after they had left, bride and bridegroom were back in Los Angeles. "Even if we don't get any sort of a honeymoon right now we're the happiest couple in the world," the new Mrs. Rose gamely told reporters. Theirs was not to be an ordinary Hollywood marriage, she added—"it's the real thing."

|||

The Roses did, in fact, seem to be as happy as any two people could be. At last Judy had found the romance she had dreamed about, that she had written soulful, tear-drenched poems about. "Would that my pen were tipped with a magic wand that I could but tell of my love for you," she had written, "that I could but write with the surge I feel when I gaze upon your sweet face. . . ." But the new Mrs. Rose needed no magic wand to say what she felt when she gazed upon David's sweet face: her eloquent and adoring eyes said it all. "She was insanely in love with him," declared her old friend Sidney Miller, and no one could have accused him of exaggeration.

Since her own house was occupied by the Gilmores and since David's house in the Valley was small and inconvenient, the newlyweds started married life at the Ambassador Hotel in downtown Los Angeles, moving, at the end of October, into a place of their own on hilly Chalon Road in Bel Air. Quickly making himself at home, David laid his railroad tracks and was soon riding his trains over the almost mountainous terrain. Judy's adjustment was somewhat harder. The house itself was her terrain, but she did not know how to navigate it, how to cook, clean, or hire help—anything. For all those domestic chores, she had always depended on her mother, and marriage had not made her less dependent, but more: now she had not only herself, but a husband and a big house to look after. She would have been lost if her mother, with her usual efficiency, had not stepped in to take charge. It was Ethel who engaged two servants to run things, and it was Ethel, living just a few minutes away, who supervised them.

Once settled, the Roses entertained with dinner parties and excursion trips on Bel Air's only railroad. The "Gar-Rose Railway," David named it, in a rather touching gesture to the bride who had given him a little train station as a wedding present. If anyone had wanted a portrait of marital bliss, it could have been found at 10693 Chalon Road. That, at least, was the opinion of those who visited there. "David was small and Judy was tiny, and they just made a darling-looking couple," said Ann Rutherford. "You wanted to pick them up by the ankles and put them on the mantel." For the first few months of their residence, Judy and David spent much of their time in their new house, near the mantel, if not on it. David did most of his arranging and composing at home, as he had always done, and Judy was enjoying a long break between pictures: *Babes on Broadway* finished shooting on October 15, and rehearsals for *For Me and My Gal* did not begin until February 19, 1942.

|||

Punctuated only by radio and publicity spots, that rare sabbatical also gave Judy an opportunity to do something close to her heart—war work. War in Europe had begun less than two months after *Babes in Arms* was completed in the summer of 1939, and war, or the threat or war, was to make its presence felt, however obliquely, in almost every movie she made during the next six years. The bugles sound loudest in *For Me and My Gal,* which is actually set during wartime—World War I. It is the story of vaudeville troupers—Judy and Gene Kelly, a newcomer from Broadway—who rise to the top, but break up when the ambitious Kelly, putting his career ahead of his country, schemes to escape service. Only after he has been shamed by Judy, whose brother has been killed in the trenches, does he repent, sail off to France and become a hero in the ambulance corps. To every young American who watched it at the beginning of another war, the picture's message was clear: do your duty.

Even the sunny *Babes in Arms* movies were affected in odd and unpredictable ways by the ongoing battles. After *Babes in Arms* itself, Mayer ordered Arthur Freed to begin *Strike Up the Band.* "It sounds so patriotic," he explained. Freed, who was always the first to agree with Mayer, instantly dumped another project, for which writers had already been hired. "I guess you're right, boss," he said. "I'll get on it immediately." So he did, and as a result of Mayer's concern, a jarring note of jingoism was inserted into a film that, stripped to its basics, is about nothing more serious than Mickey and his pals chasing girls and trying to win a high school band competition. "Look at George Gershwin," says Mickey, in a dubious tribute to the composer of *Strike Up the Band*'s title song. "Why, his music's as good as Beethoven or Bach—better, maybe. Best of all, it's American." Lest anyone miss the point, the picture ends with a raising of the Stars and Stripes, over which are superimposed the faces of Judy and Mickey: in the eyes of M-G-M's image makers, they, too, were symbols of America.

Judy, who believed every red, white and blue line that the scriptwriters handed her, did not need to see the flag waving to do what she thought was her part for her country. Without prompting from Mayer or anybody else, she made several appearances in 1941 to sell Treasury bonds and to raise money for America's friends, the embattled Britons, Greeks and Chinese. Early in December, she also made her first trip to an Army camp, traveling with David, who played the piano for her, to Fort Ord in Northern California, more than three hundred miles from Los Angeles. They were there on Sunday, December 7, when the Japanese bombed Pearl Harbor and the United States was finally yanked into the maelstrom.

Like the vaudevillian she was to play in *For Me and My Gal,* Judy now volunteered to spend much more of her time entertaining the troops. One of the first stars to respond to the War Department's call for morale-boosting visits to Army camps, she set out in January 1942, with David at her side, on an extensive and exhausting tour, journeying east to do three shows a day, eight songs a show—and that did not include appearances to sell war bonds and war stamps in the towns they passed through along the way. Unfortunately, her eagerness to help was stronger than her constitution. Her schedule was too rigorous, and the conditions, poky trains and cold, drafty halls, proved too harsh. After visiting five camps and a hospital, she collapsed at Camp Walters, Texas, with a severe case of strep throat. Forced to halt her tour, Judy returned to California in early February, pale, thin and still quite sick, yet promising to go out again when she had recovered.

She was as good as her word. Several months later, in the summer of 1942, she and David went on the road once more, entertaining at seven camps in seven states. At the end of July they celebrated their first wedding anniversary at Camp Robinson, Arkansas, where the cooks, who had learned the significance of the date, surprised them with a giant cake, complete with a tiny bride and groom perched high atop its frosty summit. The cake was more than a little late, however, and the real bride and groom must have viewed their miniature counterparts with sad irony. For the fact of the matter was that Judy and David were no longer the happiest couple in the world; they were, indeed, not happy at all.

|||

As early as April 1942, less than nine months after their flight to Las Vegas, gossips were wondering whether Judy's wan appearance was the aftermath of her bout with strep throat, or a symptom of an unhappy marriage. "Judy hasn't been well for the last few months," reported Louella Parsons, "and because she has been rundown and thin rumors have been gathering fast and furious that she and Dave Rose, her musician husband, had reached a definite parting of the ways." Never reluctant to pose an awkward question, Parsons then asked Judy whether the reports were true. "Gosh," replied Judy, "I wish I knew who started that gossip. Honestly, Dave and I haven't had any trouble and I am just starting to feel better. I wish people wouldn't try and separate us."

At least the last part of her answer was accurate. People, mostly the dark-suited people in the Thalberg Building, were trying to pry her away from David—and had been from the beginning. Still angry at her unaccustomed disobedience, Mayer and his men acted like sour in-laws, incessantly sniping at a union of which they so thoroughly disapproved. Indeed, said Hedda Hopper, "they turned on Judy like rattlesnakes. On Academy Awards night, she had sat for years at the number-one table along with the rest of the M-G-M stars. As Mrs. David Rose she was deliberately humiliated and seated at a much less desirable spot on the side and out of the spotlight. . . . They actually believed that she belonged to them, body and soul. They'd created her; why couldn't she show more gratitude?" Studio hangers-on tried to poison their relationship, added Hopper, by convincing her that David was trading on her popularity to boost his career; when she walked with him through the streets of Culver City, such people would greet her but ignore him. Judy herself thought that the studio used its influence to keep David from getting jobs.

Powerful as it was, however, Metro was not omnipotent. David did work, Judy's real friends did greet them both and Judy did attend the Academy Awards. In a neat riposte to those who had relegated her to a table in Siberia, she even invited Hopper to join her chilly exile. "Love to," said Hopper, who then told Mayer how shabbily she thought he was treating Judy. "But he was immune to shame or compassion,"

Hopper wrote in her memoirs. "I wasted my breath." The fact was that although Metro's petulance may have exacerbated the difficulties in the Rose marriage, it did not create them, and two contented people could have ignored Leo the Lion's peevish snarls. Judy and David had only themselves to blame, and their unhappiness was entirely of their own making.

There was, to begin with, the disparity in their ages. When they were dating and spending only a small part of their time together, the twelve years that divided them had seemed trivial—so Judy had liked to say, anyway. On Chalon Road, where they shared a life, the distance between them stretched wider than the Grand Canyon. If Judy had been a more mature nineteen, or if David had been a more youthful thirty-one, it might have shriveled into insignificance. But Judy was, to use her own words, "a mixed-up little girl," and David was more staid and settled than many men in their forties and fifties—inhibited, prudish and dull, Judy later confided, even in their sexual relations. "He acts like an old man," she complained to her friend Dorothy Walsh.

Yet the calendar alone could scarcely have explained the yawning gap between them, and the real difference was not so much in age as in temperament. Like her father, Judy delighted in company, in laughing and making those around her laugh. She loved to dance, and when they were first married, she unsuccessfully tried to persuade David to take lessons. But David was neither a laugher nor a dancer. He enjoyed few things more than being alone, putting on his engineer's cap and toot-toot-tooting along the Gar-Rose Railway. "Judy was outgoing, fun, vivacious, with energy to the hilt," said Dorothy Raye, a Metro dancer who knew them both. "Dave gave her nothing to attach to."

Beneath his placid exterior, his smooth, smiling imperturbability, David was as mixed up as she was. "Always churned up inside," as he himself said, he was a repository of anxieties and emotional conflicts, a man who, within a couple of years, was to be hospitalized with a nervous breakdown. The other men in Judy's life had said what was bothering them—Artie Shaw had never shut up about it. David, by contrast, dealt with his problems quietly, all by himself, venting his anger not through words, but indirectly, through long, ominous silences and acts of what psychologists call passive aggression. In perhaps the most glaring example of the latter, Judy came home one afternoon to find her grand piano lying flat on the floor—David had sawed off its legs. His only reply to her outraged screams was that he thought he could compose more comfortably lying down.

More disturbing than the things he did, however, were the things he did not do—his protracted silences. With David, the calm before the storm *was* the storm. "Sullen" was the label Martha Raye, the first Mrs. Rose, had applied to him. "Brooding" was the adjective the second Mrs. Rose preferred. Both words meant the same thing: self-absorbed to the point of solipsism, David could very well have lived alone on a desert island. Late at night Judy would find herself gazing forlornly out the window, watching her new husband riding "his little toy trains," as she later called them, in endless, maddening circles. "I am very much in love," she had said on what seemed like a long-ago day in Las Vegas. But she had not spoken for David, who, she now bitterly acknowledged, would rather be outside, running the Chalon Road Choo-choo, than inside with her. "I'm miserable," she at length told a friend. "I'm just plain unhappy."

Though he maintained his silence, David, too, had reasons to complain. One of the most prominent reasons was Ethel, who, having finally given her blessing to the marriage, automatically assumed that she would manage David's money as well as Judy's. Although he managed to evade that particular snare, David could not escape Ethel herself; whether he liked it or not, she was indispensable to the operation of his house. Yet even under her commanding eye, life on Chalon Road could be uncomfortably bumpy, and Judy, whose vision of wedlock had been all hearts and flowers, was unequal to the task of maintaining anything resembling a stable and well-ordered home. Dinner guests once knocked at the front door, for instance, to find their host and hostess already dining in bed—Judy had forgotten she had asked them. Other times, because she had not learned to keep an engagement book, she and David would invite different people for the same night, or realize too late that they had accepted conflicting invitations. The result was inevitable: needless confusion and hurt feelings.

Elsa Maxwell, the well-known forties columnist and gadabout who repeated those stories, said that she had no idea what David did wrong in their marriage, but that she did know that the Judy of those years was "completely unfitted to be a wife." Judy herself would not have disagreed with that harsh indictment—"I was in a cocoon emotionally," she admitted—and at home, as at work, she watched helplessly as other people pulled the strings. Acting as if Judy were a child of nine, the married couple Ethel had hired to run things addressed her by her first name instead of her last, as they would have done with any other employer, and generally did what they thought best, rather than what she asked them to do. She told them what she wanted for dinner; they told her what she would be eating.

Thus, to the long list of those who bullied and bossed her, the overbearing Ethels, Mayers and Busby Berkeleys, she now had to add her own servants. "Sometimes I'd, I'd, I'd want to feel—um—as though I had some dignity and was really capable," she said a few years later, still stuttering with resentment at their demeaning, patronizing behavior. "I'd get so indignant with them." But her indignation did her no good at all: they still did exactly as they wanted to do, or as Ethel had instructed them to do.

|||

Despite their problems, the Roses might have struggled on had Judy not made an unsurprising disclosure—she was pregnant. For her, the discovery, which probably occurred in the fall of 1942, must have been a moment of both joy and anxiety. Joy, because she doted on children; one of the reasons she had married David, in fact, was so that she could have a child of her own. Anxiety, because she knew that the men at Metro did not look at babies with her dewy eyes; a pregnancy, even one unaccompanied by any hint of scandal or embarrassment, was the news they had most dreaded.

It was bad enough that she had tarnished her wholesome, youthful image by selfishly taking a husband; motherhood would obliterate it altogether. "We simply can't have that baby have a child," Mayer had thundered; though he was speaking only of the character she played in *Little Nellie Kelly,* his words applied with equal force to Judy herself. What panic, then, what sweaty faces and desperate scurrying around, there must have been on the third floor of the Thalberg Building when, at the end of November, the *Los Angeles Examiner* reported the following bit of Hollywood gossip: "The rumor comes straight that Judy Garland and Dave Rose are expecting a baby."

Unsure how her undemonstrative husband would react, Judy left it to Ethel to break the news to him. She heard them speaking upstairs, then watched her mother come down alone. "Now, Judy, you understand this is impossible," Ethel said. "This baby. You can't have it."

"Can't have it?" Judy interjected. "Why not? It's mine. I have to have it."

"You don't seem to understand," her mother patiently replied. "You can have lots of babies at the right time, but this is not the right time. . . . I've talked it over with David and he agrees with me."

When she married David, Judy later said, she thought he had a "strong hand to guide me." A strong hand David did not have. In marrying him, she had stood up against the studio, her mother and even David himself, all but pushing him to the altar. Now, as he stood politely aside, like one of the audience rather than the lead actor in the intense little drama that was swirling around him, a lonely, besieged Judy reluctantly agreed to an abortion. "I'll handle everything," her mother said, and the day after that conversation, Judy sat silently in a car between her mother and her husband and was driven to what she described as a dreary little establishment just outside Los Angeles's city limits. There her pregnancy was terminated.

Terminated as well, after less than a year and a half, was the union she had bragged would be the real thing. Ailing for months, it died the moment she consented to the abortion. After that, she told June Allyson, "the marriage was never the same. Something was gone. It broke my heart." With nothing keeping them together and everything driving them apart, the Roses announced a temporary separation. "We regret that it is necessary to issue a statement saying that we have parted," they said at the end of January 1943, "but we have both agreed that a matrimonial vacation now is the only way to settle our mutual differences." The skeptics had been right all along. Judy had not been the right woman for David, and David had not been the right man for Judy.

|||

"I do like to be in love," Judy was later to say. "A woman is incomplete when she's not in love." So it was that as she was falling out of love with David Rose, she was falling in love with someone else. But unlike David, whose appeal had eluded most of her friends, her new lover was obviously, demonstrably desirable, as close to perfection as a mere mortal could be: amusing, intelligent, talented and so handsome that it could be said, without quibble or contradiction, that no man was more handsome. "The most beautiful man I ever saw. No question," adjudged Anne Baxter, one of his many lovely costars. His dark good looks, combined with a virile athleticism and a voice as warm and rich as a Brahms symphony, had made Tyrone Power—for that was the name of this paragon—into 20th Century–Fox's biggest star, several rungs above Judy herself on Hollywood's top ten list. Every time the camera lingered on his deep and ever-so-understanding eyes, millions of hearts pounded like so many libidinous tom-toms.

Imagine, then, the commotion Judy's own heart must have made when, at their very first meeting, at a party in Brentwood, Power leaned down from his slim six feet, focused those long-lashed eyes on her and all but knocked her over with praise and attention. Adding force to his words was his transparent sincerity. A week or so earlier—on October 16, 1942, to be exact—he had seen her in her first full-length adult role, as the aspiring vaudevillian of *For Me and My Gal,* and since then he had been raving about her magical transformation from awkward teenager into interesting woman. Now, here she was, here he was, and out of town for several days was his wife, a chic, glamorous French actress who went only by the name Annabella.

A better recipe for romance could not have been devised. "There was an immediate attraction between them," said Watson Webb, Power's best friend and chief confidant, "and by the time Annabella got back— and it wasn't that long—Tyrone was already pretty well smitten." By the first week of January 1943, when Power entered the Marine Corps, he and Judy were deeply in love, and Judy, who had largely forsaken the house on Chalon Road for a place of her own in nearby Westwood, was ushering a few select friends into her bedroom to show them his photograph. Where was the fun in having one of the most ravishing men in the world mad about you, after all, if you had to keep it all to yourself? "Oh, he's wonderful!" she exclaimed to her friend Anne Shirley. The last thing she saw before she fell asleep at night, Power's smiling face was the stuff her dreams were made on.

What attracted her was obvious: his unsurpassable looks and a charm so exundant that few could withstand it. It was as if a light came on whenever he walked into a room, said one woman; another recalled the aura that seemed to surround him. In such awed tones had the Greeks and Romans spoken of their gods. Few earthly men had Power's nat- ural advantages, and he was able, with no more effort than it took to flash one of his high-voltage smiles, to bed nearly every female who caught his fancy. "We've had them all, haven't we?" bragged one of his friends at the studio, pointing to a wall covered with photos of the Fox women. It was a banquet of beauties, that much-admired wall, and Power, who was only twenty-eight, had had more than his share.

What few knew at the time—some secrets were safe in Hollywood— was that the sword-wielding, fistfighting, swashbuckling hero of such adventures as *The Mark of Zorro* and *The Black Swan,* a man who insisted on doing most of his own stunts and who was to whistle through the harshest and most strenuous training the Marine Corps had to offer, had also had more than his share of men. A bisexual, Power seemed equally excited by both genders, and even he probably could not have said which he found more to his liking.

Despite his many dalliances, during three years of marriage he never before had allowed anyone, male or female, to threaten his relationship with Annabella, however. *That,* Judy did almost instantly, and he was as much in love with her—"he was crazy about her," was Watson Webb's succinct assessment—as she with him. What did Judy have that so many other, prettier and more glamorous women did not have? The answer to that puzzling question is preserved, for all to see, in *For Me and My Gal,* the movie that first piqued Power's interest: she had grown into a woman of intelligence and spunky resolve, but, through some miracle of her own making, she had managed to retain the freshness and dewy innocence of girlhood. She was Dorothy—the Dorothy of *Oz*—grown up, and the combination of youth and maturity was, for many people, infinitely more alluring than a flawless face or a voluptuous figure. "Miss Garland has the faculty (wonderful for her but tough on an audience) of melting your heart," said one critic, "and in a sympathetic part she's murder."

Murder she was for Power, in any event, touching subterranean emotions that other women had never known of, let alone aroused. He had been an object of flattery for so long that he accepted admiration as his due; what he really wanted was what he did not already possess: someone who would understand him totally and completely, with unreserved, unthinking and unstinting sympathy. He had, to quote from his favorite author, a popular novelist of the time named Mildred Cram, a "longing so intense, so consuming, that it got into his eyes and betrayed him."

It was a youthful, almost adolescent yearning that the practical Annabella, who was six years his senior, who had been married twice before and who had a daughter just three years younger than Judy, could scarcely comprehend. But Judy, barely out of adolescence herself, not only shared that longing but embraced it—her eyes betrayed her, too. She and Power thus came together not merely as man and woman, but as soul mates, celebrators of everything romantic from the wistful music of Rachmaninov to the elegiac, doom-shrouded verse of A. E. Housman. To that rather distinguished list Power added Cram's little potboiler *Forever,* a novella that Judy had not previously read, but that she could now quote word for word. Its sentimental message of love surviving death itself was as comforting to her as it was to him, as it was, in fact, to many Americans whose lives were shadowed by war in those grim years. "This is forever," sighs Cram's heroine as she walks with her lover into a pearly eternity; and forever was how long those two besotted stars also thought their own love story would last.

Where their spirits led, their bodies eagerly followed. After sharing a bed with an older, rather reserved spouse, each found the other to be an exciting and uninhibited sexual partner. Few other women had aroused Power as much as Judy did. Aware, for her part, that he was bisexual, Judy nonetheless convinced herself that she could transform him into a man who loved only women—and only one woman at that. Power gave her good reason, indeed, to believe that she might succeed where so many others had failed, and in the months after their meeting, it was his turn, for perhaps the first time, to fall under the spell of that old black magic called love.

There was just one cloud, small at first, then larger and increasingly ominous, intruding into their sun-drenched paradise: they were both married. Judy's marriage had crumbled, in her eyes, if not in the law's, before she had met Power. But Power's remained firmly intact, and as they were soon seen strolling arm in arm into the Fox commissary, alarms once more started howling in Culver City. Little Judy, screamed the men in the Thalberg Building, was endangering her career again.

|||

Metro had been wrong when it told Judy that marriage might wreck her career. Audiences liked "the now-come-of-age Judy Garland," as the studio had taken to calling her, as much as they had liked the younger version. *For Me and My Gal,* her biggest hit by far, drew long lines around the country, overturning a house record of eighteen years at Manhattan's huge Astor Theater. "Box-office honey," the editor of *Film Daily* called the picture. But if the studio had been wrong about her marriage to David, it was not necessarily wrong about her romance with Power, which *was* cause for concern. It was one thing for Judy to have publicly held hands with a man who was already rushing toward the divorce court, as David had been. It was quite another thing to break up the seemingly tranquil marriage of a popular star like Power. "To be involved with a married man was serious, something you really weren't supposed to do," said Anne Shirley. And you absolutely were not supposed to be involved with a man who was about to go off to war and risk his life for his country. Small wonder that Mayer himself summoned her to his office to warn her of quicksand ahead.

Threats and warnings had not stopped her from marrying David, however, and this time around the studio's naysayers showed uncharacteristic finesse; they were, indeed, almost diabolically subtle. Rather than trying to bludgeon her into submission, they aimed, by means of psychological warfare, to surreptitiously lead her to the conclusion they wanted her to draw: that Power was not her Prince Charming after all. Their primary weapon in this gamy plot was her studio publicist, Betty

Asher, who had previously used her persuasive arts on Lana Turner, helping to hold Turner together during her noisy breakup with Artie Shaw. Like many of those who worked in Howard Strickling's wide-ranging publicity department, Asher was not actually a publicist, someone who represented a star to the press; she was instead a kind of lady-in-waiting, a hand-holder and a fixer, someone who did whatever it took to keep her client happy and productive. The "vice-president in charge of Mickey Rooney" was how Rooney described his own publicist, Les Peterson, and Judy could have said the same about Asher.

But Mickey was shrewd enough to realize that the affable Peterson was not a real friend, that he held, along with all his other titles, that of company spy: he reported every move Mickey made to his bosses in the Thalberg Building. Not for several years was Judy to realize that Asher was doing the same thing. "She gave a report to the studio office every week on the people I saw, what I ate, what time I came in at night and what time I got up in the morning," Judy was later to say. "I can remember crying for days after I found out what she was doing to me." But by then the damage had been done.

|||

The daughter of a producer at Universal, Asher was as much a child of the motion-picture industry as Judy was. She had grown up in Beverly Hills, she had attended UCLA for three years and, until she was in her late teens, she had led the cushioned, protected life of Hollywood's junior elite. All that ended abruptly with her father's death. With no money and no one to help her—her alcoholic mother could scarcely take care of herself—she was obliged to live by her wits alone, which advised her to be hard, unscrupulous and loyal to no one. Even as she was telling Turner, who looked upon her as a close friend, how much better off she was without Artie Shaw, Asher was ringing Shaw's doorbell and inviting herself inside. "The next thing I knew," said Shaw, "we were in bed together." It thus should have surprised no one that at Metro Asher's lover was Eddie Mannix, one of Mayer's chief subalterns and a man well placed to give a girl, especially an attractive, curly-haired blonde, a helpful boost up the corporate ladder.

Though Asher was just five years older, to Judy she seemed light-years ahead in experience and worldly wisdom. Her seeming sophistication, in fact, was probably one of the reasons she appealed to Judy, who doubtless hoped that some of that polish would rub off on her. With surprising speed Asher became not only her helper, but also her friend, mentor and emotional crutch. Judy depended on her more than anyone else, and there were times when no one, not even her old friend Roger Edens, could talk to her as soothingly and as effectively. Whenever Judy suffered an attack of nerves during filming, Asher would suddenly appear on the set, as mysteriously as a genie, to calm her down. On orders from Mayer himself—"Mr. Mayer wants them left alone," Judy's directors were told—no one was allowed to interrupt their conversations, and shooting could not resume until Asher had left.

Asher's friendship with Judy was not confined to Culver City; during the time Judy was seeing Power, the two women went so far as to share quarters in Westwood. Almost inseparable, they were seen everywhere together, whispering and giggling like schoolgirls. A relationship so intense, so unusual and so conspicuous did not go unnoticed, particularly on a gossipy studio lot, and many at Metro suspected that Power was not Judy's only lover in those days.

They may well have been right. Judy was not a lesbian. Nor was she a bisexual, equally attracted to both sexes. She was indeed drawn to men as iron is drawn to a magnet. Yet, despite that, she nevertheless enjoyed an occasional frolic with another woman, as did many other women in the permissive movie colony. That Judy and Asher both sometimes had sex with other women is indisputable; that they also had sex with each other is probable, if ultimately unprovable. They were as close as lovers, in any event, and Asher, to whom Judy told all and to whom she listened most intently, had been ideally cast to play the role of the double agent who would harden her heart against her beautiful Ty.

|||

Love is supposed to bring happiness, but for Judy it brought not joy, but anxiety, confusion and long, sleepless nights. Much of her uneasiness was the product of her own impatience, and within mere weeks of their first meeting she was demanding that Power ask Annabella for a divorce. Although his marriage had grown a little stale, Power was not ready to give it up, however, at least not so quickly, and some sympathy must be extended to a man who had not only sacrificed his extraordinary career to join the Marines, but who was now also being asked to give up just about everything else—his marriage, his home and his security.

And some sympathy must also be extended to Judy, who could not get him to say yes, and who could not get him to say no. Handicapped by a constitutional compulsion to please, Power was all but paralyzed at such crucial moments. "It was hard for Tyrone to face big issues," acknowledged a regretful Watson Webb. Judy, who had fallen in love with his melting smile, did not see, or did not want to see, that his need to ingratiate himself was the obverse of his spectacular charm, that the two were bound together, one and indivisible. All Judy knew was that he refused to do what she wanted. Furious, she made what must have been a wrenching sacrifice, declining to see him when he came home from camp on weekend passes.

Perhaps never before had Judy been burdened by so much anxiety as she was in those early weeks of 1943. As if Power's refusal to commit himself were not anguish enough, she was once again enduring the daily abuse of her old nemesis, Busby Berkeley, who had started work on *Girl Crazy*. His frantic pace, even more frenzied than usual, was pitilessly hard on his two stars, Judy and Mickey. Judy was, moreover, almost undone by the six-shooters popping around her during rehearsals for his elaborate rodeo scene, "just a wreck," as one observer recalled, until Mickey put a comforting arm around her shoulder. "Honey, don't worry," he said. "It's all right."

But it was not all right. Fear and tension on the set, combined with a queasy concern about her affair with Power, had frayed her nerves beyond the breaking point, and Berkeley's dismissal, three weeks into filming, came too late to prevent Judy's collapse. Her weight dropped alarmingly, from a normal 110 pounds to ninety-four, and on January 29 she was confined to her bed for five days, warned by her doctor, sturdy old Marc Rabwin, that even after she returned to work, she should not do strenuous dance scenes for another six to eight weeks.

It was probably then, during those five days of convalescence, that Judy agreed to see Power again. Gazing into the warm and compassionate eyes that stared from his photograph near her bed, how could she have refused? Their romance resumed where it had left off, and Power, still in the grip of that old black magic, at last decided, on March 31, to grant her request and confront his wife. Over dinner at Perino's, a restaurant often favored by the stars, he gave Annabella the bad news: "I've got to tell you—I'm in love with somebody else." But Annabella, canny Frenchwoman that she was, already knew, in fact had known for months—not because of anything Power had done, but because of what he had not done. After reporting in October that he had met Judy, he never again mentioned her name. But from that moment Annabella had noticed his lack of ardor in the bedroom. It was obvious, she said, that Judy was the reason. Yet having gone so far as to bring their affair into the open, Power could not bring himself to take the next step: he was still unable or unwilling to ask Annabella for a divorce.

|||

A few days after that tell-all dinner, Power was on a crowded troop train, headed east to Quantico, Virginia, the Marine Corps officers' training school near Washington, D.C. As his train clattered slowly across the country, over the mountains and across the prairies, farther and farther away from Judy, he clutched her memory ever more tightly, and in a letter to Webb he made it clear how completely she had displaced Annabella in his affections. "I'm just the luckiest, happiest man alive today," he wrote from Indianapolis. "God—sometimes I don't think I can stand it. I do love her so." A chance to show how much he loved her came perhaps sooner than he anticipated: not long after he had settled into his new barracks, he received some startling news—she was pregnant, Judy announced. She was carrying his baby, and if he did not marry her, she would be compelled to have an abortion.

Quick divorces were not easy to obtain in 1943. Even if Annabella had agreed to one, it would have been hard, perhaps impossible, for Power to have procured it in time to marry Judy before her condition became a scandal. Judy must have been aware of that, and there is reason to suspect that she invented the pregnancy to pressure him into breaking with Annabella completely and irrevocably. But even as she was prodding him to say good-bye to Annabella, she herself, curiously enough, had neglected to file for divorce from David. Real or false, her pregnancy nonetheless pushed Power into a corner that he could not smile his way out of, and he finally asked Annabella for his freedom. His request was so tentative and polite, however, that Annabella had no trouble answering with a firm and authoritative no. Writing to Webb, Power himself confessed to a feeling of terrible depression. "I just can't see ahead at all," he said. "Everything seems so futile, and pointless."

The story of Judy and Tyrone now moved swiftly toward its climax. At the end of May, Annabella traveled to Washington to talk to her husband face-to-face. Apparently assuming that her visit signaled a change of mind—a *oui* to divorce instead of a *non*—Power urged Judy, who had just finished *Girl Crazy,* to hurry east for a victory celebration in New York. As frightened of airplanes as she was of guns, Judy nonetheless jumped aboard a plane, making the long and punishing transcontinental flight—nineteen hours, with three stops for fuel in a dawdling DC-3.

She rushed only to wait, her happiness and her entire future resting, so she thought, on one favorable word from Annabella. If Power had shown some of the resolve of his swashbuckling screen characters—the dashing Zorro, for instance—he might yet have persuaded Annabella to make that word yes. Without a script, the actor who played those dashing roles could not stand up to so determined a woman, and even at that late date, with Judy poised nervously by a telephone in Manhattan, Power was all but tongue-tied. Whenever he brought up the subject of Judy, Annabella simply let the conversation die. No she had said, and no she continued to say—*tant pis!* Her spirits sinking with every hour, Judy lingered in New York until all hope had passed; then, feeling defeated, and probably deceived as well, she returned to Los Angeles. Power had let her down, and they both knew it. Their love affair was over, and a relationship that had begun with soaring hearts and flights of verse thus ended in resentment, recrimination and an undignified muddle.

Some romances, like Judy and David's, are doomed, and obviously so, from the start. Others, like Judy and Tyrone's, bear the stamp of smiling fortune, and fail only because the lovers lack the endurance and grit to see their problems through to a conclusion. If Tyrone was shy the grit, Judy was short the endurance. Though she turned twenty-one on June 10, a few days after she came back from New York, emotionally she remained an adolescent, an impatient child who demanded too much, too soon, and, as a result, wound up with nothing. If she had waited for her man until the end of the war, as millions of other women were loyally doing, the icy barriers that blocked her way in the spring of 1943 probably would have melted to little puddles. Until the fighting stopped, Power could have been no more than a distant, absentee husband in any case, his address a remote island in the Pacific. Waiting would have cost her nothing.

Judy might have shown more patience if she had been able to ignore the poison her best friend, that artful Iago, Betty Asher, was pouring into her ear. The most damaging story Asher passed on to her, the one that killed any possibility of reconciliation, was that Power was entertaining his Marine buddies with her love letters. Such tawdry behavior was so alien to Power's character that Asher's story was almost certainly a brazen falsehood. Astonishingly, Judy believed it, however, and she was, of course, grievously wounded at being made sport of. Retaliating, as she often did, with humor, she nicknamed poor Tyrone "Tyroney the Phony," refusing thenceforth to acknowledge his cards or messages.

Just a few months earlier they had identified with the young lovers in Mildred Cram's *Forever,* whose devotion was so strong that it survived death itself. "We'll find each other. Somewhere. Somehow," the hero assures the heroine, and so, on the last page, they do. But that was a happy ending Judy and Tyrone were not destined to see, and when they talked about each other afterward, they could not hide a note of regret, which echoed through their words like the faint sound of a lonely cello, for what might have been—for the "land of lost content," as Housman so aptly named it. "It really was different between Tyrone and me," Judy was to say. "It was no small affair."

It was no small affair for Power either, and months after their breakup he confessed that she still occupied his dreams. When her latest movie, *Meet Me in St. Louis,* reached his island outpost in February 1945, he was reminded, more sharply than he probably liked, of all that he had given up. Her first color picture since *The Wizard of Oz, Meet Me in St. Louis* caught, in a way that black-and-white had never been able to do, the full vibrancy of her personality and the warmth and fire in her brandy-brown eyes. What delicious agony, then, it must have been for Tyrone to sit watching her for nearly two hours in a makeshift outdoor theater, surrounded by dozens of other men—far, far from Hollywood and even further from the good times they had shared. "My God," he wrote Webb, his words drenched with longing, "but she never looked more beautiful."

Metro's winning combination
in Babes on Broadway

CHAPTER 7

In Love with Harvard College

The end of their romance was probably harder on Tyrone, who had long, vacant hours to brood and ponder at remote and lonely bases, than it was on Judy, who was almost constantly busy, caught up, when she was not working, in the carnival excitement of wartime Hollywood. In the months since Pearl Harbor the entire motion-picture industry—studios, performers and the thousands of technicians who supported them—had been recruited for the war effort, and from Culver City to Burbank there was an almost audible, ceaseless hum from the studio moviemaking machines. Besides churning out innumerable patriotic shorts, documentaries and even cartoons, the studios released dozens of features designed to stir the soul and stiffen the backbone—films with titles like *Thirty Seconds over Tokyo, Stand By for Action, Salute to the Marines, They Were Expendable* and *A Guy Named Joe.* In a statement that might have surprised his admirals but was well received in the Thalberg Building, Winston Churchill himself said that the propaganda value of *Mrs. Miniver,* a Metro tearjerker about an English family bravely bearing up under German bombs, was worth a hundred battleships.

Even films that, like most of Judy's, ignored or scarcely touched on the war were considered essential to the battle: they raised spirits simply by reminding fighting men what they were fighting for, said General Dwight D. Eisenhower, the commander of American forces in Europe. "Let's have more motion pictures!" ordered the general. Pleased to accept accolades for doing what they had always done, and had always planned to do, the studios ascended new heights of prosperity as more Americans than ever before—ninety million of them, or nearly 70 percent of the population—lined up every week just to see a picture show. By October 1942, many of the men who would have made those films were wearing uniforms themselves. More left each day, and by the end of January 1943, both Judy's current and prospective husbands, David Rose and Tyrone, were dressed in government issue.

Those who remained did their bit in other ways. Other stars had quickly followed Judy in traveling the country to entertain homesick troops and sell war bonds to gawking civilians. At home in California, the stars assisted the war effort by doing what they did best—entertaining. Judy made frequent appearances on radio programs beamed directly to the battlefronts, shows with names like *G.I. Journal* and *Mail Call,* and, like nearly everyone else, she lent her talent to the Hollywood Canteen, which for three frantic years was probably the best nightclub in the world, a place where ordinary guys could meet and even dance with their screen favorites.

In the overheated atmosphere engendered by war, with death an unseen but palpable presence, every second was urgent and compelling, and at the Canteen, as well as at dozens of other clubs, restaurants and dance halls throughout Southern California, the crowds arrived early and stayed late. Everyone was determined to have a good time. At such a moment and in such surroundings, it would have been difficult for a fun-loving young woman like Judy to suffer very long from the pains of broken romance. And it would have been altogether impossible once her wandering, searching heart had found a replacement, initiating a relationship no less electric than the one she had enjoyed with Tyrone.

III

Her new lover, Joe Mankiewicz, was, at thirty-four, Metro's wonder boy, the producer of such memorable pictures as *Fury* and *The Philadelphia Story,* the possible successor, some thought, to the illustrious Thalberg. Mankiewicz's German-born father was a professor of linguistics at the City College of New York; his older brother, Herman, was a celebrated screenwriter, the chief author of Orson Welles's *Citizen Kane;* and Joe himself was formidably intelligent. He had entered Columbia University when he was fifteen, he had spent several exciting months in Berlin when he was nineteen, and he had begun writing Hollywood scripts when he was twenty. "Harvard College," Mayer had nicknamed him, a reference not only to his brains, but to his tweedy, pipe-smoking, professorial style.

Harvard College generally went his own way at Metro. "I've followed very few of the rules," he was to boast. In a business in which top actresses were either extravagantly flattered or outrageously bullied, often in shameless succession, but rarely taken seriously, Mankiewicz did something so unusual as to be noteworthy: he talked to them as equals, earnestly listening to their ideas about what their roles should be. They returned the compliment, and Mankiewicz gained a reputation as a man who had a winning way with the weaker sex. The result, of course, was that he was assigned more than his share of pictures with prickly and temperamental females. "Joe knows more about women than any man I've ever met," said Anne Baxter, one of his leading ladies. "We're all just glass to him, and he sees everything that makes us tick."

A man with such remarkable X-ray vision, especially an attractive man with what June Allyson called "wonderful laughing eyes," was bound to find success with women off the set as well as on, and Mankiewicz did not have to seek romance—it sought him. What looks did for Tyrone, brains did for Joe. "Everyone," recalled one woman, "was in love with Joseph L. Mankiewicz." How could Judy have been an exception?

They probably did not begin their liaison until the late winter or spring of 1943, when both were both suddenly alone, eager for companionship. Tyrone, who was away at Marine camp, was sending Judy discouraging messages about their future prospects, and Mankiewicz's second wife, the Austrian actress Rosa Stradner, was at the Menninger Clinic in far-off Kansas, undergoing psychiatric treatment for a psychological disturbance so serious that it had brought about a catatonic fit. Discovering that they had something in common, namely a sardonic sense of humor, Judy and Joe, the two who were left behind, formed an instant attachment. "We made each other laugh a lot," said Mankiewicz, "and we became used to each other very quickly." So quickly did matters proceed, indeed, that not long after Judy said her final good-byes to Tyrone she transferred her affections, fully and unreservedly, to Joe and his laughing blue eyes.

|||

For Judy, Joe was the very model of a man, the ideal that all the other men she had loved, and was to love, could aspire to but could never

Joe Mankiewicz in the early forties

quite reach. He was, to her bedazzled eyes, as witty as Oscar Levant, but without Levant's debilitating hang-ups; as intellectual as Artie Shaw, but without Shaw's sophomoric pretensions; as nice as David Rose, but without Rose's stupefying blandness; and as charming as Tyrone, but without Tyrone's sexual ambiguity. There was no question which gender Joe preferred, and the fact that he had made so many glamour pusses, a list that included Joan Crawford and Loretta Young, swoon and surrender only added to his musky appeal. In Judy's opinion, Joe, or "Josephus," as she called him in private, was nothing less than perfect. "Oh, he's so brilliant," she told her sister Jimmie. "God, he knows everything! He's the most wonderful man that ever lived!"

But if Joe was much like the men she had loved before—except better—Judy was nothing at all like the beautiful and worldly women who had attracted Joe. To him, she was instead an unspoiled creature of nature, like a wood nymph, a wide-eyed dryad he had surprised in some still, fern-shrouded glade, where she was hiding from prying eyes and grasping hands. "She had a fresh kind of a foresty look, as though there were dew on her," he said. Other, more sophisticated women his X-ray vision could see right through; but he could stare all day at Judy and fail to penetrate her mystery. She was the one woman he could not explain, and that sense of continuing complexity made her all the more interesting: she was a challenge without end. "You can write down everything Lana Turner ever thought and felt and meant, and then put the pencil down," he said. "That's it, a closed book. But I don't think anybody's going to close the book on Judy Garland."

Still, Joe did not harbor the same kind of love for Judy, tantalizingly mysterious though she was, that Judy harbored for him. Though she liked to say, and may even have believed, that he would have married her if he had been free—which, with a wife in a psychiatric hospital and with two infant sons to take care of, he definitely was not—marriage was not even a remote possibility. It was, in fact, never even mentioned; nor, as Joe recalled it, did it ever enter his mind. "I wasn't in love that way," he said. "I was in love—and I know this is a terrible analogy—the way you love an animal, a pet."

Although Judy would have been crushed by the comparison, it was not quite as terrible as it may sound. The love lavished on an animal can be as genuine as any other and, within its limits, no less intense. Indeed, Freud himself, no mean expert on such matters, spoke of his own pet, his beloved chow Jo-Fi, more affectionately than most men do of their wives. "She is a charming creature," he said, "so interesting, also as a female, wild, instinctive, tender, intelligent." Very similar was Joe's love for the wild, instinctive, tender and intelligent Judy. He may not have wanted to marry her, but he did want to see her safe and happy, protected—even if it meant jeopardizing his own flourishing career— from all those at Metro who sought to exploit her.

Yet for all his psychologizing, Joe seemed unaware that, in a curious sense, he, too, was seeking to exploit her; not for money, but for something so fundamental to his own personality that he probably would have been the last to recognize it. He hungered, this man who knew everything about women, to play Pygmalion; he had an incurable compulsion to take what nature had generously provided and to make it better, or what he imagined to be better. He had done it before, and he was to do it again; but in all his experience he was never to find another woman so packed with talent yet so eager to do his bidding as the just-come-of-age Judy Garland. He longed to mold her, and she longed to be molded. More than anything else in the world, she wanted to be his Galatea.

Most of her colleagues would have said that Judy had already reached the peak of her profession. But Joe was convinced that she could climb still higher, higher than anyone at M-G-M knew or could conceive—she could be a great actress. "To M-G-M, Judy was just a piece of equipment," he said, "a money-making device. I found myself fascinated by her, by the possibilities of a girl who obviously could act, *really* act, but who was very rarely called upon to do so." As he watched her movies, he saw a gift of fabulous promise being almost thrown away. Judy romping through a piece of fluff like *Girl Crazy*! Masquerading as a stagestruck teenager in a silly soap opera like *Presenting Lily Mars*! It was as if Sarah Bernhardt were reduced to playing radio's Ma Perkins, or Nellie Melba were forced to sing snappy little tunes for cigarette commercials. It was, to Joe's way of thinking, intolerable, if not, alas, inconceivable.

His concern did not end there, however. Disgusted by the abuse of her abilities, he was incensed by the abuse of Judy herself. With her mother looking over one shoulder, Mayer looking over the other, she was, he felt, being denied the right to be herself, being robbed of her youth as she had been robbed of her childhood. "I thought she was getting very short shrift from life!" he said indignantly. As she reached her maturity, it was time, Joe believed, for her to make her own decisions and to discover, before it was too late, her own precious identity. Who was Judy Garland? She did not know, and the answer to that question, Joe was convinced, could come only through psychoanalysis: she needed some time on the couch.

|||

For Joe, psychoanalysis was not merely a therapy for disturbed minds; it was a religion, and no Catholic, going to mass every morning and saying fifty Hail Marys every night, could have been more devout. He himself was seeing an analyst; he had dispatched his wife, Rosa, to the Menninger Clinic in Kansas; and when their time came, he was to send his sons to analysts as well. "I was a nut about the potential value of psychotherapy and the study of the human psyche," he later admitted. Like any true believer, he probably exaggerated his faith's benefits, but Joe was nonetheless right, absolutely right, in urging psychotherapy on Judy. It did not require Sigmund Freud, or Joe Mankiewicz either, to conclude that there was something amiss with a pretty young woman who peered into the mirror and saw nothing but ugliness, a performer of almost supernal gifts who doubted that she possessed any talent at all. Even Judy knew she needed help. "I wasn't too bright," she was to say, "but I knew something was radically wrong."

Joe probably advanced the idea of psychoanalysis to her as early as 1942, even before their affair began, and it was also then, most likely, that he introduced her to the eminent Dr. Karl Menninger, who was visiting from Kansas. After one session, Menninger proposed she spend several months, perhaps as long as a year, at his celebrated center in Topeka. Although she was beginning to have emotional difficulties, Menninger told her, they could probably be resolved through psychotherapy. "Just come back and work and see where all these things started," he said. "If you see what goes on inside yourself, I think you'll have no problems that you can't handle." Since so long an absence from M-G-M was unrealistic, Judy did the next best thing: at Menninger's recommendation, she began seeing Ernst Simmel, the dean of Southern California analysts and a confidant of Freud himself.

Unlike many of his colleagues in Southern California, the worst of whom were quacks and charlatans, the best of whom were often name-droppers and glory seekers, Simmel was a serious therapist with unassailable credentials. A onetime president of the Berlin Psychoanalytic Society, he had been one of the founders of a psychoanalytic sanitarium, the renowned Schloss Tegel, that was, in many ways, a model for Menninger's own clinic. Fleeing the Nazis in the mid-thirties, he soon became one of the most respected practitioners in Los Angeles, analyzing so many famous patients from the movie industry that one of them, Joe's brother, Herman, joked that, like the members of a football team, they all ought to wear sweatshirts emblazoned with the letter "S."

At the outset, anyway, Judy took analysis more seriously, sacrificing her sleep for an hour's session each morning before she went to the studio. What she said in those early morning meetings can never be known, but if her elderly Herr Doktor was doing his job properly— and his background suggests that he was—he was at the very least shining a light on her past, helping her see both herself and her problems with newfound clarity.

If such an examination is painful for the patient, it is sometimes just as painful for the patient's parents, who are also put under close scrutiny. As Judy's therapy progressed, Ethel, in any case, began noticing a change in her attitude, a disquieting hint of self-assertion. Judy had disobeyed her before, certainly, but that had been the disobedience of a child; she had never questioned her mother's ultimate authority. Now she did so, and Ethel, increasingly alarmed, summarily demanded that she stop seeing Simmel, and Joe along with him. Judy's response was what her mother had most feared—a declaration of independence. "I'll live my own life," Judy told her. "I will do what I want to do. I'm not a child. I've been married. You have to stop treating me like a little kid."

It was rebellion, a threat to her mother's own position, and an angry Ethel drove to M-G-M to alert the one man she thought could put it down, complaining to Mayer about psychoanalysis in general and Simmel and Joe in particular. Disliking independence in his employees and distrustful of analysis, as many people were in those days, Mayer concurred on every point. "Mr. Mayer and I agreed that Judy shouldn't be going to the analyst," Ethel triumphantly informed Jimmie. But what good was an agreement that left out the person who had to keep it? There was only one voice Judy would listen to, and that belonged to Joe, the source of all the trouble. Joe would have to be confronted, and the only question was how Mayer would deal with a man who was just as strong-willed, just as stubborn and just as determined as he was.

|||

The inevitable showdown came not in Mayer's vast white-on-white office in Culver City, but in a compartment on the Santa Fe line's luxurious Super Chief, speeding west in the early summer of 1943. Joe, who had been visiting his wife at the Menninger Clinic, had boarded the train in Kansas City sometime after midnight. Already aboard, by unhappy coincidence, was Mayer, on his way home after a trip to New York. Since the sleek and supremely comfortable Super Chief—"a grand hotel on wheels," the railroad liked to boast—was Hollywood's favorite conveyance, Joe should not have been too shocked when Mayer's traveling companion, the loyal Howard Strickling, knocked on his door the following day. Mr. Mayer had heard he was aboard, Strickling said, and wanted Joe to come to his compartment.

Gone were the days when Mayer patted him on the back and called him Harvard College—Joe had embarrassed him with one witticism too many. Now, wasting little time on small talk, Mayer got right to the issue: how dare Joe carry on with Judy, a woman thirteen years his junior? Thus began a bizarre onslaught, a seemingly endless stream of ancient platitudes and newer bromides of Mayer's own concoction. "He talked to me about God and motherhood and wifehood and parenthood and the studio," recalled Joe. "How when you lie down with dogs, you get up with fleas. How a fish starts to stink from the head. How you have a responsibility to your wife and when you are not with her, you must live like a monk. But what he was really saying was, 'You mustn't mess with our property.' "

Though it sounded extemporaneous, Mayer's colorful rant was, in fact, a practiced and polished performance. It was his peculiar but usually effective method of disciplining an errant employee, and it finished, as such performances usually did, on a conciliatory note. "You understand that I'm talking to you strictly as the head of a studio," Mayer concluded, a remark so sanctimonious and insincere that Joe, who had listened in amazed silence, finally spoke up. "No, you're not, Mr. Mayer. You're talking like a jealous old man." Had Joe struck him, Mayer could not have been more outraged. "Get him out of here!" he shouted to Strickling, and Joe retreated down the gently swaying corridor to his own compartment.

If it not been for the relentless Ethel, the matter might have been left there. Not only was Joe protected by a contract, but Mayer was also too shrewd an executive to dismiss one of his most important producers because of a few heated words. Ethel did not give up, however, and two or three weeks later, back in Culver City, Joe once again received a summons. Waiting for him in Mayer's office, besides Mayer himself, were Eddie Mannix, who often appeared when trouble loomed, and an unsmiling Ethel. Not bothering to rise from his desk, Mayer launched into a new diatribe even as Joe was walking through the door.

"All right," he said. "I told you on the train—stop filling this girl's head with all sorts of talk about psychiatrists. Are you her father? What's your relationship to her that you're telling her how to live her life? Don't you think her mother knows a little bit about these things?" This time Joe, having seen the show once before, did respond, trying to inject some reason into the discourse and pleading with Mayer to give both Simmel and psychoanalysis a chance. "You've never met him, Mr. Mayer. You don't know what he thinks about Judy. This girl needs help."

That was the opening Ethel had apparently been waiting for. "So!" she screamed. "My daughter's crazy!" Up to that moment, Mayer had been giving another performance, Joe later decided, a performance designed more to mollify the mother of one of his biggest stars than to frighten Joe himself. But Ethel's fury was infectious, and what had begun as a demonstration quickly turned into the real thing, with Mayer, now furious himself, joining her almost hysterical attack. It was Joe who finally put an end to the uproar with the last witticism he was ever to make at M-G-M, a line to which even Mayer could not manage an answer. "Obviously, this studio isn't big enough for both of us, Mr. Mayer. One of us has to go."

Things had got out of hand, and the result—Joe's departure to another studio—was not at all the one Mayer had intended. By the beginning of August, less than a week later, Joe had been released from his Metro contract and was working at 20th Century–Fox, which not only paid him more money, but also allowed him to fulfill his fondest ambition—to write and direct his own movies. Instead of being an avenging angel, visiting retribution on the man who had come between her and her daughter, Ethel had been an angel of deliverance, opening the door to a new, more rewarding career and a shelf heavy with Academy Awards.

|||

Though Ethel's meddling had cost Metro one of its boldest and brightest lights, it had gained Ethel herself nothing at all. Judy continued to see both Joe and her analyst, and neither her mother nor Mayer could think of a way to stop her. Conspiring together, the two of them had, in fact, only shown, far better than Joe could have done, how desperately she needed assistance to break their strangling grip. Lying on Simmel's couch on those chilly California mornings, when the grass was soggy with dew and most of her friends were still climbing out of bed, Judy did not have to reach back to childhood to find examples of her mother's manipulation; abetted by Mayer, Ethel provided them nearly every day, as regularly as the war bulletins that were broadcast on the radio.

The decision to begin therapy thus marked a critical juncture for Judy, a moment of ripe possibility. She knew she was not in control of her life, and she seemed determined to find out why. Besides seeing Simmel, she took Joe's advice and read the psychoanalytic pioneers—Freud, Jung and Adler—as avidly as she had read Housman's poems and Mildred Cram's novella *Forever* during her romance with Tyrone.

She seemed to be striving as hard as she could, and Joe, who had sacrificed his job rather than see her quit analysis, had good cause for optimism. Everything, in short, seemed to be going right, yet something was wrong, so wrong that in the end her therapy could only be termed a failure, the hopes invested in it to be dismissed, as Joe was so aptly to phrase it, as the foolish fancies of an opium dream. When Judy was finally through with Freud and his disciples, she had benefited, as she was later to say, "not one bit."

Unlike other branches of the medical arts, psychoanalysis is an intimate collaboration between doctor and patient, equal partners in a common pursuit. Properly tended, a wounded body mends by itself, without any exertion on the part of its owner. A wounded psyche, by contrast, heals only if the patient actively joins in the repair effort. Analysis will work its cure only if the patient is convinced it can work. Belief will not guarantee success, but disbelief will guarantee failure. Encapsulating those requirements in a phrase, Carl Jung said that nothing less than "perfect sincerity" is demanded from those entering psychoanalysis. One should never expect more from a patient, Freud himself cautioned, than lies within the patient's native capacity.

|||

Given the need for such a close and collegial relationship between doctor and patient, it is hard to imagine why Karl Menninger thought Judy and his friend Simmel would be a good match. The one was a bouncy product of the Swing Age, with a pronounced distrust of authority. The other was an elderly German with a thick and forbidding accent, a man whose dictatorial manner irritated even his colleagues. "The Obermacher"—the Supervisor—was the sarcastic title Herman Mankiewicz pinned on Simmel. It is likely—she herself indicated as much—that Judy viewed him just that way, not as a doctor trying to help her, but as another in the long line of those exercising control. In any event, she began defying him, as she so often defied her mother and her bosses at M-G-M, with small acts of rebellion, missing sessions and, in the sessions she did attend, inventing falsehoods about the problems that plagued her. A "big pack of lies" was how she described the accounts she gave him.

A lie told inside an analyst's office is different from one told outside: it is a symptom of illness, not a transgression against the moral code. A more sympathetic analyst might therefore have regarded Judy's big pack of lies as a clue to her underlying problems, as a key that could have opened many doors. Simmel responded to Judy's bad behavior as her mother or Mayer might have done, however, with understandable but not very professional petulance. When her friend Betty O'Kelly telephoned to cancel one of Judy's sessions, for instance—Judy was afraid to make the call herself—the exasperated Simmel took the phone from his secretary. "Will you tell Judy that I cannot help her if she does not keep appointments?" he said. He then added, in a frigid voice: "And I cannot help her if she continues to lie to me when she does keep appointments. Give her that message."

Whether Judy would have reacted differently to a less rigid analyst— or whether psychoanalysis was, in fact, beyond her capacity for looking inward—is, of course, impossible to say. What can be said is that she could not work with an analyst as starchy and imposing as Simmel. "I could never 'associate freely' with him," she confessed. "I was too self-conscious." After a promising start, she seemed to lose faith in the entire process of analysis. "Imagine whipping out of bed," she said, "dashing over to the doctor's office, lying down on a torn leather couch, telling my troubles to an old man who couldn't hear, who answered with an accent I couldn't understand, and then dashing to Metro to make movie love to Mickey Rooney." Why did she persist in a treatment that made her so unhappy? asked Jimmie. "Well, Joe thinks I ought to do it," replied Judy.

|||

It was probably a relief, then, for her to get away from such pain and pressures, leaving Los Angeles for much of the summer and fall of 1943 to enjoy a happy reunion with an old and always ardent admirer—the live audience. On June 28, she journeyed east for an outdoor concert in Philadelphia, where she performed before the largest number she had ever encountered, fifteen thousand jamming a space that was supposed to seat sixty-five hundred, with perhaps another fifteen thousand who could not get in carpeting the surrounding slopes and dales. To have said that she was a hit would have been inaccurate, wrote one reviewer; "cyclonic is the only word to describe with any degree of adequacy the 21-year-old, red-headed film star's success." If the Liberty Bell had pealed "Over the Rainbow," staid old Philadelphia could not have given her a lustier reception.

Similar hosannas were heard throughout July, as Judy followed her conquest of the City of Brotherly Love with an almost month-long tour of military bases in the East and Midwest. August she spent at home in California, but on September 4 the "amazing Judy," as one Philadelphia critic had titled her, was on the road again, this time with something called the Hollywood Cavalcade, a train full of stars—from Fred Astaire and Greer Garson to Mickey Rooney and Betty Hutton—that crisscrossed the country pitching war bonds. Ten thousand miles the stars traveled together, entertaining an estimated seven million people and selling well over a billion dollars' worth of bonds.

She could not stay away from home forever, however, and when the Cavalcade returned to Hollywood, twenty-three weary days later, Judy came face-to-face with some hard and unwelcome facts. Having completed her stay at the Menninger Clinic, Joe's wife Rosa had come back from Kansas, and it was obvious that the story of Judy and Joe was rapidly approaching its conclusion. That was fine with Joe—romance with Judy brought him more trouble than he wanted—but Judy was not so complaisant. Having found the most wonderful man who had ever lived, she was unwilling to let him escape so easily, and sometime in the final few weeks of 1943, or perhaps the first few weeks of 1944, she announced to Joe what she had earlier announced to Tyrone: she was going to have his baby. Nothing else, Judy had learned, captures a man's attention like the news that he is about to become a father.

To Tyrone, she may actually have been telling the truth. To Joe, she was either lying or fantasizing, and Joe knew it—knew it from the inappropriate times that she picked to talk about her pregnancy, knew it from the blank and noncommittal expressions on the faces of her sisters when she did. He also knew why she was inventing a story that would be so quickly discredited. "She didn't feel I took her seriously enough," he explained. Aware of all that, he was also aware, Freudian that he was, that if he called her bluff, he would only further damage her already fragile ego. He had but one choice, he felt, and that was to pretend to believe her. "She herself had to tell me it wasn't true," he explained. "It was one of those things you have to play straight through."

Even Judy realized that, this time around, there was not the smallest hope of marriage—Joe could not leave a woman who had just come out of a psychiatric clinic—and they agreed that she would have to have an abortion. Still playing it straight through, and then some, Joe joined her on a secret trip to New York, where the procedure was to be performed. To prevent word of their arrival from reaching the newspapers, Joe's friend Mark Hanna, a Manhattan press agent, met their train at one of the last stops before Grand Central Station, then drove them to his own East Side apartment. There, unbeknownst to the gossip columnists, they stayed while Judy belatedly took a pregnancy test. To their feigned astonishment, the test came back negative. Judy was not pregnant after all; their trip had been for nothing. "A little happy, a little sad," in Joe's words, they boarded a train for the return to Los Angeles, leaving New York as silently as they had arrived.

Imaginary though it may have been, Judy's pregnancy had achieved its purpose. It had made Joe take her seriously, seriously enough, in any event, to travel all the way across the continent and back on what he was certain was a fool's errand. If that was not love, it was a close approximation. For Judy, their hush-hush trip east was also her last opportunity to have Joe all to herself, and when she looked back on the days they had spent together, locked in cozy train staterooms or in Mark Hanna's Manhattan apartment, she surrounded them with a halo of rosy nostalgia, as she might have a honeymoon. For Joe, on the other hand, that peculiar journey signaled the beginning of the end. When they finally disembarked in California, he was resolved to gently lead his charming but troublesome dryad to the glade in which he had found her. "We didn't break off our affair," said Joe. "It just faded away. That was what was so wonderful about it."

|||

She could be a great actress, Joe assured Judy; but only if M-G-M started giving her great parts—parts for grown-up women, not love-starved teenagers. It was at his urging, then, that in the summer or fall of 1943 Judy gathered her courage and, for the first time, turned down a role Metro had assigned her, that the studio had, in fact, ordered written specially for her. To her suspicious ears, the character, a girl of seventeen, looked like the same part she had played a dozen times over, and the picture itself sounded like a tired old tune, heard once too often. "Perhaps M-G-M should let Miss Garland grow up and stay that way," *The New York Times* had said when it reviewed *Presenting Lily Mars* in April, and Judy fervently agreed: she was no longer willing to play dewy-eyed teenagers. *Meet Me in St. Louis,* she told the studio, would be a major setback to her career, and she would not go near it.

Logic was firmly on her side. On paper, the girl, Esther Smith, is just Betsy Booth under a different name. She is still in her teens, still in school and still mad about the boy next door, who, for much of the movie, scarcely gives her a second glance. The story line was so pleasingly familiar—"a valentine in the palm of your hand," was how its creator, Sally Benson, described it—that at one point a delighted Metro thought that it had stumbled on another gold mine like the Hardy series. *Meet Me in St. Louis* might be merely the first of many adventures for the Smith family, four girls and a boy, in turn-of-the-century St. Louis. Such a prospect, so alluring to M-G-M's accountants, did not fill Judy's heart with joy.

As they were published, one by one, in the pages of *The New Yorker,* Benson's stories did have considerable nostalgic charm, particularly for the war-weary readers of the early forties. But charm is hard to convey on the screen, and a valentine, pretty as it may be, is usually not enough to keep an audience in its seats for two hours. A movie demands a plot, and a plot was something *Meet Me in St. Louis* did not have. The world the Smiths inhabited was as sunny as Eden. Was the ketchup boiling on the stove too tart? Would Esther's date retrieve his tuxedo from the tailor in time to take her to the Christmas ball? Would Mr. Smith, who already had a good job, take a better one in New York? Those were the matters that concerned the household at 5135 Kensington Avenue in the months preceding the 1904 St. Louis World's Fair. The story line, in short, was purposefully—some thought, perversely—undramatic, thinner than the ketchup bubbling on that cast-iron stove.

Yet even if she had liked the script, Judy would have objected to what appeared to be a secondary role. It was plain to her, as well as to Joe, who was peering protectively over her shoulder, that the movie's real star would not be Esther, but five-year-old Tootie, the youngest of the Smith sisters—the young Sally Benson herself. With her winsome smile and her endlessly emotive eyes, Margaret O'Brien, who was to play Tootie, had already run away with such pictures as *Journey for Margaret* and *The Canterville Ghost,* and she seemed destined to skip away with *Meet Me in St. Louis* as well. "I don't think that I come off too well," concluded Judy, who had been around Hollywood long enough to recognize a scene stealer when she saw one.

Though she did not say so, it is likely that Judy was also unhappy that Arthur Freed, the film's producer, had given the role of the oldest Smith sister—a big part, almost as large as her own—to a total unknown, a former Radio City Rockette whose sole qualification was that she shared his bed. "A flaming rocket has burst upon Metro-Goldwyn-Mayer studios!" proclaimed Metro's publicity department, but the only one who ever felt any heat from Lucille Bremer was the love-smitten Freed himself.

Annoying as it was, the casting of Bremer at least had an explanation. More puzzling was Freed's selection of director: the shy and often inarticulate Vincente Minnelli, who had little film experience and who seemed, to Judy and many others in Culver City, an odd choice to be entrusted with such a big-budget Technicolor production. Realizing that *Meet Me in St. Louis* represented his chance to break into the front ranks, Minnelli did his best to change Judy's mind. He saw great things in the script, he told her. "In fact," he said, "it's magical." But nothing he said convinced her; Judy saw no magic, in either the director or the screenplay.

At Metro, unlike more turbulent studios such as Warner Bros., stars rarely refused an assignment, and Mayer had every right to suspend Judy for saying no to *Meet Me in St. Louis.* For once he took her side, however, informing Freed that he was forced to agree with her—the picture had no plot. But Freed was not only one of Mayer's favorites— "I've taken this boy and I've made a great producer out of him!" Mayer liked to brag—he was also one of Metro's biggest and most reliable moneymakers. After so many successes, Mayer finally decreed, the studio owed Freed a failure. Assuring Judy that the film would not ruin her career, Mayer gave his assent. Plot or no plot, *Meet Me in St. Louis* was Freed's to make.

|||

A successful producer Freed most assuredly had been. But if his biography had ended with his forty-ninth birthday in the summer of 1943, he would be remembered today more as a songwriter than as a moviemaker. Indeed, even in his palmiest days, Freed looked and behaved more like the bedraggled, sweat-stained song plugger he once had been than the high-paid producer he had become. Mispronouncing words, flashing filthy fingernails and spraying the dinner table with food when he talked, he was almost obstinately sloppy and uncouth—"a slob," as Irene Sharaff put it.

Like most of the other Metro moguls, he regarded sex as a job benefit, and Lucille Bremer was only one of many attractive women who thought the couch in Freed's office would carry them to stardom. "I have something made for just you," he promised little Shirley Temple after she moved from Fox to Metro. "You'll be my new star!" he added, forgetting that Temple already was a star. With no more prelude than that, Freed abruptly rose from his desk, proudly displaying something Temple had never seen in all her eleven years—a man's penis. But Temple's reaction, nervous laughter, was not what he had expected, and Freed indignantly ordered her out of his office. "Get out!" he shouted. "Go on, *get out!*"

The most prominent sycophant in a studio crowded with sycophants, Freed was the object of innumerable jibes. "If you want to shave Arthur Freed," went one, "you have to lather L. B. Mayer's ass." The jokes were not far off the mark, and no bulldog, panting love with every slobbering breath, could have been more devoted than Freed was to his silver-haired master. He frequently drove to Mayer's house at the beach for breakfast, sat beside him as Mayer had his hair cut in the Metro barbershop, patiently followed him around the lot, one deferential step behind, and joined him again at night for a drink in his office or a visit to the clubs on the Sunset Strip. Though the venue changed, the talk never varied—"Boss, what d'ya think?" Freed would ask, and Mayer would be happy to tell him.

Vulgar, crass, obsequious to superiors and often brutal to inferiors— that was Arthur Freed. But the authors of mighty movements and the doers of great deeds do not always look or act the way the history books would like, and Freed the vulgarian was also Freed the visionary, a man with large and scandent dreams. Although he could not put it, or much of anything else, into words, somewhere in the back of his disorderly mind he was forming an image of a new and more ambitious kind of movie musical.

|||

His vision was all the more remarkable because he was one of the chief inventors of the old-style musical he now found so tiresome. Irving Thalberg had employed Freed and his partner, Nacio Herb Brown, to write the songs for Hollywood's first all-talking musical, 1929's *The Broadway Melody,* and Freed had been involved, either as songwriter or assistant, in most of Metro's subsequent musical efforts. Yet though the first pictures he himself produced never ventured far from the tradi-tional formula, in which the romantic story was little more than an ex-cuse for songs and dances, Freed was, in fact, inching his way toward something different. "I felt a lot of the stuff they were doing in musi-cals was stale," he said. "It had become a cliché."

Since moviemaking, more than any other art form, is a collaborative enterprise, Freed could not do anything truly innovative until he had a production team of his own choosing, people not tied to the stale old ways. With Mayer's approval, Metro's money and the assistance of Roger Edens, who was his junior partner and artistic conscience, Freed therefore set out to find the best writers, musicians and designers in the country, traveling most often to New York for what he described as "a whole new crowd of people." Just as money begets money, so does tal-ent beget talent, and many of Broadway's best—Gene Kelly, Stanley Donen, Betty Comden and Adolph Green, to name just a few—were soon flocking to what had become known as the Freed Unit. So slowly that no one noticed what was happening until it had happened, Freed was building a virtual studio within the studio—"my own little Camelot," he called it.

It was about the time of *Girl Crazy* that Freed realized how bored he was with harebrained plots. By then he had not only the desire but also the means to strike out on his own—to create an original musical, right there in Culver City, that contained songs no one had ever heard before and that presented real people in real situations. Still, no one in the fall of 1943, probably even Freed himself, could have guessed that all his previous pictures had been little more than practice exercises and that now, with *Meet Me in St. Louis,* he was ready to show what he could really do.

|||

Freed had prevailed against almost universal opposition, and a tangible sign of his success soon appeared on Lot 3. There, not far from its more modest Andy Hardy street, Metro built a little bit of old St. Louis: eight imposing Victorian houses, each surrounded by a lush lawn and mani-cured shrubs and flower beds. *Meet Me in St. Louis,* the picture without a plot, was going ahead. Freed's victory had come at a price, however. Both he and Minnelli knew that they were gambling their reputations, and perhaps their careers, on the fate of a movie nearly everyone, in-cluding the star, had warned them against. If *Meet Me in St. Louis* scored a hit, it would be a long time before anyone again questioned their judgment; but if it flopped, if audiences insisted on a more con-ventional story, as most people at Metro believed they would, it would be even longer before they escaped an endless drizzle of recrimina-tions and I-told-you-so's. For both of them, the stakes could scarcely have been higher.

It must have been a great disappointment, then, to immediately stumble on one of the facts of moviemaking life: somber men in dark-blue suits can say yes to a picture, and highly skilled people can spend months readying it for the cameras, but it is the actors, quirky and often temperamental, who must appear on the screen. If they show up late for their calls, or show up unprepared, tempers flare, schedules crum-ble and carefully constructed plans are shredded into confetti. On a movie set, where dozens of people are usually working just outside camera range, time really is money, and as little as a day's delay can send the budget soaring. But that was the dismal scenario—delay and interruption, stop and go—that destiny had ordained for *Meet Me in St. Louis,* which finally began production on November 10, 1943.

At the beginning, the main problem was Judy. Accepting the role of Esther only grudgingly, she had demonstrated her displeasure, consciously or not, by arriving four hours late for her first day of rehearsal, then at least twenty-five minutes late every rehearsal day thereafter. Even more ominous was her tardiness—an hour and sixteen minutes—on the first day of actual shooting, December 7. A week later, on December 16, she pleaded illness and stayed home altogether; two days after that she was on time, but soon left for home with a migraine. The last week of the year she missed entirely, nursing one of the ear infections that had dogged her since she was a baby, in Cedars of Lebanon Hospital.

So she continued, frequently ill, more often late, during the first few months of the new year, 1944. Again and again a sleepless Judy would telephone assistant director Al Jennings—or Freed himself—in the middle of the night to say that she could not work the next morning. "I've had a violent headache all night," she might say, "and I just can't come in today." Sometimes she could be induced to change her mind; sometimes she could not. "Miss Judy Garland phoned Mr. Freed at 4:30 this morning that she was not feeling well and might not be able to work today" was a typical entry in the production notes, which provided a minute-to-minute account of every working day. "At 8 A.M. Miss Garland's sister phoned Al Jennings that Judy had been ill all night and unable to rest, and as a result could not report for work today," was another such notation.

|||

Meet Me in St. Louis was not the first movie to be slowed by Judy's illness and tardiness. During the shooting of *Girl Crazy,* only a year earlier, she had, in fact, been sick even more often—seventeen days, one more than she was away from *Meet Me in St. Louis.* Then her absences had seemed an aberration, caused, at least in part, by Busby Berkeley's

abusive behavior. Now they seemed to be part of a pattern of unreliability, the result of an increasing reliance on the uppers and downers
her mother had started her on so long before. "I've got to keep these
girls going!" had been Ethel's chirpy rationale for giving her daughters
stimulants, and a decade and more later Judy could not function without them. "I always have to be my best in front of the camera," she later
explained to a somewhat bewildered Minnelli. "You should know that.
You expect it of me too. Well, sometimes I don't feel my best. It's a
struggle to get through the day. I use these pills. They carry me
through."

Just as often they stopped her altogether, however, and her unreliability not only cost the studio money, but also irritated her fellow actors, who were forced to arrive early, day after day, then sit around in
full costume until she decided to emerge from her dressing room. After
one such delay, Mary Astor, who was playing her mother, burst through
the door to give her a sound spanking. "Judy, what the hell's happened
to you?" demanded Astor, who had also played the mother role in *Listen, Darling,* six years earlier. "You were a trouper—once. . . . You have
kept the entire company out there waiting for two hours. Waiting for
you to favor us with your presence." After responding with an infuriating giggle—"Yeah, that's what everybody's been telling me"—Judy
grabbed Astor by the hand and, in a pathetic confession of despair, all
but wept: "I don't *sleep,* Mom!"

Whatever else they did, the pills did nothing to boost her morale or
bandage her fragile ego, and, like a tightrope walker, she could be
thrown off balance by the slightest jolt. The strongest such jolt during
the making of *Meet Me in St. Louis* came from an unlikely source, the
mild-mannered, almost overly polite Minnelli. In all but the Busby
Berkeley movies, Judy's instinctive talent, combined with a photographic memory, had usually enabled her to complete each scene in one
or two takes, without much guidance from the director. "I just went out
there and did what came naturally," she proudly recalled. But Minnelli
was not pleased with her performance in either the first take or the second take—or any take after that. Though he did not say so, he thought
that the inexperienced Lucille Bremer was much better, that Judy was
making fun of her lines, whereas Bremer, who played Rose, Esther's

older sister, was reading hers with true and convincing sincerity. "She was wonderful in her approach," he said of Bremer, "believing every word she said."

It is doubtful that Judy was intentionally mocking the script, not after the first or second take, anyway. The more likely explanation is that she was unaccustomed to working with a director as subtle as Minnelli, who compared the effect he was hoping to achieve to a fugue in which his actors were expected to play off one another with the contrapuntal precision of musical instruments. In any event, Judy could not understand what she was doing wrong, and Minnelli, whose instructions were as enigmatic as haiku, was incapable of telling her. "You wished he'd come out with a statement—a noun, a verb and something to put them together," was the wry observation of Irene Sharaff, who was responsible for the film's rainbow of beautiful costumes.

As the cameras continued to shoot the same scene, take after humiliating take, an almost distraught Judy finally asked Freed to come to her dressing room. Baffled and "scared cross-eyed," as she phrased it, she announced that she had lost her talent: she no longer knew how to act. Freed assured her that she did know, and work resumed. But with the director and his star all but throwing darts at each other, the tension on the set was palpable. Quiet and restrained in public, Minnelli bitterly complained about her to Irving Brecher, the chief scriptwriter, while Judy, who returned his sentiments in triplicate, entertained the crew with malicious imitations of his maddening but sometimes comical indecision.

Even when scenes went well, however, as they increasingly did, Judy found the set of *Meet Me in St. Louis* an unnerving place to be. She did not enjoy her many on-camera exchanges with Bremer—"it's hard to act to a stone wall," was her chilly explanation—and the cruel manipulation of little Margaret O'Brien was a painful and scarifying reminder of her own childhood. To prepare Margaret for crying scenes, for example, her mother would play a nasty but effective trick on her: her dog was to be killed, she would sadly inform the child. Margaret's eyes would widen, the tears would flow and the unfortunate pooch would be reprieved until the next time she was supposed to cry, when once again it would be sentenced to die. Just watching this cynical exercise brought tears to Judy's own eyes. "It's awful! Terrible!" she would exclaim. Like her, she said, Margaret would never enjoy a normal childhood.

|||

An active romance might have made a difference to Judy, carrying her over the rough spots; but disappointment in love also added to her cross-eyed misery. Eager to end their affair on a friendly note, Joe had advised her to date other men, and Judy had dutifully, even enthusiastically, obliged. She did not, in fact, have to look far for an attractive candidate, no further than her *Meet Me in St. Louis* costar Tom Drake—the very man she was supposed to fall in love with on the screen. Just as Esther Smith pursued the boy next door, so did Judy pursue Drake, the actor who played him. The moment she saw him smile, Esther sings at the beginning of the picture, she knew he was just her style. And Drake was Judy's style. Tall, and handsome in a solid, square-jawed way, he had sympathetic brown eyes, a deep, resonant voice and a smile that was indeed engaging, slow to take shape and somewhat shy when it arrived, but altogether sincere, unlike the toothy, thousand-watt grins that blinded the hatcheck girls at Ciro's. "He's real" was all Judy said to her friend Dorothy Walsh.

Young Alfred Alderdice—Drake's original name—was, in short, a walking advertisement for all-American wholesomeness, and if she had written ten thousand pages, Sally Benson herself could not have invented a more appropriate match for Esther, or for Judy either. "She was mad about him," said Ralph Blane, who, together with his partner, Hugh Martin, wrote most of the film's songs. "Ooooh! She had to have him—that was all there was to it." Friendship led to romance, which led to bed—where the affair ended. To Drake's embarrassment and to her own dismay, Judy could not arouse him—he could not perform. Drake was an all-American boy, all right, but an all-American boy who liked other all-American boys.

A woman more certain of her sexual attractiveness would have realized that his failure in bed was nobody's fault. But Judy was angry, apparently equating her inability to excite him, or his inability to be excited, with rejection, seeing it as something akin to an insult. Though they did not know what had transpired, those on the set noticed an immediate change in the weather; the flames in Judy's eyes turned to icicles. "There was never a harsh word between them," said Al Jennings, "but Judy shut him out after that, which made Tom awfully unhappy."

|||

On a less troubled production, Judy's absences might have occasioned more frowns. But on an illness-plagued set like that of *Meet Me in St. Louis*—"the sickest picture in town," Jennings called it—they shrank into relative insignificance. Pneumonia kept Astor away for nearly a month; appendicitis, followed by strep throat, put Joan Carroll, who played the second-youngest Smith daughter, out of action for several weeks; and various ailments afflicted Harry Davenport, the septuagenarian grandfather. Most damaging of all was the prolonged absence of Margaret O'Brien. Late in the afternoon of Sunday, January 30, Margaret's aunt telephoned Jennings with the alarming news that her niece would not work the next day—or for the next two weeks. Margaret was suffering from the flu and hay fever, the aunt said, and she was being whisked away that very afternoon to the warmer, drier climate of Arizona.

Before an astonished Metro could try to stop her, Margaret and her mother were on a train heading east. New York, not generally noted for its warm and dry winters, was their real destination, and Mayer's boss, Nick Schenck, was the specialist they were traveling so far to see. Determined to get more money for her daughter, Gladys O'Brien had shut down the entire picture simply to demonstrate Margaret's importance. It was an act of breathtaking audacity; but with an expensive movie barely halfway finished, Metro could not afford to stand on principle. Schenck got the point, Margaret got the money and *Meet Me in St. Louis* got Margaret again. After a thirteen-day suspension, shooting resumed in the middle of February.

By then, nearly two and a half months into filming, the atmosphere on the set, so recently charged and turbid, had begun to brighten. "Judy, I've been watching that man," Mary Astor had responded when

Judy complained about Minnelli. "He knows what he's doing." And even Judy, who sometimes stayed late to watch the rushes, the raw, unedited footage that had been shot that day, could see that Astor was right. When the shooting finally ended on April 7, it was clear that something remarkable had occurred on that sickly and often embattled production: a movie of extraordinary power and presence had been created.

On the simplest level, *Meet Me in St. Louis* is superb entertainment— "one of the Great American Family sketches," as the reviewer for the *Los Angeles Times* instantly pronounced it. Unlike Metro's other great American family sketch, the tiresome and tendentious Hardy series, it is sentimental without being bathetic, touching without being corny, and uplifting without being preachy. "Make a bee-line right down to the Astor" was the recommendation of the equally enthusiastic critic for *The New York Times*. "For there's honey to be had inside."

Honey there was and honey there is; but there is also much more. What Freed and Minnelli had been alone in seeing was that their picture did not need a traditional plot, that the most wrenching dramas are those that involve the conflict of emotions. No plot in *Meet Me in St. Louis*? It has the most basic plot of all: the fight for survival, the struggle of the Smith family to preserve its happy, almost blessed way of life. In *The Wizard of Oz* Dorothy had to battle murderous apple trees, flying monkeys and a wicked witch before she could return home. The Smiths *are* home, and they want to stay there, stopping time in its one perfect moment, the months leading up to the St. Louis World's Fair. There is no villain but the calendar, time itself, relentless and implacable.

It is that sense of evanescence that speaks to the subconscious, giving the film a poignancy that is as sharp now as it was in 1944, that year of war and dislocation, when home, and the permanence and security associated with it, were all millions of people thought about. "If a picture doesn't haunt you a little after you've seen it, it hasn't meant much," Minnelli was to say, and by his definition, which is as good a measurement as any of a picture's enduring value, *Meet Me in St. Louis* means quite a lot. Audiences thought so, anyway, and the film's receipts soon surpassed those of any previous M-G-M release. No further proof was needed: Freed and Minnelli had not only succeeded, they had triumphed. They had been right, and everybody else had been wrong. One of the first to admit error was the star. "Arthur," Judy said after an early preview, "remind me not to tell you what kind of pictures to make."

*Their vows said, Judy and Vincente
leave for their honeymoon*

CHAPTER 8

A Marriage Made in Metro-Goldwyn-Mayer

f all the curious events that had occurred on the set of *Meet Me in St. Louis,* the most curious was this: the star and the director had forgotten their antagonism long enough to fall in love. For several weeks they kept the happy news to themselves. Judy was uncharacteristically silent, Minnelli was characteristically inscrutable, and the transition from war to peace was so slow and subtle that even the keen-eyed Ralph Blane, who had followed every movement of Judy's previous pas de deux, was surprised when he learned about what he called their "tootsie wootsie."

Judy's heart probably started to melt a little when she watched the daily rushes, for Minnelli, who had caused her so much pain and self-doubt, was doing what no other director had ever done: he was making her look beautiful. Not just pretty, or handsome, or any of the other adjectives that are attached to a merely attractive woman; but beautiful, without conditions or qualifications. Some of the credit had to go to her new makeup woman, Dorothy Ponedel, who rounded out Judy's thin lower lip and used the tricks of her trade to call attention to her dark and expressive eyes; some credit, too, had to go to Irene Sharaff, who designed costumes that disguised her short neck and somewhat odd figure. But Minnelli, who made sure that every shot was not only flattering, but tenderly embracing, was the architect of her new look, and Judy knew it. As far back as she could remember, she had wanted to look beautiful. Now, thanks to him, she did.

As their relationship began to defrost, she sometimes joined Minnelli and his assistant director, Al Jennings, along with Jennings's wife, Juanita, for dinner at a nearby studio hangout, then returned with them to watch the rushes. There was no hint of romance during those dinners, however, and sparks did not start to fly until a mutual friend, the dancer Don Loper, decided to play matchmaker and arranged a dinner on neutral territory, away from Culver City and its workaday associations. The evening was such a success that dinner together became a habit, just the three of them and Loper's date. So it continued until the day Loper phoned Minnelli to say he was sick; dinner was off. When Minnelli—or Vincente, as Judy now called him—relayed the bad news to Judy, he discovered that she was not disappointed at all: there was nothing, she replied with a chuckle, to prevent them from having dinner by themselves. Her logic was inescapable, and from then on she and Vincente usually dined alone, as Loper had apparently intended all along.

It was at that point that people began to notice. For all its worldly glamour, Metro was no different from any other nosy village; it feasted on gossip, tidbits of which were passed from set to set, lot to lot, with astonishing speed. By then Judy and Vincente, openly billing and cooing at parties, did not care who knew. Their tootsie-wootsieing did not stop with sweet talk at parties, and sometime in the spring of 1944, a few weeks after *Meet Me in St. Louis* finished shooting, they started living together. To the astonishment of everyone but themselves, they were a couple.

|||

One thing at least they had in common: childhood memories of life on the lowest rungs of show business, of falling asleep to the sound of ap-

plause rather than lullabies. Vincente's father, the son of an Italian rev-
olutionary, was a conductor; his mother, whose own family was French,
was an actress; and they met, sometime around 1900, in a small Midwestern theater, as Frank and Ethel Gumm were to do a decade or so
later. In 1902 Vincente's father and uncle formed the Minnelli Brothers Tent Theater, which, with Vincente's mother, the new Mrs. Minnelli, as its star, toured rural Ohio for the next two decades, bringing
drama, or melodrama, to such places as Marion and Sandusky,
Zanesville, Massillon and Chillicothe. Born in February 1903, Vincente, like Judy, was not much more than a baby when he was first
pushed in front of an audience. But Vincente, unlike Judy, was not a
stage natural, and he spent much of his childhood at a boarding school
or with his grandparents in little Delaware, Ohio, where Grandfather
Minnelli had settled down to teach music. And little Delaware, which
had a population of about nine thousand, as conventional a town as a
town could be, was where Vincente grew up.

By his own description, Vincente was a lonely boy. Awkward,
painfully shy and more interested in drawing and painting than in the
games that occupied most other boys, Vincente—or Lester, as he was
known in those days—spent much of his time in his backyard studio, a
converted chicken coop. A year after graduating from high school, he
took his paintbrushes to Chicago, which, strange as it might seem, provided the best possible schooling for a future movie director. Vincente's
first job, dressing windows at Marshall Field, the giant department
store, taught him how to arrange a scene in three dimensions. His second, assisting a society photographer, taught him composition and per-
spective. His third, designing costumes for the stage shows of
Chicago's biggest theater chain, Balaban and Katz, instructed him in
the dramatic uses of color, a knowledge he was to exploit so effectively
in *Meet Me in St. Louis.*

After a decade in the Second City, Vincente took his now mature
skills to New York, where he ascended the theatrical ladder even more
swiftly. Shy Vincente may have been, but he was also ambitious, determined and sometimes even ruthless in getting what he wanted. "If
there is anything I want to be known for," he declared, "it is for smart,
sophisticated productions." Within three years he was presenting such

smart productions at the new Radio City Music Hall; within four years, on Broadway.

Arthur Freed lured him to California in 1940 with what may have been an unprecedented contract. Vincente was required to do nothing but wander the Metro lot until he learned how movie musicals were made. After two years of watching and occasionally offering suggestions, he was given his first directing assignment—*Cabin in the Sky,* an all-black musical fantasy starring Lena Horne and Ethel Waters. Shot on a low budget, *Cabin in the Sky* nonetheless bears the distinctive Minnelli stamp: an easy, fluid camera style; the use of songs to help tell the story, much as dialogue does; and a fanatical eye for small details that, looked at separately, escape notice, but, added together, create an atmosphere of rock-hard, altogether convincing authenticity. *Cabin in the Sky* was both a critical and a financial success, and those, like Judy, who were later puzzled when Vincente was chosen to direct *Meet Me in St. Louis* had simply not been paying attention.

|||

Youth needs models, inspirations and ideals, and, as a young man in Chicago, Vincente had chosen his: James McNeill Whistler, the expatriate American painter who had dazzled and often outraged nineteenth-century London and Paris with his individual style and pugnacious wit. "Here was a man—and an artist—with whom I could identify," Vincente was to write in his memoirs, and it was then, in Chicago, that he discarded his provincial past and reinvented himself, as best he could, as a latter-day Whistler. By the time he reached New York, the transformation was complete. He was no longer Lester Minnelli, a timid boy from Ohio who liked to draw: he was Vincente Minnelli—artist, aesthete and man of mode.

If Whistler, who wore yellow gloves and brandished a long, wandlike cane, was a dandy, then so was Vincente, whose Metro uniform, modified for a later age and a more congenial climate, consisted of immaculate pearl-gray slacks and short-sleeved yellow shirts. If Whistler violated contemporary taste by painting the interiors of his houses in simple and arresting colors, then so did Vincente, who decorated one room of his California house in stark black and white—black walls, white furniture. If Whistler enjoyed a stylish life, then so did Vincente, who hired a Filipino houseman to see to it that things ran smoothly inside his dark and elegant walls.

He could wear smart clothes, he could live in smart rooms and he could be pampered by a smart-looking houseman, but Vincente could not copy Whistler in every respect. Whistler, for instance, was as famous for his sharp tongue as he was for his art. Vincente, by contrast, could scarcely make a point, let alone a witticism. Whistler was handsome; Vincente was not. With a receding chin, an aggressive nose and drooping eyes, he was so downright ugly, in fact, that his co-workers made jokes about him, some claiming he looked like a dinosaur, others a goldfish. Making his physical defects even more noticeable was a collection—a virtual rogues' gallery—of unconscious tics, an occasional twitch in the right eye and a continuous pursing of the mouth. "To tell the truth, I couldn't really look at him," said Kathryn Grayson, who, for a decade or more, was Metro's reigning classical soprano. "He had this affliction: he was totally unattractive."

But Vincente had still another characteristic that was, to many people at Metro, even more repellent. He was obviously, even ostentatiously effeminate, and conduct that had gone unremarked, if not ignored, in New York caused constant comment—and sometimes a disbelieving hush—in Culver City. One incident, from the early forties, can stand for many. Visiting the set of *Kathleen,* the only picture Shirley Temple was ever to make at Metro, he wore more makeup than most of the female stars: mascara, eye shadow, lipstick and a covering base—everything but false eyelashes. If he had been the ghost of Irving Thalberg, his arrival could not have caused more amazement. "There was an absolute silence on the set," recalled Dorothy Raye, one of *Kathleen*'s dancers. "I mean *silence*! Nobody had ever appeared looking like that. None of us could think of what to say."

Effeminate behavior is not a guarantee of homosexuality any more than a fullback's swagger is a guarantee of heterosexuality. But Vincente was indeed homosexual, or at least largely so. In New York, his almost certain lover had been another artist and designer, a young man so similar that they were almost mirror images. Like Vincente, his companion came from a small town in the American heartland—Hannibal, Missouri. Like Vincente, he had worked for Marshall Field and Balaban and Katz in Chicago, which is where they probably met. Like Vincente, he had been given the first name Lester, a coincidence so improbable as to defy calculation. Finally, so close was the physical resemblance that Lester Gaba—for that was the friend's name—could almost have passed for Vincente's twin.

Though Minnelli and Gaba maintained separate apartments, they were together so often that their friends always paired their names, as if they were a firmly attached couple—"Vincente and Lester." When Vincente was working at the Radio City Music Hall, Gaba could be found in the front row nearly every night, patiently waiting for him to finish his duties backstage. Though Gaba stayed in New York when Vincente left for M-G-M, Vincente did not suffer for lack of male companionship in his stylish house in the Hollywood Hills—at least two young actors confided to one of Judy's friends that they had had "a do" with him.

His colleagues at M-G-M did not need to know the details of what went on in his bedroom: most of them simply assumed that he was homosexual, not "marrying material," as one female member of the Freed Unit diplomatically phrased it. Not marrying material, in any case, was how he was generally perceived at the time he was directing *Meet Me in St. Louis*. Judy had heard the rumors, but she did not choose to believe them. To those who whispered that her new lover might be homosexual, her response was indignation. "It's not that at all!" she exclaimed. "It's just his artistic flair!"

|||

There were only two obstacles on the rosy road to matrimony. The first was an all-but-forgotten husband, David Rose, who delayed giving Judy a divorce, prompting an exasperated Roger Edens to write some new lyrics to David's *Holiday for Strings*:

> *Oh, see the little violins*
> *Enjoying sunshine at the shore.*
> *They're rid of David Rose, the bore,*
> *Who won't divorce his wife, and so*
> *Her life is at a standstill.*

Eventually David did consent, and on June 8, 1944, almost three years after he and Judy had stood before a sleepy justice of the peace in Las Vegas, a judge in Los Angeles severed the ties that bound them together. Judy was at last rid of David and his tiresome trains, always going somewhere, never arriving anywhere.

The second obstacle was not legal, but emotional. After several months, Joe Mankiewicz had come back into Judy's life. The affair that Joe was to say "just faded away" had not yet disappeared entirely, and in late spring Judy said good-bye to Vincente and resumed her romance with the man who still had first call on her affections.

Hurt and dismayed, Vincente was not too hurt to work with Judy again, however, and in July he directed her in the *Ziegfeld Follies,* a cinematic variety show that included everything from an Esther Williams water ballet to the only number Fred Astaire and Gene Kelly were ever to do together. Yet of all the film's varied and sometimes spectacular selections, Judy's ten-minute sketch—"A Great Lady Has 'An Interview' "—is the most surprising, unusual for her and even more unusual for M-G-M. It not only lampoons one of the studio's biggest stars, the stately Greer Garson, but it also satirizes the whole idea of stardom—the very ethos of M-G-M.

Affecting a grand manner and a pretentious accent, Judy's Great Lady, Madame Crematon, slithers around the set in a slinky white gown, holding a press conference in which she gives absurd answers to absurd questions. Though Roger Edens was its co-author, this delightfully wacky sketch bears the unmistakable stamp of Kay Thompson, Judy's newest mentor and the woman who, after Edens himself, was to have the greatest influence on her performing style.

If Vincente's model was Whistler, then Thompson's was Sarah Bernhardt, and, like Bernhardt, Thompson set out to become not only a star but a personality, a figure of such incandescent originality that she would outshine the ordinary twinklers who passed through the studio gates. Thus it was that Catherine Louise Fink, the blond, angular and long-faced daughter of a St. Louis jeweler, transformed herself into the sleek and dramatic Kay Thompson, flying into Culver City in the early forties like some exotic bird, a multicolored quetzal perhaps, to astonish the ordinary cardinals and mockingbirds already in residence. She was too exotic for Metro's taste, however, and instead of hiring her as a performer, Arthur Freed gave her a job as a singing coach. In her mid-thirties, Thompson had already enjoyed a full career as an arranger, as well as a singer.

Coached by Edens since she was thirteen, Judy did not need Thompson to teach her how to sing. What Thompson did was to push her singing to a new, higher level, giving it a canniness and sophistication it had not had before. Though it is impossible to pinpoint—it consisted of many small and subtle touches—Thompson's influence is most evident in Judy's increasing comfort with complicated arrangements and in her more kinetic delivery. Thompson made her more conscious of her movements, convincing her that singing involves not just the voice, but the entire body, that gestures and movements—the raising of an arm, the opening or closing of a hand, the expression on the face—are as important as tone, phrasing and volume. All that, and what Edens had taught her, too, Judy absorbed and, through some mysterious alchemy, turned into gold, accepting what suited her, rejecting what did not. She was always her own best teacher.

|||

By the end of July it was clear, even to Judy, that her affair with Joe had no more future in the summer than it had had in the previous winter. Joe was not about to divorce his wife to marry her, and their final days together had been no more than a fling, a kind of holiday before they both returned to less exciting partners. That was not the conclusion of their relationship, however, and just recalling their days together was to give pleasure to both of them for many years to come. "I guess I've had my share of affairs with women," Joe was later to say. "But they only exist as affairs with women. Every year, as I grow older, the memory of what we did and what we went through when we did it grows dimmer and dimmer. That isn't the case with Judy. I remember her as I would remember an emotion, a mood, an emotional experience that is an event."

Equally vivid was Judy's image of Joe, which, like an old photograph, wrapped in plastic and reverent good wishes, she pulled out from time to time to hold up and admire. More than Tyrone Power, Artie Shaw,

David Rose or any of the other men she had known or was to know, Joe occupied a continuing place in her heart. He was the love of her life— so she often said—and it was to him she seemed to be speaking when she slowly caressed, almost purred, the lyrics of one of her favorite songs of the forties—"Happiness Is a Thing Called Joe." In the fifties her friends Harold Arlen and Ira Gershwin wrote a new ballad for her, "The Man That Got Away." Asked to sing at Hollywood parties, she would fix her eyes on Joe, in a way that he alone would notice, and, borrowing Gershwin's mournful lyrics, remind him that, for her, no other love would ever be the same. Embarrassed, Joe would take her aside afterward and whisper crossly: "Come on! Cut the crap!" Judy would laugh, but refuse to obey. For her, Joe would always remain the man that got away.

Vincente was not to get away, and their work together in *Ziegfeld Follies* reintroduced Judy to some of his persuasive virtues. Even in her short segment he had distinguished himself, endowing her with the two qualities she most coveted, beauty and glamour. It was only natural, then, that when her next film, *The Clock,* ran into difficulties a few weeks later, it was to Vincente that she turned. Offering her the chance to play her first straight role—she was not required to sing a note—*The Clock* was the only movie she had ever lobbied for, her opportunity, she thought, to demonstrate her abilities as a dramatic actress. But now, in the waning days of August, it was in such deep trouble that it was in danger of being scrapped—unless, of course, she could convince Vincente to rush to the rescue.

Some blamed the picture's problems on Judy herself, who had made it no secret that she thought the director, the relatively inexperienced Fred Zinnemann, was not up to the job. "I don't know—he must be a good director," she told Freed, "but I just get nothing. We have no compatibility." In a conflict between a fledgling director and a major star, the star will always win, and on August 23, Freed, accepting the inevitable, fired Zinnemann and closed down the picture until another director could be found.

As far as Judy was concerned, that director had to be Vincente, and, with Freed's permission, she made her pitch to him over lunch at the Players Club. Whatever the club was serving that day, it could not have tasted as good as the sweet satisfaction Judy piled on Vincente's plate. A year earlier he had begged her not to drop out of *Meet Me in St. Louis,* and she had responded with a cold stare. Now she was pleading with him to save a picture she cared about. Such a big request from a woman who had just dumped him for another man! Rarely is a spurned lover offered such a gratifying present, and Vincente grabbed it. On September 1, *The Clock* resumed shooting with a new name stenciled on the director's chair—Mr. Minnelli.

Judy was right about Vincente: he was the ideal director for *The Clock,* perhaps the only one on the lot who could have prevented it from being drowned in a gush of sentimentality, the Metromush the studio ladled out so generously during World War II. Its teary-eyed plot, a whirlwind wartime romance, was familiar to anyone who went to the movies during those years. In New York on a two-day pass, a G.I. meets a girl in Pennsylvania Station. They fall in love, are separated, then find each other again and rush to get married, saying their good-byes as husband and wife in the same place they started, where the soldier catches a train that will carry him back to camp and, by implication, into battle. That was all there was, a patchwork of small and seemingly trivial dramas—just the sort of challenge Vincente had confronted in *Meet Me in St. Louis.*

Vincente began his rescue mission by introducing a whole cast of fascinating bit players: he was to become famous for the unusual attention he lavished on such small parts. He then gave a costarring role to a whole new character, New York itself. Meticulously re-created on Culver City soundstages, the city was more than a passive backdrop for romance; it became a lively participant, pushing the lovers together in some scenes, separating them in others. When shooting ended on November 21, it was apparent that Vincente's salvage operation had succeeded. Although *The Clock* does not merit the kind of superlatives that are attached to *Meet Me in St. Louis,* it is, at its best, so good, as James Agee, the era's most astute film critic, phrased it, that "it inspires ingratitude for not being great."

If it was not great, *The Clock* was good enough to have justified Judy's strenuous exertions on its behalf. It did exactly what she had hoped it would do, demonstrating "for the first time beyond anybody's doubt"—to quote Agee again—"that Judy Garland can be a very sensitive actress. In this film Miss Garland can handle every emotion in sight, in any size and shape, and the audience along with it." Joe Mankiewicz had been right: given a chance, Judy could be a fine, possibly even great, actress. What Joe had not reckoned with was the corollary to that proposition: she needed Vincente Minnelli to show her how to do it.

III

Not long after *The Clock* finished filming, Vincente received a gift from Judy. It was a clock—a real clock—and attached to it was a note. "Whenever you look to see what time it is—I hope you'll remember 'the Clock,' " she had written. "You know how much the picture meant to me—and only *you* could give me the confidence I so badly needed. If the picture is a success (and I think it's a cinch) my darling Vincente is responsible for the whole god damned thing." In fact, she had shown her appreciation from the day he took over, all but smothering him with gratitude. Gratitude is sometimes mistaken for love, and it is hard to say which one Judy felt. The result was the same in either case: she returned his affections, and after a brief and, for Vincente, painful detour, they once again were speeding down the road to matrimony.

This time their romance was not a secret, and during breaks in filming of *The Clock* they could be seen huddled together, deep in conversation. So smitten were they that at least once, when they thought no one was around, they moved beyond mere talk. Returning to the set during lunch hour, three extras, dressed as sailors for a subway crowd scene, were astonished to glimpse them making love in a darkened alcove. Quietly backing away, the trio took a vow of silence. "We will never say a word," said one. "We didn't see this." But the light operators, who often ate their sandwiches where they worked, on the catwalks high above the stage, did see it and made no such pledge. Within seconds everyone in the studio seemed to know what had transpired in that shadowy alcove. "Is it true?" one of the extras was asked when he walked into the music department a few minutes later. "Was Judy really going down on Vincente Minnelli on the subway set?"

Judy and Vincente were as visibly entwined as any couple could be, and at the end of November they embarked on a kind of pre-honeymoon honeymoon, a luxurious trip east, courtesy of M-G-M, for the New York opening of *Meet Me in St. Louis.* Although Judy had been there many times before, Vincente showed her a new side of Manhattan, introducing her to theater friends like Richard Rodgers and taking her to the actual spots where much of the action in *The Clock* was supposed to have occurred—the Metropolitan Museum, the Central Park zoo, an Italian restaurant in Times Square. Her pleasure was his pleasure, and he saw New York afresh through her enthusiastic eyes. When they returned to Los Angeles in early December, he continued his tutorial, ushering her through art galleries and antique showrooms and observing with joy her awakening interest in antiques, painting and jewelry—all the things that gave him enjoyment.

They had begun the year in bitter conflict. They ended it with a midnight kiss at Jack and Mary Benny's New Year's Eve party, in the company of a hundred other stars and studio executives. A week later, on January 9, 1945, just a few days before Judy was to begin work on a musical western titled *The Harvey Girls,* her first picture without Vincente since *Girl Crazy,* they announced what many had already guessed: they were engaged to be married.

|||

When he was a boy in Ohio, Vincente had experienced his epiphany: watching his mother dance around the stage of the Minnelli Brothers Tent Theater in a costume he himself had designed. His proudest moment, he called that childhood triumph, which was the key to everything that followed. Like Joe Mankiewicz, his polar opposite in so many other respects, he was a natural-born Pygmalion, a man whose ruling passion was the molding and nurturing of exceptional women. "Vincente loved someone he could make beautiful, someone he could create," said his friend Lena Horne. "He loved dressing women." Until he entered into his affair with Judy, Horne herself had been his most conspicuous protégée. Not only did he show her off to advantage on the screen, as the sensuous seductress in *Cabin in the Sky,* but he also gave her an education in living off the screen, picking books for her to read and paintings for her to look at—even teaching her the right knives and forks to use at dinner.

Some women might have resented such interference. Judy, like Horne, accepted it eagerly. She longed to be Vincente's Galatea, just as she had been Joe's. Whereas Joe had instructed her in matters of concern to intellectuals, however, Vincente unlocked the secrets of sophistication, beauty and elegance—things she really cared about. And whereas Joe had denied her his unwavering attention, Vincente concentrated on her as obsessively as he did on his work. "Vincente saw something in Judy that nobody else did," said Irene Sharaff. "I think he was truly in love with her. But I think she was in love with the idea that somebody took her seriously."

Old habits die hard, and the engagement ring on Judy's finger did not deter her from secretly entertaining other men. Her most ardent pursuer during the winter of 1945 was another man who arrived festooned with superlatives—Orson Welles. Still the dashing boy genius who had created *Citizen Kane,* Welles possessed attractions enough for any woman. But an affair with him carried a titillating bonus for Judy, and it must have thrilled her to be able to entice Welles away, if only briefly, from one of Hollywood's true sex goddesses—his wife, the supernaturally beautiful Rita Hayworth.

Their dalliance was, in any event, a dangerous game for both of them. The jealous and watchful Hayworth came close to discovering it when she spied a huge bouquet of white flowers in Welles's car, a gift for Judy. Naturally assuming the flowers were meant for her, the smiling Hayworth was about to retrieve them when Welles's quick-witted secretary, who knew the truth, ran out and removed his card to Judy, then handed the flowers to Hayworth, as if they had been meant for her all along. A similar mix-up almost brought disaster when Judy, confusing her dates, invited both fiancé and lover, Vincente and Welles, to dinner on the same night. Realizing her mistake only when she heard Vincente's car in her driveway, she rushed out the door with Dorothy Ponedel before Welles could arrive too. The stove was smoking, Ponedel told Vincente—they would have to eat in a restaurant.

|||

Louis B. Mayer had been against all of Judy's previous lovers, complaining that they were married, divorced or too old. Vincente, who, at forty-two, was the oldest of them all, was, by contrast, embraced as if he were the son-in-law Mayer had always hoped for. The reason, as usual, had more to do with dollars and cents than paternal feeling. She missed the sound of applause, Judy had told Louella Parsons, and when her contract expired in 1947, she would leave Metro for Broadway. Such news from one of the studio's biggest moneymakers had turned faces gray in the Thalberg Building, and though it could not force her to sign a new contract, Metro could give her a helpful push by encouraging her to marry Vincente. From the studio's point of view, he was the ideal suitor. How could she star on Broadway, after all, if she was happily attached to an M-G-M director?

Metro had yet another reason for approving the union. Though she had been a model of good behavior during the filming of *The Clock*, Judy was still a shaky reed on which to hang a major musical. A quiet and reliable husband like Vincente would be a steadying influence, the studio reasoned—would "straighten her out," as Lucille Ryman Carroll, the head of Metro's talent department, phrased it. As always, Louella Parsons was chosen to convey the corporate line to the rest of the world. Everyone at M-G-M, Parsons assured her readers, was delighted with the Garland-Minnelli alliance. "They say that Judy is a different girl, happy as she can be," she burbled.

"I want Mr. Mayer of my studio to be at my wedding if I get married," Judy had said before she became the wife of David Rose. But flattering words had not mollified the furious Mayer. This time he not only showed up, like a beaming father, to give the bride away, but he also presented the happy couple with a munificent wedding present— three months away from the studio for a honeymoon in New York. Their first night as man and wife was to be spent rushing eastward on the Super Chief. If Judy could not be on Broadway herself, she could at least be close to it.

The wedding ceremony took place, as scheduled, at three o'clock on the afternoon of Friday, June 15, in Judy's mother's house in the

Wilshire district—Ethel had long since moved from Stone Canyon Road. Metro's chief costume designer, Irene Gibbons, had designed Judy's dress, a smoky-gray jersey with pink-pearl beading to match her pearl engagement ring. Betty Asher was Judy's bridesmaid, and Ira Gershwin was Vincente's best man. The Reverend William E. Roberts of the Beverly Hills Community Church performed the service, at the end of which he held out a wooden staff that was to be grasped, as a symbol of the just solemnized union, by the four people standing in front of him: the bridesmaid, the best man and the bride and groom. All four did as they were directed. Then, seemingly from nowhere, emerged a fifth hand—Mayer's—to clutch the knob at the very top of the staff. "We were now man and wife in the eyes of God," said Vincente. "But what's more, we also had the blessing of a man upstairs who in many instilled far greater dread."

|||

"These were our happiest times," Vincente was to say of the first months of their marriage. Arriving in Manhattan on the morning of June 18, the newlyweds were soon eating breakfast in their honeymoon retreat, a three-story penthouse on tony Sutton Place, with terrace gardens and expansive views of the East River below. "More than halfway to heaven," murmured an admiring friend. So it was; so were they. "Right away," said Judy, "we did as we had planned—just moved in and pretended to be New Yorkers."

It was an exciting time to be in New York, which was very much the exuberant city Vincente had portrayed in *The Clock*. Germany had surrendered in May, and just two days after Judy and Vincente stepped off their train, four million jubilant New Yorkers lined the streets to welcome home General Eisenhower, the conquering commander. In August Japan also called it quits, bringing more crowds and parades and triumphant flags. Never again would that city of tall towers and even taller egos be enveloped in such a halo of friendship and good feeling. "There were no strangers in New York yesterday," observed a *New York Times* reporter the day after Japan's surrender.

Expectation was in the very air that victorious summer, as hopes long dormant suddenly revived and old lives were exchanged for new. Inhaling the rich oxygen of promise and possibility in her cottage in the sky, Judy also looked forward to a fresh start, a life free of the drugs that had imprisoned her for so many years. Walking by the East River with Vincente, she asked him to hold her hand. Then, with her other hand, she threw a small object into the rushing water—a vial of her pills. She, too, had declared victory over a cruel and insidious foe.

|||

"Whenever I came to New York before," said Judy, "I lived in a hotel—for two weeks perhaps—and rushed, rushed, rushed." On this visit she was able to slow down and enjoy herself, to be a woman of leisure with money to spend and a maid, a cook and a devoted husband to look after her. Joining in Metro's campaign to convince her to sign another contract, the usually dour Nick Schenck pasted a smile on his face and descended from his Times Square office to take her shopping at Tiffany's. "Metro wants to buy you a wedding present, Judy. Pick out something you like." Like a good girl, taught never to order the most expensive dish on the menu, Judy chose a simple gold brooch. "Nonsense!" thundered Schenck. "You must choose something much gayer." "Much more expensive" was what he really meant, and after some hesitation Judy selected a bracelet of square diamonds and emeralds, with a pin to match. It was then the groom's turn. After a similar good-mannered pause, Vincente pointed to a gold wristwatch, and that became his gift from Leo the Lion.

On their trip the previous year, Judy had met a few of Vincente's friends. Now she met the rest, including his old companion, Lester Gaba, who joined them for dinner one night. Seeing the man he obviously still loved so firmly attached to someone else was an unsettling experience for Gaba. Recalling the evening years later, he was, indeed, so saddened that tears came to his eyes. "Vincente was the only big thing in his life, and Lester was crushed," said Gaba's friend James Loyd.

But Gaba was the only one unhappy with Vincente's wife. Amazed at how quickly she won hearts, Vincente perceived that, without even trying very hard, Judy could simply will people into adoring her. "She'd been doing it all her life with far larger audiences. When all else failed—

the wit, the self-effacement, the warmth and the genuine concern for others—she fell back on her greatest weapon. How can you resist a woman when she shows you her vulnerability?" No one could. When the visitors from California strolled around the city, ordinary New Yorkers greeted her as if she actually were the girl next door. "Hi ya, Judy!" a truck driver might shout. "Howza kid?" Or, squinting as if she spied a friend she had not seen for years, a stooped old woman might ask, "Is that you, Judy?"

Denying a newspaper report that she and Vincente planned to adopt a child, Judy said that they hoped to have a baby of their own someday. "And another," she added defiantly. "And another. Until we have a good-sized family." That someday was to arrive sooner than anyone, including Judy, had anticipated. At the end of August, a week or so before they were to return to Los Angeles, she discovered she was pregnant—really pregnant this time. Phoning California, Judy said, "I'm going to have a baby, Mama." Remembering how her mother had insisted on an abortion when she was married to David Rose, she then asked a question that should have given even the thick-skinned Ethel pause: "Do you mind?"

|||

To Judy's happy surprise, however, both Ethel and Metro professed delight with her news. Hoping to use her once more before her pregnancy began to show, the studio speeded up its timetable and rushed her into her next project, a biography of Jerome Kern titled *Till the Clouds Roll By*. The picture was not so much the story of Kern's life—a woefully miscast Robert Walker played the composer—as it was an excuse for a parade of his glorious songs, which were sung by just about everybody on the Metro payroll who could carry a tune. With just three songs, Judy's part was relatively small, and Metro, still seeking to smile her into a contract, assigned Vincente to direct her, leaving Richard Whorf, one of the studio's traffic-cop directors, to handle everyone else. Beginning rehearsals on September 17, about two weeks after her return from New York, Judy went before the cameras in early October.

Clever cameramen and ingenious costume designers managed to disguise her increasingly delicate condition. But delicate it was, and after one arduous scene Judy told Dorothy Ponedel that "if I have to do this again, I don't think I can make it, because whoever is in my belly is going to come right through my navel." Judy's work ended on November 7—just in time. If filming had gone on much longer, no amount of camouflage could have hidden the fact that she was in the fifth month of her pregnancy; her baby was expected in March.

Liberated from a studio schedule, Judy was then free to prepare for a role she had long wanted, that of mother. Many newly marrieds start life in a new home. Judy and Vincente chose to stay put in his hilltop pink stucco at 8850 Evanview Drive, with its aviator's views of Los Angeles. "I like it so much I didn't want to go to a new place," explained Judy. To make it big enough for three, they bought the vacant lots on either side and expanded, building a nursery for the baby and, for Judy, a huge bathroom and dressing room, which Vincente decorated with antique glass walls and a fur-covered chaise longue. Judy's piano sat next to the bay window in the living room, which Vincente had painted dark green and furnished with black marble tables, white marble lamps and bright chintz couches.

Though she was no longer the naive teenager of her first marriage, Judy was still unable to manage servants—a cook, a housekeeper, a nurse and a chauffeur—leaving Vincente to impose what little discipline existed on Evanview Drive. A child of whim and short attention span, as Vincente described her, Judy sometimes ignored the servants to play housewife herself, scrubbing the kitchen floor one day, making chicken fricassee the next, baking a cake the day after that. Whatever she cooked was like an M-G-M production, requiring the dirtying of nearly every pot and pan on the shelves and a full crew to clean up. Vincente watched her attempts to play Betty Crocker with a mixture of amusement, resignation and dismay. His part of the household chores, he learned, was to write good reviews, passing out at least ten compliments for each dish she set in front of him. "Her desire for constant approval was pathological," he sadly concluded.

Afraid that she would lose her baby, or that it would otherwise be harmed, Judy stayed off pills, steadfastly keeping the pledge she had made in New York. "I just don't know how it's ever going to work out," she confessed to Dorothy Walsh. "I'm scared to death." But the effort exacted a price, and worry and strain, along, perhaps, with the pains of withdrawal, whirled her downward into depression. A couple of months before the birth was expected, Hedda Hopper decided to give her an unusual shower—men only, all the male stars, producers, directors and technicians Judy had worked with during her busy career. Although Hopper received an enthusiastic response—one guest was going to bring a miniature baby grand piano for the nursery—she was forced to cancel the party when Ethel phoned to say that the excitement would be too much for Judy. Writing Hopper a note of apology, Judy herself said that she would have been a dull guest of honor. "Forgive me, and after March I'll be rarin' to go. I'll be my old self again."

On the afternoon of Friday, March 8, 1946, she entered Cedars of Lebanon Hospital for a cesarean section, which was scheduled for the following Tuesday, March 12. That morning, at 7:58, she gave birth to a girl weighing six pounds, ten and a half ounces. Liza, she was named. When the pregnancy had been announced the previous summer, some at Metro, judging Vincente only by his effeminate mannerisms, had joked that it must have been the result of immaculate conception. But the tiny girl in the crib was not the product of a miracle. With dark hair, long lashes and brown eyes as big and inquisitive as a lemur's, she was, clearly and unequivocally, Vincente's child—"the most beautiful baby in the nursery," he proudly proclaimed.

|||

As soon as her baby was born, she would be raring to go, Judy had promised. But a month later she was still confined to her bed, the result of follow-up surgery to correct a problem caused by the cesarean and also of what seems to have been severe postpartum depression. While there was no reason for alarm, Louella Parsons wrote in her column, Judy had gone through "a really miserable time." Two weeks later, at the end of April, Judy did get up—too soon, as it turned out. Collapsing on a sidewalk in Beverly Hills, she was carried into a music store, where she fainted again. Ordering her back to bed, her doctor instructed her to remain there until she was fully recovered. There were so many rumors about her circulating in the weeks that followed—"the impression was given that my health was being despaired of," Judy complained—that she gave an interview to the *Los Angeles Times* just to say that she was all right. "Actually," she asserted, "I haven't felt much better than now during my whole life."

By July she was, in fact, well enough to sing on the radio and at a memorial in the Hollywood Bowl honoring Jerome Kern, who had died of a cerebral hemorrhage the previous November. By fall she seemed to have regained her strength, inviting the fan magazines to Evanview Drive to photograph her with her baby. "She really loves the water," Judy assured one reporter who watched as she gave Liza her daily bath. "I expect she'll be at least a champion swimmer." But that aquatic exercise was mostly for show. Liza's nurse usually handled such chores, and when the time finally came for the nurse to have a day off, Judy admitted to having stage fright, terrified and excited both at the prospect of spending her first day alone with her six-month-old.

For a whole year, since she had finished her part in *Till the Clouds Roll By*, Judy had not had to worry about the studio. Not since she was a baby herself had she been allowed the luxury of so much idleness. That undemanding existence was soon to end. In November she gave in to Metro's pleas and signed a new five-year contract that would carry her all the way into the 1950s. The people in the Thalberg Building had been correct in thinking that marriage would confine her to California: how could she leave both husband and baby for the bright lights of Broadway? The studio was so eager to have her before the cameras again that it tore up her old contract, which had a year to run, and almost doubled her salary, boosting her from $3,000 a week to nearly $6,000, a sum comparable to the salaries paid other top Metro stars and more than double the $2,500 Vincente was making. "She's always said M-G-M was home," Parsons told her readers, "and when you get right down to it, there's still no place like home, even to a movie star."

|||

M-G-M was indeed home. By the fall of 1946 Judy had worked there eleven years, nearly half her life. She had grown up inside its protective walls, and, like a princess of a reigning house, she had navigated the perilous passage through adolescence, broken love affairs and two marriages in full view of her colleagues. But if Metro had protected her and often catered to her, it had also imprisoned her. Nick Schenck could have given her a hundred Tiffany bracelets—could have showered her with all the treasures in Ali Baba's cave, for that matter—and it would not have made any difference: she would still be subjected to early morning calls, unrelenting pressures and what she thought were condescending attitudes. Inside those walls she would forever remain the ugly duckling, Mr. Mayer's little hunchback. The damage to her ego had been done years before, and as long as she remained at M-G-M it was past curing.

All that anger, so long festering, so long suppressed, burst out within weeks, perhaps even days, of the signing of her new contract. Almost immediately she regretted having agreed to it. With a few strokes of the pen, she seemed to believe, she had turned the key to her own prison cell. "The tension that had been building up in me against the studio suddenly seemed to have hit the boiling point" was how she herself described her emotions. "Every day when I went to work it was with tears in my eyes, resistance in my heart and mind. It gave me no pleasure."

The inevitable explosion occurred when she started her next picture, a musical version of S. N. Behrman's Broadway play *The Pirate*. A Technicolor romp along the old Spanish Main, *The Pirate* was a comedy of mistaken identities: a retired pirate, Mack the Black, who pretends to be a pillar of Caribbean society; a pretty girl, Manuela, who has fallen in love with the romantic Mack of legend, unaware that he is really the middle-aged bore her family has demanded she marry; and a conceited actor, Serafin, who makes believes he is Mack to win the girl's love. Judy was to play Manuela; Gene Kelly was the actor who pretended to be Mack; and Walter Slezak, an excellent character actor, was the real Mack. Best of all, as far as Judy was concerned, was the director—Vincente, of course. *The Pirate* sounded like such fun, said Vincente, that she was "quite certain she'd fly through the filming."

In fact, she could scarcely crawl through it. When she showed up for her first day of prerecording on December 27—songs were always recorded before shooting began, then lip-synched in front of the cameras—she was so frail and depressed that the recordings had to be junked. Partly because of her frequent absences, actual filming did not begin until well into 1947—February 17, to be exact. In all, Judy was to be gone ninety-nine days out of the 135 in the rehearsal and shooting schedule. Three years earlier, it had been Al Jennings, the assistant director of *Meet Me in St. Louis,* who had been awakened in the middle of the night with the news that Judy would not be in the next day. Now it was the turn of Wallace Worsley, *The Pirate*'s assistant director. At least two or three times a week he would be jolted out of sleep to hear her say, "I don't feel well—I won't be able to come in."

Forgotten was her pledge to stay off pills. Sometimes she appeared on the set in a barbiturate stupor. After keeping several hundred extras waiting for two hours, for instance, she arrived one morning in such a daze that she appeared to be sleepwalking, wandering aimlessly around the set until, twenty minutes later, she informed Vincente that she was going home. Other times amphetamines had the reverse effect, making her tense and occasionally even paranoid. Called upon to dance around open fires in one scene, Judy jumped across the stage in terror. "I'm going to burn to death!" she shouted. "They want me to burn to death!" Finally she was led away—crying, laughing, altogether hysterical.

She suffered a similar attack of paranoia the day Hedda Hopper visited the set. Shaking with fright, Judy declared that everyone who had once loved her had turned against her, claiming that Ethel had gone so far as to tap her telephone line. "She is doing everything in her power to destroy me," Judy said of her mother. Once again she had to be taken away—actually carried out this time—still wearing her makeup and costume, then driven home to be put into bed.

The feeling of betrayal was further fueled by a very real cause for complaint, a developing collaboration between Vincente and Gene Kelly that pointedly excluded her. No longer the green newcomer he had been when he played opposite her in *For Me and My Gal,* Kelly was now a veteran full of ideas for the picture and, more important from Judy's point of view, for the expansion of his role. Hurt at being left out of their chummy little club—they did not want to burden her, Vincente lamely explained—Judy accused them of having a lot of fun, but ignoring her. To retaliate against Vincente, the principal culprit in her eyes, she asked Kelly to help stage her numbers as well as his own—and to disregard Vincente while he was doing it. "How," wondered a puzzled Vincente, "had we come to this state of affairs where suddenly I could do nothing right in Judy's eyes?"

Good directors and film editors have salvaged many weak performances with judicious cutting, and Judy's may have been helped by such excisions. Dropped, never to reappear, were at least two numbers that fell short of her usual high standard. What helped her, however, was to hurt the picture. The loss of those numbers, combined with Kelly's voracious scene-grabbing, threw the entire movie off balance; Manuela, who should have been at the center, became little more than a secondary character. Judy's problems were reflected not in what was on the screen, but in what was missing.

Yet even if Judy had been Judy—the Judy of her earlier pictures—*The Pirate* would have been irretrievably flawed. With a few exceptions, Cole Porter's songs lacked his trademark wit and brio, while Vincente's direction veered dangerously toward the precious and exotic, allowing sumptuous sets and costumes to overshadow his story. Gorgeous to look at, the picture never quite comes together: it has frenetic movement, but no real energy.

It had no energy at the box office either. *The Pirate* was the only picture Judy was ever to make that failed to yield Metro a profit. "Vincente and I honestly believed we were being so dazzlingly brilliant and clever," said Kelly, "that everybody would fall at our feet and swoon clean away in delight and ecstasy—as they kissed each of our toes in appreciation for this wondrous new musical we'd given them. Well, we were wrong." They did not have to wait long to find out just how wrong. "Would have fallen asleep," was the comment scrawled on one preview card, "were it not for all the noise produced on the screen."

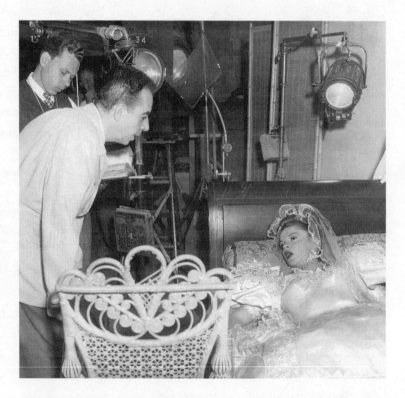

*Husband and wife, director and star,
on the set of The Pirate*

CHAPTER 9

A Hell in Heaven

o Judy, Joe Mankiewicz observed, a man meant more than love and companionship: he was her guard and protector, her bulwark against a world ever eager to exploit her spectacular gifts. She had thought that Vincente, who had brought out her beauty in *Meet Me in St. Louis,* her acting ability in *The Clock* and her sly humor in *Ziegfeld Follies,* was such a man. Now, in the weeks following the signing of her new contract, her confidence in him evaporated, vanishing so swiftly that Vincente was left stunned, shaking his head in wonderment. Part of the reason may have been that she held him responsible for the contract, that document that destroyed her dreams of Broadway glory. And indirectly he was: had it not been for Vincente—and little Liza, too, of course—she would have been looking forward to the roar of applause rather than the jangle of an alarm clock, summoning her to a job she had grown to hate and fear. Things had become so bad, she told Dorothy Ponedel, that every time she entered the studio gates she felt like vomiting.

Until *The Pirate,* the Minnellis had seen only the benefits of their professional partnership. In the winter of 1947, as Judy's emotional problems worsened, they began to see the drawbacks. The abrupt reversal was probably harder on Vincente, who suddenly found himself torn between two allegiances, to his wife on the one hand, to his Metro career on the other. His wife was in trouble, but if *The Pirate* failed, his career might also be in jeopardy. After three successful pictures, he had already suffered a bad fall with a costly curiosity called *Yolanda and the Thief.* If he now stumbled a second time, with his very next picture, Metro might agree with some of his detractors, who thought his taste too rarefied and arty for a mass audience, and never again entrust him with a big production. How frustrating and dismaying it must have been, then, for Vincente to watch Judy's erratic behavior and to realize that his future rested, as it had at the start of *Meet Me in St. Louis,* in her unsteady hands. "As director, I should have insisted on her fulfilling her assignment," he said. "As concerned husband, I couldn't. So I made excuses."

Those were harrowing months for him, "agonizing times," as he later recalled. Wallace Worsley could—and finally did—refuse to pick up the phone when Judy called after midnight with news of a migraine or stomachache that would keep her away from the cameras. Vincente did not have such a luxury. Her troubles were his as well. The first to see a storm approaching, he was also the last to see it leave. Morning to night, night to morning, his anxiety never lifted. At least twice, he and Judy were halfway to Culver City when she forced him to return home. Several times she arrived at the studio, worked for an hour or so, then asked for the studio doctor, complaining that she was not well.

If Vincente squirmed under his competing obligations, so did Judy. In her eyes, he was no longer a husband in whom she could confide, but the voice of a despised authority, the drill sergeant pounding on her dressing room door and rudely shouting: "Miss Garland, we'd like to have you on the set, please." Vincente never used her first name in front of the cast and crew. Almost overnight he had been transformed from protector to persecutor; he was the man from Metro, a studio surrogate who shared her house and bed. On Evanview Drive she felt truly alone only when she closed the door to her dressing room and bath. Those two rooms became her hideaway, a place where she could relax and lie quiet and undisturbed in the arms of her fur-covered chaise longue.

|||

By those who possess it, privacy is taken for granted, like the air they breathe or the water they drink. But to Judy, who had never known it, it was a treasure denied. For as long as she could remember she had been under surveillance, first by her mother, then by Mayer and his operatives, and now by Vincente. Judy was not imagining the prying eyes that surrounded her: they were real, everywhere she looked, a whole tapestry of them—piercing, suspicious, accusing. Now, as her problems piled higher and higher, those eyes were joined by equally inquisitive ears. Hedda Hopper had assumed that Judy was having delusions when she said her mother was tapping her telephone. In fact, someone, though not Ethel, was indeed listening.

Kathryn Grayson, who was on the other end of some of those conversations, could have testified to that. Late at night, Judy would sometimes wake her, begging her to come and sit with her. Moved by the desperate tone in her voice, Grayson would say yes. But within minutes, before she could dress and leave her house, Grayson would receive a second call, this time from either Ida Koverman or Mayer's henchman Benny Thau. "Kathryn, don't go," one or the other would sternly command. "Do Judy a favor and do yourself a favor. You have to get up at six o'clock and be at the studio at seven. You can't stay over there until two or three or four o'clock in the morning. You can't help Judy. The situation can only drag you down." Following orders, Grayson obediently returned to bed.

Who was the spy? Who alerted Metro the minute Judy put down the phone? When Grayson inquired, she was politely told to mind her own business. There were, however, only two possibilities: either someone in Judy's house, Vincente most likely, was eavesdropping; or Metro was monitoring Judy's calls with a telephone tap. Taps were illegal, of course, but the studio that made it a practice to examine its stars' personal telegrams, which was also against the law, would not have scrupled to tap their phones as well. In the Los Angeles of the thirties and forties, M-G-M did exactly what it wanted. Was Metro spying? Or was Vincente? The answer remains a mystery, but the result does not: Metro knew almost every move Judy made, every word she uttered.

Caught between his rival loyalties, Vincente did what he frequently did in confusing and ambiguous situations: he tried to muddle through, doing his best to satisfy both sides. When Judy was unable to work, he shot around her. When she was able—and she had many good days—he shot as much as he could, as fast as he could. If such a resigned and passive course satisfied M-G-M, which eventually got its picture, it did nothing for Judy, whose condition seemed to deteriorate daily. With encouragement from Vincente, who often drove her to sessions, she returned to Dr. Simmel, her analyst from the Joe Mankiewicz days. Since Simmel did not treat patients outside his office, Louis B. Mayer, who not long before had derided Simmel and all other disciples of Freud as so many quacks, also hired a second analyst, Frederick Hacker, to keep her calm on the set. Simmel was still unable to do her much good, however, and Hacker, a smarmy young Viennese who loved to gossip about his famous patients, was not there to provide lasting help, but merely to prevent her from falling apart before the picture was completed.

"The mind is its own place," wrote Milton, "and in itself / Can make a Heav'n of Hell, a Hell of Heav'n." And wherever she went, whatever she did, hell—a hell of her own manufacture—was Judy's home in that bleak year of 1947. Her friend Lee Gershwin, Ira's wife, caught a glimpse of the penal fires encircling her when Judy came knocking at her door one night, asking for a place to sleep after a fearful argument with Vincente. Lying on the couch in the Gershwins' spare room, with Lee trying to comfort her by stroking her arm, Judy began screaming—a sound of pain, torment and despair, a keening for all that was wrong in her life, that continued until she fell asleep. Muddling through, as Vincente was attempting to do, was no longer good enough for his ailing wife. To anyone who bothered to look, nothing could have been plainer: Judy was suffering a breakdown. She did not need a smooth-talking psychoanalyst to hold her hand on the set; she required several months in a good clinic, as Karl Menninger had suggested four years earlier.

|||

As it approached its second anniversary, the Minnelli marriage would most likely have been on shaky ground even had Judy not suffered a breakdown. The skeptics had been right all along—Judy and Vincente were an odd and, in the long run, ill-matched couple. Apart from the tiny girl in the nursery, they had little in common except the work that had brought them together. Now they did not have even that, and all that remained were the things that divided them, from an age gap of nearly two decades to Vincente's uncertain sexuality: neither one, the evidence suggests, received much sexual satisfaction from the other. The result was the usual friction between a husband and wife who can no longer get along, and both made frequent use of the Gershwins' spare room. Sometimes Vincente would leave Evanview Road in a fury; sometimes Judy would. "After all," she would say sarcastically, "this is your house."

By the beginning of February their relationship was showing such visible strain that Louella Parsons, who had been one of the first to give it her blessing, used her column to rebut rumors that they had separated. "Separated my eye," she indignantly declared. "Those two are in love. It's only the people who really are in love who quarrel now and then." Louella was not altogether wrong. It was true that Judy and Vincente had not separated; but it was also true that the ties that bound them together were beginning to unravel. Indeed, those bonds were already loose enough to allow both of them clandestine outside romances.

Judy, for her part, engaged in a brief but spirited affair with Yul Brynner, an aspiring Russian actor who was everything Vincente was not—young, handsome, athletic and consummately virile. The male lead in a play called *Lute Song,* a musical fantasy set in China, Brynner had already been pounced on by several Hollywood stars, Joan Crawford among them; but Judy, according to Brynner's son and biographer, was the only one he actually loved. Both apparently did their best to keep the romance quiet, but to those who could read between the lines, reliable old Louella said all that needed to be said when she reported that Judy longed to make a movie of *Lute Song*—with Brynner, of course, as her costar. In any event, Vincente, who talked in his memoir of Judy's "intense infatuations," almost certainly knew what was going on.

Judy was soon to know what was going on in Vincente's love life as well. Shortly before *The Pirate* finished shooting, she returned home unexpectedly and walked into their bedroom to change clothes before crawling wearily into bed. But that, she soon realized, was impossible, for the bed was fully occupied. Locked in loving embrace were two familiar male figures: Vincente and a man who worked for them. Violence would have been the natural reaction of most people who came upon a spouse in such a compromising position—in flagrante delicto, to use the familiar Latin phrase. But Judy's anger was directed only against herself, and the only blood she spilled was her own. Running into her hideaway, the beautiful bathroom Vincente had designed for her, she started hacking at her wrists with a razor or some other sharp object, continuing until Vincente, jumping from the bed and rushing after her, grabbed it away.

Vincente had stopped her before she could do herself much harm, and Judy's injuries were mostly emotional. When she appeared at the studio a day or so later, the bandages on her wrists were the only visible reminder of that tawdry drama. Feeling that she could not keep such a corrosive secret to herself, however, Judy did confide in another actress, who, over time, sent the tale of her horrifying discovery echoing through the Hollywood Hills. Eventually it reached the ears of Jacqueline Susann, who concocted a similar surprise for Neely O'Hara, the character she modeled after Judy in *Valley of the Dolls,* her bestselling potboiler of the mid-sixties. But Susann's fictional account is gray and pallid compared with the one Judy related to her friend at Metro. Listening with mounting indignation, the friend angrily declared: "You should have slashed *his* throat, not your wrists."

|||

Those who have never suffered a nervous breakdown—or a "major depressive episode," in current psychiatric jargon—can scarcely comprehend what it means. Those who have experienced it speak of bouts of uncontrollable weeping, an inability to sleep and a lethargy so profound that the smallest and most routine exertions, such as bathing and dress-ing, become onerous chores, while larger ones, such as going to work, become as daunting as a climb up Everest. Unable to talk or listen, read or write, many do nothing but lie in bed all day, staring at the ceiling. The world on the other side of their bedroom door becomes an un-mapped continent, an Arabia Deserta, that threatens danger with every step. "The mind begins to feel aggrieved, stricken, and the muddied thought processes register the distress of an organ in convulsion" was how the novelist William Styron described his own breakdown. "It is a storm indeed, but a storm of murk."

Judy had been trapped in the middle of such dark and impenetrable clouds since the final weeks of 1946, when she signed her new Metro contract. Now, in the aftermath of the astonishing scene in her bed-room, she was whirled into even deeper despair. "Judy Garland is a very sick girl and has suffered a complete nervous collapse," Louella Parsons reported on July 12, two days after Judy finished shooting her scenes in *The Pirate*. Parsons was not exaggerating. Now, at long last, Judy was al-lowed to go where she should have gone at the beginning of the year—into a psychiatric clinic. "Mama went away for a little while," Vincente explained to Liza. "But she'll be back very soon."

Several miles southwest of Beverly Hills, Las Campanas, the clinic she checked into, appeared pleasant enough, with rolling lawns, trees and private bungalows. But it was not the Beverly Wilshire or the Waldorf-Astoria, and early every morning Judy was awakened by a nurse rummaging through her bungalow, searching for contraband—pills and liquor. Shy and self-conscious at first, Judy eventually wan-dered out onto the lawn, where she discovered, to her surprise, that most of the other patients were just like her, not crazy, but, in her words, "desperately and impossibly exhausted."

She requested and was refused permission to see Liza. After much insisting on her part, however, as well as much whispering on the part of the doctors, her baby was driven down from Los Angeles for an emotional reunion—an outpouring of kisses, tears and laughter. It was clear that Liza, just sixteen months, had been as lonely for her mother as her mother had been for her, and when they were forced to say good-bye, Judy lay on her bed and wept. "There have been many blue moments in my life," she recalled, "but I never remember having such a feeling. It's hard to believe, but I almost literally died of anguish."

In those days there were no drugs to fight depression—the first antidepressant, Iproniazid, did not come on to the market until 1957—and whatever therapy Judy was receiving at Las Campanas was not doing her much good. On the recommendation of her newest psychiatrist, Dr. Herbert Kupper, she therefore left Las Campanas after a couple of weeks and traveled east to the Austen Riggs Foundation, a more serious clinic in the town of Stockbridge, in the Berkshire Mountains of western Massachusetts.

Unlike Las Campanas, Riggs seemed the ideal place for a successful treatment. It was in the very center of the kind of small town Judy professed to like—a town so pretty, in fact, that it might have been a product of Metro's art department—and Dr. Robert P. Knight, who treated her, was the kind of doctor she seemed to need. He was an esteemed alumnus of the Menninger Clinic—the "premier Menninger therapist and analyst," according to one history. Unlike the German-accented analysts of Los Angeles, he was a friendly, sympathetic Midwesterner, a good-looking man, several inches over six feet, at the vigorous peak of what was to be a sterling career. A frequent contributor to scientific journals, he had spent many years, moreover, studying the borderline state between neurosis and psychosis, the gray and foggy no-man's-land in which Judy seemed to spend much of her life. He was, in short, an impressive practitioner of the psychoanalytic arts, and she was obviously in the best of hands. The fact that her therapy did not go well—that it was, indeed, another failure—can be blamed on no one but Judy herself.

Frightened perhaps of the loneliness and isolation of Las Campanas, she had made the cardinal mistake of persuading Kupper to travel with her from California; she had then compounded that error by further persuading him to stay with her in Stockbridge, in a room near hers at the Red Lion Inn, almost across the street from Riggs. His continuing presence was, of course, an obstacle to Knight's own work: it was as if one surgeon were looking over the shoulder of another during a delicate operation, then grading his performance for the patient on the table. Knight apparently said as much, and Kupper returned to California.

In what can only be called another mistake, worse even than the other two, Judy soon followed him, abruptly ending her treatment and raising the suspicion that Knight had come uncomfortably close to the painful origins of her illness. But that was not the reason she gave him. "I can't stand it here in Stockbridge," she grumbled. "It's too quiet." Knight's response to this spoiled and nonsensical complaint was unanswerable. "When you don't have a lot of noise around you," he said, "the noise inside you becomes overwhelming."

|||

It was not too quiet in Los Angeles, and by late summer Judy was back on Evanview Drive, preparing for her next picture, Irving Berlin's *Easter Parade.* "She has made such a remarkable recovery that she can return months before anyone expected," wrote Louella Parsons. So, indeed, it seemed. If nothing else, the extended rest had brightened her spirits and swept away the clouds, at least for the moment. Putting aside their conflicts, the Minnellis exhibited all the signs of amity, and Judy's friends were pleased to welcome home, instead of the terrified hysteric of a few months before, the feisty young woman they had known in earlier years.

Despite all the hugs and smiles on Evanview Drive, the climate had changed, however. Judy and Vincente still shared a bed, but they no longer shared a professional life. After *Meet Me in St. Louis,* Judy's admiration for Vincente had been so great that she trusted almost no one else to direct her. Three and a half years later she continued to respect his skills as a director—but of someone else's movies, not hers. Through the good offices of Kupper, she let Arthur Freed know that she wanted Vincente, who had already been assigned *Easter Parade,* to be replaced before she started work. Giving in to her demand, an uncharacteristically chastened Freed summoned Vincente to his office. Judy's psychiatrist, Freed informed him, believed that Vincente symbolized all of her problems with the studio: it would therefore be better if somebody else directed her.

Stunned, wounded and feeling altogether betrayed, Vincente wondered why Judy, who met him every evening with a warm hello and a kiss on the cheek, had not told him herself. "Why did it have to go through two other people?" he asked himself. "Weren't married couples supposed to openly discuss such things with each other?" But when he arrived home nursing his disappointment, Judy welcomed him with her usual kiss—and said not a word about the picture. Not that night, nor weeks or months later, did either one acknowledge that she had booted him off what might well be Metro's biggest movie of 1948.

Just as bad luck had hovered over *The Pirate,* so did good luck now attend *Easter Parade.* Brought in as director was Charles Walters, a handsome former dancer—he had been Judy's partner in the finale of *Presenting Lily Mars*—who had to his credit only one relatively small movie, the recently completed *Good News,* starring June Allyson and Peter Lawford. Judy liked him, he liked her and the atmosphere on the set was so relaxed—in sharp contrast to the tension that pervaded any Minnelli production—that there was room for fun and banter. "Look, sweetie, I'm no June Allyson, you know," Judy informed Walters his first day on the job. "Don't get cute with me—none of that batting the eyelids bit or fluffing the hair routine for me, buddy! I'm Judy Garland and just you watch it." When Berlin, who inspired tongue-tied awe in most people, boldly suggested how one of his songs should be phrased, Judy walked up to him, put her face two inches in front of his, poked a pugnacious finger into his stomach and said: "Listen, buster, you write 'em, I sing 'em." Berlin was delighted: the pleasure of hearing Judy sing his songs had been the chief reason he had chosen M-G-M over 20th Century–Fox, which had also offered a huge sum for the rights to *Easter Parade.*

Even bad luck turned out to be good. On October 12, a month into rehearsals, Gene Kelly, Judy's costar, broke his ankle in a Sunday afternoon volleyball game. He would be unable to dance for months. Since there was no one on the Metro lot to replace him, it looked as if the whole project might have to be postponed indefinitely, or perhaps canceled altogether. But Kelly's accident, which seemed the worst possible news, was, in fact, the best. Kelly's unrestrained scene-stealing during the making of *The Pirate* had almost certainly exacerbated Judy's sense of being persecuted.

With a possible disaster in the offing, Freed put in an emergency call to Fred Astaire, hoping to coax him out of his premature retirement. Responding, like Berlin, to the lure of an opportunity to work with Judy, Astaire soon said yes. Four days after Kelly's accident, he was out of retirement and in Culver City, altering Kelly's routines to suit his own, quite different style. "My compliments to Gene Kelly, and I am glad he broke his ankle last year," one of the London reviewers was later to say, voicing an opinion many others shared but were too polite to utter. The more sophisticated Astaire was a far better match for Berlin's succulent melodies and the sleek and glossy picture planned by Metro.

|||

"Did he give me confidence?" asked Audrey Hepburn, who later danced with Astaire in the musical *Funny Face*. "Oh yes," she gushed, answering her own question, "from the first minute." And, from the first minute, confidence was what Astaire also gave Judy, who needed

Tramping along the avenue with Fred Astaire in Easter Parade

encouragement the way a rose, pale and drooping in the shadow of taller and more assertive plants, needs the sun. Her reaction, like that of the light-starved rose, was foreseeable—she blossomed. Indeed, for a few happy weeks she convinced herself that a love affair would soon follow. "What am I going to do about Vincente?" she fretted, though not too unhappily, to her friend the actress Sylvia Sidney. The answer was that she had to do nothing, because there would be no love affair: Astaire was a famously faithful husband, who, in Sidney's apt words, would have strayed "about as far as his toenails."

Curiously enough, a similar scenario—an older man giving a psychological boost to an uncertain young woman—was the one the scriptwriters had devised for *Easter Parade*. A famous dancer of the vaudeville era, circa 1912, is in love with his tall and willowy partner. When the partner, played by Ann Miller, accepts a part in the Ziegfeld Follies, the dancer—Astaire, of course—angrily vows that he can take any chorus girl and turn her into a headliner. Enter Judy, who becomes the Eliza Doolittle to his tap-dancing Henry Higgins, fulfills his vow and then walks him to the altar. There was no more to the plot than that. After Walters took over from Vincente, he had removed from the script the emotional subtleties and ambiguities Minnelli always found so appealing. For his *Easter Parade,* Walters wanted only blue skies.

They were what he got. The skies became even brighter after a February preview, when the audience gasped with pleasure at the concluding scene—Judy and Astaire walking arm in arm down Fifth Avenue in a spectacular re-creation of Manhattan's Easter Parade. M-G-M knew then that it had a hit; when the picture was released in July, long after Easter, the reviews, almost universally ecstatic, came as an anticlimax. Summing up the raves, the *Hollywood Reporter* said simply that "the Metro monarch has a howling success." Praising Walters, a couple of critics took an indirect but nonetheless obvious slap at Vincente; one observed that Walters had wisely avoided the "pretentious flourishes" that could easily have ruined such a simple, sunny picture. In any event, the audiences that had stayed away from Vincente's *Pirate* just a few weeks earlier thronged to see Walters's *Easter Parade,* which did indeed go on to become Metro's biggest-grossing movie in 1948.

In the glow of good feeling, Judy's behavior on *The Pirate* was all but forgotten. Working with Astaire, Berlin and Walters, she had been reliability itself, rarely sick or very late. As a result, *Easter Parade,* which went before the cameras on November 25, 1947, finished shooting on February 9, 1948, on schedule and well under budget. "How's it going, Fred?" Vincente had asked Astaire one day on the lot. "How's my girl doing?" Both pride and chagrin must have greeted Astaire's reply. "Just great!" said Astaire. "Judy's really got it."

|||

In *Easter Parade,* one reviewer exclaimed, Judy had truly come of age— she had grown into "something touching golden currency." The men in the Thalberg Building agreed, but they were thinking not of her talent, as the reviewer was, but of her singular ability to fill theater seats. With the box-office returns for *Easter Parade* coming in, the totals rising higher every week, the executives viewed her as exactly the kind of currency Metro needed in 1948, the kind they could take to the bank. For the unthinkable had happened: rich and haughty M-G-M, the only studio that had smiled through the lean years of the thirties, was suddenly in financial trouble, fighting for its existence.

The entire motion-picture industry was, in fact, under siege in that third year after the war. Attendance, which had reached its peak in 1946, had been dropping ever since, as Americans, freed from wartime restrictions, found other ways to occupy their leisure hours. Saturday night at the movies was no longer a national habit. Hollywood's most fearsome competition appeared, at first glance, to be little more than a fad, almost a joke: a big box with a tiny screen that brought fuzzy black-and-white pictures into the living room. "Who in hell," Louis B. Mayer had demanded, "is going to look at those pygmy screens?" But the answer—just about everybody—came soon enough. The million television sets of 1948 were to quadruple in 1949, and were to nearly triple again the year after that, to eleven million. To the men who ran the studios, the arithmetic was as frightening as the equations that resulted in the atomic bomb.

More bad news came from Washington, where the Supreme Court decided that it was a violation of antitrust laws—a criminal conspiracy—for the studios to own the theaters in which their films were shown. A corporation could make movies or it could show them, but it could not do both: the studios would have to sell their theaters. Though they were given some time to comply—a temporary stay of execution—the court had pronounced a death sentence on the studio system. A film featuring top stars would always find an outlet, but without their theaters, the studios would not have a guaranteed market for their other, less glamorous products, the profitable B-movies, shorts, cartoons and newsreels that helped hold up the structure. If the court's edict had come down ten years earlier, Metro, for instance, might not have been able to find an audience for the first Hardy picture, and the whole series—sixteen movies in all—might have died aborning.

Though the late forties were hard on all the studios, they were hardest by far on M-G-M, which had yet to wake up to postwar realities. A generation that had been in battle abroad and had endured privation at home found hopelessly quaint and out-of-date the sermonizing that many Metro features still spouted. "I worship good women, honorable men and saintly mothers," Mayer liked to say. But a movie theater was neither a church nor a lecture hall, and when they did leave their pygmy screens for the big one in a theater, moviegoers wanted stories that more closely reflected the gritty and often unsavory world they saw and read about every day: the greed and backstabbing in Warner Bros.' *The Treasure of the Sierra Madre,* for example, or the horrors of alcoholism in Paramount's *The Lost Weekend.*

"There are no bad M-G-M pictures!" was another Mayer aphorism, but in 1947 and 1948 Metro, which had once hogged the Oscars, received not a single nomination in any of the major categories. It was a stunning slight, proof that the men and women who ran Metro were out of touch with their colleagues as well as with their audience. Not all the stars in Culver City could overcome limp and unimaginative stories, and too many dull films, coupled with a bloated, overpaid bureaucracy, quickly translated into shrinking corporate profits. The industry leader became the industry laggard, and in 1948 Metro made a mere $4.2 million, its poorest showing since 1933, the worst year of the Depression.

Increasingly alarmed, Nick Schenck finally issued a decree: there would have to be a shake-up in Metro's high command. Mayer, he said, would have to find a new hand—another Thalberg—to oversee film production and give it the life and vigor it so conspicuously lacked. In the fat years, Mayer had been strong enough to stand up to his wily old adversary. In 1948, a year of hunger and deprivation, he did as he was told, and after receiving a couple of turndowns, he announced his choice. Dore Schary, he said, was the man to fill Thalberg's long-vacant chair. Though he was not considered one of Hollywood's young giants, as was David O. Selznick, Mayer's first choice, Schary did seem to have the requisite qualities for the job, combining the vitality of youth—he was forty-two—with the experience of age. In the early forties he had been in charge of the unit that produced Metro's low-budget productions; most recently, he had been RKO's head of production.

As proud of his high principles as many in Hollywood were of their winning racehorses, Schary was not universally admired. So widespread was his reputation for holy attitudes that one acquaintance sent Christmas greetings with a telegram rather than the usual card. "Happy Birthday" was all it said. But sanctimony did not trouble Schenck and Mayer, and Schary was lucky enough to be available at a time when Schenck was so desperate and Mayer so enfeebled that he could demand whatever he wanted. What Schary wanted, it turned out, was absolute authority over everything produced on the lot. Mayer would retain titular power, but Schary would be the real boss, czar in all but name, answerable to no one but Schenck himself. The fiefdom Mayer had ruled for so long thus fell without a struggle, like a fortress that has fought off fierce and mighty armies but, faced with sudden starvation, opens its gates to the first stranger who bothers to knock. It was that dispirited Metro that on July 1, 1948, greeted its conqueror.

The only productions Schary agreed to leave alone were the musicals, which were also the only ones that gave Leo reason to purr in those grim months. Without its musicals, Metro's small 1948 profit would have been replaced by a large loss; *Easter Parade* alone earned well over $3 million, a huge sum in the forties. That picture's success—and Metro's profit—could be attributed, in large measure, to Judy. Of all the actors and actresses employed by the studio of the stars, she was perhaps the last one who still spelled magic on theater marquees. After listing some of M-G-M's other fabled names—Clark Gable, Greer Garson, Van Johnson and Walter Pidgeon—one reporter pointed out that, celebrated as they were, they were not in the same category as Judy. According to box-office figures, he said, Judy was in a "draw class" by herself. She was, in short, not just an asset; she was Metro's prime asset.

|||

Though he was never in love with her, as Judy had fantasized, Fred Astaire did like working with her. Her showmanship, he said, was uncanny, and he regarded the numbers he did with her in *Easter Parade* as high spots in his career—exalted praise indeed. Astaire was therefore as elated as Judy was when, even before *Easter Parade* completed shooting, the studio decided to put them together again. In Garland and Astaire, Metro thought, it had stumbled on a winning combination, another Rooney and Garland—or Rogers and Astaire.

The Barkleys of Broadway, their new picture was to be titled, and it promised to be a frolic. They were to play a married couple this time around, musical-comedy stars who begin feuding when the wife, disdaining the fluff that has made them famous, longs for serious roles that will show she can do more than sing and dance. Not until the end does she realize that, for a performer, there is no ambition higher than spreading joy—"fun set to music," as her husband calls it. After the writers, those talented hams Betty Comden and Adolph Green, did a run-through of their screenplay in Arthur Freed's office, an enthusiastic Judy turned to Astaire. "If we can only do as well as they did reading those parts, we're okay," she said. With Chuck Walters directing, employing the same velvet touch that had proved so successful in *Easter Parade,* the weeks ahead did, in fact, look like fun set to music. After two of Judy's oldest friends, Oscar Levant and Billie Burke, were added to the cast, *The Barkleys of Broadway* began to assume the genial atmosphere of a house party.

A house party it was not to be, however. As much as Judy had enjoyed her collaboration with Astaire, *Easter Parade* had worn her out. Emotionally, she was back where she had been a year earlier, during the terrible days of *The Pirate*—tense, nervous and continually exhausted. In early June she pulled herself out of a sickbed to do just one number in *Words and Music,* Metro's ponderous salute to the songwriting team of Richard Rodgers and Lorenz Hart. Singing a duet of "I Wish I Were in Love Again" with her old pal Mickey—the last time they were to appear together on film—she was so pale and gaunt that not even Dorothy Ponedel's makeup wizardry could make her anything more than a shadow of the young woman who was romping across the screen in *Easter Parade.*

Given her poor health and low spirits, it was almost inevitable, then, that when rehearsals for *The Barkleys* began a week later, Judy was soon calling in sick, a refrain that was repeated with increasing frequency as June gave way to July. By now, Judy believed, she was nothing but a mechanical hoop that Metro was rolling around for its own pleasure, and it was obvious to her, if to no one else, that she would never be able to finish *The Barkleys.* "The rehearsals began," she said, "and my migraine headaches got worse. I went for days without sleep, but I kept on. I just wanted to go somewhere to lie down and stop." And stop is what she eventually did, ignoring the pleas of both Freed and Mayer, who journeyed all the way up to Evanview Drive to plead with her to return to the set.

At last, on the afternoon of July 12, the sixth day in a row she had failed to come in, Freed telephoned her doctor. "He said that she possibly could work four or five days, always under medication and possibly blow up for a period and then work again for a few days," Freed reported in a studio memo. "He was of the opinion that if she didn't have to work for a while it might not be too difficult to make a complete cure but that her knowledge of having to report every morning would cause such a mental disturbance within her that the results would be in jeopardy."

Although he was a little late in getting around to it, Freed had posed the right question, and the doctor had given the right answer: forcing Judy to continue in *The Barkleys* would be good for neither her nor the studio. She had to be removed from the picture—that much was clear. Less understandable—altogether baffling, in fact—was the callous way in which Metro chose to inform her. On July 19 it sent her a registered letter to notify her that not only had she been dropped from *The Barkleys* but her contract had also been suspended—she had been thrown off the payroll. From most valuable asset she had been down-graded to potential resource. She had been set aside for repairs, like any other piece of studio equipment.

As he had done after Gene Kelly broke his ankle, Freed quickly picked another star, hiring an airplane to fly *The Barkleys'* script to Gin-ger Rogers, who had made eight pictures with Astaire in the thirties. There she was, Rogers coyly told a reporter, lolling around her four-hundred-acre ranch in Oregon, communing "with the cowsies and the chickensies," when the precious pages arrived. Almost pathetically eager for her to say yes, the studio made an offer she could scarcely turn down—$12,500 a week, more than double what Judy had been making. For that kind of money, Rogers did not mind kissing the cowsies and the chickensies good-bye, and two days later she was in Culver City. Though she had wanted out, an envious Judy now felt left out. "I'm missing the greatest role of my career," she wailed to Louella Parsons.

Judy's troubles with *The Barkleys* did not end there, however, and a few weeks later she made the mistake of visiting the set. During a break in filming she posed for photographs with Rogers and Oscar Levant and traded jokes with her many friends on the crew. But the presence of the first Mrs. Barkley was unsettling to everybody, which was prob-ably the aim of her visit, and unnerving to Rogers, who retreated to her dressing room, refusing to go before the cameras again until Judy had gone. Taking Judy aside, Chuck Walters told her of Rogers's feelings, and a minute later a hurt and angry Judy was striding toward the door. "I've been asked to leave the set," she explained to one astonished on-looker. Astaire, who had missed the whole exchange, walked in the door as she was stalking out and saw nothing but her furious face. "What," he asked, "are they doing to that poor kid?"

|||

But the kid was no longer doing so badly. There had never been any doubt that she would quickly regain her strength if she were made to feel good, safe and secure, and that is precisely what had happened. A surprising pair of guardian angels—Sylvia Sidney and her husband, Carleton Alsop—had brought her down from Evanview Drive and installed her in their own house in Beverly Hills, where they treated her like a cherished member of their family. "I was crazy about her," said Sidney, "and I thought it would be absolutely criminal if somebody didn't do something to preserve that talent." While Alsop, a sometime agent and radio producer, fought Metro over her salary suspension, Sidney played the good Jewish mother, bringing Judy endless trays of her favorite foods. "I felt just like a goose being fattened for the market," a grateful Judy recalled.

By September that pampered goose had gained seventeen much-needed pounds, and Metro asked her to sing another song for *Words and Music*—preview audiences had complained that one number from Judy was not enough. It does not take sharp eyes to notice that the Judy who sang "I Wish I Were in Love Again" in June is not the same Judy who belted out "Johnny One Note" during the September retakes. The first Judy is distressingly thin, her cheeks heavily rouged to hide their hollows; the second Judy is blooming, the vibrant and robust star of *Easter Parade*. Such discrepancies are the bane of moviemakers, but in this case Judy herself welcomed them. The difference in her appearance between the first song and the second, she said, was the difference between sickness and health.

|||

During all of Judy's struggles with M-G-M, Vincente, like David Rose before him, stood curiously idle, a bystander rather than a helpmate and husband. "These were my most ineffectual times," he wanly admitted. If anything, his sympathies lay with the studio, and he did his best to convince her, despite ample evidence to the contrary, that Metro really did care for her as a person, and not merely as a box-office draw. Is it any wonder that, with a man like Vincente at her side, continually telling her that she was at fault, Judy felt so helpless, encircled by enemies on all sides? "There was no one to fight for me," she lamented, and it is impossible to say she was wrong.

For half her life, since the death of her father in 1935, Judy had been seeking someone to replace him, someone who would advise and protect her. So her psychiatrists had told her; so she believed; and so she behaved, falling in love, time and again, with older and presumably wiser and stronger men. In one way or another, all had disappointed her. From Artie Shaw and Oscar Levant to David Rose and Vincente, she had demonstrated infallibly bad judgment in her search for a masculine protector. Now, with Carleton Alsop, she was to have such a protective shield.

Trying to make sense of her tangled finances, Alsop quickly learned that her financial health was as precarious as her physical and emotional. M-G-M's zealous accountants, he discovered, had tallied up the cost of every minute by which she had delayed *The Pirate* and *The Barkleys of Broadway,* as well as every day she had been away at Las Campanas and Austen Riggs, the two psychiatric clinics. The total of what Metro's money people called "retroactive penalties" came to approximately $100,000, an enormous debt that was to be deducted from her salary when she did start working again. "I don't believe you have any legal claim for taking that penalty," Alsop informed Mayer. "And I feel strongly enough about it that we may just have to establish that point in a law court."

Alsop delivered his threat with a smile, however, inducing Mayer to devise a solution that satisfied everybody: he gave Judy bonuses for her two songs in *Words and Music,* a sum sufficient to cover most, perhaps all, of Metro's claims. Thrilled that she had at last found a man who could stand up for her against Mayer and the studio, Judy prevailed upon Alsop to become her permanent agent and manager. But Alsop truly was like a father—Judy nicknamed him "Pa"—and, unlike the other men in her life, he could stand up against her as well, steadfastly refusing to bow to her tantrums and neurotic anxieties. When Vincente could not handle her, which was frequently the case, he telephoned Alsop, who showed up, even in the middle of the night, to give her a verbal spanking. "Now, goddamn it, Judy," Alsop would say, "you go back to bed and go to sleep, or get your ass up and go to work." Cursing him in return, Judy, more often than not, would nevertheless do as she was told.

|||

The musical comedy Arthur Freed had bought for her—she was to play the gunslinging Annie Oakley in Irving Berlin's Broadway hit *Annie Get Your Gun*—was not ready when she reported for work again, sleek and rested, in the fall of 1948. Taking advantage of the delay, Joe Pasternak, whose production unit rivaled Freed's, borrowed her for *In the Good Old Summertime,* a tuneful remake of Ernst Lubitsch's 1940 comedy, *The Shop Around the Corner.* If Freed was the bold pioneer of the movie musical, then Pasternak was the genial guardian of the old order. "Pasternak Land," his part of the Metro lot was named, a reference to his light, schmaltzy comedies, which always seemed to take place in a smiling country where even the snow was as sweet as powdered sugar. "I want to make folks forget about troubles," was Pasternak's unapologetic explanation. "Let the newspapers take care of fact." *Presenting Lily Mars,* the only other picture he had done with Judy, had been just that kind of confection. So was *In the Good Old Summertime,* an old-fashioned romance about two feuding clerks in a music store who fall in love with their anonymous pen pals, unaware that they are, in fact, corresponding with each other.

Familiar with the problems that had bedeviled other productions Judy had been in, Pasternak saw to it that the atmosphere on the set was as sunny as that on-screen, extracting a pledge from everyone involved, from the director, Robert Z. Leonard, to Judy's costar, Van Johnson, to treat her gently. "There was never a word uttered in recrimination when she was late, didn't show up, or couldn't go on," said Pasternak. "Those of us who worked with her knew her magical genius and respected it." As a tangible symbol of that respect, he gave orders for one red rose to be placed in her dressing room every morning, along with an unsigned card that read: "Happy day, Judy." Mystified, Judy assigned Dorothy Ponedel to ascertain the identity of her secret admirer; but not even Ponedel, whose sources spanned the Metro lot, could learn his name. The result of all that kind attention was a Judy who was rarely ill and a production that was completed five days ahead of schedule. "What did you do to Judy?" a delighted Mayer asked Van Johnson. "We made her feel needed," Johnson answered. "We joked with her and kept her happy."

Those high spirits were reflected in the film itself, and when *In the Good Old Summertime* opened at Radio City Music Hall in July 1949, one of Judy's songs, a boisterous rendition of "I Don't Care," elicited a spontaneous burst of applause from the audience—a sound rarely heard in the dark recesses of a movie theater. Further rounds of applause came from the reviewers. "Great troupers come seldom in a theatrical generation," wrote one, "but when one does arrive on the theatrical scene there is no mistaking the special magnetism that is their art. If ever there existed doubts that Judy Garland is one of the great screen personalities of the present celluloid era the opportunity to alter the impression is offered in 'In the Good Old Summertime.' "

|||

Arthur Freed was in enthusiastic agreement—he said so many times. Even so, it was not in his blunt, obstinate and often crude nature to do anything out of the ordinary, as Pasternak had done, to make Judy happy. With *Annie Get Your Gun,* which finally began production in March 1949, he did just the opposite, in fact, hiring the one director in Hollywood most likely to cause her anguish. That director was Busby Berkeley, of course—the same Busby Berkeley who had caused her so much grief on the *Babes in Arms* series, the same Busby Berkeley whom Freed himself had fired three weeks into the filming of *Girl Crazy.* Freed could not have made a worse choice, or one more puzzling and perverse, and catastrophe arrived with foreseeable speed—on only the second day of shooting, April 5. As it happened, Berkeley's first victim was not Judy, however, but Howard Keel, the tall, strapping baritone who played the cowboy lead. Instead of allowing Keel to slowly trot his horse across the soundstage, as both prudence and the smooth floor dictated, Berkeley ordered a faster and more dramatic gallop. The unsurprising result was that the poor animal slid and fell, taking Keel down with him.

"He'll be all right! He'll be all right!" Berkeley shouted as Keel was carried away.

"Buzz, his leg's broken," retorted Al Jennings, *Annie*'s assistant director, who had cut the boot off the actor's injured leg and knew what he was talking about. "He won't be all right." His leg encased in a cast, Keel was out of action, and for several weeks the cameras had no one to focus on but Judy.

A reasonably contented Judy, the Judy of *Easter Parade* and *In the Good Old Summertime,* might have soldiered through the more intense schedule now assigned her. But for Judy there was no contentment, reasonable or otherwise, in the spring of 1949. Her marriage to Vincente was in its last days—on a treadmill to disaster, as Vincente aptly described it—and the Minnellis rented a second house on Sunset Boulevard, so that, after a fight, Judy would have a place to get away. Relations turned particularly bitter in March when Vincente, alarmed by an upsurge in consumption, snatched away her pills. Though he acted in her best interest, Judy did not see it that way, and at the end of the month she announced their separation. "I'm very sorry, but it's true," said Judy. "We're happier apart."

Despite such turmoil, until Keel's accident Judy had seemed equal to the demands of what promised to be a difficult picture. During prerecording sessions—she recorded the picture's entire score between March 25 and April 1—her voice was strong and vibrant, as sassy as a trumpet in Berlin's humorous songs, as tender as an oboe in his romantic ballads. As shooting began, however, she seemed unsure of herself, tiptoeing around the character rather than jumping into her role as she usually did. Portraying the blustery, gun-toting Annie was a stretch for her, different from any part she had ever before attempted, and she seemed uncertain how to proceed. She was also intimidated, she confessed, by the prospect of playing a role so strongly identified with a powerhouse like Ethel Merman, the original Broadway Annie.

Even the best actors sometimes find themselves lost and confused when they venture into unfamiliar territory, and it is the director's job to lead them down the right path, avoiding quicksand on one side, dangerous precipices on the other. Another director—a Vincente, for example—might have guided Judy through the treacherous spots in *Annie Get Your Gun,* pointing out the possibilities of a Garland Annie, an Annie more vulnerable and therefore more sympathetic and believable than Merman's had been. A comparison of the different ways the two women rendered Annie's songs—both versions have been preserved—suggests, indeed, that Judy could have put her own stamp on the role.

That old World War I parade master, Busby Berkeley, was more ac-

252 | *Get Happy*

customed to giving marching orders than to offering guidance, however. He did not instill confidence; he destroyed it. "This monster treats me the same as when I was fifteen!" a bitter Judy complained, and his bullying soon did to her fragile ego what it had previously done to Keel's strong body. "Judy would come to work feeling fine," said Jennings, who had last worked with her on *Meet Me in St. Louis.* "Then Buzz would see her, and he would start screaming and yelling and hollering the way Buzz did. Ten minutes later I would be called to her dressing room. 'I'm sick,' she would say. 'I can't stand it. I've got to go home.' And that would be the end of that."

The scenes that Berkeley did manage to shoot filled her with dismay. Ever since she had arrived at M-G-M, Judy had yearned to be glamorous, to wear costumes designed by Adrian and other top designers. Starting with *Meet Me in St. Louis,* she had finally got her wish. Now, playing a smudge-faced and disheveled Annie, she was back where she had started, looking and sounding exactly like little Sairy Dodd, the pigtailed, barefoot hillbilly she had portrayed in *Pigskin Parade.* Watching herself in the daily rushes, she shrank into her chair with stunned embarrassment, then turned to Berkeley. "How could you make me look so bad?" she hotly demanded.

The destructive behavior she had exhibited on the set of *The Pirate,* then on *The Barkleys of Broadway,* now reemerged. She began to arrive at the studio late or not at all, often staying home, unable to rise from her bed. Her weight dropped to ninety pounds, and even her hair began to fall out, a side effect, most likely, of her profligate use of amphetamines. In an effort to lift her out of her depression, a new doctor, Fred Pobirs, persuaded her to undergo a series of electric shock treatments, a total of six. But if all that voltage did any good, it was not apparent to Jennings. Once again, as in *Meet Me in St. Louis* days, he was being awakened in the middle of the night—and occasionally two or three times a night—by her frantic phone calls, moaning about a migraine or wistfully wondering whether the morning would bring sunshine or clouds. Not that it much mattered: on a Busby Berkeley set, the weather was always turbulent, the menacing sound of thunder never far away.

Freed could have intervened to stop Berkeley's abuse, but in at least one instance he himself was equally brutal. He happened to be on the set one day when, too tired (and perhaps too drugged) to continue, Judy slid to the floor with the cameras rolling. Rather than help her to her feet, a furious Freed rushed over and shook her by the shoulders. "What's the matter with you?" he snarled. "Get up off your ass and let's film this scene."

In the end, it was Berkeley's incompetence, not his treatment of Judy, that brought about his demise. To everyone's astonishment, a director whose reputation rested on his fluid and freewheeling use of the camera had succumbed to a kind of paralysis. He, too, seemed trapped in the shadow of the Broadway musical, directing his film version as if it were still confined to a handkerchief-sized space in a Times Square theater. "There was no real action, nothing," said Jennings. "It was as if he were photographing a stage play." Watching the rushes, Freed reluctantly agreed. He fired Berkeley on May 3, then put in an emergency call to the man who probably should have been in charge from the beginning—Chuck Walters.

After seeing the footage Berkeley had shot, Walters concluded that nothing, not so much as a skinny inch, was worth saving. "My God—it was horrible!" he said. "Judy had never been worse. She couldn't decide whether she was Mary Martin, Ethel Merman, Martha Raye or herself." Trying to give her the help she should have received weeks earlier, he made it his first task to invite her into his office for nearly three hours of intense discussion. "It's too late, Chuck," Judy sadly replied. "I haven't got the energy or the nerve any more." Nor had she. "I couldn't learn anything," she recalled. "I couldn't retain anything. I was just up there making strange noises. Here I was, in the middle of a million-dollar property, with a million-dollar wardrobe, with a million eyes on me, and I was in a complete daze. I knew it, and everyone around me knew it. But I desperately tried to go on. I knew that if I didn't finish this one, it was the finish of me. So I kept on."

|||

But not for long. Less tolerant of Judy's problems than Mayer had been, Schary himself met with her, then telephoned Nick Schenck in New York to offer his own solution: she should be removed from the picture. "This is a tough one," he said. "But our feeling is to take her out because otherwise you're going to be in a hole—and you won't have a movie." To which Schenck laconically answered: "Do what you have to do." The decision to fire Judy had thus been made, and its implementation awaited only the right opportunity. Poised and ready, Metro found that moment on the morning of May 10, when Judy, who was due on the set at nine, did not even drive through the gate until ten-ten. Waiting for her in her dressing room, where Pasternak's rose had once winked a friendly greeting, was a warning letter from the front office. "We desire to call your attention to the fact," it said, "that on a great many occasions since the commencement of your services in 'ANNIE GET YOUR GUN,' you were either late in arriving on the set in the morning, late in arriving on the set after lunch, or were otherwise responsible for substantial delays or curtailed production, all without our consent." Any further tardiness, the letter added, would result in her suspension.

Considerably chastened, Judy rushed to the set, rehearsed until the lunch break, then responded immediately when Jennings called her at one-twenty for her first scene of the afternoon. Before she could leave her dressing room, however, there was a knock at the door. Assuming that her absence from the set meant that she was late, two men from the front office handed her a second letter, notifying her that since she had not heeded the earlier warning, she was being taken off the picture. Still a third man, realizing that the first two had jumped the gun, huffed and puffed onto the set seconds after they had left for her dressing room. "Oh, they weren't supposed to deliver that letter yet," he said.

They succeeded in their mission, nonetheless. Although it was premature, and therefore not legally binding, that second letter sent Judy into hysterics. When Jennings, on orders from Mayer, who knew that the legal niceties had to be preserved, summoned her to the set a second time, at two o'clock, she angrily refused, vowing not to return "now or ever again." Those were the rash words the studio wanted to hear, and she was not allowed to retract them. Appearing on the set ten minutes later with the breathless message that Judy had changed her mind and would soon follow, Dorothy Ponedel was surprised to see both the cast and crew heading for the exits. "Where's everybody going?" she asked Jennings.

"They're all through," he told her. "We're finished."

"Well, get them back. Judy's on her way."

"Too late," Jennings replied. "Too late."

And too late it was—too late for Metro, too late for Judy and too late for common sense: for the second time in less than a year, she was suspended, off the payroll. The next day the studio sent a memo to all those who might have dealings with her: "For your information Judy Garland's contract has been suspended as of May 10, 1949. She is not to be called or requested to render services of any kind whatsoever unless the matter is cleared with Mr. Mannix or Mr. Schary." Betty Hutton, a brassy-voiced comic who was undiplomatic enough to say that she had been praying for the role, became the new Annie. "I'd stand on my head in Macy's window to get that part," said Hutton. "There never will be another character like Annie Oakley—a regular barrelhouse sort of dame." A barrelhouse sort of dame was the Annie she played, crude and broadly comic, without the subtlety and pathos a healthy Judy might have given the portrayal. Released in 1950, the picture was a huge success anyway, making more money than any previous Freed musical and putting Hutton herself on the covers of several national magazines.

For Judy the studio had no further plans. "Judy Garland out of Films for Year," read the front-page banner headline in the *Los Angeles Examiner*. Although she publicly accepted all blame—"I've been a bad girl," she admitted—Judy was portrayed in the press as spoiled and temperamental, a performer unworthy of sympathy, according to Louella Parsons. "Certainly," said the indignant Parsons, "after all the breaks she has had at M-G-M they have a right to expect her to cooperate and not fail to report for work."

Grim costume shots for _Annie Get Your Gun_

CHAPTER 10

"I Am an Addict"

A year earlier, in the summer of 1948, a local scandal sheet, *Hollywood Nite Life,* had printed three front-page articles about the drug problems of one of the world's biggest stars. "Miss G," the paper had helpfully dubbed her, on the unlikely chance that any of its readers had trouble guessing her identity. Although Judy's surrender to pills was well known within the industry, never before had it been advertised to the public—in bold, black headlines, moreover. Suddenly one of Hollywood's worst-kept secrets was secret no longer: the girl next door, wholesome and winsome Judy Garland, was a drug addict. Those who read the articles—and everyone in town seemed to have done so—now had an explanation for her erratic behavior on the set: she was, as *Hollywood Nite Life* indelicately phrased it, a "pill-head."

What was startling to Judy's fans, however, was an old and increasingly tiresome subject in the Thalberg Building, where Mayer had convened many high-level meetings to consider one topic: how to wean Judy away from drugs. "We did everything we could to try to get her back to normalcy," said Lucille Ryman

Carroll, who, as head of the talent department, attended such sessions. "We spent several years trying to straighten her out." More than once Judy herself was summoned to the meetings in Mayer's office, only to annoy and frustrate everyone present by blandly insisting that she did not need straightening out—she was not a drug addict. "No, I'm not taking anything," she would say. If anyone accused her of lying, which everyone knew she was doing, she would, in Carroll's words, "just open those big brown eyes and look at us."

But it did not require the services of Metro's spies to ascertain that Judy had organized a supply system that Metro's own purchasing department might have envied, that she had not one doctor prescribing for her, but four, five or more, and not one pharmacy filling her prescriptions, but nearly every one listed in the Yellow Pages. The Alsops saw just how many suppliers she had lined up when she stayed with them during her *Barkleys of Broadway* crisis. Each evening, between seven and eight o'clock, something like half a dozen motorcycles would roar up their driveway, bringing drugstore deliveries from miles around.

Judy was not the only one in Hollywood who was hooked on pills, of course. Nearly everyone was ingesting some kind of sedative or amphetamine—"bolts and jolts," they were called. The bolts, the sedatives, were the most sought after; the stars were willing to try almost anything that promised a good night's sleep, an absolute necessity in a business that required bright eyes at dawn. Noël Coward, for instance, blessed Marlene Dietrich for the gift of a magical suppository. "I rammed it up my bottom," he reported to his diary, "and slept like a top." Judy was satisfied with the more conventional sleeping pill. What else can you do, she asked a fan magazine, when you are working so hard? "Golly," she added, "you know you just have to have sleep."

|||

If Judy was not the only star consuming drugs, she was the most visible. So insatiable was her appetite that even her network of doctors and drugstores could not keep up with the demand, and what she could not buy, she would beg, borrow or steal. At parties, for example, while most people were having fun downstairs, she was upstairs prowling the bathrooms, shamelessly burgling medicine chests—she even stole allergy pills. The day after escorting her to a gathering at Rosalind Russell's, Evie Johnson, Van's wife, received an irate call from the hostess.

"Jesus Christ, Evie! Why didn't you warn me?"

"About what?" inquired the astonished Johnson.

"About Judy!" Russell exploded. "She rifled my medicine cabinet. It's empty!"

Mornings would sometimes find her knocking on Gene Kelly's door—the Kelly house was midway between her own house and the studio—to ask if she could use the bathroom. Kelly's wife, Betsy Blair, would say yes, then be surprised to watch her brush past the downstairs bathroom and boldly march upstairs to the Kellys' private bath. Only when her husband began noticing the disappearance of his sleeping pills did Betsy learn that a weak bladder was not the real reason for Judy's visits. Word of her acquisitive habits soon got around, and when Judy was expected, bathrooms were emptied of almost everything but shaving cream and toothpaste.

Desperate people do desperate things, and nothing Judy did in her pursuit of pills, no matter how humiliating or outrageous, seemed to embarrass her. William Tuttle, who became head of Metro's makeup department, caught a glimpse of that desperation when he accidentally dropped one of his own Benzedrines. Like a dog jumping for a scrap, Judy grabbed it almost before it hit the floor. Still, nobody wanted to be blamed for giving her drugs, and after *Hollywood Nite Life* shone the spotlight on the pill-popping "Miss G," the real Miss G felt a chilly breeze when she walked to her table at Ciro's or the Mocambo. "It was a terrible thing in this town," said Judy, "because people really stayed away from me as though I were a leper." It was harder still to shrug off the even more frigid reaction of her own daughter. On one particularly bleak day, Liza joyfully jumped into her arms, then instantly recoiled, screaming in shock and horror at the foul smell emanating from her mother's pores—the unpleasant by-product of a knockout drug with the fearsome name paraldehyde. "Ye gods!" exclaimed Sylvia Sidney, who witnessed that pathetic scene. "It had the most awful odor."

Sidney was also present for another, equally scarifying encounter. After examining a bedridden Judy at the Alsop house, a group of doctors compared notes at the far end of her darkened bedroom. Hearing their whispered buzz, Judy sat up and glared at them. "There is something you fools do not understand," she said. "I am an addict. And when I want something, I can get it."

||||

After the debacle of *Annie Get Your Gun,* Nick Schenck and Dore Schary were ready to throw her to the wolves, Judy said, and so it seemed. Her pleas for reinstatement were rejected, and in the week or so that followed her suspension, it appeared that all her fears had been realized—that *Annie,* in fact, had put an end to her career. A defeated, "tragic little figure" was how Hedda Hopper described her during those desolate days, a Judy dressed for January, in a sweatshirt and windbreaker, in the middle of May—a Judy who looked middle-aged at twenty-six.

Rescue from that enveloping blizzard came, and none too soon, from an altogether unexpected source: Louis B. Mayer. A monster in so many ways, the old lion had a soft spot for the sick and distressed; he was, at heart, as sentimental as his movies. It was he who had paid the bills of Marie Dressler, that hatchet-faced comedienne of the thirties, when she was dying of cancer; and it was he who had insisted that Lionel Barrymore be given good roles even after arthritis confined him to a wheelchair. Now Mayer was concerned about Judy. "She is in a terribly bad way," he told Katharine Hepburn. "She has made us millions of dollars. We should be able to help her." But Mayer, who could obtain an answer to the most obscure question by simply picking up the phone, was stumped when it came to helping Judy. "What do you think should be done?" he finally asked Carleton Alsop. Alsop's answer was perhaps too obvious to have occurred to anyone before. "Why don't you," he said, "get her away from all the sycophants and the doctors who give her these pills?"

It was a good idea—common sense, really—and Mayer quickly accepted it, recommending that Judy travel all the way across country to a Boston hospital he himself had visited earlier in the year. Going still further, he also suggested that she see his personal physician—a woman, at that—Jessie Marmorston. With Judy herself in full and grateful agreement, the sole obstacle was money. Judy had none. She was, in her own words, "stony broke," without the wherewithal to travel much beyond the county limits. Not knowing where else to turn, she put pride aside and requested a loan from the studio that had just suspended her. "By all means," said Mayer. "That's the least we can do for you, is to pay for your hospital bill." But Schenck, whom he called for approval while Judy was still sitting in his office, was not so generous, sounding as much like Scrooge as Scrooge himself. "Mr. Schenck suggests that you go to a charity hospital, because we're not in the money-lending business," Mayer said after he put down the telephone.

In the end, however, Schenck did come through—Mayer had promised to pay her bills out of his own deep pockets if he refused—and on May 27, Judy, accompanied by her faithful companion, Carleton Alsop, boarded the Super Chief for Boston.

Unlike Las Campanas and Austen Riggs, Peter Bent Brigham, which she entered on May 29, the day she arrived, was not a psychiatric clinic, but an ordinary hospital. "There's nothing the matter with my head," Judy stoutly maintained. "It's my body that's tired." She was at least half right, and after a series of tests, she was put on a regimen to restore her weight and energy: three big meals a day and lights out at nine o'clock, whether she was sleepy or not. She had to relearn how to eat and sleep, Judy's doctors explained to her.

Free to come and go as she pleased, she relaxed for the first time since her honeymoon with Vincente, attending baseball games and enjoying luxurious weekends at the Hotel Ritz Carlton with the Alsops—Sylvia was playing in summer stock outside the city. Vincente called from time to time, and Frank Sinatra, with whom Judy, like so many of her friends, had had a brief romance, telephoned every day and visited once, keeping her hospital room filled with gifts—flowers, perfume, bed jackets and phonograph records, along with a machine on which to play them. In June, Judy went to New York to meet Liza, whose nurse had brought her all the way from Los Angeles to help celebrate her mother's twenty-seventh birthday. After a few days in Manhattan, mother and daughter traveled north to Cape Cod for a lazy vacation by the ocean. But it was neither the days in New York nor the weeks on Cape Cod that Liza remembered; it was their farewell in Boston, that tearful hour when Judy's nurse gently pulled her one way, back to Peter Bent Brigham, and Liza's nurse pulled her the other way, back to California.

|||

At the beginning of her stay at Peter Bent Brigham, Judy had been sent to the children's hospital next door for a brain test, an electroencephalogram. As word of her presence spread through the wards, the small patients, many of whom were retarded or brain-damaged, begged to see her. Happy to oblige, Judy patiently made the rounds on each floor, ending in the ward housing the youngest, the four- and five-year-olds. "Hello, Judy!" they yelled, unable to hide their excitement. Such a greeting, so spontaneous and sincere, was the very medicine she needed, and she returned every day thereafter. "If I was cured at Peter Bent Brigham, it was only because of those children," Judy later declared. "They were so brave, so darling." Like draws to like, deep to deep, and Judy was most drawn to a dark-haired girl with eyes so frightened that she turned her head away as Judy drew near. So badly had her family treated her that the girl had not spoken for two years. It was with her that Judy spent most of her time, not at all bothered that the girl never once broke her silence to respond to her stories of Liza, *The Wizard of Oz,* Clark Gable, Mickey Rooney and the Gumm family's vaudeville act.

By the end of August Judy had recovered her weight and energy, and it was time to say good-bye. On her last day in Boston, she paid her final visit to the children's hospital, where each of the patients, scrubbed and smiling, held a tiny bouquet of flowers in her honor. "Well, my friend, I'm going now," she said to the girl who refused to speak, "and I want to thank you for all you've done for me. I'm going to miss you." As Judy leaned over to kiss her, the girl reached out and clasped her as tightly as she could, and all the words she had not uttered for so many months poured out in a seemingly endless torrent. "Judy!" she screamed. "I love you! I love you! Don't leave! Don't leave!"

Watching that poignant drama, the rest of the ward was all but awash in tears: the nurses cried, the other children cried, Alsop cried and so, of course, did Judy. When Alsop warned her that they would miss their train, Judy waved him away. "Well, we'll just have to miss it," she said. "I'm not going to leave this child right now while she's talking." And there she remained for the next two hours, listening to her little friend's excited babble and bringing the nurses over, one by one, so that the girl would continue to speak even after Judy herself had returned to California. There had been other gratifying moments in her life, Judy later said, but nothing approached that one. "I didn't give a goddamn how many pictures I'd been fired from. I had done a human being some good. She had helped to make me well, and I had helped her."

|||

Released at the end of June, *In the Good Old Summertime* had once more demonstrated Judy's appeal at the box office, and she soon began hearing friendlier sounds from Culver City: Metro wanted her to do another movie. Judy was eager to resume work—the catastrophe of *Annie Get Your Gun* had clearly frightened her—and she interrupted her eastern idyll for two weeks of story consultations at the studio. She dutifully returned to Boston to complete her treatment, however, and when she came back to California in early September, she was feeling better than she had in months, perhaps years. Peter Bent Brigham seemed to have succeeded where the psychiatric clinics had failed. "I'll never work or worry so hard again," she vowed. "It's too wonderful to feel good."

Since one of Arthur Freed's pet projects, a high-gloss remake of *Show Boat,* that greatest of all American musicals, would not be ready for another year, she was rushed instead into *Summer Stock,* another of Joe Pasternak's congenial confections. Judy was to play a Connecticut farmer who loans her barn to a troupe of actors, then steps in to save their show when the star, her spoiled younger sister, walks out. As he had done with *In the Good Old Summertime,* Pasternak assembled a cast and crew Judy knew and liked—Gene Kelly, Phil Silvers, Eddie Bracken, Marjorie Main and Gloria DeHaven. Chuck Walters was to direct, and Al Jennings, the patient recipient of so many late-night phone calls on previous pictures, was to be his assistant director. Louis B. Mayer himself came down to the production office to ensure that the right attitude prevailed. "We're going to bring Judy back," he said, "and I want everybody on the set to cheer her on and make her feel happy." Informed that Jennings knew her best, Mayer fixed him with his owlish gaze and said: "Then you be the head cheerleader."

There was only one problem. In one respect, Peter Bent Brigham had done its job too well. Those three big meals a day had restored the weight Judy had lost and then some—a lot, in fact. Thin and frail when she had left Los Angeles in May, she was plump and robust when she came home three months later, too heavy, by fifteen pounds or more, for a woman who was supposed to excite Gene Kelly more than the slim and pretty Gloria DeHaven.

|||

She had not been so overweight since she was in her early teens, and the studio did what it had done then: it ordered her to lose the pounds. "Excess Baggage Banned," read the headline in the *Los Angeles Times*. A crash diet followed, and the old illnesses and frenetic pill-popping followed that. "The less I ate, the more nervous I became. Then the migraines started to come back, and then no sleep. It was like a bad dream that I thought I had put away. I was in the trap again." And so was Metro. Even as rehearsals began, the betting around the lot was two-to-one that *Summer Stock* would never be completed.

Judy seemed determined to prove the doubters right, calling in sick so frequently that Kelly organized basketball games in the main rehearsal hall to maintain morale. "Please, just knock on wood," Chuck Walters would say when she did appear. "She's here." Even then, she often ignored scheduled calls, however, and Jennings and others had to coax or fool her into performing. For a barnyard scene, for instance, the company traveled to the San Fernando Valley, only to find Judy so sick when it came time to shoot that she had to be helped to the car that was to drive her home. Hiding his dismay, Jennings nonetheless persuaded her to stay a few more seconds, long enough to hear her playback, the song she had recorded weeks earlier and had been brought to the Valley to lip-synch for the cameras.

"Gee, that's great!" Judy said when she heard her own voice, lush and vibrant, booming across the yard.

"Why don't you climb onto the tractor and rehearse it for a minute?" suggested the wily Jennings. She did as he requested, and just as he had anticipated, she soon forgot how sick she had been, not only remaining to finish the shot but even comforting him when a technical glitch forced her to do it again. "Don't worry," she earnestly assured him. "We'll get it."

Sometimes she really was ill or incapable, so drugged and unsteady that she had to depend on supports to keep herself upright. Most frightening were her episodes of hallucination, first noticed on the set of *The Pirate.* "What am I doing here?" she inquired in the middle of one *Summer Stock* scene, suddenly looking around in bewilderment. "Why doesn't Vincente take me home?" At another point she believed that everyone on the production was standing around her, pointing disapproving fingers in her direction. "Everybody is against me here!" she wailed to Sydney Guilaroff, Metro's chief hairdresser. "I know they're trying to get rid of me. Nobody cares about me! Nobody!"

The truth, as far as the other actors were concerned, was the exact opposite. Far from pointing their fingers at her, Judy's colleagues did their best to make her laugh. Phil Silvers came in on his days off to cheer her up, and young Carleton Carpenter wrote an encouraging song. "Don't be afraid, baby, let go o' your heart," it began. Carpenter even attempted to rescue her in his dreams, trying, over and over, to pull her out of an imaginary drug den—her dressing room. "I had to get her out of there," he said, "away from the narcotics—but I couldn't." Nor could anyone else.

If the cast of *Summer Stock* was on Judy's side, many in the Thalberg Building were not, and the production notes were even more thorough than usual, obsessively documenting each second of delay that she caused. The mood of official displeasure was reflected in Louella Parsons's column. Parsons said that although she had never before publicly spanked Judy—actually, she had whacked her hard on several occasions—she would do so now. "I can't understand her attitude after all that has been done for her," Parsons went on to complain. "Even the people who sympathize with her can't understand her actions toward the studio."

One who no longer sympathized was Joe Pasternak. The "laughing Hungarian," as he was sometimes called, was now all frowns and gloomy sighs, her ardent supporter no longer. "That's all, I can't take it any longer," Pasternak told Mayer at last, suggesting that Metro close down the picture. "I quit." But Mayer refused to allow that or to give up on Judy. "Sit down," he said. "This little girl has been so wonderful. She's made us a lot of money, and she's in trouble. We've got to help her." To which he added, in grim conclusion: "If you stop production now, it'll finish her."

Mayer, who still retained vestiges of his former authority, had his way, and filming proceeded in starts and stops, like an unreliable car struggling toward its destination. Suffering all of a sudden from an ulcer, an ailment he blamed on Judy, Chuck Walters found it almost galling to watch the dailies: the film he saw emerging in the screening room was another of Joe Pasternak's airy delights, with nary a hint of the torment on the set. Although Judy was indeed too heavy, she seemed fine otherwise, in good voice and good spirits. "How dare this look like a happy picture!" Walters would find himself saying, all but shaking his fist at the screen.

At least Walters knew that his misery would cease when the lights were doused and the sets were struck. Judy did not have that comfort. Drinking too much at the traditional end-of-the-picture party, she threw herself into the lap of Saul Chaplin, one of the movie's two music directors. "I'm a fat slob!" she cried, digging her head into his shoulder. "I'm so ugly and untalented. They're going to find me out!"

|||

The cheers that had gone up when shooting ended in the spring of 1950, long past schedule, changed to groans a few weeks later, when Metro decided that the film demanded a dramatic concluding number. Judy, who had gone to the seaside resort of Carmel for a long rest, would have to be called back. It was left to Walters to break the bad news to the star herself, who surprised him with her cheerful, even enthusiastic agreement. She set only one condition: the number would have to be "Get Happy," a song from a 1930 Broadway revue, music by Harold Arlen, words by Ted Koehler, that she had always wanted to sing. This was a demand Metro could gladly accept, and Judy canceled her vacation to return to Culver City.

In a Hollywood musical, even a three-minute segment, which is all "Get Happy" was, could call for months of preparation. The Pasternak crew did not have that luxury. Saul Chaplin quickly wrote an arrangement, Walters himself did the staging—Nick Castle, who had choreographed all the other songs, had decamped for another project—and teams of set designers, electricians, costumers and cameramen hurried to make sure everything would be in order for the first day of shooting. As was so often the case, Judy, the quickest of quick studies, breezed through the prerecording, not even requiring a rehearsal. As was also so often the case, however, she fell apart at the climactic moment—the first time she was called before the cameras. She was, in fact, so drugged she could scarcely stand, let along nimbly dance her way through a circle of eight dinner-jacketed chorus boys.

"Put her up there!" a furious Pasternak ordered anyway. "Shoot the number. I want everybody to see what's happened to her."

"Joe, you can't do that," Jennings pleaded. "You just can't do it. You'll hate yourself if you do." Pasternak reluctantly conceded, but Jennings then had to calm an equally furious Judy, who, unaware of her hapless state, also wanted to go ahead, retreating only when Jennings invoked technical problems that could not be corrected until morning. "I'll be on the set and ready at nine o'clock in the morning," she angrily declared, "and you'd better be ready to shoot!"

If she could get at least one great song across, Judy had told Vincente, she would be satisfied with *Summer Stock,* which she quite rightly considered an amiable trifle, beneath the abilities of everybody involved. "Get Happy," she hoped, would be the number that made the whole effort worthwhile, and to everyone's astonishment, she showed up early the following morning to start it, just as she had promised.

Unable to lose much weight during the many months Metro had been screaming at her, she had watched the pounds melt away in Carmel, where there was no one to harass her. The Judy who strode onstage that morning in late spring was therefore not the same Judy who had stood there a few weeks earlier. Slim and supple, she had been taken out of overalls and matronly dresses and put into a costume that

Taking off her overalls and showing her legs for "Get Happy"

would have been previously impossible: a tight-fitting man's dinner jacket over a still tighter leotard. She wanted to show off the legs that one besotted literary critic compared to a couplet by Alexander Pope—"beautifully and smoothly turned." Topping off her new wardrobe was a hat, a black fedora, which she tipped provocatively—insouciantly—over her right eye. She looked so strikingly different from the chubby Judy who was seen in the rest of the movie that many people later assumed that "Get Happy" was unused footage from a previous production.

When Judy, rakishly exuberant, concluded, "Get Happy" was everything that she had wished, or could have wished. The very definition of a showstopper, it was the perfect ending for *Summer Stock,* the best part of the picture by far. It was also the perfect ending for Judy's career at M-G-M—the last number she was ever to do for the studio of the stars.

|||

At the conclusion of *Summer Stock,* it was clear, both to Judy's doctors in Boston and to her hard-nosed bosses in Culver City, that Peter Bent Brigham had not been able to correct what Dore Schary uncharitably called her "catalogue of ills." To effect a permanent cure, as well as to protect one of its most important assets, Metro now did what it probably should have done seven years earlier, when Karl Menninger had first made the recommendation: it volunteered to give her a year off at full salary, and to pay all of her medical bills too. There was only one catch to that generous proposal: she would have to undergo a strict regimen of treatment, presumably at Menninger's or some similar clinic.

An offer that might have been accepted in 1943, however, when it came from a man she believed she could trust, was coldly rejected in 1950, when it came from Schary, a man she had reason to distrust. Indeed, Judy may well have suspected that, once inside a psychiatric clinic, she would not be let out—a justifiable fear given the fact that her own mother had looked into the possibility of having her forcibly committed, traveling all the way to Topeka to make inquiries of Menninger himself. Now, when Metro made the suggestion, Judy was indignant. "I'm not crazy," she told Schary, who promptly washed his hands of her.

When a relationship is over, it is over, and it is futile to try to prolong it. Irritating habits that were ignored, or regarded as charming eccentricities, during the good days suddenly become incitements to scorn and fury, sparks for harsh words and angry actions. In such a charged atmosphere, even a minor infraction can become a casus belli. And that was where Judy and M-G-M stood with each other in the uneasy spring of 1950. Their romance had long since ended, and though neither was yet willing to acknowledge it, a breakup was inevitable. All that was lacking was an excuse, and that came soon enough.

|||

After she finished "Get Happy," Judy returned to Carmel, where she planned several weeks of rest and relaxation. Her doctor recommended a vacation of at least eight months, and Metro, which had no immediate plans for her, seemed in no hurry to put her back to work. Scarcely had she become comfortable in her picturesque retreat, however, than she received a phone call from the studio. Eight days into rehearsals for Arthur Freed's *Royal Wedding,* June Allyson had announced that she was pregnant—she would have to drop out. Was Judy well enough to take her place? In what she was later to term "one of the really classic mistakes" of her life, Judy said yes, and on May 23 she was back in Culver City, rushing to rehearsals and preparing to do another picture with her old friends Chuck Walters and Fred Astaire.

This time her arrival was not met with universal joy. Like a veteran still limping from his battle wounds, Walters begged to be relieved: his health, he said, could not stand the strain of directing another movie with Judy. "I've got an ulcer," he cried to Freed. "I'm a wreck! Not two in a row with Judy—I can't." Freed reluctantly released him and assigned the director's job to a promising novice, twenty-six-year-old Stanley Donen, who until then had been chiefly known as Gene Kelly's collaborator and assistant. But it was Judy, not Donen, who was on trial.

For the first week she passed every test, punctual to the minute. She was half an hour late on June 1, however, and later still on June 2, when she was called for eleven, but failed to arrive until midafternoon—two-fifteen. By the third week of June, the last week of rehearsals, her energy was clearly flagging, and, over Donen's objections, she gained Freed's approval to work half-days, a reasonable request given her famous ability to learn routines after only one or two run-throughs. She had, in fact, already mastered the picture's complicated score. "Oh," exclaimed Saul Chaplin, "she sang the songs so brilliantly!"

Though she came in late—by anywhere from fifteen minutes to three hours and fifteen minutes—on nine of the eighteen days she worked, Judy's record on *Royal Wedding* was nonetheless better than it had been on most of the films she had made since *Girl Crazy.* But Dore Schary's efficiency-minded M-G-M was not the same studio that had produced those earlier films, a fact that Freed was reminded of, if any reminder were needed, by the memo from the front office that laid out the schedule for *Royal Wedding.* "IMPORTANT! PRODUCTION!! INFORMATION!!!" it proclaimed in a red banner, three inches high. The letter went on to say that the studio was "making an all out effort" to speed up filming—and knew it could count on Freed's cooperation.

Judy was a symbol of the wasteful old days, and her smallest misstep was now noted and the memo dispatched to half a dozen eager executives. Consciously or not, the new regime appeared to be itching for a confrontation, and the combative Donen was pleased to provide it. On

June 16, at the end of that third week, he demanded that she come in
the next day—a Saturday—for an hour's rehearsal. "If she doesn't come
in tomorrow," he warned Freed, "it's going to be a nightmare."

And so it was, but for Judy, not for Metro. Pleading illness, she
stayed home. Though it was only the first day she had missed entirely—
and only an hour's work, at that—she had handed the studio the excuse
it apparently had been waiting for. Within hours, a telegram, dated that
very day and obviously readied in advance, arrived on her doorstep
from Metro's corporate office in New York: "This is to notify you that
for good and sufficient cause and in accordance with the rights granted
to us under provisions of Paragraph 12 of your contract of employment . . ." She had, in short, been suspended once again.

In baseball, Hedda Hopper was quick to observe, it's three strikes
and you're out. "With Judy Garland," she added with a succinct finality,
"it's the same." Hopper was merely saying what Judy and everybody
else in Hollywood knew: this suspension was different from the previous two. This was to be her last. There would be no more chances.
Judy was being kicked out of the only real home she had known since
she was thirteen.

|||

So distraught that she had to be put to bed under sedation, Judy had
dried her tears by Monday afternoon and was steady enough to discuss
her post-Metro prospects with Vincente, Carleton Alsop and her secretary, Myrtle Tully. Although she was, for the moment, unemployable in
the motion-picture industry, the outlook was less bleak than she
seemed to think. Hollywood was not the only place in which she could
find pleasure and profit. Broadway beckoned and, across the Atlantic,
the Palladium, London's premiere variety house, had long been paying
her court. There was also an altogether new stage for entertainers—
television. As soon as it heard the news of her firing, NBC, in fact, offered her a contract, guaranteeing to make things enjoyable for her.
"Cheer up," said the telegram from NBC, "we all love you." One
world had locked her out, but the doors to several others were ready to
spring open at the mere mention of her name.

That was the argument reason would have made, and that, or something like it, was probably the argument presented to her that Monday afternoon in her living room on Evanview Drive. But Judy was not listening to reason. Around six o'clock, not long after Alsop had driven to Culver City to try to obtain a reversal of her suspension, she impulsively ran down the hall to a bathroom, locking the door behind her. "Leave me alone, I want to die!" she screamed as Vincente and Tully scurried after her. When she refused to open the door, Vincente broke it down with a heavy chair and saw what he had feared—blood. Smashing a water glass against the sink, Judy had scraped its jagged edge across the right side of her throat. "I wanted to black out the future as well as the past," she later explained. "I didn't want to live any more. I wanted to hurt myself and others."

Calling with the bad news from Culver City—her dismissal was final—Alsop heard the rumblings of still worse disaster on Evanview Drive. "Get over here as fast as you can!" screamed the frantic Vincente. Alsop rushed back to find not one hysterical Minnelli, but two— though a sharp slap on the face quickly returned Vincente to his senses. After that, the two men bundled Judy up, hid her on the floor of a car and drove her to the house she had rented on Sunset Boulevard. Waiting there was her doctor, Francis Ballard, who examined her neck and saw that, despite all the excitement, she had not seriously harmed herself. Slightly scratched, her throat required nothing more than a Band-Aid. He had done more damage to himself shaving, Alsop wryly observed.

That should have ended the matter. But someone, perhaps inadvertently, tipped off the newspapers, which quickly transformed those tiny abrasions into huge front-page headlines. "Judy Garland Cuts Throat Over Lost Job," shouted the tabloid *Los Angeles Mirror*. "Judy Garland Slashes Throat After Film Row," headlined the *Los Angeles Times*. So it continued for the next several days, as the papers explored her downfall from every angle. "Hollywood Heartbreaks—Story of Fame, Fortune and Despair," was the title of one article, which included Judy in a long and pathetic list of actresses ruined by the movies, everyone from Frances Farmer, who was confined to an asylum, to Olive Borden, a star of the silents, who died, penniless and almost alone, in a tiny room in a downtown mission. It took a war—North Korea invaded South Korea on June 25—to push Judy and her travails onto the back pages.

|||

A suicide attempt, even one as halfhearted as hers had been, has many motives. Judy was doubtless telling the truth when she said that she had wanted to die. But she was probably also telling the truth when she whispered to Dorothy Ponedel that she had been trying to gain public sympathy—and to put the blame for her suspension on M-G-M. If she was unable to achieve her first goal, Judy succeeded admirably in her second.

Florabel Muir, the *Mirror* reporter who first broke the story, set the pro-Judy tone of the coverage when she wrote that her desperate action was "a black reproach" to all of Hollywood, but a particular embarrassment for M-G-M, which had asked her to work against her doctor's advice. When one of Louis B. Mayer's racehorses, a mare named Busher, injured her leg, Muir noted, Mayer had put her to pasture for more than a year, until she had fully recuperated. "It would seem," Muir tartly remarked, "the same consideration could be given to the little Garland gal whose golden voice and great acting ability are worth saving perhaps as much as Busher was." Also in Judy's corner was Hedda Hopper. After saying that Judy's was "the greatest talent ever developed in this city, and I've known them all," Hopper, too, chided Metro. "Poor little Judy," she concluded. "So much talent, so much pressure, so much bad advice."

Seeking to counter such sentiments, the studio that was so adept at protecting its stars now proved equally skillful at smearing one of them. In a lengthy statement, Metro portrayed Judy as a reckless ingrate, an emotional cripple whom it had often employed against its better judgment. Denying her the respect suffering is usually accorded, the studio did its best to turn her troubles into a public joke. "Judy, as everyone who knows her realizes, is a very hysterical girl," one unnamed executive told Louella Parsons, the only columnist Metro could count on to relay its side of the story without blinking. "At least ten times before she has pretended to end her life when she was in trouble with the studio." In like manner, Ralph Wheelright, a balding, bespectacled Metro press agent, lifted his pudgy chin to show photographers exactly where Judy had cut herself, creating a picture so comical that it seemed designed to make her brush with tragedy seem slightly ludicrous. "Goddamnit," Alsop bitterly complained, "how could you do such a fucking, stupid thing, and do it to Judy?"

The answer, which even the canny Alsop had not yet grasped, was that Judy was now perceived as a liability: she had outlived her usefulness; she was expendable. "I tried to do everything in my power for Judy," said Mayer, neatly absolving himself of any responsibility. "I couldn't have done more if she had been my own daughter."

|||

"Judy's the bouncy type," said Carleton Alsop, who had, indeed, witnessed some remarkable recoveries. "She'll snap out of this in a hurry." But Alsop was wrong. Judy did not snap out of it in a hurry; she remained in bed for several days, with nurses in constant attendance. In a pattern that was repeated over and over, she was awakened to eat, then, when she soon started to cry, was given a sedative that put her back to sleep. "She apparently still doesn't know whether she wants to go on with life," Alsop was finally forced to admit. The newspapers and their blaring headlines were kept away from her, and Judy believed that the baskets of telegrams that came to the door every day were all in response to her suspension.

A year or so earlier Mayer had pleaded with Katharine Hepburn, that paragon of Yankee virtue, to give her a helping hand. "Do you feel that you could do anything?" he had asked. After talking to her, however, Hepburn had decided that there was nothing she could do: someone like Judy, she explained, was a full-time, twenty-four-hour-a-day job. Oddly matched as they were, the two women nonetheless became good friends, and when Judy was fired from *Annie Get Your Gun,* Hepburn had offered her the use of her homes in Connecticut and Manhattan. Thus it was that on the morning after Judy's encounter with the broken glass, the invincible Kate was the first notable to be allowed into the house. Looking not at all like a movie star—her freckled face was bare of makeup, her red hair flew in the breeze and her angular body was clad in a sweatshirt and slacks—she beat her way through the assembled press and threatened death to the first photographer who dared to take her picture. Hearing the commotion outside, Judy awaited her arrival with both anticipation and apprehension. "Oh, golly," she thought, "here comes Hepburn health."

Then, with the brisk authority of a celery tonic, Hepburn marched into Judy's bedroom. "Oh, dear, dear, you rally are sick," she said. "I think you'd better come stay at my house for a few weeks." Judy translated that as an invitation to six weeks of basic training—sit-ups, weight lifting and regular dunkings in Hepburn's pool—but before she could say no, Hepburn remembered that she was about to start a movie and would be unable to play drill instructor. Next to come through the door was someone equally formidable, Judy's earliest advocate at Metro, Ida Koverman. Sent by Mayer, Koverman, too, refused to talk to the gathered newshounds. "You have your job to do and I have mine," were the only words that tough old Scotswoman would give them.

Though no other friends were let into the sickroom, many people seemed genuinely touched by Judy's plight, and expressions of sympathy came in from all around the world. One of Florabel Muir's readers telephoned the reporter to say that Judy's voice had brought her not only pleasure but hope—that after hearing Judy sing "Over the Rainbow" in *The Wizard of Oz,* she had been able to overcome some very rough times. "I wish that song could do the same for Judy," the caller added wistfully.

|||

Everybody, it seemed, wanted to help. At one of Los Angeles's evangelical churches, Judy's name went up on a blackboard along with those of other unfortunates, earthquake victims and the like, for whom the congregation was urged to seek divine intervention. Jane Russell, whose luxuriant bosom had made her RKO's leading sex symbol, was one of those who bowed their heads on her behalf. As she prayed, Russell later wrote, she heard a command from the Lord: she was to give Judy a heavenly message. Following orders, Russell reached Judy by phone— a minor miracle, all by itself—then, after describing her mission, relayed the message. "The Lord is my shepherd," went the familiar words of the Twenty-third Psalm, "I shall not want. . . ." Judy gave a slight gasp, mumbled a polite thank-you and hung up.

By late July, Judy was well enough to travel with Liza to Sun Valley and Lake Tahoe, then, a few weeks later, to New York with Dorothy Ponedel and Myrtle Tully. It was in Manhattan, amid Gotham's asphalt and concrete, that her injured ego received the medicine it most needed—adulation. Assuming she would go unrecognized, she sneaked into a Times Square theater for an afternoon showing of *Summer Stock*, only to be spotted as she was leaving, and embraced by an excited crowd, clapping and shouting encouragement. "We're all for you, Judy!" one person said. "Keep your chin up!" advised another. Another outpouring of warmth and affection came at a Broadway play; as she made her way to her seat, cheers resounded through the theater. Buoyed by such receptions, Judy finally did bounce back, just as Alsop had predicted. Confident—even ebullient—she returned to Los Angeles in mid-September, prepared at last to confront her future: it was time to write finis to her Metro career.

Not long after her brush with suicide, Mayer had paid her a visit. What they said to each other has not been recorded, but their meeting, which lasted an hour and fifteen minutes, was emotional—Louella Parsons got that description from Mayer himself. "Judy Garland has fifty years more to live, if she obeys her doctor, and I believe she will," Mayer said afterward, and, in accordance with this generous sentiment, he persuaded Nick Schenck to keep her on salary, or part salary, until she was on her feet.

Three months later, when her health had returned, Metro agreed not only to cancel her contract, which had more than a year to run, but to forgive the several thousand dollars she still owed for her trip to Boston the previous year. On September 29, 1950, the studio officially released her from any further obligations, "with reluctance and regret," as Mayer generously phrased it, "and with a view to serving her own best interests." Fifteen years after her father had driven her through that storied gate on Washington Boulevard, a small girl with a large voice, she was free, no longer answerable to anyone but herself. In times to come, Judy would look back on M-G-M—her alma mater, she would call it—with a mixture of bitterness, rue and more than a little nostalgia. But at that instant her chief emotion was relief, and all she could say was, "Isn't it wonderful!"

|||

"In an oblique and daffy sort of way, you are as much a national asset as our coal reserves," Billy Rose, the Broadway impresario and columnist, had written. "Both of you help warm up our insides," he had said. "And the day you stop making pictures you're going to take a lot of warmth out of the lives of the millions of Bills and Betties who live in furnished rooms and cook their breakfasts on hot plates—me-and-my-shadow folk, for whom a Judy Garland movie is the best available substitute for the kiss in the dark that never happens." Now, that gloomy day had dawned. Judy had stopped making pictures for all those Bills and Betties, and who was to blame?

The easy answer was Metro, more specifically Dore Schary and the ungallant Stanley Donen, who had delivered the fatal wound with conspicuous and unseemly haste—and over nothing more serious than an hour's missed rehearsal. Behind them stood Schenck and Mayer, who had long been aware of Judy's addiction to drugs, but who had chosen, until it was too late, to stand by, scolding rather than helping. No less an authority than Harry J. Anslinger, the U.S. Commissioner of Narcotics and the highest drug enforcement officer in the nation, had put them on notice. Concerned about her well-being—"I believed her to be a fine woman caught in a situation that could only destroy her," he said—Anslinger had traveled from Washington to New York to talk to Schenck in person.

Anslinger knew Judy's story in detail—knew both where she was obtaining drugs and why—and he, too, suggested that the only way she could shake her habit was to spend at least a year in a sanitarium. Anslinger's long experience and weighty credentials meant little to Schenck, however, who had all but sneered at such an outlandish recommendation. "I've got fourteen million dollars invested in her," he had said. "I couldn't afford your plan. She's at the top of her box office right this minute." To Anslinger's outraged retort that Judy's death, from suicide or a drug overdose, would cost him his fourteen million in any case, Schenck had philosophically replied: "We'll have to take that chance."

There was blame enough for everybody, Judy's mother not excluded. But in the end, the responsibility for Judy's departure belonged not to M-G-M, but to Judy herself. She did not want to stay at Metro; she had not wanted to since 1946, when she signed the contract the studio had now so kindly canceled, and she had regretted and fought her decision ever since. For her, she said, M-G-M was not a golden fiefdom; it was a haunted house, where every time she entered, she felt like screaming—again and again. Nor did she consider herself a privileged princess, waited on "hand and foot," as Stanley Donen was to claim. In her eyes, she was more like a prisoner.

If Judy symbolized the old M-G-M, her exit symbolized its demise. Its structure remained—some of Arthur Freed's best pictures were, in fact, yet to be made—but not its spirit. More interested in educating audiences than entertaining them, Schary let performers' contracts lapse, and, one by one, the studio of the stars said good-bye to its most valuable creations, its Gables, Garsons and Tracys. "Isn't God good to me?" Mayer had often exclaimed, but as he watched his power daily dwindling, he must have harbored some doubts. About Schary, all he could say was "I was a sheep who invited a hungry wolf to dinner."

Less than a year after Judy left, the embittered Mayer gave Schenck—"Mr. Skunk," he called him in private—an ultimatum. "It's either me or Schary," he said. "Which?" For Schenck, who had been conspiring against him for more than twenty years, the choice was obvious. Mayer represented the past; Schary, who had succeeded in reversing the studio's financial losses, was the present. The outcome, as Mayer should have realized, was foreordained, and his resignation was immediately accepted, effective August 31, 1951. "I know how you and Nick schemed to kick me out, you son of a bitch," he snarled at Schary. Then, as the offended Schary angrily stalked away, Mayer shouted after him: "Sit down and I'll tell you everything, you little kike." Beaten at last, the wounded old lion had nothing left but his roar.

Helped up by Buddy Pepper
after an unplanned landing at the Palladium

CHAPTER 11

Resurrection

I n Hollywood, Judy had been written off by just about everybody—"still a mixed up dame" was the contemptuous appraisal of one record company executive. The chief dissenter was Judy herself. "The slate of the past is wiped clean," she defiantly declared. "Insofar as I'm concerned, the world is good, golden, and glorious. My best years and my best work lie ahead of me, and I'm going to give them everything I've got." To do that, however, she had to leave Hollywood, with its skeptics, pessimists and bad memories, and at the beginning of October, a few days after Metro's announcement, Judy and her companions, Myrtle Tully and the omnipresent Dorothy Ponedel, once again boarded a train for New York. "What I want to do now," Judy said before heading east, "is to rest and have fun."

That is exactly what she did. Not long after she alighted at Grand Central, her old friend Fred Finklehoffe, a screenwriter on several of her early movies, received a telephone call. "Freddie," Judy said, "let's go out on the town." Finklehoffe was not the only one to receive such a summons, and Judy's escorts were soon being listed in the gossip columns, causing caustic comment back home. Vincente, said one writer, had to be "the most broad-minded husband in the land." But that was not quite the case. Vincente was not so much broad-minded as he was indifferent, as eager as Judy to bring their partnership to its conclusion.

Their marriage, like their movies, was a product of M-G-M, and it was probably inevitable that when Judy broke with the studio, she would also break with Vincente. In her mind, the two were one. What rankled most, perhaps, was her discovery that Vincente's real spouse, the one to whom he had pledged his primary allegiance, was the studio. He was, in fact, to remain under contract to Metro for a total of twenty-six years, longer than any other director; he outlasted not only Judy, but Louis B. Mayer, Dore Schary and that master conniver, Nick Schenck himself. A man whose odd clothes and face makeup had once caused a minor scandal was thus to become the quintessential Metro director, almost as much a symbol of M-G-M as Leo the Lion. No roar was ever to be heard from Vincente, however, and a career of such durability was not made by talking back to the people in power. For Judy, the sad corollary to his remarkable endurance was that not once during the five years they were together had Vincente stood up for her against Mayer, Freed or anyone else in the Thalberg Building.

"Judy needed a strong man, someone to lean on," one of her friends explained. "And Minnelli, though understanding and anxious to help, was sort of an ethereal guy. He wasn't strong enough to cope with Judy and her problems." Vincente himself acknowledged as much. "I'd obviously failed Judy," he admitted in his memoir, adding that he could not overlook the bleak fact that the years of their marriage were also the years in which she had seemed least able to cope with the world. "It was an indictment I couldn't ignore."

It is probably safe to say that, on balance, they had failed each other in equal measure. If Vincente had disappointed her, so had Judy disappointed him, worn him out with her scenes and suicide attempts, one crisis following another in never-ending succession. It was tiring to live in the path of a perpetual hurricane. If they stayed together, Vincente had finally come to realize, their life would always be marred by her indulgences and compulsions. Still, he might have accepted all that. What he could not accept was her almost gleeful admission, her "shocking confession," to use his words, that she had lied to her many psychiatrists—that she had not really tried to get well. For that, Vincente said, it was "damn near impossible" for him to forgive her.

Their once-promising collaboration was now only a memory, and on December 21, 1950, they announced the end of their marriage. "So characteristic of quiet, gentle Vincente Minnelli that he never said a word when Judy Garland walked out," clucked Louella Parsons, who made it clear whose side she was on. "Perhaps Vince was too easy and too gentle with her." Although they were always to remain friends, for Liza's sake, if not for their own, occasionally one or the other would let slip a disparaging remark. "Oh, Vincente Minnelli," Judy would say, with more than a hint of sarcasm, "the man with perfect taste." With Judy gone, Vincente would look for another Galatea, a woman his perfect taste could mold into a beautiful work of art. But Judy's search for a protector had already ended: she had found a man who was neither quiet nor gentle. She was in love again.

|||

Her new love's name was Sid Luft—Michael Sidney Luft—and Judy had actually met him in 1937, when she was making *Broadway Melody of 1938* and he, a strapping young man of twenty, was working for Eleanor Powell, the picture's star. They met a second time eleven years later—at a bowling alley, of all places. "She thought I was a conceited ass," he said, "and I thought she was a shrimp." Those negative opinions were radically altered, however, on their third meeting, in the fall of 1950. Also visiting New York, Luft saw Judy enjoying herself with Freddie Finklehoffe, his friend, too, at an East Side hangout called the Little Club. He went over to their table, said his hellos and asked if he could sit down. Finklehoffe, who was hoping to keep Judy to himself, did not waste words on polite excuses. "I don't want any traffic with you at all, Sid," he said. "Get lost." But Judy, who later said that she fell in love with Luft even as he stood there looking down at her, laughingly intervened. "Of course, let him sit down, Freddie," she said, and Luft pulled up a chair.

Judy and Luft were soon going out by themselves, and when Luft returned to Los Angeles a couple of weeks later, Judy quickly followed. Their romance continued to blossom in its new venue, and weeks before she and Vincente announced their breakup, Judy moved out of the house on Evanview Drive—she had already given up her house on Sunset Boulevard—and into an apartment of her own in West Hollywood. As surprised as her friends had once been by her engagement to Vincente, they were still more shocked by her affair with a man one magazine forthrightly labeled "Mr. Wrong." But whether Sid was Mr. Wrong or Mr. Right—or, like Dr. Jekyll, both in equal parts—was never to be precisely established, by Judy or anyone else. What was clear was that in Sid, who had a boxer's biceps and bulky build, she had discovered a man who would, quite literally, fight for her.

Sid was so fond of a good scrap that one amused writer had honored him with a prizefighter's nickname—"One-Punch Luft." On two occasions he had turned posh Ciro's into a boxing arena; his last match, in the spring of 1950, created such a ruckus that almost a thousand of the club's glamorous patrons screamed, shouted and shoved one another aside as they climbed onto tables for a better look. Now, back in Los Angeles at the end of October, One-Punch Luft was in the papers again, this time for breaking the nose of Jimmy Starr, a Hollywood columnist, on the sidewalk in front of the Mocambo, in full view of anybody who happened to be passing on Sunset Boulevard. One thing could be said for certain about Judy's new lover: he was a volcano who could erupt at any time.

|||

His father had owned a jewelry store, his mother had run two dress shops, and Sid had grown up in the leafy, WASP-y suburbs of Westchester County—Yonkers, Bronxville and New Rochelle—just north of New York City. Inviting as they appeared, in the twenties and thirties those were inhospitable precincts for Jews, and from the time he was five, Sid was made painfully aware that he was different, or, in his words, "a Jew—a little Jew." Not about to be pushed around by anybody, he started toting a gun, a .22-caliber revolver, before he reached puberty. "Boy, 12, Walking Arsenal," read the newspaper headline after the police confiscated it, an action that may have prevented serious bloodshed when an older, bigger boy attacked him at an ice rink the following year. "Hey, Jew, get off the ice!" the boy yelled, then, whacking him with a hockey stick, proceeded to beat him up.

Nearly choking on his hate, Sid vowed to make himself powerful enough to kill, even without his revolver, and he embarked on a rigorous course of weight lifting, exercise and boxing lessons. Three years later, so muscular that he could walk up stairs on the palms of his hands, he approached his assailant, by this time a husky nineteen. "Remember me?" Sid asked, then took his revenge, returning, with compound interest, all the blows he had received on the ice those many months earlier. That, at least, was how Sid told the story of his stormy teenage years, and, to judge by his later history, most of what he said was probably true.

Sometimes, in fact, it seemed that Sid had been born angry—angry at his tormentors, angry at his circumstances and, perhaps most of all, angry at his father, who would not defend him. By choice coincidence, the relationship between the Lufts, Norbert and Leonora, was much like that between Frank and Ethel Gumm: the husband weak and passive, the woman strong and aggressive, a go-getter. Sid made no secret which parent he favored, and as much as he worshipped his doting mother, that Bronxville Brünnhilde, so, to the same degree, did he disdain his too-docile father. Indeed, when Norbert Luft accused him of some misdeed, Sid, then fifteen and well on his way to becoming a muscle man, threatened to light a real fire under what seemed like a classic Oedipal conflict. "You're accusing me of something I didn't do," he told his father, as he made his hands into furious and very visible fists. "And if you keep on doing it, I'll hit you." Taking him at his word, Norbert backed down, which probably made Sid despise him all the more.

As they move into manhood, many men learn to control such youthful hostility, diverting it into healthier and more productive paths. Sid did not. He not only retained his early rage, but put it on such frequent and ostentatious display that it is almost superfluous to suggest that it was a cover for deep-rooted insecurities: a truly secure man does not need to raise his fists at every slight, actual or imagined. "A professional he-man," was how Joe Mankiewicz, that grizzled veteran of the analyst's couch, characterized Judy's new lover.

Yet many women like a belligerent swagger, particularly when it is combined with charm, penetrating brown eyes and more than passable good looks, and not long after he graduated from high school, Sid was the boyfriend and secretary of the tap-dancing Powell. Pleased with her acquisition, Powell told a reporter that when she took him on a trip to Havana, Sid's athletic rumba "made the cheeks of the caballeros blanch with envy." There was obviously more to young Sid's job than answering the mail.

Flying had been Sid's obsession since boyhood—in California he logged something like four hundred hours in the air—and in 1941, months before the United States entered World War II, he traveled to Canada to join the already embattled Royal Canadian Air Force. Returning to California after Pearl Harbor, as a test pilot for Douglas Aircraft, he was severely burned in the crash of a light bomber, an experience that profoundly changed his priorities. From then on, Sid said, he concentrated on only one thing: survival.

|||

In November 1943, several months after that skirmish with mortality, Sid married Lynn Bari, a star of B-pictures at 20th Century–Fox. After the war he tried to find a place of his own in the movie business, and he did manage to produce two modestly successful pictures, *French Leave* and *Kilroy Was Here,* for tiny Monogram Pictures. When he met Judy in New York, Sid, a keen fan of the horses, was attempting to put together a third picture, a biography of sorts of Man o' War, perhaps the most famous of all American racers.

Most of Sid's projects, including that Man o' War movie, collapsed before leaving the starting gate, however. The problem may have been, as some suggested, that he was lazy, unwilling to give his ideas the time and effort they demanded. Or it may have been that too many of his enterprises involved what could be termed sharp practices, dealings that, though not necessarily illegal, made sober-minded people hesitate before handing him checks. "A slicker, always off on some dream of a big deal" was how Judy's friend Eleanor Lambert remembered him.

If he was not a movie mogul, Sid acted like one. A stylish dresser, with a fondness for expensive silk shirts, he could often be seen at the racetracks, Hollywood Park or Santa Anita, sitting in a box with the real moguls and sometimes winning or losing thousands of dollars in an afternoon. Like many of the rich, he also maintained his own racing stable, even if it consisted of a mere three horses. Louis B. Mayer and Jack Warner could afford hay, oats and big losses at the pari-mutuel windows. Sid could not, and in 1947 an irate Lynn Bari filed for divorce, doing her best to portray Sid, that model of tough-guy masculinity, as nothing better than a kept man. "During our marriage I was the only breadwinner in the family," she declared, adding that she had put her assets under both names solely because he had pleaded: he wanted, he had told her, to be considered "a man of property."

Forgetting such humiliating comments, the two eventually reconciled, and a year later Bari gave birth to their only child, John Sidney Luft. But the differences that had surfaced when Bari filed suit were never repaired, and three years later, just a few weeks before Sid and Judy came together at the Little Club, Bari again asked for a divorce. This time, alleging "eight years of slavery," she did not change her mind. "He'd leave the house in the evening 'to get a newspaper,' and he'd come back at 6 a.m.," Bari told a Superior Court judge. "He didn't care about a home. He preferred night clubs, and I didn't."

Judy did—and she preferred Sid, as well. "Judy, don't mess with him," Finklehoffe had warned her. "He's trouble." But after what she regarded as fifteen years of bullying by M-G-M, Sid was the kind of trouble she wanted, a man who would stand at her side, fight her battles and, if need be, pound his fists into the faces of her enemies. For Sid, unlike Vincente, she felt not a tepid affection, but an unrestrained and uninhibited passion. "Judy was so crazy about this guy called Sid Luft that anything he did she would ask for more," complained Dorothy Ponedel. "He had her hypnotized."

|||

Though Judy had found a new man, a new career eluded her, and at the beginning of 1951 the question remained: what would she do with the rest of her life? "What is happening to Judy Garland?" one Hollywood columnist demanded. "Where will she wind up?" Judy must have wondered herself, and for all her confident talk she could not hide that she was frightened—and had good reason to be. At twenty-eight, she knew just one thing: how to make movies. With several proposals from which to choose, she was guaranteed an audience. But how long could she keep it? Could a woman with her record of unreliability be counted on to appear on time for a performance? And every performance thereafter? That was a question no one, including Judy, could answer.

"I'd like to go to England," the fifteen-year-old Judy had wistfully remarked in only her second movie at Metro, *Thoroughbreds Don't Cry.* "Maybe I will someday with a show." Now, half a lifetime later, she had that opportunity. Rejecting all the offers from her own country, she chose the one from England: $70,000 for four weeks at London's Palladium, the last great variety house in the English-speaking world. Nearly two decades after she had left, Judy would be returning to her roots—vaudeville.

"The history of my life is in my songs," she was to say, and the act she put together was a biography in song. With the help of two of the brightest talents in Culver City, Roger Edens and Chuck Walters, she selected highlights from her fifteen years in film, from "You Made Me Love You," which she sang in her very first movie for Metro, *Broadway Melody of 1938,* to "Get Happy," which she sang in her very last, *Summer Stock.* There were several from those in between, including two from *Meet Me in St. Louis* and two renditions of "Over the Rainbow," which was not only her signature song, but a particular favorite of Londoners, who had been comforted, during the dark days of the Blitz, by its sentimental message of hope and longing. She was, in short, producing, directing and starring in an M-G-M musical in miniature—*The Judy Garland Story,* it might have been called. Hollywood may have declared her anathema, but Judy was still a movie star, and a movie star was what people expected to see.

Despite their impending divorce—a judge dissolved their marriage on March 29—Judy also asked for advice from the master of the Metro musical, driving up to Evanview Drive with her pianist, her old friend Buddy Pepper, to give Vincente a special preview. Perfectionist though he was, Vincente could come up with no more than one suggestion.

Because she was often referred to as the greatest entertainer since Al Jolson, he said, she should include "Rock-a-bye Your Baby with a Dixie Melody," one of Jolson's standards. Reviewing the performance she gave that evening, Vincente said that Judy's voice "was better than ever, for it had a new-found maturity. The heartache in the sad songs and the frenetic drive of the upbeat numbers created an extraordinary impact. She'd developed marvelous gestures which put the stresses on the most unexpected words. The effect was awkward and occasionally graceless, but strangely, it was right."

|||

The patterns of the past are sometimes harder to break than the bars of a jail cell. Despite Vincente's praise, despite her own hard work and the effort and sweat of Edens and Walters, Judy began having second thoughts. Although she had sung on the radio many times, she had not performed before an audience, paying to hear her alone, since the summer of 1943, when she sang at Philadelphia's Robin Hood Dell. What if she went all the way to England and nobody wanted to hear her? "I've

A walk on the deck during the voyage to England

heard that the British can be awfully quiet if they don't go for an actress," she had fretted when first approached by the Palladium.

Though Sid and her agent, Abe Lastvogel, did their best to reassure her, Judy seemed prepared to cancel the whole trip until Fanny Brice, her costar in her third Metro movie, *Everybody Sing,* came crashing through her door. Placing her hands on her hips like an exasperated mother, Brice all but shouted: "Good lord, girl, do you think you're the only person on earth who has problems? I know every heartache in the book. But I never sat down on my heels and gave up—and you're not going to either! Not if I have to get out my old spanking brush and give it to you where you need it most. Now, you keep your head up and your eyes on tomorrow—and the hell with yesterday."

Fearing Brice and her old spanking brush perhaps even more than she did the standoffish English, Judy kept to her plans and traveled to New York with her three companions—Myrtle Tully, Dorothy Ponedel and Buddy Pepper—for their March 30 date with the French liner *Ile de France.* "Honestly, I've hit my stride," she said shortly before sailing, revealing not a hint of anxiety. "Things have been pretty rough these past few years, but I've snapped out of my depression. I'm in fine voice, I've lots of energy—and well, the future looks fine."

She would need that good humor when she read what the London reporters were to write in the days before her opening. For several years, since the time of *The Pirate,* her weight had gone up and down almost as fast as a yo-yo—thin, fat, thin, fat. When she disembarked at Plymouth, the yo-yo was stuck at fat: she was as heavy as she had been a year earlier, during the first weeks of *Summer Stock.* "Plump and jovial" was how one paper described her. "Tubby," said another. To all of which Judy had the perfect, unanswerable comeback. "I may be awfully fat," she admitted, "but I feel awfully good."

Her fans—most of England, it seemed—would not have minded if she had been as big as Big Ben, just so long as she sounded like Judy Garland. As she walked down its gangplank, the *Ile de France* wished her well with a long blast from its horn, while the other ships in Plymouth harbor spelled out her name in nautical signals. Smiling crowds stood at the pier, and hundreds more waited at the train station in London, merely to say hello.

The one she really wanted to hear say hello, however—Sid, of course—had stayed behind in New York. On Judy's instructions, Dorothy Ponedel had telephoned him from the ship, midway across the Atlantic, and had begged him to join her. After settling into London's Dorchester Hotel, Judy had Ponedel call again—Judy needed Sid for emotional support, Ponedel told him. The second call persuaded him, and within hours he was on a plane to England. Thus it was that on opening night, Monday, April 9, Judy had everything and everyone she desired. As she and Pepper walked arm in arm to the stage, she made a small confession, however. She felt, she said, as if she were walking to her execution.

|||

Storytellers cherish that dramatic moment when a courageous person takes on the odds. A Stanley, setting off through unexplored jungles in search of the missing Livingston. A Lindbergh, slowly rising from Roosevelt Field on his lonely flight to Paris. A Ben Hogan, so severely injured in a car crash that he has been told he will never play again, walking onto a golf course to win the U.S. Open. Soldiers and statesmen, adventurers and athletes. Those are the heroes who make the blood race, who bring a tear to the eye and who inspire poets and playwrights and filmmakers. But what of the writer and artist, the composer and entertainer, who risk career and livelihood to try something radically new? Are they, too, not brave, those explorers of the mind and the imagination?

And what of a Judy Garland, fired by M-G-M, written off by Hollywood and "on the slippery slope to a fadeout," as she so accurately phrased it? How much courage must it have taken for her to have walked onto the storied stage of the Palladium that evening in early April? As the orchestra began playing her entrance music, Buddy Pepper, who was waiting for her at his piano, peered back into the wings and saw her mouth form just two terrified words—"Oh, no!"

If courage is not the absence of fear, but its defeat, then Judy displayed courage that night, going ahead despite an attack of nerves so serious that it made her choke on several words of her introduction. "Never mind!" came the shouts from out front. "You're doing a good job." Thus encouraged, she went smoothly ahead until, just after the fourth number, she twirled to make a brief exit. As she turned, she tripped and fell—landing smack on her backside. Seeing that she was hurt only in her dignity, Pepper let out a whoop of laughter as he rushed to pick her up, and Judy laughed with him. "That's one of the most ungraceful exits I ever made," she said—the cue the audience was waiting for. Suddenly that huge theater was one happy howl. Of such accidents are triumphs made, and from then on, from the first row in the orchestra to the last row in the second balcony, the Palladium belonged to her.

Still, it was not until Judy had started her final number—"Over the Rainbow"—that Pepper, like a soldier too caught up in the battle to know which side is winning, began to appreciate the dimensions of her victory. Even before she concluded, the audience was roaring its approval, a sound so ear-shattering that Val Parnell, the Palladium's managing director, called it the biggest ovation he had ever seen or heard. Her eyes misting, Judy could doubtless have said the same. In return, she offered the only gift in her possession—a promise to sing her heart out.

She kept her word, selling out her entire run at the Palladium—two shows a night and two matinees a week. "I doubt if Sarah Bernhardt, Jenny Lind and Vesta Tilley would ever have asked for more from their admirers" was how the *Evening Standard*'s critic characterized her almost ecstatic reception. When she had finished in London, Judy proceeded to conquer the rest of England—and Scotland and Ireland too—with a week each in Glasgow, Edinburgh, Manchester, Dublin, Liverpool and Birmingham and one night in the seaside resort of Blackpool. "Not bad for a kid from Lancaster, California, hmmm?" she joked to Pepper.

What would happen to Judy Garland? a Hollywood columnist had demanded in January. Her British audiences had now answered him and all the other doubters. "Where do I go from here?" Judy herself asked. "One thing is certain. I have found out where I belong—out there under the limelights singing for my supper. I have been asked to make more movies, and of course I will. Maybe I'll make one over here. But from now on it's the stage that has first call on me."

III

It was almost inevitable that, given such sentiments, Judy would follow up her British successes with stage appearances in America. But what kinds of appearances? And on what stages? Those were the questions she was asking herself when she set sail for New York on August 7. Some were urging her to tour the United States with one-night stands based on her Palladium act; *Inside U.S.A.,* it was to be titled. But Sid and Abe Lastvogel had a better idea: a single stage in a single city—New York. There was only one problem: vaudeville was dead, and Times Square, its onetime capital, no longer possessed a variety house like the Palladium. The greatest of them all, the Palace, on the southeast corner of Broadway and Forty-seventh Street, still stood, but as a movie theater, and a seedy, woebegone movie theater at that.

That was its sorry condition, in any event, when Sid passed by on the afternoon of August 12 and, in a moment of inspiration, stopped at a pay phone to call Sol A. Schwartz, the president of RKO Theaters, which owned the Palace and many other movie houses. Though Sid did not know it, Schwartz had long wanted to restore the Palace to its former vaudeville glory, and within five minutes the two were exchanging hellos in the lobby. "Sid," said the eager Schwartz, "are you thinking what I'm thinking?" Sid was, of course, and two weeks later *Variety* announced that, after eighteen years, vaudeville would return to the Palace, with Judy Garland topping the bill. On the evening of Tuesday, October 16, Judy would at last realize her fondest ambition—to see her name in lights on a Broadway marquee.

Rushing back to California, she once again enlisted the Freed Unit to help put her act together. Roger Edens wrote introductions, Chuck Walters did the staging and Irene Sharaff designed some of her costumes. At the piano, taking the spot once occupied by Buddy Pepper, who complained that Sid had shortchanged him during the British tour, would be a distinguished Freed alumnus: Hugh Martin, co-author of the *Meet Me in St. Louis* songs, which would be a prominent part of her repertoire. As work progressed, it was evident that the Palladium had merely been a rehearsal for the Palace. Not only would her New York show be at least ten minutes longer, forty-five minutes in all, but it would also be considerably more elaborate. In London, Judy had been by herself; at the Palace she would be assisted by eight chorus boys and a partner. Dirtying his face, Walters himself would join her for "A Couple of Swells," the tramp number she and Fred Astaire had romped through so exuberantly in *Easter Parade.* Broadway was where her show would be playing, but Culver City was where it had been manufactured.

As Judy prepared her act in Los Angeles, RKO prepared the Palace in New York. On October 4 the house went dark; workmen hurried in to give it a much needed face-lift. Crystal chandeliers were returned to their proper places, new carpets were laid and fresh coats of paint were applied to every wall in sight. But if RKO was gambling thousands of dollars on Judy, Judy herself was wagering much more. Anywhere else, a flop might be forgotten. At the Palace it would gain a perverse immortality. A hit, on the other hand, would reverberate equally loudly. There was no escaping the core of the matter: it was on the island of Manhattan, and nowhere else, that the new Judy would succeed or fail. "The Palladium experience was grand," wrote the Broadway columnist Dorothy Kilgallen, "but it was, after all, England. New York is the terrible, wonderful test."

|||

Nobody knew that better than Judy. When she arrived in New York in the second week of October, she was suffering from such a bad case of pre-curtain jitters that Hugh Martin asked his music-minded friends Bob and Jean Bach to divert her with a party the night before the opening. "She's going to be appearing before strangers," he said, "and it might just ease things if she could groove a little bit." Arriving without Sid, Judy sat in the living room of the Bachs' brownstone apartment in Greenwich Village, and, sipping bourbon and singing "Over the Rainbow," she did groove—and after the party grooved some more.

As the hosts were emptying ashtrays and preparing for bed, Jean Bach looked out the window and saw Judy's limousine still waiting to take her home. Suspecting she might have fallen asleep, the Bachs searched every corner but found no Judy. They did not realize what had happened until they heard their front door slam the next morning. Judy had spent the night outside on their terrace with another of their guests, one of her long-ago lovers, that bouncy butterball from Georgia— Johnny Mercer. Fortunately for her voice, which was to be actively employed a few hours later, the skies were clear and the temperature was warm, never dropping below fifty-four degrees.

It was even milder when the taxi carrying Judy and Chuck Walters neared the Palace the following evening, only to find the street blocked off. "What the hell's going on here, driver?" inquired an angry Walters. "Everybody's here for Judy Garland's opening," replied the driver. There was, in fact, no rush. Judy was last on the bill, preceded, in true vaudeville fashion, by five acts: a sextet of teeterboard acrobats, a brother-and-sister dance team and no fewer than three different sets of comics. Introduced by her eight chorus boys, Judy came on after the intermission. Too heavy still, she forestalled any whispers about her weight by dismissing it with a joke, as she had done at the Palladium. "Call the *Mirror,*" she sang, "call the *News,* tell 'em I've another nineteen pounds to lose." The real songs quickly followed, some made famous by Palace headliners of the past—"Shine On, Harvest Moon," for example, which was Nora Bayes's signature song, and "My Man," which was Fanny Brice's—and some, such as "The Trolley Song," made famous by Judy herself.

At the end came her two big production numbers, "Get Happy" and "A Couple of Swells," after which, still wearing her tramp costume, she sat down at the front of the stage to sing her own signature song. Slow and subdued, almost a whisper at the start, her rendition of "Over the Rainbow" was like the final scene of a play, the scene that draws together half a dozen different threads and provides the audience with the quiet catharsis it needs after such an emotional outpouring. Night after night, the result was the same: tears streaked down Judy's cheeks as she tried to follow her rainbow, and many more tears—a rivulet, then a salty waterfall—came from all those watching and hearing her.

When she was through, the Palace, in the words of one reviewer, was "bedlam superimposed on bedlam," giving her an ovation that one reporter clocked at three minutes and eighteen seconds, something close to eternity as time is measured in the theater. The critics joined in the applause the next day. Vaudeville, dead for eighteen years, turned out to have been a sleeping beauty, said one. "The kiss that awakened this beauty last week came from plump and lively Judy Garland—singing and dancing at the Mecca of old-time vaudevillians, New York City's Palace Theater." RKO's gamble had paid off—and so had Judy's.

As lines formed at the box office, her run, originally scheduled for four weeks, was extended, then extended again, and again after that. Despite a brutal schedule of two shows a day, during that entire period she revealed only one sign of the troubles that had attended her at M-G-M: a collapse onstage in November, the product of exhaustion and a new doctor's prescribing too high a drug dosage. Returning after a few days, she continued, at a slightly slower pace, well into 1952. " 'JUDY' BREAKS ALL-TIME LONG RUN RECORD AT PALACE! 12TH TERRIFIC WEEK!" proclaimed the ads at the beginning of the new year.

For the Palace, Judy had been perhaps too successful: a replacement was all but impossible to find. Knowing that, after such a triumph, even a modest hit would look like failure, every star Sol Schwartz approached shied away, horrified at the dismal prospect. "Who can follow that?" demanded Betty Hutton, who, with almost obscene glee, had grabbed at the lead of *Annie Get Your Gun* two years earlier. "If you did four flips in the air, cut your head off and sewed it on again," said Hutton, "it wouldn't mean a thing."

It was Judy, not the public, who finally called it quits. After nineteen weeks and 184 performances, she lowered the curtain at last on February 24. At the end of that final show, the audience, some three thousand, including standees, rose and serenaded her with "Auld Lang Syne," a gesture that caused her to place one foot behind the other, like a little girl, and grin in delight—then cry, with equal delight. "Shout; for the Lord hath given you the city," Joshua told the children of Israel. But Judy did them one better. To take title to New York, all she had to do was sing.

|||

Judy's conquest was so complete that critics and commentators, hard pressed to account for it, eventually gave up, likening it to a miracle—and miracles can only be described, not explained. "Where lay the magic?" inquired a bewildered Clifton Fadiman, who saw her not at the opening, but many weeks later, at a point when many shows have lost that first-night fervor. "Why did we grow silent," Fadiman went on, "self-forgetting, our faces lit as with so many candles, our eyes glittering with unregarded tears? Why did we call her back again and again and again, not as if she had been giving a good performance, but as if she had been offering salvation?"

Since she had received similar receptions in Britain and Ireland, the answer could not be found in a quality unique to New York, its press or its people. Nor, since she was to cast the same spell in many places during the years that followed, could it be found in anything particular to the time, or to big cities, or to a special group. Young and old, male and female, city folk and small-town dwellers, the sophisticated and the unsophisticated: when they were in a Garland audience, all were self-forgetting, their faces lit as with so many candles. Judy's appeal was universal.

Where, then, lay the magic? The question puzzled Judy herself. "I have a machine in my throat that gets into many people's ears and affects them" was one of her less than helpful answers, although it was true that she had a most remarkable musical instrument, a warm, viola-like vibrato—vibrato is a gentle fluctuation in pitch—combined with the blasting force of a trumpet. The sound that emerged was what the critic Henry Pleasants called "the most utterly *natural* vocal production" he had ever heard. "Probably because she sang so much as a child, and learned to appreciate the appeal of her child's voice, she made no effort as she grew older to produce her voice in any other way," wrote Pleasants in his astute critical survey, *The Great American Popular Singers*. "It was an open-throated, almost birdlike vocal production, clear, pure, resonant, innocent."

Voice alone barely began to explain the magic, however. Several of her contemporaries also possessed remarkable machines—some better, in fact, than Judy's, with wider ranges and more artful technique—yet failed to raise the blood pressure in the seats out front. But Judy was not merely a singer; she was a singing actress. "Good singing is a form of good acting," she declared, and she did the reverse of what most other singers do. She put the words before the music, instead of the other way around, treating the lyrics with all the reverence due them, as one of her longtime arrangers, Nelson Riddle, so aptly phrased it. "I really mean every word of every song I sing, no matter how many times I've sung it before," Judy herself said to one interviewer. "The whole premise of a song is a question, a quest," she told another, making the same point in a slightly different way. For her, a song was not just a song; it was a story, and neither she nor her audience could ever be sure of the ending. Or so she made it seem.

Yet all of that—her voice and the way she used it—still only partially explains Judy's peculiar magic. Nora Bayes, her most illustrious predecessor at the Palace, probably came closest to an answer when she said that the real artist confides a secret to the audience, embracing it as an old and trusted friend. The secret varies from performer to performer, and Judy's was so obvious that few could see it: she was desperately in love with those who came to see her—and she had been since she was two years old. Metro had torn them apart before their romance reached full bloom, but now that they were together again, she and her audience, Judy realized how much she had missed it, how lonely she had been without it. Her second secret was less obvious: she needed her audience more than it needed her. She was happy—"truly, truly happy," to use her own words—only when she was onstage. Offstage, Judy was uncertain who she was. Onstage, she knew. All those who applauded her, who stood up and cheered, were doing more than thanking her for a memorable performance. They were providing her with an identity.

And so, to a lesser degree, was Judy providing them with one. In her songs they heard not just her triumphs and disappointments, but their own as well. As she exposed her inner emotions, so, too, did they expose theirs, if only to themselves. As Judy confessed her vulnerability, they, for perhaps the first time in their lives, also confessed theirs. Contributing to that revival-meeting atmosphere was her studied informality. Pausing between numbers, Judy made jokes, wiped her sweaty brow, drank a glass of water and took off her shoes, which she complained were hurting her feet. Emotions flowed in both directions, and, as the show progressed, between artist and audience occurred a kind of chemical bonding, an exchange that infused both with new energy. "It was like breathing again," Judy herself said, "having people let me know

I still meant something to them; that they loved me and still wanted to hear me sing."

|||

With the inquisitive tools of modern electronics, scientists can now trace the path sound takes on its journey from the ear to the brain. Received by receptors called hair cells, it proceeds to the snail-shaped cochlea. From there it goes to the cochlear nerve, then on to the temporal lobe, on again to the auditory cortex—then finally to its ultimate destination in the frontal lobe, that part of the brain that lies behind the forehead. Like passengers in an airliner, who can see lights being turned on in the dark cities below, researchers can peer through flesh and bone to watch a sound switching on the brain's biological circuits. What happens next, what the brain makes of that sound, science cannot say, however, and no one knows—probably no one will ever know—why one sound is considered an unpleasant noise while another produces a sensation of melting, exquisite joy.

"A dominant aspect of human biology": that is how one eminent doctor, Lewis Thomas, characterized music, and although its influence cannot be measured, as most other aspects of biology can be, music does have strange and uncanny powers. Very often, indeed, it is the sole key to otherwise impenetrable areas of the brain, to remote regions that remain detached from the centers of thought and reason. Buried deep inside the brain's tender folds and crevasses, those areas, an inheritance from primitive ancestors, respond to a song or a bar of music long after the reasoning centers have surrendered to internal catastrophes. Stroke victims who have lost the ability to speak can yet sometimes sing; Alzheimer's patients who must wear tags to remind them of their names can yet remember complicated lyrics from once-popular standards.

If music works such wonders on the ill, is it any surprise that it also has extraordinary effects on the well? Or that, more than any other stimulus, it awakens sleeping memories? A childhood outing, a first kiss, a wedding, a funeral: all flitting souvenirs, perhaps, as elusive as fireflies until a snatch of music captures and returns them to their owner. The beat of the heart. The act of breathing. The movement of the legs in walking. Each has its own rhythm, and each is part of that larger musical instrument, the human body. When the rhythms are off, illness enters; when they stop, so does life itself.

In an attempt to restore sick bodies to their rightful rhythms, the physicians of the pharaohs, it is said, sang, rather than recited, their prescriptions, for words without music, they believed, lacked the capacity to heal. How good their remedies were for bringing down fevers and mending broken bones is hard to say, but that they were on to something, those Egyptian sawbones, could clearly be seen on the faces of those leaving Judy's performances at the Palace. As they walked through the lobby, they displayed not merely smiles of happiness, the customary reactions after a good show, but the ecstasy of deliverance. They had not attended a concert; they had participated in an incantation, a rite more ancient than the pyramids themselves. Her altar may have been a stage on Times Square, with the subway rumbling underneath and taxis honking outside, but Judy had more than a little in common with those shamans of old Nile, chanting their cures in the crouching shadow of the newborn sphinx. She was not singing songs: she was dispensing spiritual health and enlightenment, sustenance for the soul. And therein lay the magic.

|||

If New York was the terrible, wonderful test for Judy, then Hollywood, where she took her show next, would be a trial, like performing in front of a skeptical family that, in recent years, had witnessed only her humiliations. But this time Metro would not be around to pick her up. She would be all by herself, on the stage of Los Angeles's cavernous Philharmonic Auditorium, half again as big as the Palace, with nothing but air between her and the audience. "I'm nervous all right," she confessed as she waited for the big night—Monday, April 21. "I always am for an opening. But it's not the kind of nervousness that makes you sick. It's a kind of joyous nervousness."

All of Southern California seemed to share that pleasurable anxiety. Hundreds waited for the box office to open—twenty-five hundred tickets were sold within an hour—and nearly everyone she knew, from Lana Turner and Joan Crawford to Arthur Freed and Louis B. Mayer, was planning to attend her first night. Most of Los Angeles and Pasadena society, that WASP-y elite that rarely mingled with the vulgar movie folk, was also coming, together with a passel of swells from out of state—Henry Ford II had ordered a plane to fly him and his friends from Detroit. The Garland show was fast shaping up as a curious combination of Hollywood premiere and social event, and the local newspapers dispatched their society editors, along with their critics and feature writers, to cover what one of them was to call "one of the most heterogeneous and interesting audiences we have ever seen in Los Angeles."

Bolstered by her successes in London and New York, and with Sid at her side, the newly confident Judy was up to the challenge. The outcome of the evening was thus never really in doubt, and even Arthur Freed, who was not renowned for his tender heart, was observed to blubber when she dangled her feet over the stage and launched into "Over the Rainbow." The following day's front pages told the rest of the story. " 'Rainbow' Girl Finds Pot o' Gold," declared the headline in the *Herald & Express*. "Judy Garland Scintillates in Philharmonic Comeback," said the more sedate *Times*. But the *Hollywood Citizen-News* put it best, as well as most succinctly—"Judy Returns In Triumph." Could any four words have sounded sweeter to a woman, who, just eighteen months earlier, had been pronounced dead by those very same papers?

Four weeks Judy played to sold-out houses at the Philharmonic; then, on May 26, she moved north for four more weeks at the Curran Theater in San Francisco. So well had she done on both coasts that plans were afoot to take her show to other parts of the country as well, starting with Chicago in September. But those schemes had to yield to a higher plan. Judy was pregnant—she probably had been since February or March—and she would soon have to give up her strenuous routine. Although she had made no secret that she expected to marry Sid, she had probably not anticipated that the wedding date would arrive so swiftly. Yet there it was and on Sunday, June 8, midway through her San Francisco engagement and just two days shy of her thirtieth birthday, Judy and Sid drove a hundred miles south, to the small town of Paicines, where they promised to love and cherish each other at the ranch of one of Sid's friends. "It was," said the bride, "a beautiful wedding and a beautiful day."

That was a distinctly minority opinion, however, and not many in Hollywood saw much to admire in the union. "If Judy had a dollar for every friend who's whispered in her ear that Sid was a far-from-ideal matrimonial bet, she'd have a hefty bankroll to show," said one fan magazine. A columnist was openly disdainful. "So Sid Luft," was his sarcastic wedding present, "is what a girl finds over the rainbow?"

|||

Judy, in fact, did not need anybody to whisper in her year. During the nearly two years they had been together she had seen firsthand why so many people distrusted Sid. The first disquieting sign probably came in London, where Sid, who had assumed control of her finances, managed to find his way to the best tailors and shoemakers on Savile Row, yet scrimped on the paychecks of the faithful little entourage that had accompanied Judy from America—Buddy Pepper, Myrtle Tully and Dorothy Ponedel. Not even given the wherewithal to eat, poor Pepper was reduced to scrounging meals from Tully and Ponedel, who were at least allowed to order from hotel room service. Angry and puzzled both, Ponedel finally confronted Judy and demanded to know what was happening to the piles of cash the Palladium was dumping in her lap every week. "All my money is tied up in an attaché case," replied Judy, "and that is tied to Sid's wrist." And that was where it remained, in London, New York and Los Angeles. With Sid writing the checks, Judy soon gained an unenviable reputation for shortchanging many of those who worked for her.

A second disturbing sign came on October 1, 1951, a few days before Judy left California for her opening at the Palace. Driving home after a late dinner at a restaurant called the Ready Room, Sid ignored a stoplight at the intersection of La Cienega and Beverly Boulevards and slammed broadside into one car, which then careered into another. "I had a beer—well, maybe three," admitted Sid. "I can feel it, but I'm not drunk." Although there was only one slight injury, a dispute erupted in which Judy smacked one of the other drivers, a seventeen-year-old, and broke his glasses. When a passing dentist volunteered that he had seen the collision and that Sid was at fault, an indignant Sid popped him too, breaking his nose, as well as his glasses.

Two hours later, at 3:15 A.M., Sid was booked on four counts— drunkenness, drunken driving, driving without a valid license and carrying a concealed weapon—and shoved into a jail cell until his lawyer arrived with bail money. It is hard to say who was more befuddled that night, Sid or the dim-witted cops who did not even think of searching his car until he asked whether anybody had seen his gun. The dutiful gumshoes then peered under the front seat of his car and discovered a loaded .38-caliber revolver—one of two, it transpired, that had been reported stolen from Douglas Aircraft during the period of Sid's employment. Most of the charges were eventually dismissed, and Sid was let off with a $150 fine for drunken driving.

Still more ammunition against him was provided by Lynn Bari, who, early on, took Judy aside and presented a list of an ex-wife's complaints. Judy did not listen, of course. "You're bitter," she said, "so you see everything in a distorted light. He's a wonderful guy. I've grown to understand him better than anyone ever has." Such condescending comments could only have made Bari more hostile, and when she read, months later, about Judy's sellout crowds, she took Sid to court, claiming that, as a participant in Judy's profits, he could now afford to pay more for the support of their three-year-old son, John. In 1951, her lawyers pointed out, Sid had spent almost twice as much—$4,329.25, to be exact—on his three racehorses as he had on his own son. Asked how much he received as her manager, Judy, who testified for half an hour, looked hopelessly blank. Sid handled her finances, she said simply, and he could "draw anything he needs."

Quickly pouncing on this vague statement, Bari's lawyer, S. S. Hahn, denounced Sid as a Machiavelli who was able to make Judy do whatever he wanted. "I'm sorry to say that all the money Judy makes goes into Luft's pocket," he said. Apparently persuaded, Superior Court Judge Louis H. Burke ordered Sid to double his support payments, to $400 a month. The judge also let it be known that his opinion of Sid was not much higher than Hahn's. Sid had been a very uncooperative witness, said Burke, and his testimony had been "nowhere near the truth."

Whether Sid was right, wrong or somewhere in between was a question of no concern to Judy, who knew at least one thing to be true: he had restored her to life, something no one else had been able to do. Without him, she might never have finished her British tour. Without him, she would never have played the Palace, or the Philharmonic, or the Curran. Without him, she might already have become one of Hollywood's has-beens. "None of this would have been possible without Sid," she said. "He and I have accomplished so much in the last year. He's the kind of person you can lean against if you fall down. He's strong and protects me."

Sid had realized something that had escaped everyone else, including Vincente. Much of Judy's self-destructive behavior was a rebellion against a lifetime of taking orders: she was allergic to anything that even hinted of coercion. Perhaps because he suffered from the same condition, Sid perceived that the best way—indeed, the only way—to deal with her was to leave her alone, to let her do exactly what she wanted. The prime example of the pressure she so intensely resented was the never-ending scrutiny of her waistline. Sid was the first to tell her to gobble up—to take that second helping of mashed potatoes if she wanted it. He did not care how heavy she was, Sid assured her, and neither did her audiences—an optimistic assumption that long lines at the box office soon confirmed. "I want to protect her from the trauma she once knew," he said. "I don't want her to be bewildered or hurt again. I want her to have happiness."

Any good manager might have said much the same. But Sid had something else in his favor. In London, when Dorothy Ponedel complained about not being paid, Judy quickly shushed her. "I know what's going on, Dottie," she said, "but I love the guy."

*Chatting with James Mason
on the set of A Star Is Born*

CHAPTER 12

A Golden Deal and a Death in a Parking Lot

She had passed all of her tests, she had survived all of her trials, she had stared down all of her critics, and when she returned to Los Angeles at the end of June, Judy claimed her reward: a new movie contract. Wasting no time in capitalizing on the excitement aroused by her appearances at the Palace and the Philharmonic, Sid had struck a golden deal with Jack Warner, the Louis B. Mayer of Warner Bros. "Your artistry goes beyond the capacity of words," Warner wrote Judy. "I sincerely believe you are one of the greatest entertainers the world has ever known. What more can words say?"

Nothing, when dollars said it so much better. Under their new agreement, the Lufts would become moviemaking partners with a studio now stronger than Metro itself. Warner Bros. would provide the cash, soundstages and technicians, while Transcona, the Lufts' newly formed production company, would actually produce pictures—their contract spoke of as many as nine. If their features made money, both would share in the profits; if they lost, Warner Bros. alone would suffer. Sid and Judy could not have asked for better terms.

Three stories already had tentative approval. One was the saga of Man o' War, which Sid had been peddling around town for years. The tragic history of the Donner Party, the westbound settlers who met death in the snowy Sierra Nevada, was the second. And a musical version of *A Star Is Born,* Hollywood's favorite picture about Hollywood, was the third. Since acquiring Judy was the only reason Warner Bros. had consented to such a generous arrangement, *A Star Is Born* was the first to get under way, with Judy, of course, playing the star. Preliminary work began that very fall, just as she entered the final weeks of her pregnancy. For once, she was eager to begin. "I used to be scared to death of people and really scared of lots of things, but not any more," she said. "That concert tour gave me courage I never had before. I sort of grew up in the last couple of years."

The collaboration with Warner Bros. was one result of that new-found maturity, promising not only to restore Judy's name to movie marquees, but also to give her the financial independence she had always longed for. Because she and Sid would be the heads of a corporation—they would control 70 percent of Transcona; two friends would own the rest—they would be employers rather than employees, the ones who gave orders rather than the ones who took them. With most of their money coming from profits rather than salaries, they would, moreover, avoid paying personal income taxes, which, in the fifties, were almost confiscatory for those in the highest brackets. Mired in debt a year before—Sid alone owed $60,000—the Lufts seemed destined to become rich, movie moguls in their own right. At that lucky moment, with good fortune smiling everywhere she looked, Judy gave birth to her second child, another daughter. Born on November 21, 1952, at St. John's Hospital in Santa Monica, she weighed six pounds, four ounces and was named Lorna—Lorna Luft.

|||

A new baby. A new husband. A new career. For Judy, there had been a parade of triumphs, all made sweeter by the disasters that had preceded them. But nothing, it seemed, could assuage her gluttonous sense of inadequacy, her oppressive feeling of self-contempt. Defying logic and the counsel of common sense, the same old problems persisted, impervious to triumphs, unyielding to the seductive songs of ordinary happiness. Like a virus in the blood, a dark mood would unexpectedly seize her, and she would almost hunger for self-destruction.

One episode, which occurred in late 1951, during her months at the Palace, can stand for many. She had spent the afternoon seeing a revival of *Meet Me in St. Louis,* the film in which she looked most attractive. It was a festive occasion, shared with friends, but that night, as she sat in her dressing room, preparing to go onstage, she stared into the mirror and began sobbing. "I'm not beautiful anymore," she said. "I just want to forget everything." And with that, she grabbed the hot curling irons from her hairdresser and, until he snatched them away, held them close to her face, as if she intended to burn herself.

In the days after Lorna's birth, that virus returned with more serious results. Aggravated, apparently, by postpartum depression, it was further inflamed by Sid, who was in San Francisco watching one of his horses run the day she carried Lorna home from the hospital. "I had to bring my baby home myself," she said reproachfully when he did return. Although she seemed to forgive him, a day or two later she once again went into a bathroom and made cuts on her neck. "Judy," said her doctor, "you keep this up and you're going to hurt yourself."

Her spirits soon recovered, the virus disappearing as quickly as it had appeared, and by the end of the year she was well enough to travel with Sid and baby Lorna for a New Year's celebration in New York. But there, on the afternoon of Monday, January 5, she received genuinely bad news from California, news that was not only to send her into another emotional tailspin, but was to torment her for weeks, and perhaps years, to come. Early that morning, as she was hurrying to her job at the Douglas Aircraft factory in Santa Monica, her mother, the seemingly indomitable Ethel, had collapsed in the company parking lot, dead of a heart attack at fifty-nine.

Flying back to California the next day, Judy met with her sisters, Sue and Jimmie, to make plans for the funeral. Forest Lawn's Little Church of the Flowers, where they had said good-bye to their father seventeen years earlier, was the site they chose, and two days later, at noon on a gray January 8, an old family friend, a Presbyterian minister from Bakersfield, conducted the services. Their mother had always been their chief topic of conversation—"Guess what she did to me!" one or another would exclaim when they met—but Ethel's girls did little talking on that gloomy Thursday. All Judy, who had refused to speak to her mother for many months, could say was "I didn't want her to die."

|||

Judy may not have wanted her mother to die, but she had wanted her to disappear—to stay far away from her, her husband and her children. The road to that painful juncture was a long one, and, had no one else been involved, Judy might not have arrived there at all. But someone else—Liza—was involved. Not satisfied with having been a stage mother, Ethel seemed bent on becoming a stage grandmother as well, and, at the end of the forties, while Judy was still married to Vincente, she began to push Liza as she had once pushed Judy.

Watching the two in the same room was, for Judy, childhood revisited, the release of a hornets' nest, a swarm of stinging memories, and she found her mother's behavior so "deeply neurotic," as she put it, that it made her ill even to see grandmother and granddaughter together. So strained was the atmosphere that when Ethel came to dinner, sullen silence presided, and though "their proud spirits would never allow either of them to admit it was a tragedy," said Vincente, the relationship had deteriorated beyond salvation.

Eventually silence gave way to violent arguments, and the breach became unbridgeable. Most of her friends thought that Ethel was a tank who could ward off all blows; but rejection by Judy, final and irrevocable, was one disappointment too many: she cracked and tried to kill herself, swallowing half a bottle of sleeping pills with a whiskey chaser. She was saved from the effects of that lethal combination only by Jimmie's timely rescue, and, with no further reason to stay in California, Ethel soon followed Jimmie and Jimmie's second husband, Johnny Thompson, to their new home in Dallas.

Texas was not her address for long, however. Within hours of Judy's own attempted suicide in June 1950, Ethel was back in California and, despite clear signals that she was not welcome, bulldozing her way into Judy's house on Sunset Boulevard. Before long, one newspaper reported, she was "in complete charge of the situation." That, of course, had been the problem all along, and when her mother later returned to Los Angeles to stay, Judy would have nothing to do with her. "Judy didn't want anybody meddling," said Johnny Thompson. "And Ethel did meddle—although she always thought it was for your own good."

For much of Judy's Metro career, her mother had also been on the studio payroll, going home in the late forties with $150 a week, a spare but livable income by the standards of the time. That modest sinecure ended when Judy left Culver City, and in the spring of 1952, nearing sixty and in poor health—she suffered from high blood pressure, diabetes and an ulcer—Ethel found herself working at Douglas Aircraft for less than half that, a mingy $61 a week. There had scarcely been a time that she had not worried about money, fighting to keep herself and her family afloat; now, it seemed, she had lost the battle. "Poor Ethel!" exclaimed her friend Dorothy Walsh. "Her life was a real struggle. She tried so hard."

Unable even to keep up the premiums on her life insurance, which was to provide her burial money, Ethel sought help from Judy, who was then singing to sellout crowds at the Los Angeles Philharmonic. Judy still refused to see her, however, and Ethel got no further than Sid. Though he agreed to make her insurance payments, Sid balked at her additional plea for a loan of a couple of hundred dollars. "I'll tell you what," he said offhandedly, "we'll send you twenty-five dollars a week."

Hurt and insulted by his casual condescension, Ethel angrily walked away, and a few days later, on May 2, the *Los Angeles Mirror* ran a story about the estrangement between mother and daughter. In case any of its readers missed its message—that Judy was ungrateful—the paper spelled it out in unmistakable sarcasm. "While Judy Garland is busy making her 'comeback' and some $25,000 a week," said the caption under its picture of Ethel, photographed behind her desk at Douglas, "her mother, Mrs. Ethel Gumm Gilmore, works quietly at Douglas Aircraft in Santa Monica as a clerk for about $1 an hour take-home pay."

The *Mirror* visited Ethel again on June 12, after it learned of Judy's marriage to Sid. "Garland's Maw Blisters Luft—Judy's Mother Says Luft Is a Nogoodnik," proclaimed the *Mirror*'s front page, in letters large enough to announce a declaration of war. "Well, I'm not surprised," Ethel said when she was told about the wedding, "but I've been hoping it wouldn't happen. He's a bad guy. I couldn't tell Judy anything. She has to learn everything the hard way. She's a big girl now—30 years old the day before yesterday—but when will she grow up?"

Once released, Ethel's resentment could not be contained; in the weeks that followed she poured out a torrent of bitterness and bile. "Judy and I never had a quarrel, she just brushed me off," she complained to the gossip columnist Sheilah Graham. "If you have a daughter, don't let her sing or dance," she advised Graham. Sounding more defensive than she probably realized, a response, perhaps, to whispers that she had not been the most affectionate of mothers, Ethel maintained that Judy's problems were not the result of too little maternal love, but of too much—she had spoiled her. "Judy has been selfish all her life. That's my fault. I made it too easy for her."

Some wedding present her mother had dispatched! A slap in the face could not have been more hostile, and although she remained mute in public, Judy was savage in private. "My mother's a fucking riveter at Douglas," she said, "and that's where she belongs. It's too good for her." But when Lorna was born in November, Judy exacted her revenge, informing the hospital that her mother was not to be permitted to see her new granddaughter. That was the most hurtful action she could have taken, and Ethel, who conveniently ignored the harsh words that so recently had tumbled out of her own mouth, was appropriately wounded. "What have I done wrong?" she wailed to a friend. "What did I do that she hates me so?"

Americans have always idealized that abstract figure, the mother—"her very name stands for loving unselfishness and self-abnegation" was Theodore Roosevelt's platitudinous tribute—and in the days after Ethel's death, the newspapers raised the same questions. Why had Judy turned on the woman who had started her on her spectacular career? How could she have stood by and watched her own mother, who had contributed so much to her success, conclude her life so pathetically—broke, angry and alone? Even a few of Judy's friends attacked her for what they saw as ingratitude, if not outright matricide. Apparently forgetting their night of alfresco passion before her opening at the Palace, a drunken Johnny Mercer confronted her as she walked into a party.

"Why did you let your mother die in a parking lot?" he snarled. Judy's sorry reply was to burst into tears and retreat to a bathroom, where, following a now familiar pattern, she cut her wrists, bringing an ambulance screaming to the door. "Naturally," said the host, "the incident was so macabre that everyone left."

|||

It was fitting that Ethel died, as she had lived, rushing to beat the clock. Never was there a time, even in those last discouraging months, when she was not engaged in a frenzy of movement. No one, in fact, had ever been able to keep pace with the Ethel Express: not Frank Gumm, not Sue or Jimmie, and not Judy, who had been chained to it nonetheless, bouncing along like a dejected caboose, since she was two. Judy could not recall a time, indeed, when her mother was not forcing her to do something she did not want to do, subjecting her to pressures that few adults, let alone children, ever encounter.

Other women her age could look back on picnics, parties, first dates—the multitude of everyday experiences Judy had been denied. But the lack of those pleasures would have counted for little if Ethel had not also deprived Judy of something much more valuable— responsibility for her own life. Her take-charge mother had made almost all her decisions for her. The few decisions Ethel did not make, Metro did. Judy had had even less chance than most young stars to grow up. Now, at the age of thirty, it seemed she never would. And for what had she sacrificed? Money? Fame? Power? Judy believed she knew. "Maybe I fulfilled Mother's ambitions," she said with quiet bitterness, "and maybe she fulfilled hers."

Mothers usually protect their children. Ethel did the opposite, and no conquistador, hacking his way through soggy jungles or scaling icy Andes heights in search of Inca gold, could have been more ruthless. Yet of all Ethel's betrayals, one stands above the others as permanent indictment: it was she who had forced Judy to take drugs; it was she who had made her a slave to a kaleidoscope of brilliantly colored pills and capsules. What had she done to cause Judy to hate her? Ethel had inquired. What could Judy have answered? That there was not one reason, nor two or three, but thousands, one for every pill she took.

"As is the mother, so is her daughter," says the Old Testament, and Judy, in the end, proved no less obstinate than her mother. "She was a lonely and determined woman," Judy said, "and I guess I'm the same way." For most people, the years bring a mellowing. Anger cools, quarrels recede, wounds heal. Battlefields become sacred shrines, and one-time enemies exchange embraces rather than blows. Nostalgia rules. Where Ethel was concerned, however, Judy's heart only hardened. As she grew older and better realized the damage done to her, she seemed to dislike her mother more and more, finally arriving at a point where she blamed her mother—"this hideous woman, this outrageous, awful woman"—for nearly everything that had gone awry in her life.

"Nothing, ever, wipes out childhood," wrote Simone de Beauvoir, a statement that is as melancholy, yet as incontestable, as a tolling church bell. Judy, certainly, knew it to be true, and nothing, ever, was to wipe out the injuries inflicted on her by that ambitious little dynamo, her mother.

|||

"A career is a curious thing," says Norman Maine, the movie-star hero of *A Star Is Born*. "Talent isn't always enough. You need a sense of timing—an eye for seeing the turning point—or recognizing the big chance when it comes and grabbing it." The person to whom he is giving such perceptive advice is Esther Blodgett, the character Judy was to play. But he might as well have been speaking to Judy herself, for in 1953 she, too, had arrived at a turning point. If her remake of *A Star Is Born* succeeded, her career would be secure as far as she could see; if it failed, she really would be through in Hollywood. She had been given a second chance; a third would be in the nature of a miracle. Her whole future was riding on just one picture, and Judy knew it. *A Star Is Born*, she told one columnist, could not merely be very good—it had to be the greatest.

A product of some of the brightest talents in the business, the original, made in 1937, scarcely needed improvement. David O. Selznick had produced it, William Wellman had directed it and Dorothy Parker was one of those who had shaped its shrewd and knowledgeable script. Janet Gaynor, the recipient of the very first Oscar for best actress, for

1927's *Seventh Heaven,* had played Esther, the Midwestern innocent who dreamed of movie glory. Fredric March, who was to win an Oscar for 1946's *The Best Years of Our Lives,* had played Norman Maine, the alcoholic Pygmalion who not only transforms Esther into a star—Vicki Lester—but makes her his wife as well. What elevated that otherwise predictable plot above the ordinary was the rude reversal of fortunes in the picture's second half. Maine, the matinee idol, finds his own career falling as fast as his wife's is rising, and, rather than ruin her prospects, too, he drowns himself in the waters off Malibu.

The birth of one star inevitably meant the death of another—there was limited space in the Hollywood heavens—and in a town where many careers had plummeted as precipitously as Norman Maine's, *A Star Is Born* was a film that had touched many. Belying his cynical screen reputation, Humphrey Bogart, for instance, ran it on a home projector every Christmas, crying each time as if he had never seen it before. It was a movie both loved and admired, and anyone who attempted to do it again, with music no less, was following a tough act indeed. But that was the challenge chosen by Judy and Sid, who was assuming Selznick's role as producer.

"Those two alley cats can't make a picture," Arthur Freed said of the Lufts, and he may have been right. But the crafty cats at Warner Bros. could. With the studio's help, Judy and Sid assembled some of the finest talents of their own day. Moss Hart, whose collaborations with George S. Kaufman were among Broadway's wittiest plays, was hired to revise and update the script. Harold Arlen and Ira Gershwin were picked to write the songs, and George Cukor, whose very name signified class and distinction in the movie world, was brought in to direct. So it went down the credit list, the best being added to the best.

The only real problem was the male lead. Who could play Norman Maine? It was a difficult role, requiring a combination of bluster and sensitivity, egotism and charm. Cary Grant, the personal favorite of Judy and Sid, refused the part; so did Marlon Brando and Laurence Olivier. Tyrone Power and Richard Burton were busy on other projects. Three stars who did want the job—Bogart, Frank Sinatra and Errroll Flynn—were turned down. "Understand Want Me for Star," the vacationing Flynn telegraphed Warner Bros. But he was wrong. "James

Mason Set Starborn," replied the studio. And so Mason, an English actor who had not attracted much attention in the United States—the German field marshal Erwin Rommel in *The Desert Fox* was probably his biggest role—was offered, and instantly grabbed, the lead in the most talked-about picture of the year.

By autumn everything was in place. Even before the first scene was shot, *A Star Is Born* had the look of a champion. Everything about it—script, songs, cast and crew—had the feel of quality, Hollywood moviemaking at its very best. As an expression of his regard, Jack Warner assigned Judy the dressing room that had belonged to Bette Davis, the onetime queen of the Warners lot, and on Monday, October 12, Judy went before the cameras for the first time in more than three years. The bad habits of the past seemed behind her, and shooting progressed smoothly until, about ten days later, Warner Bros. abruptly slammed on the brakes. *A Star Is Born,* it decreed, was not to be filmed in the traditional way, but with an entirely new process called CinemaScope. The most important movie in Judy's career was caught in the middle of the biggest cinematic revolution since the introduction of sound.

|||

The revolution had been under way for more than a year, in fact, since the premiere, on September 30, 1952, of *This Is Cinerama,* which used a wraparound screen and three projectors to give filmgoers the illusion that they were watching a film in three dimensions. In the ensuing months other gimmicks were tried and discarded—one required viewers to wear special stereoscopic glasses—before CinemaScope emerged as the wide-screen victor. Using a camera with a new kind of lens, it projected images two and a half times as wide as normal, making the traditional, almost boxlike screen seem small by comparison: in CinemaScope, spectaculars really did look spectacular. Audiences were captivated, in any event, and after seeing box-office figures for the first CinemaScope feature, a biblical epic called *The Robe,* Warner Bros. belatedly embraced the new technology for *A Star Is Born.* Everything that had already been shot was scrapped—a loss of close to $300,000, or about 10 percent of the budget—and filming was started all over again.

Hardest hit by the changeover were Cukor and his crew, who had to learn, on the job, a whole new way of shooting a movie. Because the CinemaScope picture was shorter as well as wider than the conventional one, sets had to be squeezed—the top lowered and the bottom raised—to show both ceilings and floors. Nor was the CinemaScope lens as versatile as the old one. Sam Leavitt, the cameraman, was informed that he would cause distortion if he moved the camera up or down or zoomed in for a close-up—or did much of anything, in fact, but hold it stationary, pointing straight ahead. Cukor grumbled about such unaccustomed constraints, but either ignored or successfully navigated around them. "Don't worry," he told Gene Allen, his inventive production designer. "We'll make up the rules for ourselves."

|||

The least of Cukor's problems—for the first few weeks, anyway—was Judy, who belied her reputation for tardiness by usually reporting to the set on time, or nearly so. Her newfound reliability did not denote a reformation in character, however; it merely meant that she had found a new man—Harry Rubin was his name—on whom she could lean. Hired to supervise the electrical renovation of the Lufts' new house in Holmby Hills, Rubin, a self-described "Brooklyn bum," had stayed on as their all-purpose helper, a combination of majordomo and Mr. Fixit. When Judy failed to appear on one of the early days of filming, it was Rubin to whom Sid immediately turned. "See what the hell's going on!" he ordered.

What was going on, Rubin quickly discovered, was a hostile standoff at the Lufts' house. Judy was frightened of any speed much greater than thirty miles an hour, and the driver assigned to ferry her to the studio in Burbank knew only one route—a fast-moving freeway. "Do you know how to get to Warner Brothers without going on the freeway?" Judy asked Rubin. When Rubin assured her he did, she said, "Well, then, let's go!" and stepped into his car. After that, Rubin, that most unlikely of all duennas, rarely left her side.

Not even Rubin could cure her insomnia or keep her away from drugs, however. By the second week of November, Earl Bellamy, *A Star Is Born*'s assistant director, was being awakened by the excuses so familiar to his counterparts at M-G-M. "Miss Garland phoned Earl Bellamy at 4:45 this morning," reported one typical memo, "and told him she had a 'cold' and would not be in to work today."

Still, when she did show up, Judy brought to the set a concentration and intensity new even to her. Watching her play Norman Maine's grieving widow near the movie's end, Cukor said he felt that he was in the presence of some awful cataclysm of nature. "It scared me," he said. "I had goose pimples, it was so extraordinary." Not satisfied with just one take, no matter how good, Cukor instructed her to do the grieving scene a second time—and witnessed an equally terrifying, slightly different eruption. "Oh, that's nothing," joked Judy when Cukor confessed how powerfully she had affected him. "Come over to my house any afternoon. I do it every afternoon." She paused and gave him a meaningful look: "But I only do it *once* at home."

Yet even Cukor lost patience when, toward the end of production, she abandoned any pretense of reporting to work on time. "About three weeks ago, strange sinister and sad things began happening to Judy," Cukor wrote their mutual friend Katharine Hepburn. Judy would insist that she was too exhausted to work, he told Hepburn, then head straight to the racetrack; she would call in sick, then be seen that night at the Mocambo. "This is the behavior of someone unhinged," he said, "but there is an arrogance and a ruthless selfishness that eventually alienates one's sympathy."

Impatient at the best of times—one acquaintance compared him to a Mexican jumping bean—Jack Warner became increasingly exasperated. When a griping call from Judy interrupted his Saturday tennis game, he responded in kind. "Judy, you've given us a lot of trouble," he said. "We gave you everything you wanted, and now you're calling up to complain to me. I don't like to be disturbed at my home. Don't bother me again. You were utterly spoiled by the people at M-G-M. You've cost us a hell of a lot of money by going over schedule on this picture. That's all!" And bang!—down went the phone. Most of Warner's fury was directed not at Judy, however, but at her husband. "A charming fellow, Sid," Warner sneeringly wrote in his autobiography. "He's one of the original guys who promised his parents he'd never work a day in his life—and made good."

Despite everything, filming finally ended on March 17, 1954, and after viewing the rough cut a week later, everybody was suddenly all smiles: the picture was worth the wait. *A Star Is Born* was a movie of singular power and appeal—a winner, as Cukor confidently proclaimed to Moss Hart. All that was required, it was agreed, was one more number, four or five minutes at most, to show an audience reacting to Vicki Lester, so that those watching *A Star Is Born* could understand what propelled her to the top. Excited by what he had seen, but nervous nevertheless, Warner accepted Sid's suggestion that instead of inserting a number with only one new song, which audiences might reject, they guarantee success by including several favorites—a whole medley of proven crowd pleasers, much like Judy's stage show. It would, as Sid later said, be almost a movie within the movie.

About to leave for vacation in Europe, Cukor raised two serious objections. He argued, first, that such an elaborate number, which would run four or five times as long as the one originally proposed, would unnecessarily lengthen an already long picture and would force cuts in other, more essential areas. He contended, second, that a number on such a grand scale would disrupt the film's narrative flow, destroying the pace and rhythm he and Hart had so carefully constructed. "Big mistake," agreed Ira Gershwin.

Mistake or not, the number went ahead with flash, flourish and a vigorous new creative team. The always reliable Roger Edens and his gifted young collaborator, Leonard Gershe, put the segment together, and Richard Barstow, the picture's choreographer, directed. Thus it was that on June 30 shooting began on what was to be called the "Born in a Trunk" sequence, fifteen minutes in which Judy could display her dazzling collection of talents.

Desperate to finish, and fearful that Judy might return to her cunctatory ways, Warner did something that would have been astonishing for any studio, and that seemed unthinkable for one as parsimonious as Warner Bros. Ignoring the costs of overtime, he allowed production to proceed on Judy's insomniac schedule, with work starting late in the afternoon or evening and continuing until one, two or even four o'clock in the morning. At last, at two-forty-five on the morning of Thursday, July 29, 1954, the "Born in a Trunk" number staggered to completion. Nine and a half months after it had begun, *A Star Is Born* was finished.

|||

"Don't let 'em cut a minute of it," Judy's fans shouted as she walked out after the first preview, which took place just four days later, on Monday, August 2. "We could sit through four hours more!" Maybe so; but few others could. Although the audience reaction was enthusiastic—almost frenzied, in fact—*A Star Is Born,* as the director himself conceded, was far too long. "Neither the human mind nor the human ass can stand three and a half hours of concentration," George Cukor wrote Moss Hart.

Complaints about the picture's length had been circulating for several months, and Jack Warner, who mistakenly fancied himself a film editor, had already chopped out many minutes. Only at the preview was Cukor able to see what damage he had done. "He snipped here and there, seemingly without reason," Cukor angrily told Hart. "He succeeded in muddying things up, making scenes pointless and incomprehensible—all this without losing any footage to speak of." The director's angry objections restored many of Warner's excisions, and Cukor himself then sat down in the editing room. He had just seven weeks to make the necessary cuts before *A Star Is Born* was to be unveiled to the world, on September 29 at Hollywood's Pantages Theater.

Producers usually supervised such efforts—David O. Selznick oversaw every second of *his A Star Is Born*—but Sid had other plans. Despite heated protests from a weary Judy, who wanted to relax at home, he had accepted Warner's invitation, a kind of peace offering after the squabbles of filming, for them to join him on the French Riviera. "What you should do is stay here with Cukor and help cut the picture," said Judy, who had been around the industry long enough to know what producers were supposed to do. "Judy, I've had it up to my fucking gourd," replied Sid. "I'm beat. I'd like to go away someplace. Let's go, we'll have some laughs." So Cukor was left alone to wield the pruning shears.

Everyone who had been to the previews agreed that Cukor had lived up to his lofty reputation. A finely wrought film, *A Star Is Born* was a masterful blend of music and drama, each performance as carefully shaded as a figure in a Rembrandt painting. But those subtle touches, that careful chiaroscuro, came at a price, and a typical Cukor scene lasted longer on-screen—often much longer—than it would have if it had been shot by almost any other major director. In directing the first *A Star Is Born,* for example, William Wellman required only nineteen and a half minutes to end the tale after Norman Maine gets into a scuffle at Santa Anita. Even without musical interruptions, the same scenes and essentially the same dialogue consumed twenty-seven and a half minutes under Cukor's direction, longer by more than 40 percent.

Cukor's leisurely style had worked well in straight pictures. Never before had he directed a musical, however, and both Sid and Warner should have realized that a musical, which had to make room for songs as well as narrative, demanded a director with a brisker touch. Compounding their error, and apparently giving little thought to the consequences, the two had made Cukor's task much harder—and the movie much longer—by their insistence on the "Born in a Trunk" number. Superb as it was, it gobbled up fifteen precious minutes without contributing much to the telling of the story.

The result of Cukor's cutting was still a very long film. At three hours and two minutes, it was an hour and eleven minutes longer than the original *A Star Is Born* and far longer than any of Judy's other movies—an hour and four minutes longer than *Meet Me in St. Louis,* for instance. What, Noël Coward was to ask, had happened to the famous American sense of timing? "Every song was attenuated to such a length that I thought I was going mad," groaned Coward. "One in particular, 'Born in a Trunk,' started brilliantly but by the time it was over and we had endured montage after montage and repetition after repetition, I found myself wishing that dear enchanting Judy was at the bottom of the sea."

|||

Extravagance also marked the picture's opening, "probably the most remarkable premiere ever held in the film city," according to the *Los Angeles Times*. Klieg lights whitened the sky, an estimated twenty thousand people waited outside the Pantages, and both TV and radio networks broadcast from the lobby. "Welcome Judy," proclaimed a huge sign over the entrance to the Cocoanut Grove, where eight hundred select guests partied afterward, and in the following weeks there were "Welcome" signs everywhere for Judy and her movie. "Brilliantly staged, scored and photographed," burbled *Life* magazine, which put her on its cover. "One of the grandest heartbreak dramas that has drenched the screen in years," said *The New York Times*. There were only a few quibbles about length. "A mighty long gulp of champagne," said *Time,* which quickly added that, like champagne, *A Star Is Born* was hard to refuse.

Though James Mason also received warm rounds of applause, most of the attention was directed at what *Time* called "just about the greatest one-woman show in modern movie history." Yet even if she had never sung a note, Judy would still have dominated the screen, asserted Moss Hart. "It is a curious instinct that she possesses," he told one columnist. "Give her a scene and instinctively she'll play it right. Watching her, you get the almost weird impression that she's—I don't know quite how to explain it—but it's something like a great musician plucking strings on a harp."

Celestial sounds also came from theater box offices. Contrary to the studio's fears, the audiences, like the critics, did not seem to object to such a long musical. "Sockeroo" was how *Variety* described the receipts in Los Angeles and San Francisco, "mighty" in Detroit, "whopping" in Seattle, "terrif" in Cincinnati and "wow" in Louisville. And in New York, where the film premiered on October 11 at not one but two Times Square theaters, business was "radiant." Jack Warner, who had gambled more than $5 million on the picture, had won his bet, and so had two hungry alley cats, Judy and Sid. *A Star Is Born* was a hit, perhaps even the biggest hit of the year.

|||

Warner Bros. had other ideas, however, and less than two weeks after the Los Angeles opening, while the critics were still raving, while the public was still clamoring, it rushed to turn victory into defeat. The problem, as always, was length. The critics and the public may not have been unhappy with a three-hour picture, but many theater operators were. They could run *A Star Is Born* only three or four times a day, they grumbled, rather than the five or six times they could run a conventional, two-hour show. That, of course, meant a commensurate loss of revenue.

One obvious answer, which had worked well with other high-visibility features, was for the studio to have treated *A Star Is Born* as a special event, with reserved seats and higher-than-usual prices. Another answer was to have simply brushed off the complaints with the argument that it was better to have packed houses three times a day with *A Star Is Born* than half-empty ones five or six times with something less popular. But Harry Warner, Jack's older brother and the actual head of the studio, rejected those reasonable suggestions in favor of one that was totally unreasonable: rather than make the schedule con-

The studio boss, the star and the producer—Jack Warner, Judy and Sid—at the Star Is Born premiere

form to the picture, he said, make the picture conform to the schedule. *A Star Is Born,* he decreed, would have to be cut.

To order such major surgery on a movie that had already been released, reviewed and embraced by the public was so capricious that it defies easy understanding. Indeed, it was so rash and reckless, so out of character for sober, stolid Harry, that it is tempting to speculate that it was not an ordinary business mistake, but the product of an ancient sibling rivalry: Harry's hatred for his parents' darling, his flamboyant, joke-cracking younger brother. Overlooking Jack's many achievements, Harry saw him only as an egocentric, womanizing wastrel—and constantly told him so. "I'll kill you, you son-of-a-bitch!" Harry once screamed, dropping his dark-suited dignity to chase Jack through the Burbank lot with a lead pipe. Jack escaped; *A Star Is Born* did not. Now, with his order to slice and dismember, Harry was doing his best to kill the picture with which his despised brother was most closely identified.

Who determined what sections were to be removed is unclear— Cukor was in India, working on his next production, *Bhowani Junction*—but someone lopped off large chunks, for a total of almost half an hour. Left in were most of the big, spectacular scenes, including the "Born in a Trunk" number; taken out were many of the small, intimate scenes that explained character and motivation. "A star is shorn," said Bosley Crowther, the *New York Times* critic, who went on to say that "every cut leaves a gaping, baffling hole. Not only the emotional pattern but the very sense of the thing is lost." The crippled survivor of such mindless butchery was, for Cukor, a source of endless sorrow, and neither he nor Judy could bear to watch it. "*Marvelous* things were cut out," said Cukor, "marvelous, marvelous."

Most depressing of all was the disposition of those marvelous things. The discarded footage was not stored in the studio vault, a simple enough thing to have done, but destroyed—recycled for its silver content. Thus, unless someone finds a print that escaped the studio dragnet, the celluloid equivalent of the yellowing manuscripts that are occasionally discovered in the attics of great writers, no one will ever again see the *Star Is Born* that caused such excitement in 1954. "It is our destiny to be always in the hands of assassins," cried the Italian director Luchino Visconti, when his own spacious masterpiece, *The Leopard,* was also mutilated by its American distributors. And "assassin" is not too strong a word to apply to rusty-minded Harry Warner, the man who, through error or subconscious design, killed *A Star Is Born*.

The studio's folly was soon evident. Instead of increasing box-office receipts, the cuts, which were the object of wide and almost always unfavorable publicity, did the reverse, and after a few frantic weeks, attendance dropped dramatically. "Congratulations!" an irate moviegoer wrote Jack Warner. "It isn't easy to foul up a great picture, but you people out at Warner's seem to be doing a bang-up job. . . . Don't you think people in Podunk are going to feel cheated when it reaches them in its butchered up version?" These remarks proved prophetic, and one manager in Podunk country—the state of Maine—said the studio should at least have given theaters a choice between the two versions of *A Star Is Born*. He reported that he had received many letters and phone calls from customers who refused to pay full price for a less than full movie. "Consequently," he said, "we lost money on the picture." And so did Warners.

|||

Judy, the Associated Press had said, was "virtually a lead-pipe cinch" to win an Academy Award, and though the truncated *Star Is Born* was largely ignored, she and James Mason both received nominations. But Judy herself was forced to spend one of the most momentous evenings of her life not at the Pantages Theater, where the awards were to be given, but in Cedars of Lebanon Hospital. There, on March 29, the day before the big night, she gave birth to her third child, the boy she had so fervently desired: Joseph Wiley Luft, five pounds, eight ounces. If she could not go to the Oscar ceremonies, however, the ceremonies could go to her. Certain of the outcome, NBC had gone to the expense of erecting a tower outside the hospital so that its camera could peer in her third-floor window and catch her happy reaction when she was declared the winner.

That moment was never to come. The name that was announced belonged to Grace Kelly, who, playing against type, had portrayed the dowdy wife of an alcoholic in *The Country Girl*. Even as Kelly was walking to the stage, the TV technicians were leaving Judy's room, along with the camera into which she had been expected to smile and the microphone into which she had been expected to mumble her gratitude. Her friends and fans were as stunned as she was. "This is the biggest robbery since Brinks," wired Groucho Marx, and even John Kelly, Grace's father, seemed embarrassed by his daughter's unexpected triumph. "There should have been two awards," he graciously acknowledged, "and Judy Garland should have had one of them." In fact, there should have been only one award. Good as it was, Kelly's performance did not begin to approach Judy's, which, even in its abridged form, showed immeasurably greater depth, range and amplitude.

But if Judy had been robbed, who was the thief? Some believed that it was Judy herself. Her colleagues, they suspected, were punishing her for what they thought had been unprofessional conduct on the Warners set—and several Metro sets before that. Cukor, on the other hand, was convinced that the culprit was Warner Bros., whose clumsy cutting had eliminated much of the warmth and humor of her characterization, its subtlety and nuance. Beyond that, by making such public amputations, the studio had signaled its lack of confidence in *A Star Is Born,* the most expensive film it had ever made, and everyone connected to it. Warners had repudiated its costly problem child, and so, in March, did those who bestowed the Oscars—Hollywood liked winners, not losers. Even the film's theme song, the raw and haunting "The Man That Got Away," was passed over for a trite jukebox jingle, "Three Coins in the Fountain."

"I admit I want to win very badly," Judy had said, and whatever its cause, her rejection left her devastated. "It confirmed her belief that the industry was against her," said Lauren Bacall, whom she had asked to accept the award in her absence. "She knew it was then or never. Instinctively, all her friends knew the same. Judy wasn't like any other performer. There was so much emotion involved in her career—in her life—it was always all or nothing. And though she put on a hell of a front, this was one more slap in the face. She was bitter about it, and, for that matter, all closest to her were."

Yet Judy's chagrin over the loss of the Oscar was small compared with her disappointment over the fate of *A Star Is Born,* to which she had indeed given her all. A year of her life, as well as all her hopes and dreams, had gone into it, but in the end she was left with nothing: no award, no money and no prospects—Warner Bros. had seen enough of the Lufts. "It's only the beginning, folks," she had said at the Pantages premiere, certain that there would be many more such gala openings. But she was wrong. Blamed, however unfairly, for the film's many delays, she was once again unemployable in Hollywood. What had gone wrong with *A Star Is Born*? Sid offered perhaps the best, if also the most heartbreaking, explanation. "We did too much of everything," he later confessed. "Too much movie and too much music. It was good too much."

|||

Only six months earlier, when *A Star Is Born* was breaking box-office records, the Lufts were speeding along the road to riches, with a mountain of dollars, as green and inviting as the Emerald City of Oz, awaiting them at the end. Now, in the spring of 1955, they were confronted with an unpleasant fact: they were broke, really and truly broke. Hauled into court yet again by his ex-wife, Lynn Bari, this time for failing to contribute to their son's college education fund, Sid said that he could not afford even the stipulated $500 a year, for he and Judy were living on borrowed money themselves. As if to prove that dolorous point, a deputy sheriff waylaid him in the courthouse corridor to present a second allegedly unpaid bill: $600 owed on a grand piano.

Under the limelights, singing for her supper—that was where she belonged, an ebullient Judy had said in 1951, after her opening at the Palladium. What she could not have guessed was that in four short years she would have no choice: she would be singing not only for her supper, but for the suppers of three children, a husband and more than half a dozen servants and helpers. Whether she liked it or not, she would be spending the rest of the fifties in nightclubs, concert halls and sports arenas, serenading the world—just a wandering minstrel girl, as she liked to say.

With no money in the till and a sheriff, or at least a deputy sheriff, banging at her door, Judy began planning her new act during the winter, even before the Academy Awards. In July she took it on tour, visiting seven West Coast cities, from San Diego to Vancouver, British

Columbia. Though she sold out in the south, in San Diego and Long Beach, she had a mixed reception in the woodsy north; in Seattle, the box office was so poor, in fact, that a second night had to be scratched. That spotty record, combined with logistical difficulties, put the quietus on plans for a subsequent tour of the East and Midwest, leaving the Lufts as strapped at the conclusion of the summer as they had been at the beginning.

Enter a savior: television, a medium Judy had hitherto avoided. TV shows were not taped before broadcast in those days, and the prospect of performing live in front of a national audience terrified her. Now she had no alternative, and when CBS held out a bag of money, $100,000, for a single program, a ninety-minute version of her Palace act, she quickly grabbed it. A little nervous itself, CBS smothered her with kindness. What would it do, after all, if its star stayed home the night of the broadcast with one of her infamous migraines? To prevent such an untimely attack, Paul Harrison, the show's director, sat down with his technicians before the first rehearsal and laid down the law: they would have to be careful what they said and did around her. Judy was like a child, he said, and the slightest criticism, even a helpful reminder that her nose was shiny, might cause her to walk off the set and never return. "But remember," Harrison added, "she's one of the greatest talents any of you will ever work with. Keep that in mind and love her."

All the love in the world could not cure Judy's jitters—"I'm the original stage fright kid," she joked a few days before airtime—and no one at the network ever knew how close the broadcast had come to disaster. Sometime around dawn on September 24, just a few hours before her flickering image was supposed to appear on millions of TV sets, Judy took an overdose of sleeping pills that left her not only groggy, but virtually speechless for most of the day. During the final run-through she astonished CBS executives by not uttering a word, pointing to her throat and pretending that she was saving her voice for the real event. Not until the curtain went up did her voice reappear, hoarse and raspy at first, then progressively stronger and smoother.

She could have croaked like a frog, however, and still have obliterated the competition; she drew a viewership of forty million, triple the number watching either of the other two networks. Signing her up for three more such shows, one a year through 1958, CBS wasted no time in putting her before its cameras again. It broadcast her second special, just thirty minutes this time, only six months later, on April 8, 1956.

A debut of another kind followed in July, when Judy made her first appearance in what was, for entertainers, the land of the big bucks: Las Vegas, Nevada. The new earnings record she set there, $55,000 a week—$5,000 more than anyone else had ever received—was the confidence builder she seemed to need. "I've never seen her like this," exclaimed Sid, "so happy, singing like a lark, no problems—and at an opening yet!" She attracted so many people to the New Frontier that its grateful owners took out an ad in a trade paper: they wished, they said, that she could stay forever. But five weeks was all Judy could give them, and at the end of September she was back in her most cherished venue, renewing her love affair with New York audiences at the Palace. Booked for eight weeks, she stayed seventeen, almost as long as she had on her first visit. "New York is good for her," said Sid. "It's one place faster paced than she is."

|||

For Judy, 1956 was the last unblemished year of the decade, however, the last year of uninterrupted good news, and the succeeding years alternated, in perfect but monotonous rhythm, between success and failure, fair weather and foul. The first days of the very next year, 1957, began, indeed, with the termination of her lucrative television contract, the result of a rancorous dispute with CBS over the format of her third special. CBS wanted one kind of show, Judy and Sid wanted another and, rather than give in, the network canceled both her show, which had been scheduled for February 25, and her contract. "We just think she doesn't want to work," an unnamed CBS spokesman told a reporter for the *New York Herald Tribune*. Judy, he volunteered, was "known for a highly developed inferiority complex," and that, along with her fear that she was too heavy, may have led to the impasse.

Unwilling to leave bad enough alone, the Lufts pounced on these disparaging comments, claiming libel as well as breach of contract, and sued CBS for $1,393,333. But all they wound up with was a hail of unfavorable publicity. When Marie Torre, the *Herald Tribune* reporter, refused to reveal the name of the anonymous CBS spokesman, she was held in contempt of court and sent to jail for ten days. "I'm sorry if anyone has to go to jail," said Judy, who did not sound very sorry. "But if she wants to go, and be a martyr, I guess she will." There was no doubt who had the world's sympathy. The Joan of Arc of her profession, the sentencing judge called Torre, who left behind two small children when she donned her blue-and-white-striped jail uniform. Dorothy Kilgallen doubtless spoke for many when she wrote: "I must say I never thought I'd live to see the day when anyone would be tossed into the jug for saying Judy Garland had problems."

To the columnists she may have sounded like the Wicked Witch, but to the public, she was still golden-voiced Judy. She made her second appearance in Las Vegas in May 1957, then, in the months that ensued, sang all over the United States: in Detroit, Dallas, Philadelphia, Washington, D.C., and Los Angeles, too, where, for more than a week, she sang outdoors at the Greek Theater. In October she journeyed to London—her first visit since Palladium days—for what *Variety* described as a "devastating triumph" at the huge, three-thousand-seat Dominion Theater.

|||

Still, the monotonous rhythm persisted, like the ticking of some perverse clock. Devastating triumph was soon followed by equally devastating failure, and Judy ended 1957 as she had begun it, with a bitter and, for her, losing argument. On New Year's Eve, six days into a three-week engagement at Las Vegas's Flamingo casino, she got into a shouting match with some unruly patrons.

"Why don't you shut up?" Judy demanded.

"Why don't *you* shut up?" someone shouted back.

"I don't have to sing for you people," Judy responded.

"We don't have to listen to you, either," came the even nastier reply.

Nor did they. Judy not only departed the stage, but Las Vegas as well, forfeiting $100,000 and generating a new flurry of unflattering headlines. "Judy Garland Quits Vegas Show in Huff," said the *Los Angeles Mirror News*.

Three months later there was another scene on another stage, clear across the continent in Brooklyn, New York. Ten days into a three-and-a-half-week engagement at the vast seventeen-hundred-seat Town and Country Club, Judy sang two songs and stopped, unable to continue, she said, because of laryngitis. But the real strain was financial. Judy said she had not been paid, while Ben Maksik, the club's owner, said she had. As always, the sole winners were the lawyers, who busied themselves with liens and lawsuits, and the newspapers, which had more fodder for uncomplimentary stories. "Judy Garland," wrote the Broadway columnist Earl Wilson, "is close to hitting the bottom of the show business ladder for the second time in her career."

If failure attended her successes, however, so, too, did success attend Judy's failures. By July she was in top form again. Though she had gained so much weight since *A Star Is Born* that her once-vibrant eyes had become mere slits in a huge moon of a face, no one seemed to mind. The more there was of Judy, the more audiences seemed to like her, and night after night she brought star-packed crowds to Los Angeles's Cocoanut Grove, where she had last sung when she was nine years old. Moved by what it termed the heart-lifting sight of a comeback, the *Los Angeles Examiner* honored her with a teary editorial that gave an inky smile to "talent emerging from eclipse." She bathed in that bright light for the rest of the decade, in 1959 making much-praised appearances in all three of America's major opera houses—New York, Chicago and San Francisco. In New York, her seven nights at the Metropolitan grossed an estimated $190,000, close to a record for any theater, anywhere.

*Party time with Clifton Webb,
Merle Oberon, Van Johnson
and Noël Coward*

The Holmby Hills Rat Pack

've found our house," Judy exclaimed in the summer of 1953, and it was in that house, into which she and Sid moved soon afterward, that they resided for the rest of the fifties. Located in Holmby Hills, a privileged pocket between Beverly Hills and Bel Air, Judy's discovery had been built by a mogul from the old Hollywood—Hunt Stromberg, producer of such Metro hits as *The Thin Man* and *The Women*—and it seemed just right for two moguls from the new Hollywood, which Judy and Sid confidently expected to be after the release of *A Star Is Born*. It was large—"baronial" was how Jack Warner described it—and it had such old English elegance that it could have sat as comfortably in Surrey or Sussex as it did at 144 South Mapleton Drive, two doors south of Sunset Boulevard.

That English accent did not appeal to Sid, however. Doing his best to expunge it, he replaced the garage with an open carport, he paved over the quaint cobblestone driveway, and he brought in truckloads of dirt to do away with the slight slope in the backyard, obliterating Mrs. Stromberg's garden in the process. Inside, he bleached the dark wood paneling to blond, and he transformed Stromberg's private pub into a suburban den, with a record player, a TV set, a mirrored bar and a fourteen-foot couch, long enough to seat the Lufts, their collie, Sam, and their entire staff. Nor did Sid stop there, and for the next several years his family lived amid the noise and dust of construction. As soon as one section was redone, he would summon the contractors and start on another. "Sid took a castle and made a stable out of it," said Harry Rubin, who watched, with mounting disbelief, as walls were torn down in some places, then put up in others. "I had no class, but even I knew what Sid was doing was wrong."

In such a big house, there was a room for each of the children, including Sid's son John. Judy and Sid had separate suites, each with a bedroom, bathroom and dressing room. Hers sparkled with mirrors; his gleamed with rich, well-polished mahogany. The neighborhood was full of familiar faces. Next door, where Mapleton met Sunset, was Judy's old friend Lana Turner. Instead of borrowing a cup of sugar, Judy wryly observed, she would reach across the fence for some of Turner's sex appeal. In the other direction, two doors down, was the whitewashed brick French colonial that belonged to Humphrey Bogart and his wife, Lauren Bacall; and not far from them were Walter Wanger the producer and his actress wife, Joan Bennett.

Nunnally Johnson, screenwriter of *The Grapes of Wrath* and *How to Marry a Millionaire,* among other films, also lived on that stellar block. So did Gloria Grahame, who had won the 1952 Oscar for best supporting actress in Vincente Minnelli's *The Bad and the Beautiful;* Art Linkletter, host of NBC-TV's *People Are Funny;* and two illustrious songwriters, Sammy Cahn and Hoagy Carmichael. Bing Crosby, who, a few years earlier, had given Judy work on his radio program when no one else would hire her, was also a resident of South Mapleton, and his four boys could often be seen and heard racing their cars—Chevy Corvettes—down the street.

|||

The Crosby boys' hot-rodding may have awakened some people on South Mapleton, but not Judy and Sid, who joined other hard-drinking late-nighters to form Hollywood's most exclusive social club: the Holmby Hills Rat Pack, which included the most celebrated rodents on earth, next to Mickey and Minnie Mouse. Yet it was, really, only a group of friends who, with neither plan nor purpose, frequently found themselves in the Bogarts' den, lifting a glass at an hour when most people in Los Angeles, that city of early risers, were pulling up the covers. The Bogarts had a rule: "If the light over the front door was on," said Bacall, "we were home and awake and a chosen very few could ring the bell." Their light burned often, and among those chosen very few were Frank Sinatra, the David Nivens, the Mike Romanoffs—he owned the group's favorite restaurant—and Irving Lazar, the diminutive Hollywood agent. Swifty, Bogart nicknamed him, so quick was he at striking a deal.

And Judy and Sid, of course, although Sid was more tolerated than welcomed. Indeed, Bogart, who needled everyone, took special delight in attacking Sid. "Do you sing?" he demanded. Then, before Sid could respond, he answered his own question. "No, you don't. Then why the hell are you making a living off a singer?" Ridiculing Sid's fondness for conspicuous consumption—custom-made shirts, bespoke suits and bench-made English shoes—Bogart, who had been born to wealth, tartly informed him that class could be neither bought nor acquired. "And I can tell you that you don't have it, my friend," he savagely concluded, "and you never will." A man incapable of turning the other cheek, Sid retaliated in his usual way, picking Bogart up after one such assault and pinning him against a wall. If the gibes did not stop, Sid told that cinematic tough guy, he would split his head open. Bogart laughed—he appreciated dramatic gestures—but continued the razzing.

He did his best, on the other hand, to prop up Judy's unsteady ego, telling her that she had "more goddamn talent" than anyone else in town and presenting her with a pair of trick dice from his movie *Casablanca*—they always turned up a lucky eleven. But talent, Bogart added with a nudge, was no good in a living room; "you've got to get out there and do it." When Judy did do it, in Long Beach in the summer of 1955, the whole pack showed up to give her a boost, traveling in luxury of course: they had a bar on wheels, which is to say, a bus

With Janet Gaynor, heroine of the first A Star Is Born

stocked with the essential potables. "What fun we had with it all!" said Bacall. "We were an odd assortment, but we liked each other so much, and every one of us had a wild sense of the ridiculous."

And fun they all had until February 1956, when Bogart, the head of the pack, the man who provided the taste and tonic that made it more than a drinking club, was notified he had cancer, the disease to which he succumbed the following January. The Rat Pack died with him, and although others—Dean Martin, Peter Lawford, Sammy Davis, Jr., and the omnipresent Sinatra—later adopted the title, their loud, all-male crew lacked the same style. Missing was what Bogart called class.

|||

As far as the major studios were concerned, Judy was a disaster to be avoided, along with typhoons and earthquakes. All the more remarkable was it, then, when a South Mapleton neighbor, Nunnally Johnson, did something even he admitted he might live to regret: he offered her the lead in his own production, *The Three Faces of Eve.* Based on an actual case in Georgia, *The Three Faces of Eve* was the story of a woman with a triple personality, and Johnson thought that Judy—"the queen of all the psychopathic cases," as he dubbed her—would be a perfect fit. Judy thought so, as well. After reading the script and watching film clips of the real Eve as she moved in and out of her various identities, she assured Johnson that she could, as she emphatically expressed it, "kick the shit out of that part." But the casting was perhaps too good, and the role of Eve was probably too disturbing a reminder of the divisions in her own personality—the many faces of Judy Garland. She passed up the part, passing up as well, perhaps, the Academy Award that went to Joanne Woodward, Johnson's final choice for Eve.

Johnson was not the only one in Hollywood who believed that Judy had several loose screws. Psychoanalyzing her had long been a favorite pastime in a world crowded with people who were in analysis, who had been in analysis or who expected to be in analysis. "Schizophrenic" was the word most frequently attached to her. A psychiatrist who had actually treated her—California analysts were notoriously gabby—disputed that amateur diagnosis, however. "Schizophrenic," he explained to a writer from the *Saturday Evening Post,* suggested a dual identity. For Judy, he said, a new term would have to be invented. "We would need a word that means a personality that's split at least five ways," he said. Whatever the arithmetic, there was no doubt that there were too many Judys: one beguiling, one selfish; one rational, one irrational; one proper, one improper. The list of her contradictions was almost endless, indeed: there were enough Judys to fill the stage of the Palace.

If Nunnally Johnson saw the psychopathic Judy, another South Mapleton neighbor—Lana Turner's daughter, Cheryl Crane—saw the charming one. "Wonderful in every way" was how Crane characterized her, a woman so full of fun and laughter, so different from her own mother, that Cheryl wanted to trade places with her playmate Liza. Judy's own children saw that smiling figure as well. But they also knew a woman Crane would not have recognized, a drugged and depressed Judy who sometimes stayed in bed for days, allowing only the maid, the cook and Harry Rubin to tiptoe silently into her room. "Shh!" the children were told. "Mama's sleeping."

Judy's intake of drugs and alcohol was probably no greater than it had been when she was married to Vincente; but it was no smaller, either. In alcohol, the choice was usually between vodka and Blue Nun, a sweet and inexpensive German white wine, and she made sure that one or the other was never more than an arm's length away. During shooting of *A Star Is Born,* for instance, her thermos contained not water, but a stiff combination of vodka and grapefruit juice. Later, for the picture's premiere, Judy asked Michael Woulfe, her dress designer, to make her a hand muff big enough to hide a bottle of vodka, which was to be her tranquilizer during the more than three hours she was to sit in the Pantages Theater, anxiously awaiting the reaction of her friends and colleagues.

In drugs, she had a wider selection: Nembutal, Seconal, Tuinal, Demerol and Dexamyl—they sound like a recitation of kings from the Old Testament—were her daily companions on South Mapleton. Like Vincente before him, Sid tried a number of ruses to curb her appetite for those dangerous concoctions, hiring nurses to dole them out and persuading druggists to give her half-doses: they would mix the real stuff with innocuous, similar-looking substances like milk sugar, and then hope she would not detect the difference. But Judy outwitted the nurses, and she almost always knew—her body told her—when she was being cheated. In desperation, Sid sometimes even sneaked into her room when she was out, confiscating not only the pills and capsules in her medicine chest, but also those she had ingeniously hidden—taped inside drapes or under carpets, placed inside the mattress of her bed, buried in her bath powder. "You're a gumshoe, Sid," was her weary comment after one of his raids. "You missed your calling."

Occasionally, as she did during her 1955 tour, she reacted with righteous anger to such draconian tactics. "Where are they? Where are they?" she was heard screaming a few minutes before the curtain was to go up in one auditorium in the Pacific Northwest. "And don't give me that 'show must go on' shit!" And that night the show did not go on:

denied her pills, she denied her services, claiming she was sick and refusing to perform. Carried to an ambulance in a stretcher, she smiled bravely to her worried fans, never letting go of the glass of vodka hidden under the gray hospital blanket. "God bless," she whispered. "God bless."

|||

"I think Sid is just—well, just everything," Judy told a columnist at the beginning of 1955. "He's a good husband. He's a good father. He's smart. He's good at almost everything. He knows what's right for me. He's just the right man for me, that's all." That was quite an endorsement, but Sid did, indeed, give Judy something no other man ever had: continuous, unremitting attention. All the others with whom she had been involved—from David Rose to Tyrone Power, from Joe Mankiewicz to Vincente Minnelli—had enjoyed full and successful careers of their own. Sid did not. Judy was his career. She sang; he managed. She did not want to know about fiscal matters; he did, down to the penny. Theirs was more than a marriage; it was a business partnership—"Mr. and Mrs. Luft, Inc.," as one newspaper characterized it.

By the middle of the decade, however, Luft, Inc., that highflier of the early fifties, had lost altitude and appeared headed for a crash. The problem was not the usual one, a lack of income. Judy's performances brought in a cascade of dollars, well over $600,000 in 1956 alone, according to Sid—and that was probably a conservative estimate. Whatever the exact amount, it was a staggering figure in the Eisenhower era, when the Lufts had to pay only $120,000 for 144 South Mapleton, an expensive house in one of the most expensive neighborhoods in one of the most expensive cities in the United States.

Yet however many dollars poured in, however many records Judy smashed at the Palace, in Las Vegas or London, they were never enough. Always teetering on the brink of ruin, the Lufts lacked even the funds to finish furnishing their downstairs rooms. In September 1956, that year of the big bucks, a visiting reporter, Joe Hyams, was astonished to note that, three years after they had moved in, their huge living room contained only two items—a Ping-Pong table and the piano Sid had been dunned for in 1955. "Judy Garland is almost broke," wrote Hyams. "Although the Lufts live in a big home it is un-furnished; she has a remarkably small wardrobe; they have no money in the bank." When Judy visited New York, she did not even carry cash to buy lipstick, borrowing pin money, $30 or $40 at a time, from C. Z. Guest, one of her socialite friends.

Those debts, like many others, were never repaid, and the list of those who had claims on the Lufts grew ever longer. Some merely shrugged their shoulders, as Buddy Pepper had done when he thought Sid had shortchanged him at the Palladium in 1951. Others, the Warner brothers among them, were not so forgiving, and on one thing Harry and Jack were in accord: they despised Sid Luft almost as much as they despised each other. Five thousand dollars was piddling change to a man as rich as Harry was; but that was the sum, money loaned during the making of *A Star Is Born,* for which a furious Harry took Sid to court in 1955.

Owed six times that, brother Jack not only sued, but also attacked Sid in his autobiography, all but branding him a cheat and a con man. What seemed to gall Jack most was not, in fact, the money; it was the belief that he had been taken for a ride. Sid, he said, had also pried money out of him, $30,000, during the making of *A Star Is Born.* Then, as soon as the picture was finished, Sid had announced that he had just bought a racehorse for more than half that amount—$18,000. Al-though every girl could not be a Judy Garland, Jack bitterly observed, he was glad to say that a man like Sid Luft was equally rare.

In 1956 a foe even more formidable than the Warner brothers was complaining about the Lufts: the Internal Revenue Service demanded nearly $21,000 in back taxes. A year after that, in 1957, an interior dec-orator claimed $8,500 for work he said he had done on their house. So strained were the Lufts' finances that in October 1957, shortly before they were to sail for England and Judy's engagement at the Dominion Theatre, a beleaguered Sid found himself writing $15,000 in bad checks to cover expenses. All that saved him from possibly serious legal conse-quences was an accident at New York's Belmont Park in which Rover the Second, a racehorse in which Sid owned a half interest, broke his leg. By happy coincidence, poor Rover had been insured for $30,000; Sid's half was just enough to cover the checks.

Rover died only once, however, and back at South Mapleton the un-paid bills continued to accumulate. In 1958 not one but two tax collec-tors returned, the IRS delivering a past-due notice for more than $17,000, the State of New York adding another for $8,700. New York declined to wait any longer, in fact, for payments owed from Judy's first appearance at the Palace, refusing to allow her to leave the state until she had either paid up or posted a $10,000 bond. Unable to do either, Judy was forced to hand over her costumes and jewelry, right down to the wristwatch her mother had given her on her twenty-first birthday. To a reporter for the *New York Journal-American,* she admitted the in-escapable. "So I'm broke," she said. "But I'll get along—I always have. Nobody has to worry about me."

Where did Judy's money go? How did a woman who, as Sid told one reporter, had earned more than a million dollars in the previous three years, wind up in such a terrible and humiliating fix? The *Los Angeles Examiner* put into a headline the obvious question: "What Happened to the Million Dollars?"

|||

Much of the million went, of course, to taxes, the Lufts having been unable apparently to find the tax shelters in which many other high earners stashed their dollars. Much also went to that big house on South Mapleton, which had a mortgage and a payroll of eight: a butler, a gardener, a cook, an upstairs maid, a downstairs maid, a nurse, a nanny and an all-around man—the plain-spoken Harry Rubin. Was such a big staff necessary? Rubin thought not, and he was probably right. At least, none of the Lufts' neighbors, who lived in houses of equal size, required such an army of servants.

Except for her pills and doctors, Judy herself spent little. That re-markably small wardrobe Joe Hyams had mentioned consisted largely of the ski pants she wore around the house. Rubin bought them, a half-dozen at a time, at a sports shop on Wilshire Boulevard. By contrast, Sid—that "reckless spender on horses and living," as Lynn Bari had called him—had a remarkably large wardrobe, his drawers and closets all but bursting with his specially made shirts, suits and shoes. While Judy traveled without even enough cash for a taxicab, her husband's pocket was usually bulging with hundreds, sometimes even thousands, of dollars. If Sid ever went without anything, in short, he kept the fact secret. It probably astonished no one that he was one of the first in Hollywood to buy a kind of car rarely seen on American streets in those days, a shiny black Mercedes-Benz. "It's nouveau riche," Judy said when he brought it home, "but I love it!"

Before the Bogarts bought their own house on South Mapleton, an anxious Bogie had told Lauren Bacall to check with their business manager, Morgan Maree, to make sure they could afford it. Only after Maree had said yes did Bogart allow her to go ahead with the purchase. Watching the Lufts throw dollars around gave such a cautious man the shivers, and Bogart took Sid aside for a short lecture. "Listen," he said, "you've got to get straightened out. Go to my business manager." To Bogart's annoyance, however, Sid soon tired of the budget Maree imposed, and the spending resumed, unabated and unrestrained.

Many of those greenbacks were strewn around the pari-mutuel windows at Santa Anita and Hollywood Park, where Sid, "a gambling man who can kill $10,000 in an afternoon," as Hedda Hopper described him, was virtually a permanent resident. Indeed, one of Jack Warner's complaints had been that Sid was always away, sitting comfortably in his box at Santa Anita, when there was an emergency on the set of *A Star Is Born*. How much money was wasted on what *Time* magazine termed Sid's "unhappy knack of betting on also-ran horses" will never be known—it is doubtful that Sid himself knew. It was enough money, in any event, for Judy to cite it as one of her reasons for filing for divorce in February 1956. "Nobody ever made money on horses," she cried. "I can't stand it."

She could stand it, however, and after three days she withdrew her suit. "I love Sid and he loves me," Judy explained to Louella Parsons, "and I don't think we were ever so glad to see each other in our lives." But nothing, not even the threat of a breakup, could curb the gambling habit that had precipitated the suit. Six months later, when Judy gave her first show in Las Vegas, Sid apparently lost so much at the New Frontier's gaming tables that she was obliged to do an extra show simply to erase his debts. "You could hear her shouting all over the theater," said Robert Street, one of her chorus boys. "She was furious—and you couldn't blame her. There she was, used again."

Years later a friend was to tell Sid that many people were convinced he had stolen from Judy. But that, in Sid's view, was an impossibility. Despite a prenuptial property agreement that erected a brick wall between their finances—"The earnings of each of the parties shall be and remain their separate property," read a key sentence—Sid regarded Judy's money as his own. He could not have robbed her any more than he could have robbed himself. Sid was both too proud and too defiant to tell his tale-bearing friend that simple fact, replying instead: "Fuck 'em! People want to believe what they want to believe. I can't straighten them out. I am what I am. I've lived my life, and I've lived it very, very well. And that's it."

|||

In a 1955 article for *Coronet* magazine, Judy spelled out what she thought women wanted from men. What she was really describing, however, was what she herself wanted from a man. One of her odder requirements was an occasional fight. A "good tiff," she said, clears the murky atmosphere from a marriage in the same way a cool breeze blows away foul air. This was dubious wisdom, at best, but at least Judy practiced what she preached—and then some. The Lufts were so often embattled that 144 South Mapleton could have been declared a war zone; their tiffs were not mere breezes, but raging hurricanes that sent everyone around them running for refuge.

Nor did they care who heard or saw. On a trip to Long Island, to the posh precincts of Southampton, where Judy sang at a birthday party for Henry Ford II, they made such a ruckus that they were asked to leave the Irving Hotel. At a party at Chasen's, a favorite hangout of the stars, the Lufts exchanged words so raw, wrote a columnist for the *Hollywood Reporter,* that they could have been lifted from the pages of a Mickey Spillane thriller—Spillane was the writer whose novel use of obscene language shocked readers of that decorous decade.

Claiming that Sid had beaten her and locked her out of the house, Judy spent many nights on Van and Evie Johnson's living room sofa, having thrown pebbles at their bedroom window to wake them up. Whether Sid actually beat her is hard to say, but that she was often terrified of him was clear enough. "Get that son-of-a-bitching pig away from me!" she would scream, begging for help from Harry Rubin. But Sid, too, had reason to yell for help. More than once Rubin saw Judy, small as she was, give him a sound wallop or send something heavy flying in his direction.

Though the two younger children were usually only dimly aware of what was happening, Liza, who turned ten in 1956, was not, putting both hands over her ears when the wrangling reached its highest volume. Even the pugnacious Sid was sometimes overwhelmed by the battles at South Mapleton Drive, packing his bags and leaving town, usually for a distant racetrack. "After two or three days he got itchy and moved on," said Rubin. "He spent as little time with Judy as possible."

|||

What Sid did during his many trips away from home he discreetly kept to himself, but Judy's extramarital adventures can be recounted with near precision. Like many other stars, Judy had always been attracted to her leading men, casting soulful eyes at everyone from Mickey Rooney and Tom Drake to Peter Lawford and Fred Astaire. Before making *A Star Is Born,* she had informed one friend, with an almost despairing sigh, that she would probably also have an affair with James Mason. And so she did, just as she had predicted. Frank Sinatra, an old romance from the forties, reappeared in Judy's life about the same time, and although she had spoken enthusiastically about the virtues of oral sex— "It's really healthy!" she had told Harry Rubin—Judy was disappointed when she discovered that Sinatra, who agreed with her wholeheartedly, wanted nothing else. "I'm worried about Frank," she confided to Rubin. "All he wants is blow jobs."

"What's wrong with that?" Rubin demanded.

"Well," Judy replied, "you've gotta fuck once in a while, too, you know." Rubin also became one of her lovers. "Are you feeling frisky?" she would inquire, certain of the answer. And off they would go.

Judy felt frisky with others as well, including, almost certainly, at least two or three women, the only relationships about which she remained mum. When Rubin informed her that he had heard she was involved with another woman, her response was uncharacteristically vague. "You know," she said, "when you've eaten everything in the world there is to eat, you've got to find new things." Women were, in any event, never more than a side dish on Judy's menu—men were always her main course—and although a few always followed her around from city to city, she was not drawn to lesbians. One, in fact, gave her a possibly lasting fright by trying to rip off her clothes in a restaurant lavatory—she actually succeeded in tearing Judy's blouse—and Judy was saved from further trauma only by the belated intervention of Rubin and the restaurant manager.

Yet however many other lovers Judy had, Sid remained number one. "At least he does everything the way I want it," she grudgingly explained to Rubin. She was speaking of sex, of course, but what most seemed to excite both Lufts was not some bedroom trick, some exotic toy or novel position; it was the sound of battle. Guided by their own *Kama Sutra,* they equated wedded love with wedded combat, the latter acting as an incitement, an aphrodisiac, to the former. After Sid returned from one of his trips, or at the end of a particularly spirited argument, lovemaking was as certain as sun after rain. "It was almost like a cycle," said Rubin. "After the fighting stopped, they'd jump in the sack for about three days, and it was 'honey,' 'baby' and 'dear.' Then they got too close to each other, and it would start all over again."

That cycle eventually included a trip to divorce court. In February 1958, for the third time in two years, Judy summoned her lawyer, Hollywood's most renowned counselor, Jerry Giesler. Though no one, including Giesler, took her seriously on this third go-around—"Divorce Bug Again Bites Judy Garland," said one newspaper—Judy herself seemed in earnest. Alleging, for the first time in public, that Sid had physically abused her, that he had even attempted to strangle her, she obtained an order of protection and hired private detectives to keep him away from the house. "You don't know that sonofabitch," Judy told Giesler. "He gets into rages that are unbelievable." Still, no one was surprised when she changed her mind six weeks later, announcing that she was giving her marriage yet another chance.

Played too often, even the most exciting scenes become boring, and

With Liza and Frank Sinatra at her Cocoanut Grove opening in July 1958

as the fifties neared their end, the Luft marriage approached its final hours as well. As in most such stories of a relationship gone bad, there was blame enough for both. For Sid, there had been few surprises. Judy's troubles had been headline news long before he married her. The only thing he could not have known—no one on the outside could have—was how voracious her need was, how dangerous it was to come too close to that whirlpool of want and vulnerability.

Judy, however, had been surprised by Sid. If nothing else, she had expected such a famous brawler to give her security. But Sid had provided just the opposite, allowing hundreds of thousands of her dollars to slip through his hands and disappear, leaving her as destitute at the end of the decade as she had been at the beginning. What should a woman expect from a man? That was the question Judy had asked in her *Coronet* article. He must be the leader, had been her answer. If he were not, "nothing else really matters—not money, not brains, not beauty. No, not anything." In those sentences she had written the epitaph to her own marriage. For all of his schemes and deals, his tough talk and quick fists, Sid was a follower, not a leader—and nothing else really mattered.

|||

Despite the bouquets of raves that were thrown her way at the end of the fifties, Judy said she sometimes felt as if she were singing in a blizzard, scarcely knowing where she was or what she was doing. And for good reason: she was sick, and getting sicker every day. The pounds she had put on after *A Star Is Born* had hidden a serious illness, a malfunction of the liver. She was not merely fat; she was bloated with the fluids her liver was no longer capable of removing. By November 18, 1959, when she finally entered Doctors Hospital in Manhattan, Judy was in pain, her eyes glazed, her limbs stiff and swollen and her memory failing—she was probably not many days away from death. "I don't think she'll make it" was one doctor's gloomy prognosis.

For seven weeks Judy lay in bed, the fluids slowly being drained from her enfeebled body. She was suffering from acute hepatitis, probably caused, or at least exacerbated, by years of pill and alcohol abuse. Still very ill when she left the hospital on January 5, 1960, she was immediately ferried to Grand Central Station and a train that would speed her west, home to California. With her Judy carried some heavy baggage, her doctor's somber warning that she might have only five years to live. Even if she survived longer than that, he cautioned, she would remain a semi-invalid, unable to sing or perform.

Judy's initial reaction was surprising but understandable: she was relieved. "You want to know something funny?" she later confessed. "I didn't care. I just didn't care. All I cared about was that my children needed me. Suddenly the pressure was off." All her life Judy had been working; now she could rest.

For several months, through the winter and spring of 1960, that is exactly what she did, slowly recuperating from her brush with death. In at least one way she was her mother's daughter, a small woman of mulish strength and resilience. By summer she had largely recovered and was eager to perform again. Without her voice, she was no one; a Judy Garland who could not sing was not a Judy Garland at all.

Her first formal outing came in July, when she sat between Adlai Stevenson and Senator John F. Kennedy at a fund-raising dinner for the Democratic Party, which was meeting in Los Angeles to choose its 1960 presidential candidate. An ardent Democrat—she had broken down on the set of *The Harvey Girls* when the death of Franklin D. Roosevelt was announced—Judy made no secret that Kennedy was her choice. Peter Lawford, Kennedy's brother-in-law, had introduced them six years earlier, at the New York premiere of *A Star Is Born,* and the senator and the star had become good if oddly matched friends. "He's magnetic. He's tough. He's mature," said Judy. They remained close even after Kennedy's inauguration, Judy frequently telephoning the White House to ask the President's advice on how to deal with the difficult people in her life. Kennedy, for his part, sometimes called her for a private concert—a few bars of "Over the Rainbow" sung a cappella over the phone.

|||

During her months of enforced inactivity, Judy had had time, as well as reason, to look closely, perhaps for the first time, at who she was and where she was going. That reassessment led to at least one clear conclusion: it was unhealthy for her to live in a town obsessed with box-office returns and television ratings. By prevailing standards, she was worse than dead; she was a has-been. "I was liked in California but nobody needed me," she explained. "The phone never rang. In Hollywood I was somebody who *had been* a movie star." It was, she realized, time to leave.

For everyone, there is a place to which the heart turns in times of trouble, one spot, even if it exists only in the imagination, where the sun always smiles and the clouds roll by simply for decoration. For Judy, that place was the city that had resuscitated both her confidence and her career, and it was to London that she had looked during her months of recovery. "I want to get off by myself and think about the future," she told Sid. Thus it was that on July 11, 1960, a woman who was afraid of airplanes and never traveled alone did both, boarding a jet plane and flying, all by herself, to the one place in the world she believed would provide her with peace and contentment.

London did not disappoint her. In the months that followed, the English embraced her as warmly as she embraced them. She enjoyed weekends at the country house of her old friend the actor Dirk Bogarde—"the only really enchanting woman in the world," Bogarde called her—and she laughed through evenings with a still older friend, Noël Coward. Indeed, Coward was almost as delighted by Judy as he was by himself; of all the famous people he knew, she was the only one he allowed to speak without interruption. "You are probably the greatest singer of songs alive," Coward assured her, "and I . . . well, I'm not so bad when I do my comedy numbers."

Reviving with her spirits, her voice was soon restored entirely—it was better, perhaps, than ever—and on the evening of Sunday, August 28, she once again stepped onto what was, for her, sacred ground, the stage of the Palladium. Although there had been little notice, that big house was packed to the last row in the top balcony, giving her such a joyous reception that she was induced to return the following Sunday, when she received an equally enthusiastic response. Almost immediately London had worked its magic, and almost immediately Judy decided that henceforth she would make her home in the place where she felt most at home: she would move to England. She had not renounced America, she told English reporters—she still felt very American. It was, rather, that she liked life better in England. "The tempo is slower, yet it stimulates me and puts me in a *VERY* happy frame of mind."

Sid joined her in August, and in September, after renting a spacious house in Chelsea, they sent for Liza, Lorna and Joey. That fall Judy also took her songs to the Continent. American musicals had never found favor with the French, as they had with the British, and Judy's first concert in Paris, on October 5, aroused so little interest that, to fill all the seats in the Palais de Chaillot, Sid was forced to give away hundreds of free tickets. Just one performance was enough to ignite a fire, however. On the second night, October 7, the box office was mobbed, and the audience cheered her through eight curtain calls. "Now we know," said one critic, "why she is called Miss Show Business in America."

With John F. Kennedy, Danny Kaye and JFK aide David Powers in the White House, November 1962

Responding to a request from the Kennedy campaign, Judy also found time to sing for American troops stationed in West Germany. She traveled to Wiesbaden at the end of October, a few days before absentee ballots were to be sent home. It was thus with special pride that, two weeks later, she celebrated Kennedy's victory at an election-night party in London's Savoy Hotel. The next day she telephoned the Kennedy compound in Hyannis Port, Massachusetts, where Kennedy had gone to hear the returns. "Greetings, Mr. President," said Judy. "Hello, Madame Ambassador," replied Kennedy.

|||

For ten years Sid had been Judy's lover and manager, roles so inter-twined that it was impossible to separate one from the other. Now he wanted to strike deals of his own, and he thought he had a sure moneymaker, a novel system that would give airline passengers a selection of music at their seats. Sid could not make the rounds of the airlines and manage Judy, too, however, and at the end of 1960 he convinced her to accept a replacement: Freddie Fields, who had just left the Music Corporation of America, the Goliath of talent agencies, to start his own

company. For a 10 percent fee, Fields would oversee a performer's entire career, becoming manager, mentor and guide—everything but
mother and father. With Fields in charge, an entertainer would be free
to do nothing but entertain.

To such a lofty ambition Judy held the key. Though he had never
wanted to have more than a dozen clients—a select dozen, of course—
Fields had thus far been able to recruit only two, Phil Silvers and his
own wife, the singer Polly Bergen. Acquiring Judy would give his
struggling company the credibility it was so clearly missing. At Sid's behest, Fields flew to London to make his pitch, and in December, Judy
designated Fields her "sole and exclusive Manager." What Judy almost
certainly did not know was that Sid was also to receive a fee. In exchange for handing Fields his biggest client, Sid was later to say, Fields
promised to give him a thousand dollars for "each single television
show or theatrical performance" in which Judy appeared, plus another
half a million dollars for such things as Judy's musical arrangements
and lighting charts. Sid may have relinquished his role as her manager,
but he did not want to give up his share of her profits.

Though Sid's motives were not altogether pure, his choice of Fields
was sound, and as much as Fields needed her, Judy needed him, or
someone like him. The truth was that, under Sid's haphazard direction,
her career had wandered aimlessly since the mid-fifties. Despite two
Hollywood marriages, Sid had never grasped a simple but crucial
axiom: a show-business career has to have a shape and a purpose. An
entertainer who merely follows the dollar signs, as Judy had been
doing, may do well for a few years, but is likely, in the end, to wind up
broke and unremembered.

Fields claimed a broader vision. He was not a job hunter, he declared
years later, but an opportunity seeker, a man who had a plan. His plan
for Judy had the logic of necessity: he was going to show the world that
the unreliable Judy of the bad old days had vanished and that a new
Judy—a "completely revitalized" Judy, as Fields called her—had taken
her place. He proposed to work her so hard that, by the end of 1961,
even the most cynical skeptics would be bidding for her talents.

Returning to the United States, clutching his passport to the
future—Judy's signed contract—Fields wasted no time in making good

on his promise. By the second week in January he was able to present her with the beginnings of a new career: a wide-ranging concert tour; a small but key role in one of the most prestigious movies of the year, Stanley Kramer's *Judgment at Nuremberg;* and CBS's agreement to a new Garland spectacular. "With Freddie, something clicked," said Judy. "He seemed to know how to do exactly what I could not do: channel my work."

To hold her hand—she still required constant attention—Fields took in a partner, another high-powered defector from MCA. Even smoother and more charming than Fields himself, David Begelman also delighted her, and Judy was heard to sob with happiness, thrilled at having discovered her saviors at last. "You two are the luckiest thing that ever happened to me," she cried. "Leopold and Loeb," she nick-named them, an affectionate if somewhat ambiguous reference to the teenage geniuses who had murdered a Chicago neighbor just to prove that they were smart enough to get away with it. Not yet forty, Fields and Begelman were also young, smart and, beneath their well-tailored suits, ferocious—just the agents Judy wanted.

The only one who was not pleased with their cozy relationship was Sid, who had issued the invitation, then found himself excluded from his own party. She no longer wanted Sid involved in her professional life, Judy told Fields. Excluded, too, was any prospect that Sid would continue to receive a share of her profits. If there had ever been a gen-tlemen's agreement regarding Sid's fee, Fields chose to ignore it. In-stead of the huge sums he had expected from Fields, all Sid ever got for his gift of Judy was a measly thousand dollars.

|||

Nineteen sixty-one, Judy was to say, was the best year of her life—the year in which everything finally went right. "Completely revitalized," Freddie Fields had called her, and as she began her concert tour in Jan-uary, it was clear that whether he had known it or not, Fields had been telling the truth. The first critic to note the alteration was in Texas, one of her earliest stops, where the reviewer for the Dallas *Times Herald* wrote that though she had been fine in 1957, on her previous visit to the Big D, she was now a wonder, displaying a hundred times more fire, warmth and greatness. In Houston, where she appeared two days later, on February 23, the response was perhaps even more enthusiastic.

Elated by such shouts of approval, Judy stopped singing only long enough—for two weeks in March—to make her first picture in six years. A movie with a mission, *Judgment at Nuremberg* attempted to explain the seemingly unexplainable: how decent Germans could have been seduced by the dogmas of Nazism. To do that, screenwriter Abby Mann had chosen to focus not on the first and most celebrated Nuremberg trial, in which Hitler's top henchmen were prosecuted, but on a later round in which German judges were put into the dock.

To play his leads, Stanley Kramer, who produced as well as directed, had brought together a formidable cast: Spencer Tracy, Burt Lancaster, Marlene Dietrich, Richard Widmark and Maximilian Schell. For two lesser roles, emotionally disturbed victims of Nazi brutality, he had chosen Judy and another famously disturbed actor, Montgomery Clift. "He treated me like an actress," Judy said of Kramer, grateful that someone in Hollywood would give her another chance. "And what it did for me! If Stanley ever wants me to play a leper on Molokai, I'll do it."

Only once, on her first day of shooting, did the new Judy cause any of the old consternation—and that was a false alarm. For six takes she tried to cry, but the required tears refused to come. "Damn it, Stanley," she at last complained, "I can't do it. I've dried up. I'm too happy today to cry." The floodgates finally opened on the seventh take, and though her three scenes were to take up no more than fifteen minutes on screen, they packed enough raw emotion—"she gave the impression," said Kramer, "that she almost wanted to be hurt"—to bring her a nomination, if not the Oscar itself, for best supporting actress.

|||

After a brief family vacation in Florida, Judy resumed a tour that was to last for many months, sending her to every corner of the continent, from San Antonio to San Francisco, from Manhattan's Carnegie Hall, with its flawless acoustics, to outdoor arenas like the Hollywood Bowl, where she gamely sang through lightning, thunder and two hours of a drizzle that soaked both her and her audience. "Judy Doesn't Fizzle in a Drizzle," applauded the *Los Angeles Times*. Though she missed a few engagements, particularly toward the end of that relentless schedule, she did not fizzle anywhere. In a year of high spots, however, one, the tallest peak in the range, towered above all the others: Sunday, April 23, 1961—Carnegie Hall.

|||

Schoolteachers like to tell their students that because human perfection is an impossibility, the word "perfect," when it is applied to the achievements of men and women, should always be modified by an adverb such as "almost" or "nearly." Fair enough, but how, then, would the schoolteachers describe Judy Garland at Carnegie Hall? She had been superb, genuine and touching, at the Palladium in 1951, and better still at the Palace a few months later. There had also been many other "almost perfect" or "nearly perfect" appearances in the years that had followed. But the Carnegie Hall performance was to stand alone. It was so good that it could not have been better, and it therefore needs no modifier: it was, even by the strictest definition, perfect. Two decades earlier, Al Jolson had called Judy the greatest female singer he had ever heard, adding only that what she was then was yet nothing compared with what she one day would be. That day, that moment of apotheosis, had now arrived.

For more than two and a half hours, from eight-forty-five until eleven-twenty, with just one intermission, she was onstage alone—Judy without comedians, acrobats, bicyclists, dance teams, chorus boys or jumping dogs. Judy without her tramp costume, her dirty tear-stained face or her legs dangling over the edge of the stage. Judy without gimmicks, in short, singing twenty-six songs, from some of her old favorites, like "You Made Me Love You" and "The Man That Got Away," to others she had rarely sung before, such as the Gershwin brothers' "A Foggy Day" and Noël Coward's bittersweet "If Love Were All." After the twenty-fourth number, she confessed that she had almost run out of songs. "Just stand there," came a reassuring shout from one of the boxes. Judy did better than that, however, belting out two more, "After You've Gone" and "Chicago." A year earlier she had questioned whether she would ever sing again. But at the end of a concert of extraordinary length, her voice sounded as strong as it had at the beginning.

There was, in fact, magic in Judy's singing that night. Her pipes, as *Variety* called them, had ripened into the rutilant maturity of midsummer—she was to turn thirty-nine in just eight weeks. Yet they still retained, undiminished, a springlike freshness. Her voice had achieved greatness in the past, but only occasionally, never for a whole evening, never through twenty-six numbers. At Carnegie Hall, greatness, true greatness, was hers, and on that soft April night in Manhattan she ascended to heights untrodden by any of her contemporaries. Her mastery of herself, her songs and her audience was complete.

Secure in the snug embrace of a hall beloved by all musicians, warmed by the smiles flashing from every seat, she could, it seemed, do anything, from Broadway brass to whispered ballads, pure and plangent. All that—Judy triumphant! Judy *in excelsis!*—can be heard on the recording that was released by Capitol Records the following July, when it quickly rose to the top of the charts. What cannot be heard— what only those present could see—was Judy in action, dancing, prancing and strutting. She was her own chorus line, her own comedian and acrobat; she was all of vaudeville wrapped up into one small package.

To say, however, that Judy gave a perfect performance that night is accurate, but curiously insufficient. What made the one hundred and fifty-five minutes so electric was something everyone could share— something everyone can still share: a human triumph, a triumph not of combat or competition, but of spirit and determination in the service of art. In one bright evening, all of Judy's potential, a lifetime of waiting, had blossomed into thrilling, exuberant flower. It was as if, after years of trying, and after several signal successes, a writer, or a painter, or a composer had at last brought everything together—talent, experience and the artist's anguish—to produce one great and definitive work. That was Judy at Carnegie Hall. She had shown what she could do and what she could be, and, through the miracle of her music, she had opened a brief, shivery window into a realm beyond ordinary understanding.

|||

Carnegie Hall was validation, proof that Judy really had changed. "The new new Garland," one magazine dubbed her. Fields's strategy had worked, and reporters, who are almost as excited by comebacks as they are by downfalls and disasters, rushed to her side. All the articles that appeared in the ensuing months were flattering; several were shrewd and insightful. But the most revealing look at the phenomenon of the Garland concert—that combination of "revivalism and the ancient rites of Dionysus," as one magazine called it—came not from a reporter sitting in the audience, but from a screenwriter standing backstage at one of her performances in New Jersey, where he was gathering material for a movie, *The Lonely Stage,* that Judy was scheduled to make several months later.

The screenwriter, Mayo Simon, arrived at the concert hall in the afternoon, as the lights were being adjusted and the orchestra was starting to rehearse. Wearing a babushka and looking, in Simon's opinion, like "dumpy Gussie Schlump, the woman who cleans up after the show," the star herself did not arrive until seven-thirty, half an hour before the curtain was supposed to go up. Though her stage fright was notorious—Judy herself joked about it—she seemed not at all nervous that night. Sipping a glass of white wine in her dressing room, she gossiped, told stories and managed to ignore both the clock, which soon announced eight, and the sound of clapping that followed from her impatient audience a few minutes later. Finally, at eight-thirty, she jumped up. "Let's do a show!" she exclaimed, and disappeared behind a screen to don her costume. When she emerged, she had discarded the babushka, but, to the disappointed Simon, who had expected some magical mutation to have taken place behind that screen, she still looked like Gussie Schlump. Where, he wondered, was the woman who was causing such hysteria night after night?

But the sorcery was not in her costume or makeup. Now, as she stood in a corner of the stage, listening to her overture and waiting for her entrance cue, Judy underwent an amazing metamorphosis. Straightening up, she appeared to become both taller and thinner. "It was stunning," said the astonished Simon, "the most fantastic transformation I have ever seen. It was like watching Mr. Hyde turn into Dr. Jekyll, or seeing black-and-white change into Technicolor. When she walked out onstage, she was not just a wonderful singer; she was a presence!" Through an act of will or alchemy—or perhaps both—the ugly duckling had become a swan, and Gussie Schlump had become Judy Garland.

*A face-off with Sid
in a London recording studio, 1962*

CHAPTER 14

A Standoff at the Stanhope and the End of Sid

ike the calendar, Judy's career can be neatly divided into decades, each following an increasingly familiar pattern: a brilliant start, several years of spectacular success—and then disaster. The forties, her movie-star years, had begun in a flurry of excitement, but had concluded in heartbreak and recriminations. The fifties saw resurrection on the stages of the Palladium and the Palace, but they, too, ended in sorrow, with her doctors despairing of her life as she lay immobile in a New York hospital.

And now the sixties had brought a second miraculous recovery, the clamorous triumph of Carnegie Hall and a welcome back to both movies and television. After *Judgment at Nuremberg,* Judy was to provide the musical meows for Mewsette, a sexy French cat in a feature-length cartoon, *Gay Purr-ee,* that boasted eight new songs by Harold Arlen and E. Y. Harburg. She was to make *A Child Is Waiting,* her second picture with Stanley Kramer and Abby Mann. And then, in the spring of 1962, she was to fly to England to star opposite her old friend Dirk Bogarde, in *The Lonely Stage—I Could Go On Singing,* it was later to be called.

Sandwiched between *Gay Purr-ee* and *A Child Is Waiting* was an hour-long TV show, with guest appearances by two of the day's hottest entertainers, Frank Sinatra and Dean Martin. As impressed as everyone else by her remarkable revival, *Time* magazine anointed her with a title—"Judy Garland III."

Through all the years, the relentless cycle of ups and downs, there was, however, one constant. Judy did well only when she felt confident—and she only felt confident when she was holding the hand of a man she could trust. "Only *you* could give me the confidence I so badly needed," she had written Vincente at the end of work on *The Clock;* but when her confidence in him vanished, so had her marriage, her M-G-M career and her emotional equilibrium. Along came Sid with a new boost to her ego, sending her soaring through the first half of the fifties. When her faith in him disappeared, buried under an avalanche of debts, her career, marriage and self-esteem started to disappear as well.

Freddie Fields and David Begelman had come next. It was they who had made Carnegie Hall possible, and it was they who had enabled her to pay off that pile of debts—$375,000, by her estimate. "I hated owing money," she confessed. "It's—humiliating, especially if you're capable of *not* being in debt." In Dallas, where she was publicly embarrassed by the presentation of a hotel bill left over from her 1957 visit, she grumbled that despite the many thousands she had made, she had never actually seen any of her money, had never touched it to know it was hers. Always ready to humor her, Fields and Begelman, those two Johnnys-on-the-spot, listened to that complaint and came to her room after the concert with exactly the right medicine for such psychic pains—a brown paper bag bulging with that night's receipts. "I'd never seen so much money," she said. "I giggled like a schoolgirl, throwing it in the air and letting it cascade down around my head."

Only when it was too late did Sid wake up to what he had done in giving up his manager's title. Judy now looked not to him, but to Fields and Begelman for guidance and protection. A title was not all Sid had given up, however, and it was probably not a coincidence that Judy ceased to love him at about the time she discovered she no longer needed him—in January 1961, to be precise, a few weeks after Fields had been hired. She took a walk through the streets of a snowy Manhattan, she said, and in that whirl of white, suddenly realized that, after ten years, she did not "give a damn" about Sid.

|||

From the beginning, the Lufts, with their loud arguments, separations and skirmishes with creditors, had provided rich copy for the gossip columns. It was perhaps not surprising, therefore, that Sid, who was accustomed to so much noise in his marriage, seemed deaf to a genuine howl of distress. He may not have understood how troubled the relationship really was until July 1961, when Judy pointedly excluded him from a family vacation on Cape Cod, where she had taken a place just a hundred yards from the Kennedy compound. Showing up nonetheless, Sid checked into a motel and telephoned her; but her voice was so chilly that he kept his distance for a couple of days. When he finally did visit her, she had warmed only slightly, greeting him with the cool politeness she might have shown a casual acquaintance.

"You know, Sid," she said, after pouring him a drink, "I'm going to divorce you."

Spoken so matter-of-factly, her words unsettled him perhaps more than any others she had ever uttered, and Sid returned to his lonely motel room, opened a bottle of liquor and promptly proceeded to fall apart. In an instant, Judy had reversed the roles of a decade, and it was Sid who called her, sobbing uncontrollably. "Sid, what's gotten into you?" she asked after rushing to his side. "I don't know," he cried. Remaining until he had regained his composure, Judy then left, still cool and unruffled.

That icy reserve thawed somewhat in the fall, when the Lufts tried yet again to bridge their differences. "You just don't toss ten years of marriage aside easily," Judy explained. In December, when she fell ill in Europe, a few days after the Berlin premiere of *Judgment at Nuremberg*, Sid went all the way across the Atlantic to bring her home. He then stayed to celebrate the Christmas holidays with her and their children, Liza included, at a house Judy had rented outside New York, in suburban Scarsdale. When Judy flew to Los Angeles to work on her CBS special and *A Child Is Waiting*, Sid followed her there as well, bringing the whole family together in a house less than a mile north of their previous address on South Mapleton. That house had been sold several months earlier to pay off lingering debts—three mortgages, eighteen attachments, numerous liens, unpaid child support for Sid's son John and loans from two of Sid's friends.

Taping the first week in January, Judy almost waltzed through her television show, which went on to smash an opposition that included NBC's popular western series, *Bonanza*. Signs of trouble, hints of the old Judy, began to resurface during filming of *A Child Is Waiting*, which was set in a school for retarded children. Stanley Kramer, who had made her feel so secure in *Judgment at Nuremberg*, was busy with another project, and he had assigned the directing chores to a brash newcomer, John Cassavetes. Unlike Kramer, Cassavetes believed in keeping his actors off balance, convinced that from nervousness would spring spontaneity.

From Judy and her costar, Burt Lancaster, he received little but resentment, however. "That boy doesn't know what he's doing," Lancaster complained to Abby Mann. "I'm going to kill him," Judy herself said. She settled for infuriating him instead, frequently arriving late and unprepared, using that old but always reliable weapon, passive aggression. Unhappiness ruled from beginning to end—and well beyond—and everyone involved, Cassavetes included, was dissatisfied with a film that offered a glimpse into a world few moviegoers knew or, as dismal box-office returns were to demonstrate, wanted to know.

|||

How much problems on the set contributed to discord at home—and vice versa—is hard to say, but by the end of March it was clear that the Lufts had failed in their attempt at reconciliation. Leaving their rented house in Bel Air, Judy moved into the Beverly Hills Hotel for a couple of weeks, then flew by herself to New York, where she hoped to relax before traveling on to England and another difficult role in *I Could Go On Singing*. Not long after she landed in New York, she collapsed, however, the strain of working almost nonstop for more than fifteen months having caught up with her at last. Admitted to Manhattan's Columbia Presbyterian Medical Center on April 15, she spent a week recovering from what was apparently simple exhaustion.

Despite all the signs to the contrary, Sid expected to join her in Europe, where he was still hoping to peddle his stereo system to the airlines. Arriving with the children from Los Angeles, he packed everybody but Liza, who stayed with friends, into a suite in the Stanhope Hotel on Fifth Avenue. Judy joined them there on April 22—but on a different floor. She would take Joey and Lorna to England by herself, she declared. Sid angrily rejected the suggestion, finally refusing to let them out of his sight.

The standoff at the Stanhope ended on the evening of Saturday, April 28. Three times that day Judy had summoned the police, but nothing she could say or do was sufficient to prod them into yanking her children away from Sid. Realizing that more drastic measures were demanded, she then appealed to her New York lawyer, who, wasting no time, marched into the Stanhope's lobby with a squad of four—two private detectives and two city policemen. At seven o'clock Judy appeared outside Sid's suite. Assured that she was alone, the suspicious Sid let her in and quickly closed the door, which was the signal for the assembled gumshoes to tiptoe from their hiding places and take up position. Five minutes later they heard what they had been waiting for—the sound of shouts and falling furniture.

"Get in, you guys!" the lawyer ordered the two detectives. "That's what you're here for!"

Whether Sid opened the door or it gave way to a battering ram of beefy shoulders is in dispute—but open it did. "The bastard hit me!" Judy screamed as her rescue crew rushed in. "He slapped me!" As Sid stood by helplessly, Joey and Lorna were hustled away to one of the two limousines parked outside—Liza was in the other—and by eight-forty-five Judy and her brood were airborne, on their way to England. She had won; her children were hers. "My marriage is finished," she said from the safety of her London hotel. "It's over. It lasted eleven years and it would take eleven years to tell you what went wrong."

|||

Judy had won a battle, but the war dragged on. Claiming that she had hired "goons" to hold him down while Joey and Lorna were carried off to England, a still-seething Sid swore that they would not remain there very long. And five days later he followed them to London, determined to take them home. But Judy again thwarted him. Persuading the London High Court to make them its temporary wards, she made certain that neither parent could take the children out of the country until legal hearings had been held, a process that would probably consume many weeks, conveniently concluding about the time she had finished *I Could Go On Singing*—and would be ready to return to America anyway. "Whatever happens and wherever I go in the world," she declared, "my children will go with me."

Neither the edict of the court nor the presence of round-the-clock detectives did much to alleviate her anxiety, however. In constant fear that Sid would somehow find a way to snatch her children, Judy found no haven even in London. The self-confidence engendered by a year and a half of unbroken success had shown signs of cracking on the set of *A Child Is Waiting*. Now, with a bellicose Sid pounding on her door, it crumbled into dust, taking with it the recently constructed wonder known as Judy Garland III. As she started work on *I Could Go On Singing,* the new new Garland reverted to old old habits, and what might have been a congenial set—her leading man, Dirk Bogarde, was one of her most cherished friends—turned instead into a hair-raising ride on a runaway roller coaster, "ricketing and racketing," as Bogarde phrased it, to its disastrous end.

Bogarde had been hearing warning bells for several months, from the moment Judy had telephoned from America, begging him to join her in a movie she described as terrible, but which, since it would be shot in England, she wanted to do anyway. They had been eager to work together from their first meeting, in 1956, at a New Year's Eve party in New York. Beel, Bogarde's country house in Buckinghamshire, was Judy's first destination when she went to Europe in the summer of 1960, and the lazy days she spent there, walking Bogarde's dogs, sitting in the sun and visiting villages that dated back to the earliest Henrys, probably persuaded her that England was the utopia for which she had so long been looking. What Bogarde himself most remembered from that summer was shared laughter. Judy, he wrote, was "without doubt, I suppose, the funniest woman I have ever met. We seemed, in that July, to laugh endlessly."

|||

I Could Go On Singing did not pretend to be anything other than a soap opera. Judy was to play a singer, Jenny Bowman, whose long-ago romance with an English medical student produced a baby boy. More interested in her career than motherhood, Bowman gave the boy to his father, relinquishing all claims and promising that she would never try to see the child again. Now, fourteen years later, she has had second thoughts. She goes to London to sing at the Palladium and to beg her former lover—Bogarde—to let her see their son. Just once, she pledges, will be enough. It is not, of course, and that first meeting leads to many scenes of soppy melodrama before the final one, which finds Bowman standing on the stage of the Palladium—alone again.

From such a theme, the mother longing for the love of her lost child, Hollywood had often spun box-office gold. But Judy saw nothing sparkling in the screenplay of *I Could Go On Singing*—"a load of shit," she called it. Though the producers, two young Americans, had agreed to make changes, chiefly in Judy's dialogue, Bogarde knew that these would not be enough to satisfy her. Keep the new version away from her, he urged them, until he had had an opportunity to talk with her and the two of them had made their own revisions. Though she was all smiles on her initial, get-acquainted visit to the studio, the Shepperton complex outside London, Bogarde knew something was bothering her. That afternoon, alone in her room, he discovered what it was. His advice had been ignored, and she had read the new script, which she found just as objectionable as the old one. "I can't play this crap," she hissed. "I'm not going to do this fucking script."

In times of acute distress, some people take to their beds, closing the door and pulling up the covers. Judy, however, inevitably rushed to the only room where her mother and Louis B. Mayer's spies had dared not intrude—the bathroom. So it was that after making that angry pronouncement, she marched into her bathroom, slammed shut the toilet lid and sat down. There, in the only place where she felt secure, she began to sob, her face pale and her body shaking. "She was in despair," said Bogarde, who sat next to her on the edge of the bathtub. "In despair for her children, in despair because she didn't have anywhere to live—Sid had made her frightened of going back to America—and in despair because of a script she loathed. Everything was on top of her. She felt trapped."

Over the course of the next hour Bogarde did his best to calm her, reading her a few pages of his own suggested script changes, alterations that reflected her own expressions and verbal idiosyncrasies. "Hey! It's good!" she exclaimed, and, drying her tears, joined him in rewriting other scenes as well.

"We're very funny," he said. "We could be a team, Bogarde and Garland."

"No, no, no, no!" She laughed. "Garland and Bogarde."

|||

Before she had arrived, the producers had filled Judy's dressing room with flowers, cases of Blue Nun wine and boxes of Bendicks chocolates. Bogarde himself had given her an emerald brooch with a bluebird design—a token of the movie's first song, "Hello, Blue Bird"—and Ronald Neame, the director, had flashed his considerable charm. "The

In London with Dirk Bogarde, Lorna and Joey, 1962

theory was that if we all just loved and admired her enough, everything would be okay," said Mayo Simon, whose screenplay had drawn Judy's ire. "It turned out that there wasn't that much love in the world." That was a lesson learned almost immediately. Several hours after the first day's shooting, Judy was in a hospital, the result of an overdose of pills—another attempted suicide. Her anemic excuse, presented to Bogarde two days later, was that Neame had not been effusive enough, that he had not, for all his charm, extended the warm hand she felt she deserved. "I'm a goddamned star," Judy told Bogarde. "I need help."

The atmosphere surrounding the picture was thus clouded from the start, and from then on very little Neame did met with her approval. On good days Judy called him "pussy cat." On bad days he was that "goddamned British Henry Hathaway"—Hathaway was an American director renowned for his bluster—and Judy tried to have him fired. "Who is smoking a cigar?" she would bellow, knowing full well that Neame was the culprit. "I will not have anybody smoking cigars! I had too much of that when I was young."

Irrational and often paranoid behavior had bedeviled Judy while she worked on several earlier pictures, of course, but this time there was a difference: she was also frequently mean, nasty even to lower-level members of the crew and studio staff. "Here's Dorothy Adorable!" she would ominously announce, as if introducing the evil twin of little Dorothy in *The Wizard of Oz.* "Watch out!" And watch out everyone at Shepperton did, because when Dorothy Adorable walked through the door, trouble came with her. In Hollywood, star trailers boasted private toilets; in Britain they did not. Convinced that she was not receiving the respect she was due, Dorothy Adorable retaliated, as a belligerent child would, by using her wastebasket as a toilet. This caused confusion as well as consternation: who was to be assigned the unpleasant task of carting away Judy's deposits? By that time a weary Neame was beset by so many other problems that he said to himself, "Well, I'm not going to get involved with Judy's chamber pot!"

Try as he might, however, he could not escape Judy's fierce temper. Furious because he had called her to the studio on an afternoon she wanted off—she had spent the morning seeing Liza off at the London airport—she angrily snapped at him when he asked her to repeat a scene: "You said the first take was lovely, and unless you tell me what was wrong with it, I do not intend to do it again. I-am-not-coming-back-until-I-am-treated-like-a-lady!"

Chaos bred chaos, and some scenes that Judy would or could not do had to be dropped entirely, which probably accounts for the picture's peculiar and uneven pace. After that dramatic exit, for example, she did not come back to the set for nearly a week, entering a hospital again, two days later, on July 5, to recover from a second attempted suicide. Banging her head against the bathtub taps, she had not only knocked herself out, but had opened a wound that had colored the bathwater a vile scarlet. And that was not the end of her self-abuse; within the next month she twice again tried to do herself serious harm.

"How are things going today?" one of the producers was asked.

"Pretty good," came the pleased and somewhat surprised response. "She hasn't tried to kill herself today."

Perhaps most frustrating to Neame and company was the vision of what might have been, because when she was good, Judy was so good that, in Bogarde's words, "she left you breathless." At the beginning of their collaboration, Judy had urged Bogarde to write a scene to match Vicki Lester's wrenching monologue in *A Star Is Born,* the moment when she tells the head of the studio how agonizing it is to watch Norman Maine slowly destroying himself. Bogarde did as she requested, and the result of his efforts is one of the most arresting scenes in Judy's long film career. Jenny Bowman's mission to London has ended in failure—her young son refuses to leave his father to join her on tour—and while hundreds are expecting her to appear at the Palladium, she finds herself in a hospital, nursing a sprained ankle. Enter the boy's father, her onetime lover, who reminds her that she is keeping an audience waiting.

"I don't care if they're *fasting!*" Bowman shouts. "You just give them their money back and tell them to come back next fall. . . . I can't be spread so thin. I'm just one person. I don't want to be rolled out like a pastry so everybody can get a nice big bite of me! I'm just me. I belong to myself. I can do whatever I damn well please with myself, and nobody's going to ask any questions!" It is an eruption of astonishing force, all the more powerful because not only were the sentiments

Judy's—so were the words. Bogarde had not written dialogue; he had transcribed it, transforming ordinary soap opera into naked documentary. It is not Jenny Bowman exploding in that hospital room. It is Judy Garland.

A scene of such length—it lasts seven minutes, almost three minutes longer than the comparable scene in *A Star Is Born*—usually requires three or four setups and possibly three or four days of work as well, as the director films from different angles and ranges. But as action progressed, Neame realized that what he was watching was a kind of magic. Instead of stopping the camera where he had planned—"I knew that I would never, ever, get anything like that scene again"—he nodded to his cameraman to keep rolling forward, closer and closer to his two stars. Quick to catch on, the cameraman signaled, in turn, to an electrician, who hastily put a diffuser over a light that otherwise would have been too hot for close-ups.

And all the while, as that frantic dumb show was being played out behind the camera, Judy and Bogarde were enacting an intense drama in front of it. What had begun as a diatribe gradually turned into a love scene, a scene of particular poignancy because it is clear that both people know from the start that it will conclude with a parting—that the only lasting relationship Bowman can have is the one with her audience. Though few other actors could have responded with Bogarde's instinctive intelligence, the laurels belong mostly to Judy, who, as Bogarde himself phrased it, traversed an actor's universe, "from black farce right through to black tragedy, a cadenza of pain and suffering, of bald, unvarnished truth." Many in the crew, who had scant reason to like Judy, nevertheless found themselves with moist eyes when she was through. What had happened? one of them was asked as he left the set. "A miracle," he answered.

A miracle of a different kind came at the end of July. Filming was at last completed—*I Could Go On Singing* had survived Hurricane Judy and had wobbled into port. "Well, that's it, Judy, darling," said Neame after the final shot, a simple close-up on the studio lawn. "We're finished—really, really finished. The picture's done." Looking at him, then at the crew, Judy slowly walked away, saying only: "You'll miss me when I'm gone."

|||

The British court did just as Judy had anticipated, and in the middle of August she was allowed to take her children back to the United States. Lake Tahoe, that shimmering blue oasis in the Sierra Nevada, was where they were bound, and there, braced by the scent of pine and warmed by mountain sunshine, Judy finally escaped the fog of anxiety and insecurity that had enveloped her in London. Returning to the concert circuit in mid-September, she proved such a smash at the Sahara in Las Vegas that a four-week engagement was extended to six.

Love plus Appreciation equals Performance: $L + A = P$. That was the equation that lay behind both Judy's successes and her failures. If she felt loved and appreciated, she could perform wonders; if she did not, the equation was reversed and catastrophe would inevitably follow. Quick to grasp that elemental truth, Stan Irwin, the Sahara's executive producer, coddled and cosseted her like a favorite child, going so far, during her last two weeks, as to schedule her show to fit her insomniac's clock. Two-thirty was the time she bounced onto the stage—two-thirty A.M.! But the canny Irwin knew what he was doing. Even at that drowsy hour Judy filled the house.

Jack Paar, the era's reigning television talk-show host, had also figured out Judy's motivating math, and when she appeared on his *Tonight Show* in early December, he all but threw bouquets at her feet. Though she sang three songs, Paar was more interested in her speaking than her singing voice. "One of the great talkers in show business," was how he introduced her, and talk she did. She told stories of her days in vaudeville, of Happy Harry, the world's most depressed comedian. She told stories of her school days at M-G-M, of Lana Turner, Mickey Rooney and Deanna Durbin. Durbin, she confided, with a small, malicious smile, had come to Culver City possessed of just one eyebrow—though that one was a whopper that stretched from ear to ear. On a later occasion Paar asked if one of her friends was a nymphomaniac. "Only if you can calm her down," Judy shot back.

The appearance of such a relaxed and engaging Judy—"a picture of mental and physical health," *Variety* called her—was widely noted. Capturing the moment, Fields and Begelman approached the three networks with an astonishing proposal: a Judy Garland show not once or twice a year, but every week during the TV season—twenty-six weeks in all. Even more astonishing, the networks took them seriously, entering into a bidding war which CBS won only by offering an unusually rich contract. Judy was guaranteed somewhere between $25,000 and $30,000 a show, as well as full ownership of the tapes. After CBS was finished with them, Judy's corporation, Kingsrow Enterprises, could sell them again and again in syndication.

Judy was back on the road to riches from which she had been so precipitously bumped by the financial failure of *A Star Is Born.* If her show ran for only two or three seasons, she would be secure for life. "David Begelman told me there was no reason I shouldn't have a steady home with my children," she said, "be very rich, and do a weekly show—that I should have been very rich a long time ago, like Bob Hope or [Perry] Como."

|||

Long before *The Judy Garland Show* went on the air—at nine o'clock on Sunday, September 29, 1963—television insiders were writing its obituary. "The Great Garland Gamble" was how *TV Guide* billed it. Judy, said the skeptics, could not keep up with the murderous weekly pace. A day missed on a movie set could be costly, but was not necessarily catastrophic. On TV, even with shows taped in advance, it could be both. A network had an hour to fill, and performers were obligated to fill it whether they were well or ill, ready or not. The question in many minds was not whether Judy would collapse, but when. "Thousands of dollars were bet in Las Vegas that I wouldn't even do the first three shows," she said. "They thought that I wasn't going to finish a performance or even show up."

Thanks in part to George Schlatter, the show's producer, who all but drowned her in love, flattery and every comfort a spendthrift network could provide, she did both. When she arrived at Television City, CBS's vast production facility in Los Angeles, she was happily surprised by a dressing room as big as a small house: forty feet long, with wall-to-wall carpeting, antique marble tables, a piano, a stereophonic sound system, a bar and a refrigerator stocked with Blue Nun.

Thrilled by the attention, Judy was also thrilled by Schlatter, who joked when she was tense, rushed to her new house in Brentwood when she was anxious and at all times made sure that everybody treated her like a star. Slimmed down to a hundred pounds, she looked the role, more attractive than during the filming of *I Could Go On Singing*—more attractive, in fact, than she had been at any time since *A Star Is Born*. When taping began, on June 24, she was in fine form, clearly delighting in the company of her first guest, Mickey Rooney. And so she remained through June and July, "having a ball," as Schlatter phrased it.

The predicted disaster struck on August 2, at the end of the sixth week. It came not from Judy, however, but from CBS, which surprised everyone, including the advertisers, by firing Schlatter and most of his team. His mistake, in the network's eyes, was to try to make each week the equivalent of an opening night at the Palace, a "special event," as he called it. But television viewers, CBS argued, were creatures of habit. They did not want special events, at least not every week. When they sat down to watch a program, they expected the same comfortable and familiar feeling they had when they put on their slippers.

"Judy Garland will have to adjust to television," said CBS's president, James Aubrey, Jr.—"the Smiling Cobra," he was nicknamed, so quickly and ruthlessly did he strike. "Television is certainly not going to attempt to adjust to Judy Garland." For five weeks, for all of August and part of September, production was halted while CBS installed a new crew. "I was stunned and bewildered," said Judy. "It came as such a shock."

The show's new producer, Norman Jewison, shared the network's pretzels-and-beer philosophy. *The Judy Garland Show* required not only a more conventional pattern, he was convinced, but a more conventional star. Judy was too glamorous and needed to be brought down a peg. "In TV," Jewison explained, "you have to make the sacred cow less sacred." He did that by throwing her onto the barbecue and making her the butt of an endless barrage of humorless, denigrating jokes—reminders that she had recently been fat, that she had a reputation for unreliability and that she had made more comebacks than a revolving door. "This isn't the original, this is the twelfth Judy Garland," said

Jerry Van Dyke, the show's woefully miscast comic. "The original," he added, "went over the rainbow years ago."

|||

The root of Judy's problems with the network was that, for some still-unexplained reason, Aubrey not only disliked but despised her. Nothing she did could please him. On the one hand, the network—and Aubrey *was* the network—charged that she was unapproachable. On the other, it complained that she was too friendly, that she touched and kissed her guests too much. In reply to such criticism, all Judy could offer was the truth. "It's pure affection," she said. "I'm a woman who wants to reach out and take 40 million people in her arms." Hurt and offended, yet realizing that her future lay in the network's hands, she nonetheless promised to do as she was told. "CBS," she said, "knows more about television than I do."

Perhaps, but the network of *The Beverly Hillbillies* did not know much about Judy or the kind of show she could and should have done. Nor, as it turned out, did Jewison, who was no more able than Schlatter to come up with a viable formula. In their frantic efforts to find one, his writers each week churned out so many scripts, each one on a different color paper, that they once ran out of hues and had to return to plain old white. Sometimes Judy did not even know what songs she was supposed to sing until just before the taping. In a perhaps overly candid interview, she said that if things continued as they were, she herself would switch to *Bonanza,* her chief competition. "We're in trouble," she warned, "unless we all calm down a bit."

By prearrangement, Jewison departed after the thirteenth episode, which was taped in November, and turned over the remaining thirteen to yet a third producer, Bill Colleran. Dismayed by what both of his predecessors had done, Colleran promptly threw out Jewison's bad jokes and awkward gimmicks and put more emphasis on music, where the focus should have been from the start. He arrived too late, however. By December Judy and the network were almost at war. A calming influence during the summer and fall—she had even telephoned him from the set—had been John Kennedy, who advised her how to deal with a corporate despot like Aubrey. But on November 22, Kennedy was assassinated. "It's like—it's like hopelessness without hope," was Judy's confused, yet altogether lucid, reaction. Trying to repay Kennedy's kindness in the only way she knew, she planned an entire program of patriotic songs in his memory. But CBS responded with a loud no. By the time the show was broadcast, she was informed, Kennedy would have been forgotten.

In 1963, no series had a chance of beating *Bonanza,* and the best Judy's show could have hoped for was a respectable second. It did not achieve even that, and by the end of the year, with its ratings scraping the bottom of the charts, *The Judy Garland Show* was vying with ABC's *Jerry Lewis Show* for the title of costliest flop in the history of television. Whether *The Judy Garland Show,* broadcast on a different evening, with a more sympathetic and supportive network behind it, could have survived is impossible to say. Though it had many bad moments, it had enough good ones—a few were even glorious—to indicate what it might have been. There was the night, for example, on which Judy and Barbra Streisand sang in duet, then joined Ethel Merman for a trio—the three belters in one place and at one memorable time. And there was the picture of Judy alone, all but shouting "The Battle Hymn of the Republic," CBS's sole concession to her plea for a Kennedy tribute.

But if Judy had done a number with Gabriel and a choir of angels, Aubrey's face would have remained the same unyielding granite. He did not want to move her show to another night, and he did not want to give it another year, or even half a year, to find its way. Aubrey did not want to do anything, in fact, but kill it. "I won't have that cunt ruining my Sunday night!" he declared, and in January 1964, CBS startled no one by announcing that one season would be enough for *The Judy Garland Show.* The March 29 broadcast would be the last.

Though Judy's morale had revived a little at the beginning of the Colleran regime, it collapsed again under the weight of ever more bad news. The doubters were at last proved right—she was often late and unreliable—and tapings went into overtime, "golden time," as TV people call it. At the final taping, she was so distracted—she did not appear either drunk or drugged—that she started a song only to stop it. In the end she stopped entirely, unable to complete a full hour. Colleran was forced to pad the last show with segments from earlier episodes.

Worse was to come, however. When she returned to her dressing room, she found an orchid plant, with a sarcastic, even sadistic, note from Hunt Stromberg, Jr., Aubrey's chief henchman. "You were just great," said Stromberg, who had been monitoring the night's disastrous progress and had obviously been enjoying her humiliation. "Thanks a lot. You're through."

|||

In the obscure recesses of their hearts, Judy once wrote, all women realize—"know, know, *know*," she all but shouted—that the male must lead, the female must follow. That is the way it must be, she added, because women are by nature "dreadfully insecure" and they depend on men to provide their safety and security—even their meaning. "Don't yield your leadership" was her plea to the opposite sex. "Don't hand us the reins." That was Judy's philosophy, her creed, her faith—her everything—and though her own experience had proved it wrong again and again, Judy continued to cling to it, like a religious fanatic whose eyes, turned to heaven, never stop searching for a miracle.

Despite the mess in which he had left her finances, despite the welter of divorce suits and ugly public accusations, despite the lessons of history and common sense, a part of Judy still believed that Sid might be her miracle man. Indeed, even in his mid-forties, he remained the tough, quick-fisted guy who had first won her admiration. "Sid Luft in Wild Fist Fight at Night Club" was the headline dominating the front page of a Los Angeles tabloid in November 1962. Sid, it seemed, had accosted another patron at the Slate Brothers Club, demanding an apology for sarcastic comments he had heard the man had been making about him. When the other patron, a movie producer, angrily refused, Sid did what came naturally—at least to him. "I am not a man who can stand that sort of thing forever," he said, "so I hit him."

Though Sid's attack may have reaffirmed Hollywood's generally low opinion of him, it may have had the reverse effect on Judy. That barroom brawler was the One-Punch Luft with whom she had fallen in love, a man capable of providing the support his estranged wife required to survive the frenzy of a weekly television series. It was perhaps not surprising, therefore, that another, considerably smaller headline appeared a few weeks later. "Judy Garland and Sid Luft Reconciled," said the *Los Angeles Times* on February 14, 1963—Valentine's Day, appropriately enough.

A house was purchased in another ritzy area just south of Sunset Boulevard, at 129 South Rockingham Avenue in Brentwood, and in June, on the weekend of Judy's forty-first birthday, the Lufts held a housewarming party. Their family was together again. The only flaw in this otherwise happy picture was the inescapable fact that no woman, not even one as emotionally hungry as Judy, could have more than one miracle man at a time, and Judy already had hers—David Begelman.

|||

In many ways the two men now crowding her life were mirror images. Both were Jewish, with roots a few miles north of Manhattan, Begelman's in the borough of the Bronx, Sid's in the adjacent part of Westchester County. Though neither could be called handsome, both were charming, with an undeniable appeal to women. Both had expensive tastes—in clothes, cars and style of living—and both were big spenders, even if the money they were spending was not their own. And both had gambling habits that would keep them almost constantly in debt, scrounging for dollars.

There the similarities stopped, however, and Begelman possessed something Sid lacked altogether: the showman's natural instinct, the gut feeling that, in later years, was to make him a genuine Hollywood mogul, in charge of two major studios, Columbia and M-G-M. That showman's instinct was already evident in 1961 when he heard sounds he did not like as he was putting together her concert tour. "Her orchestra sounds godawful," he told his friend Mort Lindsey. "You've gotta help me." As a result of Begelman's tireless wheedling, the talented, unflappable Lindsey did come to the rescue, and for the next several years he gave Judy probably the best accompaniment she had ever enjoyed.

Unlike Sid, who seemed just as content to peddle stereo systems to airlines as he was to manage his wife's career, Begelman was in love with show business. Thrilled merely to be on a stage, he would often stand in for Judy before her concerts, mimicking her movements and even singing her songs while the electricians were adjusting their lights. Perhaps his most important attribute, however, the one that separated him from many other agents with keen ears and eyes, was his willingness to do anything a client needed to keep performing. What Judy needed, of course, was love, and love was what Begelman provided—or so she thought.

From her need and his willingness to satisfy it was born a romance that obsessed her for many months to come. A decade earlier, Dorothy Ponedel had complained that Judy had been hypnotized by Sid. Now it was Begelman's turn to play Svengali. When they were together, Judy's eyes never left him. Whatever he wanted, Judy did. "David's the boss," she told one of her fans. Comforted by the bare knowledge that he was her lover, she would sometimes order her maid, Alma Cousteline, to call and ask him to hold his mouth near the telephone while she was falling asleep. "I just want to hear him breathe," Judy said. Without Begelman's assistance, it is doubtful that there would have been a Judy Garland III—or a Carnegie Hall concert, or the three movies and television series that came after.

|||

It was now that Judy brought back Sid, who hated the man who so often had occupied his wife's bed. Certain that Begelman was pocketing money from her company, Kingsrow Enterprises, he saw a way to exact revenge, and he convinced Judy to allow a Beverly Hills accountant to audit the books. The accountant, Oscar Steinberg, issued his report on June 27, and even Sid may have been surprised by the large number of suspect entries uncovered. Begelman had, for example, written thirteen checks on the Kingsrow account, a total of $35,714 made out to cash and noted in the ledger book only as "Protection." Another check, for $10,000, made a curious migration. It went from a Begelman account held in trust for Judy, to Begelman's private account; it was then withdrawn, disappearing without explanation.

Other checks had similarly odd histories, the most peculiar of which belonged to one for $50,000. According to Begelman, that check had gone to a blackmailer who had threatened to release a photograph of

Judy, nude from the waist up, that had been taken while she was lying unconscious in a London hospital. Whether there was such a picture is impossible to say; what can be said is that Begelman pocketed most, if not all, of the $50,000. No chicanery, however small, was beneath him. Not only did he sneak in a double commission for her appearance on the Jack Paar show, but he also kept for himself the new Cadillac the show's producers had thrown in as a bonus. Unaware that Begelman's spiffy new convertible was really hers, Judy had to buy a new car when she moved west to begin her television series a few months later.

The pattern of deceptions and thefts Steinberg disclosed was almost identical to the one Columbia Pictures discovered nearly fifteen years later. Too late to help Judy, the Columbia auditors revealed Begelman for what he really was: a forger, an embezzler and a liar of heroic dimensions. Ashamed of his lack of education, Begelman had, for instance, compensated in his usual way, inflating a brief military training course in New Haven into a Yale degree. After his friends had digested that fabrication, Begelman then gave himself an additional degree from the Yale Law School.

To Sid's bitter disappointment, Judy chose to ignore the evidence, however. Taping of her series had begun only three days before she saw Steinberg's report, and she wanted nothing to disrupt its smooth progress. "Look," she told Sid, "suppose he did steal $200,000 to $300,000: sweep it under the rug now. I'm going to make $20 million on these television shows. What is $300,000?" To that cynical response there was no adequate answer, and on July 1, three weeks after their housewarming party, an angry Sid left Rockingham Avenue to cool down. When he returned a few days later, he found that his clothes had been put into storage.

Another attempt at reconciliation had failed. There were to be no more. After two and a half years of saying good-bye, Judy finally meant it. Liar and thief though he was, Begelman had won the day.

|||

Thanks largely to Judy's initial backing, Begelman and Fields had gained other prestigious clients, and now they were focusing their attention on the less troublesome newcomers. In the chaotic months that followed the firing of George Schlatter, they were, in fact, often un-available. She could get the President of the United States on the phone more easily than she could her agents, Judy complained. With no one standing between her and an increasingly hostile network, she was in the place she most feared: all by herself, with no one to defend her. On that painful night in March 1964 when she taped her last show—when she most needed their support—her agents were on the other side of the continent for the gala Broadway opening of *Funny Girl,* starring their newest and most promising client, Barbra Streisand.

Fields was callous—ungrateful, without question. But what can be said of Begelman, who had made love to Judy only so he could rob her? Who had vowed his support, then dumped her? Evil wears many faces, but it is perhaps most sinister when it is seductive, when it smiles and beguiles and flatters, professing love and admiration and sovereign kisses. Milton must, indeed, have had someone much like Begelman in mind when he described one of the fallen angels, the smooth and splendid Belial in *Paradise Lost.* "A fairer person lost not Heav'n," said the poet; "he seemed / For dignity compos'd and high exploit." But be-neath Belial's sleek exterior, "all was false and hollow." False had been Begelman's promises to Judy. Hollow had been his pledges of rewards and riches.

Men must lead, women must follow, Judy had said, but where had Begelman and Fields led her? After all her hard work, concerts, movies and TV shows, she was worse off in 1964 than she had been in 1961. Three weeks after the broadcast of her final show, the sheriff was once again knocking at her door, demanding payment on debts of nearly $70,000, probably a fraction of what Begelman had stolen. But he had robbed her of more than money. He had stolen her hope of financial se-curity, her very future.

A kiss for City College's
"Best Actor of the Year,"
Mark Herron, 1964

A Need to Be Needed and a Disaster in Melbourne

need to be needed," Judy confessed to one of her lovers. "I need to be wanted." That meant, of course, what it had meant since she was a teenager, competing for men with Lana Turner. For Judy, sex had an extra dimension: to give pleasure to a man was validation of her worth as a woman, as a human being even; it was the proof she required, ever and always, that she was something more than Mr. Mayer's little hunchback. That need to be needed was what had made her so vulnerable to a predator like David Begelman. It was that need that sometimes caused her humiliation. One ugly-minded lover bragged that after she gave him oral sex, for example, he made her sing "Over the Rainbow" so he could hear those famous words sung through a mouthful of his semen.

In any event, the ranks of her lovers grew considerably in the sixties. One was Bobby Cole, a piano player she heard in New York and took west to work on her television show. A second was John Carlyle, an attractive and witty actor who had fallen in love with her when he worked as an usher at her first Palace show. A third was André Phillipe, a French actor and singer who performed duets with her in her CBS dressing room. "A marriage of sounds" was how Phillipe characterized their relationship. Even more melodious music connected her to Glenn Ford, one of Hollywood's most durable leading men. On a photograph of herself that she gave him, Judy wrote: "You have my heart and I adore you."

At the very beginning of 1964—at a New Year's Eve party given by Ray Aghayan, the costume designer for her TV show—Judy met a man who, unlike Ford or any of the others, was prepared to give her what she most needed: unflagging attention. His name was Mark Herron, and he appeared to be everything any woman could ask for. Tall, slim and good-looking, he had inquisitive brown eyes and dark brown hair and was, in the eyes of one reporter, as "handsome as a soda-pop ad." His virtues did not end there, however. Herron was also well-mannered, intelligent and amusing, qualities that during his drama school days had invariably landed him the leads in sophisticated drawing-room comedies. Originally from Tennessee—not far from where Frank Gumm had grown up, in fact—Herron, like Frank, retained a slight Southern accent, just a hint of old magnolia. His single obvious drawback, one that the newspapers never failed to note, was his age: he was only thirty-three, seven years Judy's junior and therefore, as innuendo would have it, a hanger-on, a user, a gigolo.

A decade earlier, when he was the star of Los Angeles City College's drama department, Herron—Truman was his first name in those days—had seemed destined for acting glory. "Best Actor of the Year," the department had named him in 1952, and even before he received his degree, Herron had won minor parts in two films. After graduation came a signal honor, an invitation to join the select group that studied with one of the world's finest actors, Charles Laughton. A still-greater prize came Herron's way in the summer of 1956, when Laughton took him east for his Broadway revival of George Bernard Shaw's *Major Barbara*. Herron was apparently not ready for such a high-powered production, however—he was to play Barbara's stuffy brother Stephen—and less than three weeks before the Boston tryout, he was fired. He was never able, so it seems in retrospect, to regain his momentum. Eventually moving to Italy, he dubbed Italian films into English and played a small role in Federico Fellini's *8½*.

That was as close as Herron was to come to the fulfillment of his early dreams. Always promising, he was, like so many others in his perilous profession, always disappointed, and the night he met Judy, he was still searching for a role that would ignite his moribund career. Judy soon asked him to move into her house on Rockingham Avenue, then invited him to join her on the concert tour that was scheduled to begin—so pressing was her need for cash—a few weeks after her final show. But this time she was not going to Las Vegas, New York or even London. She was traveling to the other side of the world, to the very antipodes—Australia.

|||

Judy, said Harry M. Miller, the thirty-year-old impresario who had invited her, was "the one person Australia had never seen and would love to see," and events soon proved him right. All three of her concerts, two in Sydney and one in Melbourne, quickly sold out, and she arrived to a press reception that eclipsed that given the Queen of England the previous year. "A Knockout," the *Sydney Morning Herald* called her first show, in the tin-roofed Sydney Stadium on May 13. Her second show, three nights later, received an even more enthusiastic response, as if all those, ten thousand strong, who had missed the first, had been jealously hoarding their cheers. "I'll keep singing until the roof falls in," Judy declared, and, taking her at her word, they refused to let her go. "More, more," they shouted. Those, however, were the last cheers she was to hear in that vast country, and in Melbourne, Australia's second city, she was to discover just how fast an audience's love can turn to hate.

Disaster is usually woven from several threads, unrelated yet combining to form a pattern of chaos and calamity. So it was with Judy's misadventure in Melbourne. Priding themselves on their egalitarianism, Australians allowed no one, including Judy, special treatment. Though she had never had a problem passing through customs in any other country, in Australia she did, the inspectors at the Sydney airport going through her bags and confiscating the small pharmacy they contained—the uppers and downers she needed simply to live, let alone perform. A panicked call to a Sydney doctor, a Chinese abortionist, brought a fresh supply, but the unfamiliar dosages almost guaranteed an overdose.

Adding to her tension was the abrasive, frequently hostile tone of much of the Aussie press, which was deeply suspicious of all foreign entertainers, convinced that anyone who would travel so far was either greedy for money or unemployable everywhere else. Nor did Judy sweeten the mood by arriving late for her one press conference. One reporter, Charles Higham, likened the event to a rugby match, with the forty or so reporters, who had had too long to drink too much, jostling roughly around her. "Look this way, Judy!" commanded the photographers. "C'mon, give!" As often as she tried to pull Mark into the pictures—"He will be a great star on Broadway," she said—just as often was he pushed aside, until his once bright smile melted into a look of helpless misery. "Oh, my God, this is so awful!" Judy whispered to Higham. "Is it always like this here?"

It seemed it was, and even Miller could not resist a sharp jab. Exasperated by her refusal to return to the stage for encores at the end of her first concert—"she was exhausted, like a piece of paper, with no energy at all," explained Higham—Miller proved that a bark can be worse than a bite. "Listen, they're going crazy," he told her. "Only a jerk singer like you could produce such a response." Unable to believe what she had heard, Judy asked him to repeat himself. Miller did, and was rewarded with such a mighty face slap that, as he ruefully admitted, his ears were set ringing.

|||

Hurt and angry, and weary still, Judy thus arrived in Melbourne, and, to the outrage of the local press, locked herself in her suite at the Southern Cross Hotel for the next thirty-six hours. Now the mishap at the Sydney airport had its belated and disastrous effect. She took too many of the Chinese doctor's pills—"she was pissed out of her brain," as the blunt-spoken Miller phrased it—and on May 20, the night of her performance, Judy had to be virtually dragged from her room, not showing up at Melbourne's Festival Hall until an hour and seven minutes after the curtain was supposed to go up.

If she had done nothing but sing, the audience, so close to riot that the nervous management had brought in forty policemen to keep order, probably would have forgiven her even then. But singing seemed to be the last thing she wanted to do. In a mood that Mort Lindsey, her conductor now for three years, had never seen, she was more disposed to clown around, snatching his baton and pretending to lead the orchestra herself. "You are late," someone yelled. "I could not get out of that hotel," Judy answered. "Have another brandy," someone else suggested, as the crowd of seven thousand began heading, one by one, for the exits. "Where are you going?" Judy inquired of one departing group. "We're going home and you should, too," came the answer.

A bad performance deserves bad reviews. But not since 1880, when it had hanged Ned Kelly, Australia's Billy the Kid, had Melbourne meted out the kind of punishment it now gave Judy. Had she thrown a kangaroo on the barbie while singing obscene words to the national anthem, she could not have aroused more patriotic indignation from the Australian press. Her bizarre behavior was viewed not as a personal failing, but as a deliberate insult to the nation, the latest from a series of American stars who, according to the *Melbourne Truth*, regarded folks Down Under as "a bunch of ignorant hicks."

That anger was not confined to the editorial pages. As she walked toward her plane at the Melbourne airport, Judy heard a chorus of jeers, a brutal good-bye from two hundred people who had come to wish her ill. Small wonder that in Hong Kong, where she and Mark flew on May 23, she complained that she was not feeling well. What was she suffering from? she was asked. "Australia," Judy replied.

|||

Another kind of storm arose in Hong Kong, as Typhoon Viola sent ninety-mile-an-hour winds and rains raging across the island, threatening to crack open the windows of the suite Judy and Mark shared on the twenty-second floor of the Mandarin Hotel. Unable to leave the hotel, they thoughtfully surrounded themselves with a pile of books and magazines and prepared to sit out Viola in comfort. But there was no comfort to be found, inside or out. When she opened *Time,* Judy discovered a snide account of the Melbourne debacle, which the magazine contrasted, rather cruelly, with Marlene Dietrich's almost simultaneous triumph in Moscow. "At 41, Judy Garland may have gone over the rainbow for the last time," the *Time* story began, and as Judy read it in that exotic city, with the very floor swaying beneath her, she finally cracked. "We can't go on this way," she screamed. "Gimme those pills and we'll die together!" Mark pulled her into bed instead, and they clung together under the covers, like two lonely and frightened children, praying for the peace of morning.

Unwilling to wait, Judy slipped into the bathroom sometime during the night and swallowed enough Tuinals to send her sprawling to the floor. That was where Mark found her several hours later. No ambulance could move through the typhoon's fury, but with help from the hotel staff, Mark was able to lift her into a wheelchair and push her himself to nearby Canossa Hospital. For a long time it appeared that rescue had come too late. She lay in a coma for more than fifteen hours. At one point, in fact, Mark was told she was dead, a message that was flashed around the world.

That was wrong, though not by much. Once again her remarkable constitution pulled her through. When Judy finally awoke, she began, as she had so many times before, a quick and almost miraculous recovery. On June 1, four days after Mark had pushed her comatose body through the hazardous streets, she was back in her hotel, making calls and issuing orders. "She's getting mean as hell again," Mark wrote a friend in Los Angeles, "which means she's getting well again, thank Christ!"

|||

Her successes in the early sixties had interrupted but not changed the wearisome rhythm that had come to govern Judy's life. As predictable as the tides, as insistent as a metronome, that pitiless movement all but guaranteed that failure would follow success—success, failure. After her fiasco in Melbourne, it was inevitable that she would soon enjoy a triumph; inevitable, too, given her itinerary, that she would enjoy that triumph in London, the scene of so many treasured moments. What was not inevitable was the way in which it came, unplanned, unscheduled and unexpected, like a burst of blissful sunshine after the weather forecasts had called for rain.

"I've been told not to sing for some time because I've been very ill," Judy sadly announced when she arrived in Britain on June 30, and for once London could not shake her depression. Three weeks later, she was, indeed, in a psychiatric nursing home, the result of another half-hearted suicide attempt—she had cut her wrists again. Her wounds were not serious, however, and even her doctor could not prevent her from leaving her bed long enough to drive to the Palladium for the "Night of 100 Stars," British show business's annual charity fundraiser.

Like most of the other stellar one hundred, Judy was there only to be seen. Like them, she was expected to do nothing but say hello, then sit down and watch the show, the high point of which was to be that year's sensation, the Beatles. But a frail hello was not what those sitting out front wanted to hear from Judy. "Sing, Judy, sing!" they shouted, all but rioting when she walked away from the microphone. "We want Judy!" they chanted until the organizers were forced to push her back. "Over the Rainbow," she sang, then, on demand, an encore of "Swanee." But still the cheering continued, going on so long, in fact, that the rest of the program had to be scratched. She had sung many showstoppers in her long career, but never before had Judy actually stopped the show. "It's nice to be home again," she said.

In just a few minutes an audience in London had restored what an audience in Melbourne had so abruptly stolen—her self-confidence—and with Mark at her side, Judy rode the rest of the year on a wave of excitement. She traveled to Rome and Athens, she cut a new record and, in November, she twice returned to the Palladium to share the stage with a promising newcomer—Liza. "Terribly good, isn't she?" said the proud mama after Liza, already a polished performer at eighteen, set that old house rocking with a voice as powerful as a trumpet. "Beautiful" was the word Mark used to describe the final five months of 1964, and Judy seemed to agree. All her old friends said that she had never looked better or happier, Mark bragged to John Carlyle. "They say it's thanks to me. That of course gives me a huge amount of pride. I hope it's true. I try. And I love her more each day."

If the rhythm—high to low, low to high—stayed the same, the tempo did not. Sometimes, in the mere space of a week, she could travel that bumpy road from success to disaster—or back again. "Judy Begins with Failure, Ends in Triumph" was how the *Toronto Star,* for instance, summarized her week at the O'Keefe Centre in February 1965. Her Monday opening was terrible, said the *Star,* and she canceled two shows on Wednesday. But by Saturday, closing night, she was in top, exuberant form, joyfully bouncing through thirty minutes of encores. "The question then is which is the real Judy?" the paper's critic asked in some exasperation. "Was Monday just a bad night—made worse by a cold and laryngitis? Or was Saturday the exception, one of those occasional big nights that pop up as a career declines?" The answer was that both were the real Judy. Though the good performances still outnumbered the bad, no one, including Judy herself, could predict at the beginning of the night which kind she was about to give.

|||

Singing is a physical act, and singers, like athletes, have limited working lives, almost all losing some of their vocal agility by their mid-forties. In Judy's case, the aging process was accelerated by a style of singing, flat-out and full-throated, that, over the years, had demanded too much of those tender membranes called the vocal cords—her machine, as she liked to say. "My, I'm a loud lady," she joked. "No crooner, I." Perhaps even more damaging had been her style of living, too many drugs over too many years. Indeed, in the sixties she added to her pharmacy a new, amphetamine-like drug—Ritalin—that actually speeded up the destruction, making her throat perpetually dry.

At its zenith in 1961, when she appeared at Carnegie Hall, Judy's voice had already lost some of its radiance by the time she began her TV series in 1963. By 1965, when she appeared in Toronto, her machine had become a quirky and often undependable instrument, rich and velvety on the best nights, harsh and strident on the worst. The quality of the sound is never the full measure of any singer, however, and through force of personality and manner of presentation, the exceptional ones—Judy, most conspicuously—continue to give enjoyment long past their prime. Youth may have the muscle, but age has the experience, the artistry and understanding that come only with time.

Such distinctions were, for some, beside the point. For her most fanatical fans, Judy was always magical, an object of worship and veneration. They attended every opening night and, like participants in some ancient mystery rite, showed all the signs of cultish delirium, applauding and jumping out of their seats with excitement before she so much as opened her mouth. That many of these fans were homosexual provoked disapproving sneers from more than one national journal. Writing in *Esquire,* William Goldman, for instance, spent an entire article fulminating about the "flutter of fags" who came to the Palace in the summer of 1967, Judy's third visit to that lucky stage. "The boys in the tight trousers" was *Time*'s equally disparaging phrase.

Seeking explanations for her homosexual following, both magazines indulged themselves in psychological mumbo-jumbo. But the true explanation was perhaps too obvious to catch the attention of such flatulent minds. The homosexuals of that closeted era identified with Judy because they, too, were the objects of demeaning jokes and casual contempt—for proof, all they had to do was read *Time* and *Esquire*—and they derived comfort and inspiration from her ability to survive similar assaults. As many times as she fell down, Judy always managed to pull herself up—and they hoped that they would do the same. Many heterosexuals, the great majority of her audience, made the same identification, of course. Judy's appeal breached all borders.

Year after year she crisscrossed the continent, giving concerts in big cities and small, performing in theaters, auditoriums and stadiums and singing under roofs, open skies, canvas tents and one huge dome—Houston's Astrodome. Steadier work might have relieved some of that increasingly onerous burden, but producers, who were happy enough to hire her for guest appearances on TV, shuddered at the prospect of offering her long-term jobs. Turned down for several movie roles—Mama Rose in *Gypsy* was one—Judy was also rejected by Broadway, vetoed even as a replacement for Angela Lansbury in Jerry Herman's long-run hit, *Mame.* "If it all falls apart because she doesn't show up on opening night," Herman's producers told him, "we will have destroyed everything we all worked so hard to create."

Some of those who did give her jobs had cause to regret their generosity. In November 1965 she won praise and plaudits for hosting *Hollywood Palace,* ABC's Saturday night variety show. But her second appearance, in the spring of 1966, saw her lock herself in her dressing room midway through taping—"That beautiful voice! It's gone!" she was heard to cry—and refuse to come out until someone climbed through a hatch in the ceiling and opened the door from the inside. Because of such delays, taping did not conclude until one-thirty in the morning, four hours late.

Angry because ABC had forced her to perform despite a case of laryngitis, Judy took her revenge, staying behind after everyone else had gone home and all but wrecking her expensively decorated dressing room. She smeared its paintings with lipstick, she dumped ashes and cigarette butts between the keys of its piano and she set its sink and toilet to overflowing.

Yet there remained a few who were either brave or foolhardy enough to give her another chance, and on March 1, 1967, 20th Century–Fox announced that it wanted her for one of its splashiest productions, the film adaptation of Jacqueline Susann's *Valley of the Dolls,* which included the pill-popping character Neely O'Hara, modeled after the young Judy herself. Too old to take that part, the real Judy was to play Neely's nemesis, a bold and brassy Broadway star named Helen Lawson.

Small as it was, with less than ten minutes on-screen, it was a good role that demanded little and paid well, $75,000 for about ten days' work. Treating her like visiting royalty, the studio provided her with everything but a scepter and crown. Someone mentioned that she was an avid pool player—together with a few male friends, she often visited the pool halls along Santa Monica Boulevard—and when Judy opened the door of her dressing room, there, right in front of her, was a pool table, complete with cue sticks and balls.

Trouble began on the first day of shooting, however. From Betsy Booth in the Hardy series to Jenny Bowman in *I Could Go On Singing,* Judy's characters had always been sympathetic. Now she found herself incapable of playing one who was unsympathetic, who was, in fact, a certifiable bitch. "Just a little bit stronger, Judy," Mark Robson, the director, would patiently say. "Just a little meaner." But try as he might, Robson could not obtain what he thought should have been Helen Lawson's nasty snarl. Judy, it seemed, did not want to end her film career as the Wicked Witch. "I don't want to be a harridan on the screen," she explained, "and I don't think people want me to be."

One day of frustrating takes was enough for her, and after that Judy could not be pried out of her dressing room. The morning she was finally fired, Abby Mann, her friend since *Judgment at Nuremberg,* happened to walk by her dressing room. Unconscious after yet another overdose, she was sprawled out on the pool table Fox had so considerately provided, her dress disheveled, pulled up so high that Mann could see a dark fringe of pubic hair.

|||

Some artists are blessed with ignorance. Though they know the difference between good and bad, they cannot distinguish between good and brilliant and, as a result, find good quite sufficient. Judy was not so fortunate. However slurred her words, however shaky her walk, she did know the difference—her ear, that spiteful organ, told her—and she was mortified when she fell below her own sometimes unreachable standards. She thus knew—all the time, she knew—how badly she was doing during her second appearance on *Hollywood Palace.* "Oh, Bill, that's terrible," she exclaimed to William Harbach, the show's producer, as she came to the end of her opening number, "What the World Needs Now," a new, slightly complicated jazz waltz by Burt Bacharach and Hal David.

That she could not get it right obviously rankled, and at four-thirty in the morning a night watchman saw her emerge at last from her dressing room. Slamming the door behind her, she staggered onto the stage, which was lit, as all stages are at such an hour, only by a work light—a naked bulb atop a pole. Grabbing the light as if it were a microphone, so that her face was the only thing visible in the vast blackness of that empty theater, she slowly began singing, "What the world needs now is love, sweet love. . . ."

|||

Several times in the sixties Judy sat down to write her autobiography. "I think I've got something to write about at last!" she said excitedly, speaking into the tape recorder to which she was confiding the story of her life. "It's going to be one hell of a great, everlastingly great book, with humor, tears, fun, emotion and love." When the news got out that she had begun working on it, publishers from several continents snapped to attention, and Judy, assured of a best-seller, interviewed possible ghostwriters. With the help of one of them, her old friend Fred Finklehoffe, she actually put words on paper—remarkably candid and revealing stories about her childhood, Metro-Goldwyn-Mayer and her first two marriages. Judy did, indeed, have something to write about.

Sixty-eight pages of that everlastingly great book were all she managed to finish, however. "When you have lived the life I've lived," she reluctantly conceded, "when you've loved and suffered, and been madly happy and desperately sad—well, that's when you realize you'll never be able to set it all down. Maybe you'd rather die first." But there may also have been another explanation for her decision to stop. When she began her book in 1960, its final pages would have been upbeat, full of hope. When she abandoned it in the late sixties, that happy ending had disappeared. How, after all, could she have concluded? By saying that she was broke and increasingly desperate?

For that was the case. When she and Mark completed their eight months of globe-trotting and returned to California at the beginning of 1965, welcoming them home were all the old problems: lawsuits, creditors and battles with Sid. The only good news was that her fights with Sid were about over. On May 19 a Superior Court judge granted her a divorce, along with custody of Joey and Lorna. She had already announced her choice of a fourth husband, and six months later, on November 14, she and Mark said their vows in the Little Church of the West, a small commercial wedding chapel on Las Vegas's neon-lit Strip. How did she feel? Judy was asked. "I feel like Mrs. Herron," she answered. "I'm so happy."

If that was so, it was not so for very long. Despite his good looks, his fine manners and his intelligence, Mark was not the ideal mate Judy had thought he was, and the mystery is not why they married, but why they married when they did, after so many months of miserable cohabitation. The complaint, on Judy's side, was mostly about sex—or the lack of it—and she later claimed that the marriage was never consummated. That may have been true. Until he met Judy, Mark's sexual experience had almost certainly been limited to other men, most notably

Henry Brandon, a highly regarded character actor, and Charles Laughton, whose interest in him had not been entirely professional.

Judy was also to allege that Mark had married her only to further his career, and his career *was* probably part of his motivation. But most relationships are combinations of advantage and affection, and the fact that Mark had hoped to make use of her did not prevent him from loving her. He said he loved her, anyway, and those who watched him meekly accept her abuse and hostility were convinced he was telling the truth. "Mr. Herron, don't let it upset you," said Judy's maid, the faithful Alma Cousteline, when she saw him crying after one of Judy's tirades. "Well, it does upset me," Mark replied. "I love Judy, and I don't want her to be like this. I don't know what to do. I just don't know what to do."

|||

Nor did anyone else, for the condition from which Judy was suffering—probably manic-depression, or bipolar disorder, as psychologists and psychiatrists often label it—grew worse after her return from England. By whatever name, her illness led to extreme and unpredictable mood swings: happy to sad, playful to mean, lethargic to restless. During the sluggish periods, she would sometimes stay in bed for days, denying entrance to her bedroom to everyone but Alma and Lionel Doman, her butler and houseman. During the unsettled periods, she would do just the opposite, roaming the house in sleepless agitation and alienating everyone she knew with middle-of-the-night phone calls, often threatening suicide. Such Jekyll-and-Hyde conduct, typical of those who suffer from manic-depression, was, in Judy's case, doubtless exacerbated by drugs. In addition to all her other pills and capsules, she was apparently now also using heroin and morphine, both of which Alma found in the garage.

Anger, more potent than the most powerful drug, was the chief fuel for her illness, however, turning what might have been a manageable fire into a roaring, five-alarm conflagration. Anger at Begelman and Fields. "They took me for a ride," she shouted into that sympathetic tape recorder. "They used me. They sold me out." Anger at Sid, who was "just as bad or worse." Anger at Mark, whom she derided as a "faggot." Anger even at her adored audiences. "I've sung. I've entertained. I've pleased your children, I've pleased your wives, I've pleased you! You sons-of-bitches!"

New rage was piled atop old rage, old rage atop even older rage, resentment and rancor growing higher and higher until, at last, they formed an edifice, a skyscraper of fresh hurts and ancient grievances, that overshadowed everything else in her life. "I'm goddamned mad!" she screamed. "I'm an angry lady! I've been insulted! Slandered! Humiliated! I wanted to believe, and I tried my damnedest to believe in that rainbow that I tried to get over—and I couldn't! So what! Lots of people can't. . . . I hate anybody's guts who used me, because I wanted to be a nice girl."

In the past her fury had been directed only against herself. Now she was a danger to everyone around her. "I have felt the wind of the wing of madness," wrote Baudelaire, and many years later and half a world away, that same wind whistled through the dry canyons and arroyos of the Hollywood Hills, through palms and eucalyptus and across habitations of such riotous variety that even Baudelaire might have gasped in wonder. And there it touched Judy, too.

|||

The most convenient target of her anger was Mark. Judy was willing to push his career, it became evident, only as long as it was an appendage of her own. If Mark attempted to do anything by himself, even something as modest as appearing in a local production of Noël Coward's *Private Lives,* she did her best to sabotage him, if only by interrupting him when he tried to memorize the script. Too timid to object, Mark finally went elsewhere to learn his lines, discovering, on his return, that Judy had registered her disapproval of his absence by tossing his clothes into the swimming pool. Fished out by Lionel, who laid them on the lawn to dry, they shrank to a size only a child could wear, the tweed overcoat Judy had bought him in London being nibbled down to a fuzzy jacket.

When all her other stratagems failed to gain her the attention she craved, Judy injured herself, then accused Mark of attacking her. Responding to a frantic late-night phone call, one chivalrous friend rushed to Rockingham Avenue to find her face all bloody—Mark's work, she said. Only later did Alma and Lionel show the friend the stucco wall, still bearing traces of dried blood, against which Judy had rubbed her cheek until it was raw. On another occasion Alma actually caught her nicking her face with a razor. "Do you see what Mark Herron did to me?" Judy indignantly demanded, not at all embarrassed or nonplussed.

Against such madness, Mark had little defense. "It hadn't been too bad to fight with Sid Luft," said Judy, somewhat wistfully. "He could fight back." Mark could not, and his answer, finally, was to keep his distance. His absences from Rockingham Avenue became more and more frequent, and in April 1966, five months after their wedding, he and Judy separated. Mark went back to Henry Brandon, with whom he was to live until Brandon's death, twenty-four years later. Judy turned to a new lover, a young publicist just a few years out of Dartmouth, by the name of Tom Green. About all she could say of her fourth husband was that she could never find him. "I used to hear from him once in a while. I think he called from a phone booth on casters."

|||

Joey and Lorna, who turned eleven and fourteen in 1966, could not make a similar escape. They were the real victims of Judy's worsening condition, and for them the house on Rockingham Avenue was a battlefield from which there was no exit, a place in which tension was constant and scenes of violence and destruction were common. Almost any bad news, any slight or disappointment, might send their mother on a rampage, causing her to smash dishes, vases and anything else that was handy.

Destroying bric-a-brac is childish, but harmful only to the bric-a-brac. Setting fires is insane, a danger to life as well as property. But at least twice Judy did exactly that. She set the first one during a vacation with Mark in Hawaii, when she lit a match in his closet, then quietly sat in the sun until the firemen showed up. When Steve McQueen, who was staying next door, arrived first, Judy tartly suggested he mind his own business. "Don't be a hero, Steve," she said. "This isn't the movies. Just sit down and wait for the fire department like everyone else." The cottage survived, but Mark's clothes were destroyed, and so, to her chagrin, were Judy's, ruined by smoke.

Her second arson, a year and a half later, lacked those small comic touches. Anger at Tom Green was the spark, and Judy's own bedroom was the target. "Miss Garland's room is on fire!" screamed Alma when she saw smoke coming from under the locked door. Unable to break through, Lionel and Esteban Matison, a young visitor from Mexico, ran outside and smashed open a rarely used door to her dressing room. By then nothing in the room, including Judy, could be seen through the smoke; Matison found her, unconscious in a closet, only by crawling on the floor. Too exhausted by then to carry her, he could only haul her out by her hair. Her bedroom was gutted, but the rest of the house was unscathed.

The staff was burned by a different kind of fire. When one of the maids announced she was quitting, Judy reacted as if she had been assaulted. Picking up the nearest weapon, a turkey leg on her plate, she threw it at her, then, as the maid was driving away a few minutes later, hurled a rock at her car, cracking the windshield. The children's nanny, Mrs. Chapman, was subjected to even rougher treatment. Calling her "a Texas bitch," Judy kicked her in the leg while she was ironing clothes, then hastily retreated when Mrs. Chapman brandished the hot iron. Judy had not surrendered, however, and resumed her attack as Mrs. Chapman was leaving, this time flinging a butcher knife at the departing car.

Is it any wonder that Joey and Lorna, the mute witnesses to such scenes, were afraid of their mother? Is it any surprise that when they came home from school, they listened for sounds of trouble before going inside? Or that when they went to bed, they shivered, afraid of what the night would bring? Sharing a room near the kitchen, far away from Judy's own room, they never knew when she would wake them, sometimes hysterical, sometimes hallucinating. On those nights, her children could hear her coming, like an approaching thunderstorm, and they pulled the covers over their heads, praying that she would turn around. "It will stop," was Lorna's mantra. "It will stop."

Children react to stresses in mysterious and unpredictable ways, and, close as they were, Joey and Lorna responded differently to their never-ending anxiety. A pretty girl with blue eyes and honey-brown hair, Lorna took after her mother only in voice. "Daddy, I've got Mama right here," she told Sid, tapping her esophagus. "Right here in the throat." In every other respect, however, she resembled her father, and she reacted as he had done at the same age, with tough talk and sullen stares. If she did not despise her mother as Sid had despised his father, Lorna regarded her with decidedly mixed feelings. Judy went east to spend the Christmas of 1966 with Tom Green and his family—the children were to go to their father's for the holidays—and Lorna all but exploded with fury when she did not receive a final good-bye. "That bitch!" she exclaimed.

His mother's darling, the one she was always holding and cuddling, Joey suffered perhaps even more. "Biblical looking" was how Judy described him—a reference to his dark hair and almond-shaped eyes—and like the young David, whose soft harp soothed the melancholy of King Saul, so did the mere presence of Joey bring Judy a measure of peace. At night she would pull him into her bed for comfort and company, even if that meant waking him, tired and protesting. He was the one she worried about. "Take care of my Joey," she would say when she went away.

What armor is strong enough to protect against a love both so extravagant and so irrational? There is none, and Joey's defense was to put up no defense at all. He was unnaturally innocent, incapable of guile, and, in contrast to Lorna, always presented a sunny face to the world. The tragedy for him, and for Judy too, was that fear prevailed over love—he seemed happiest when she was away.

|||

No matter how often she went on the road, however, no matter how hard she worked, Judy remained mired in debt. "Judy Garland Is Broke," proclaimed the front page of one tabloid, which went on to say, all too accurately, that she owed money, and lots of it, to virtually everyone, from the Internal Revenue Service, the main claimant, to Sid, who, incredibly enough, was in line for $150,000 in fees for past managerial services.

It was at such a moment, the fall of 1965, that Tom Green, a conventional young man from Lowell, Massachusetts, stepped into the mael-

strom. The product of Catholic schools and Dartmouth, where he had
been president of his fraternity and a member of nearly everything else,
Green was good-looking and personable, well suited for his chosen
field, public relations. Hired by Guy McElwaine & Associates, Judy's
prestigious Hollywood agency, in the summer of 1965, he appeared, at
twenty-six, to be a golden boy with a golden future. Flattered when
McElwaine assigned him to handle Judy's publicity, he soon wondered
why he, the newest and least experienced member of the staff, was
given such an important client. Once asked, the question answered itself. Judy was no longer deemed worthy of the attention of more senior
associates.

Nor, Green learned, was that an unusual response. "Everybody was
dropping her flat because she was broke," he said. "Nobody would
help. She couldn't get anybody on the phone. Everybody was, like,
never home." The few friends who did answer were polite but refused
to give her what she most needed: money. One, the daughter of a
Metro mogul, raised her hopes by actually coming to the house; but
what Miss Moneybags offered, Judy did not want. "She's just like all
the other dykes that wanted me to go to bed with them," Judy bitterly
complained.

The most telling rejection, however, the truest indication of how far
she had fallen, came from a man, little known in Hollywood or anywhere else, named Wayne Martin. "Judy's No. 1 Fan" was the title he
gave himself, and he had been avidly following her career, collecting
photos, clippings, records and other memorabilia, since 1937. "Judy-
land," Martin called his living room, so crowded was it with Garland
paraphernalia, much of which Judy herself had given him. But when a
terrified Judy sought his aid in confirming a report that other fans were
planning to kill her—to put her out of her misery, it was said—Martin
shied away. His Garland collection, he explained, was like a sundial—
"it only records the hours that shine"—and Judy's shining hours were
behind her. He did not want to get involved, Martin informed Green:
he preferred to remember Judy as she had been, not as she was.

As he observed that phalanx of suddenly frosty faces, Green was
filled with indignation, quitting his job because he felt that even his
own firm was mistreating her. Mark Herron had wanted Judy to help

his career. Tom Green, that Lancelot from Lowell, sacrificed his career to help hers. "I told her I would do my best to get her life in order," he said. "I was genuinely stupid enough to think I could help." In the grip of the strongest of all human emotions—the desire to salvage another soul—Green embarked on a holy mission: the reclamation of Judy Garland.

Where the heart led, the body followed, and in the spring of 1966 Judy and Green became lovers. At the beginning, at least, theirs was a passionate affair, and in that decade of free and uninhibited love, they seemed to make love everywhere, Judy even disappearing under the tablecloth at a Santa Monica restaurant to perform oral sex while Green was picking at his appetizer. Forgetting the second course, they jumped into his snappy new Pontiac convertible and raced back to Rockingham Avenue. "I have the unfortunate habit of not being able to have an affair with a man without being in love with him," Judy had once said, and, true to her habit, she was soon talking marriage. "If the captain of a ship can marry you," she asked in December 1966, as they were speeding east on the Super Chief, "why can't the engineer of a train?" Green could not think of a reason, and the engineer was pleased to preside over a mock wedding in the dining car.

Arriving in Lowell, an industrial city twenty miles north of Boston, they acted, at any rate, as if they really were married. "You know, I get so tired of being Judy Garland," Judy told Green's conservative, Catholic family. "What I am is a very proper lady, and I'd just like to have that recognized." Worried that, as a Protestant with a bad reputation, she might not be welcome at Christmas Eve mass, she called the head of the archdiocese, Cardinal Cushing himself, to ask if she could attend. "Of course," said the cardinal. "God loves everybody." Thus assured, Judy accompanied the Greens to midnight mass, then, as they were leaving, joined Green in making angels in the snow, just as she had done when she was a little girl in Minnesota. "She was," said Green, "delighting in being normal."

|||

A taste of normalcy was all she was to have, however. When she returned to California in January, Judy was forced to face the brutal truth:

she was virtually destitute. "How long can you last without dough?" she plaintively inquired, and the answer—not very long—soon presented itself. The people who had helped to keep the house running—the milkman, the bread man, the laundryman, the pool man and the gardener—had already vanished, and now even food was a luxury. The arrival of the smallest windfall brought a rush to the market, usually for the makings of chili, one of Judy's favorite dishes. During her absence, Sid had helped, after his own fashion, responding to Alma's urgent phone calls by delivering a quart of milk and breakfast cereal—sometimes popcorn. But to keep the children fed and clothed, Alma and Lionel, those two almost saintly black people, had to dig into their own pockets. "Lionel, go get this child some hose," ordered Alma when she saw that Lorna's stockings were full of holes. "She can't go out looking like this."

With money borrowed from his wealthy father, Green, too, struggled to keep the household together. Others did what they could, and some of Judy's fans took turns paying telephone and electric bills. All their efforts, however, only postponed the inevitable collapse. "Where did all my money go?" asked Judy, picking up the carpet and peering underneath, as if searching for a missing stash. "Do you see any? I made millions, and I don't know where any of it is!"

To keep up her spirits, Judy kept a scrapbook of comically macabre news stories. There was, for example, the girl who was bitten to death by the black widow spiders that had made a home under her beehive hairdo. And there was the London train wreck in which the injured were carefully laid out on an adjoining train track—only to be killed by the train that came rushing to their rescue. "Every time she'd get really, really depressed," recalled her friend Doug Kelly, "Judy would whip out her scrapbook and say, 'Look at this! You think *I've* got troubles!' "

|||

But Judy's troubles were, in fact, as poisonous as an army of black widow spiders, and in the spring of 1967 she was forced to sell her house. She had never liked the place anyway, Judy publicly asserted, transforming despair into humor, as she so frequently did. But when she was alone, talking into her tape recorder, she revealed how she actually felt—heartbroken and humiliated. "How do you act when they take something from you that you thought belonged to you?" she wondered. "Are you supposed to laugh—or sing?" She answered her own question, and, without any accompaniment, launched into a song—a dirge, really—from *Porgy and Bess.* "Ole Man Sorrow's come to keep me company," she sang, "whispering beside me when I say my prayers . . . marching all the way with me, telling me I'm old now since I lost my man."

Embracing the star of Flora, the Red Menace
at the Broadway opening, May 1965

Liza—Riding a Whirlwind

or every star that rises, another must fall. That was a law as old as Hollywood. Judy knew it—it was, after all, the theme of *A Star Is Born*—and so did everyone else. But how could she have guessed that she herself was destined to stumble? Or that, through a cruel and unsparing irony, her own spectacular decline would be matched, headline for headline, by the no less stunning ascent of her own daughter? For that was, indeed, what happened. "Liza's a Girl Riding a Whirlwind," declared one admiring paper, and while the folks on Rockingham Avenue were scrounging for dollars to buy chili, a fresh, slim Liza was pictured on the front page of the New York *Daily News,* cavorting on a Riviera beach as she prepared to wow an audience in Paris.

Liza had, in fact, been preparing to wow audiences all her life. Making her screen debut when she was only two and a half—she appeared for a few seconds at the end of *In the Good Old Summertime*—she had virtually grown up in M-G-M's magic factory, spending much of her time there even after Judy was fired. She sat in Vincente's lap as he rode his director's boom; she made

friends with the actors and technicians; and she spent rapt hours in studio rehearsal halls, watching Fred Astaire, Gene Kelly and Cyd
Charisse practice their routines. At home she had a more convenient
model, and late at night Liza would sneak down the stairs to hear her
mother sing at parties. Years later, one guest could still recall her intense
dark eyes, not merely observing, but staring, studying and memorizing
her mother's every gesture and movement.

Only seventeen when she appeared in a 1963 Off-Broadway revival
of *Best Foot Forward,* Liza was on Broadway itself at nineteen, winning a
Tony, the theater world's Academy Award, for her performance in another musical, *Flora, the Red Menace.* "Can you believe that's Liza up
there?" Judy asked, in a happy daze of awe and wonder, at *Flora*'s opening. Then to Donald Brooks, the show's innovative young costume designer, she excitedly whispered, "We did that! You got her up there
looking the way she does. And I got her up there because I'm her
mother and conceivably her inspiration—the heck with her motivation." Separate careers in movies and nightclubs followed, and before
she had even reached her majority, Liza was earning, according to one
estimate, $400,000 a year.

Judy liked to brag that she had spared Liza the hardships she herself
had suffered as a child. True enough, but she had burdened her first-
born with a different set of miseries, responsibilities so heavy that they
would have crushed most adults. In a strange reversal of roles, Liza became almost a mother to her mother. She was the one who helped to
manage the staff on Mapleton Drive. She was often the one who made
sure that Joey and Lorna got off to school on time and that they were
fed when they came home. "It was as though Liza had become the
mom and Judy the child," said Mike Selsman, one of Judy's press
agents. "It was sweet, kind of nice to watch, but a little disturbing to
someone like me, who had come from an ordered background."

Liza's heaviest burden, however, was the maintenance of a permanent death watch: it was her duty, she believed, to protect her mother
from herself, to ensure that she did not kill herself. The only girl in Los
Angeles with her own stomach pump, Liza probably saved Judy's life
on several occasions, climbing in her bathroom window when she sus-

Liza and her new husband, Peter Allen, visiting Andy Warhol's Manhattan studio, December 1967

pected she had taken an overdose, and once even holding on to her feet when she was threatening to jump from a hotel window. In public, Liza tried to make light of such horrific chores. But the emotional cost was staggering. "It's just so terrible because I love her so much," she confessed in a shaky voice to one friend. "And I don't know what to do."

|||

The child most like her, Judy called Liza, and the similarities were striking. Not only did they have the same unusual physique—a big chest, a short waist and long legs—but they shared the same likes and dislikes, even the same neuroses. Liza, too, was convinced she was ugly, a belief that was to make her, like her mother, eternally insecure.

Mother and daughter also responded to the same kind of man. It was Judy, in fact, who chose Liza's first husband. Peter Allen was a twenty-year-old Australian singer and dancer she saw performing during her stay in Hong Kong and subsequently invited to London. She needed a new opening act, she said, and he and his partner, Chris Bell—the Allen Brothers, they called themselves—would be it.

Matchmaking was what Judy really had in mind, however, and she was certain that Allen—with his ginger hair, lopsided smile and infectious exuberance—was the ideal mate for Liza. Allen himself seemed to agree. Sitting at a piano when Liza first walked into the room, he greeted her with the appropriate Gershwin tune—"Isn't It a Pity? (we never met before)." Liza apparently thought it was a pity as well. Joining him at the keyboard, she started singing, putting words to his music. From such harmony did love arise, and two and a half years later, on March 3, 1967, Judy's matchmaking was rewarded with a New York wedding.

At this point, the parallels between Liza's life and her mother's became, perhaps, too exact. Just as Judy had surprised Vincente with another man twenty years earlier, so now, barely three weeks into her marriage, did Liza come upon Allen in an equally compromising position. Thus it was that three generations—grandmother, mother and daughter—had found themselves in almost identical predicaments, their marriages blighted by their husbands' preference for men over women. Ethel with Frank. Judy with Vincente. And now Liza with Peter. As if under some mysterious curse, all three women were doomed, it seemed, to make the same mistake.

Lifting a peculiar situation into the realm of the bizarre was yet another unwelcome connection between mother and daughter. Unbeknownst to either of them, the men they were sleeping with—Mark and Peter—were also sleeping with each other. It was Mark who, wandering into the Hong Kong nightclub where the Allen Brothers were appearing, had first met Peter. And it was Peter's performance in bed, not onstage, that had excited him. He and Peter had made love in Hong Kong, they had made love again in London, and they had most likely continued to make love still later in the United States.

|||

A huge betrayal, Liza was to call her dismaying discovery, though she, too, had had ample warning that the man of her dreams had romantic dreams of his own—and that they did not necessarily feature her. Yet Liza's marriage survived for three more years, and for a very good reason. Not only did she love Peter, but she depended on his brash Aussie assurance—he was her rock, she said—to keep her mother at a safe distance. At twenty-one, an age when most people start to take on the responsibilities of adulthood, Liza did the reverse. She decided, for the first time in her life, to act like a child. She had, in short, stopped being a mother to her mother.

By 1967 Judy was on her own, as far as her older daughter was concerned; Liza became one of those people Judy often had trouble reaching on the telephone. Peter answered the phone in their Manhattan apartment, and if Judy was on the line, he would say that Liza was out. If Judy telephoned the building's front desk, the doorman would be more blunt. "Miss Minnelli is not accepting any calls from her mother," he would say. When Judy was able to get through, the conversations were not always pleasant, Liza even rejecting her mother's sobbing request for money to pay her utility bill. "She doesn't want to have anything to do with me," wailed Judy, hurt, resentful and, above all, uncomprehending.

After that, Judy could sometimes be heard making harsh and spiteful comments about her older daughter—"ugly things," to use Alma's phrase. As Liza pushed her away, Judy devoted more of her praise to her second daughter. After hearing Lorna belt out her numbers in a school production of *The Unsinkable Molly Brown,* she turned to Doug Kelly and gleefully exclaimed: "Fuck Liza! This one's going to pay my rent!" Still, relations between Judy and Liza were never completely severed, and every chill was followed by a thaw. When Liza's first album was released, Judy was once again the proud mama. "Liza has a lot to learn," she concluded. "But she's doing well and she'll get better."

|||

When she lost her house in the spring of 1967, Judy also lost the last semblance of normal existence. For the next two years she was little more than a vagabond, darting from town to town, hotel to hotel. With no one else to turn to, she had asked Sid to manage her career again, and in an effort to outwit the IRS, he had persuaded her to sign over her earnings to a corporation—Group V, it was called—owned by his friend Raymond Filiberti. Though Group V would pay Judy only $1,000 per concert, a figure that would rise to $1,500 after the first twenty-five, it would take care of all her expenses: hotel, food, clothing—everything. No longer would Joey and Lorna have to subsist on chili; Group V would buy the groceries.

Anybody but Sid would have been put off by Filiberti's mud-spattered credentials, which included a year in a federal jail for having transported stolen securities across state lines. But for the first several months, Filiberti nonetheless did what he had said he would do, renting Judy a Manhattan town house off Fifth Avenue, then a suite in the St. Moritz Hotel, across from Central Park. With Tom Green keeping a careful watch on her drugs, Judy also fulfilled her part of the bargain. She undertook a punishing round of concerts that included four triumphant weeks at the Palace, and she made an appearance on the Boston Common before her biggest live audience ever, 100,000 people, many of whom sat through two downpours merely for the pleasure of seeing her in person. "It was as if her voice had come out of the long years past," marveled the *Boston Globe*'s critic. Presenting her with a souvenir of the city, a silver Paul Revere bowl, Boston's mayor, John F. Collins, was even warmer. "We have taken you to our hearts," he said. "God love you and bring you back to us."

But Judy's dealings with Group V grew increasingly chilly, becoming downright frosty in October, when she got into a screaming match with Filiberti's wife on a flight to London. Though Judy initiated the battle, suggesting that Mrs. Filiberti close her "flapping mouth," Sharon Filiberti, seventeen years younger and ten inches taller, gave perhaps better than she got, deriding Judy as an "old worn-out bag" and a "broken-down singer." Drinks, as well as words, were tossed, and by the time the plane landed in London, Judy was so upset that she turned right around and took the next flight back to New York.

Relations with Group V deteriorated still further in the weeks that followed. Judy missed three performances at Madison Square Garden's Felt Forum, and after breaking into her drug bag while Green was asleep, she made a disastrous appearance in Baltimore, wandering around the stage and muttering, just as she had done four years earlier in Melbourne. "Almost a classic tragedy" was how John Carlyle's father, who lived in Baltimore, characterized the "*very* sick" woman he saw that night. "Who's the son of a bitch behind all this?" he asked Carlyle.

That was, indeed, a question, and when Filiberti failed to pay her expenses at the St. Moritz in March 1968, Judy's arrangement with Group V all but collapsed. Unless her bill was paid immediately, Green was informed one morning, the doors to her suite would be locked and even Joey and Lorna, who had left for school, would not be allowed back in. Having spent everything he had on Judy and her children— close to $60,000, by his calculation—Green then remembered that Sid had raised cash in another emergency by pawning Judy's jewelry, which he later returned without her ever having known that it had been gone. With that example in mind, Green hocked two of her rings, then raced back to the St. Moritz with enough cash, a thousand dollars, to prevent her eviction.

This time Judy did notice that her rings were missing, however, and on Thursday night, April 11, she had Green arrested for grand larceny. Hauled off to the city jail in lower Manhattan, he was, as a reward for his good deeds, put in a cell with eleven others—a car thief, a wife beater and numerous snoring drunks. Though Judy had previously announced that she would marry him in the chapel at Dartmouth College, she now dismissed him as nothing more than an employee. So much for their late-night vows aboard the Super Chief; so much for Christmas with his family, for midnight mass and making angels in the snow. So much, indeed, for the career Green had sacrificed on the altar of Judy Garland.

Once unleashed, paranoia finds betrayal everywhere, and before it had spent itself, Judy's rage took still another victim: a female fan, Nancy Barr, who, like Green, had also provided Judy with money, time and energy—even, by Barr's account, a brief sexual relationship. Barr's sin? She had bailed Green out of jail, an act that automatically put her on Judy's enemy list. During the days that followed Judy frightened her with so many hate-filled phone calls—she would sic the Mafia on her, Judy screamed—that Barr developed a nervous condition, a spastic colon. "I loved Judy," she said, "but I could not cope with her. I wore out." So said everybody who tried to help Judy hold her tattered life together.

|||

Judy had survived so many crises and had made so many comebacks that it was hard for many to see that her situation had changed, that she had run out of options—perhaps even out of time. One by one, those who loved her either left voluntarily or were forced to leave: Liza, Tom Green, Nancy Barr and, finally, Joey and Lorna. For years Judy had fought Sid for custody, afraid that he might take their children. Now she herself pushed them away, several times actually kicking them out of their rented quarters and forcing them to seek haven in Liza's apartment on East Fifty-seventh Street.

The first to flee was Joey. Probably not knowing who he was, his mother chased him around their apartment one wild night, then, as he leaped out the door and stumbled down the stairs, she hurled a butcher knife at him, aiming well enough that it brushed his hair. Barefoot and wearing nothing but a pajama bottom, the terrified Joey ran three or four blocks through the dark and snowy streets of Manhattan until, at three o'clock in the morning, he reached the safety of his father's hotel.

Next to depart was Lorna, who, tough as she was, was not tough enough to withstand such ceaseless anxiety and so many sleepless nights. The result was three days in a hospital with what she called "a type of mental breakdown." That was followed, a few months later, by a panicked call to her father in Los Angeles. "Dad, I have to come live with you in California," she cried. "I have to come with you right now, today, tonight." A few hours later she was on a plane headed west.

New York, Boston, Los Angeles. Judy now went from one to another, so restless that she could not remain very long in one house or apartment, or even in one city. And all the while she was so broke, sometimes with as little as five dollars in her purse, that she had to plead for her meals and rooms. "I'm a great star," she had told Nancy Barr.

"Look what I've given to everybody. Where are all the fans? Where are they now that I need help?" A collapse during a performance at New Jersey's Garden State Arts Center in June sent her to Boston's Peter Bent Brigham Hospital, but she soon left to board another plane. The woman who had always traveled with mountains of luggage landed in Los Angeles with nothing more than a shopping bag stuffed with skirts, blouses and pills.

John Carlyle put her up for a few days, then passed her on to his friends Tucker Fleming and Charles Williamson, who had a larger, more secluded home in the Hollywood Hills. "This is the proper way of living," Judy said approvingly as she looked around her hosts' well-ordered house. She had flown so far mainly to see Joey, and Fleming and Williamson made sure she did, treating them to dinner at the Factory, a popular discotheque in West Hollywood. There, to the applause of the other dancers, mother and son did an old-fashioned fox-trot. When he grew up, Joey vowed, he would be a banker; then his mother would never again have to worry about money. "Did you hear what he said?" a tearful Judy asked her hosts. "What a wonderful son I have!"

A proper way of living did not suit Judy for very long. "It's just like the Christian Science Reading Room here," she soon complained to Fleming and Williamson, and returned to Boston, where she had rented a one-bedroom apartment in the new Prudential Center. Eager for a good night's sleep, her hosts were happy to wave farewell. "Judy made you feel you had run a two-minute mile," said Fleming. "We have met any number of people who have said, 'Ooooh, I wish I had known she needed help. *I* would have taken care of her.' Nonsense! Nobody could have done it."

|||

New candidates always appeared, however, and several weeks later in New York, Judy met another young man, John Meyer, who was eager to try. Meyer's story was to resemble Tom Green's in everything but length, all the emotions Green had experienced in two and a half years being compressed into less than two months, from the middle of October to the middle of December. Within minutes of their introduction, Judy and Meyer, a piano player and songwriter, were talking like old friends. Within hours, Judy was living with him in his parents' apartment on Park Avenue. Within days, they were engaged to be married, and Meyer, like Green, had embarked on a holy crusade: the salvation of Judy Garland. "She can be greater than she's ever been, and I can help her do it," he told a dubious friend. "I can help her get back up there."

The first job Meyer got her was not much of a step up: an engagement at Three, the gay and lesbian bar where he played the piano. Jackie Scott, one of the bar's owners, at first turned him down, appalled at the thought that a woman who had filled the Palladium, the Palace and the Hollywood Bowl was reduced to selling her songs in a two-room bar on East Seventy-second Street—even if it was Scott's own bar. But when a friend pointed out the obvious, that Judy was desperate for money, Scott relented, and for two or three weekends Judy showed up around midnight, sang a couple of songs to adoring crowds, and walked out with a hundred dollars, her only income safe from the IRS. After that, Meyer aimed higher, arranging appearances on three national television shows and—his crowning achievement—five weeks at the Talk of the Town, London's premier supper club, at a salary of approximately $6,000 a week.

For Meyer, the exaltation of a relationship with Judy—"she lived in four dimensions," he said—soon gave way to exhaustion, and a man who had astonished people with his nervous energy was suddenly struggling to stay awake. Judy had worn him out, too. A case of the flu ended their affair. While Meyer was in bed, fighting off a fever, Judy discovered another savior in another piano player: Mickey Deans, the night manager of Arthur, a smart Manhattan discotheque in which she had spent many late hours. Now it was Mickey Deans who would accompany her to London. Now it was Mickey Deans—DeVinko was his real last name—whom she wanted to marry. "I finally got the right man to ask me," she said. "I've been waiting for a long time."

*Clasping hands with her fans,
as Nancy Barr and Joey Luft look on
from the wings, the Palace, 1967*

CHAPTER 17

Mine Eyes Have Seen the Glory

A cool cat," John Springer, one of the owners of Arthur, called Mickey Deans, who was thirty-four and darkly good-looking, with blue eyes and a voice so deep that it seemed to echo from the depths of a cave. And cool Deans was, which meant that there was apparently no problem he could not effortlessly solve—or find someone who could. A broken television set? A stalled car? A dispute with a landlord? Deans could help. A frantic telephone call in the middle of the night, saying that Judy Garland needed pep pills so she could board a plane for California? Deans could help with that, too. Such a phone call from a friend had introduced them, in fact: Deans had rushed to her hotel suite with a bagful of amphetamines.

Deans, in short, was a Mr. Fixit. Whether it was seeing to the comforts of the VIPs who crowded the dance floor of Arthur, or turning away the gate-crashers who hoped to join them, Deans was the man in charge. And he knew it. Not merely confident, he was cocksure. "If I was dead broke," he liked to say, "I'd go out and set up a fucking hot dog stand on the corner, and within six months I'd have turned it into a fucking chain." Given to blunt talk peppered with profanity—his mother complained that he sounded like a hoodlum—Deans bore more than a passing resemblance to Sid Luft.

Though he had been seeing Judy for many months, their friendship turned serious only when she told him that she was about to leave for England. "I'm going to miss you," Deans replied, then impulsively added: "Why don't we get married?" He did not have to ask twice. Forgetting the ailing John Meyer, Judy had immediately announced the joyful news to one of the columnists who frequented Arthur, and less than two weeks later, on the evening of Friday, December 27, the excited lovers left for London, where they planned to become husband and wife.

With a new man on whom to lean, Judy was all confidence, and her opening at the Talk of the Town provided yet another English triumph, a night that was, in the words of one reviewer, "part happening, part experience, and all nostalgia." As her run continued into the new year—1969—she started showing up later and later, however, and eventually even her loyal English fans grew restive. Although Robert Nesbitt, the club's producer, pushed the curtain back from eleven to eleven-thirty to accommodate her, she still could not arrive on time. Finally, in late January, she met open hostility, a mini-Melbourne. As she began her first song at twelve-twenty A.M., fifty minutes late, a few rowdies made obscene gestures and pelted her with breadsticks and cigarette packages. "If you can't turn up on time, why turn up at all?" one well-lubricated young tough demanded, then, before anyone could stop him, grabbed her microphone and shook her by the shoulder. "That's it," said Judy. "I have had enough." And she walked off, not to return for several days.

|||

Despite a snag in their wedding plans—the papers certifying Judy's divorce from Mark had been held up in California—Judy and her Mickey decided to solemnize their love anyway. A little after three o'clock on the morning of January 9, they stood before the altar of St. Marylebone parish church, the Georgian building in which, more than a hundred years earlier, two other lovers, the poets Elizabeth Barrett and Robert Browning, had also been united. "What about a witness?" Judy asked. "God is our witness," responded the young Anglican priest, Peter Delaney, who performed a full religious ceremony. Two months later, on March 15, Judy and Mickey made their union legal, repeating their vows in the Chelsea Register Office, then holding a reception at Quaglino's, a big, fancy restaurant in the West End.

The choice of such a large, formal room was a mistake, however, only serving to emphasize how many of Judy's friends now did their best to avoid her. Of all the famous names invited, not one walked through Quaglino's door. The American singer Johnnie Ray, who had been famous in the fifties, did attend, but his presence was partly a matter of business: he and Judy were scheduled to tour Scandinavia the following week. "I can't understand it," said a disappointed Judy. "They all said they'd come." Champagne bubbled in rows of untouched glasses, the band played to an empty dance floor and the soaring wedding cake remained largely uneaten.

After that dismal celebration—"the saddest and most pathetic party I have ever attended," asserted one London columnist—the happy couple flew to Paris for a brief honeymoon, then journeyed on again to Stockholm, the first stop on the Scandinavian tour. Although an overdose of sleeping pills caused Judy to cancel the engagement in Gothenburg, Sweden's second-largest city, the other three concerts—in Stockholm, Malmö and Copenhagen—were unqualified successes. When she finished in Stockholm, she was applauded for twelve full minutes. "Of course she was fabulous," said one paper, as if any other outcome had been inconceivable.

Not that all the Viking enthusiasm helped much with her finances. "She was almost broke through mismanagement, but I intend to change all that," Mickey told a reporter, and he briskly worked to put together some moneymaking ventures. One was a documentary, *A Day in the Life of Judy Garland*. A second, which he was discussing with American promoters, was a chain of Judy Garland movie theaters, five hundred in all, across the United States. To reap her share of the profits—"a million dollars over the next year without singing a note," boasted Mickey—all Judy had to do was show her face a few times. Cool cat though he was, Mickey was no businessman, however, and his grandiose schemes, which were, like Sid's, one part logic to three parts wishful thinking, died aborning.

|||

"I don't know if London still needs me," Judy said, "but I certainly need it! It's good and kind to me. I feel at home here. The people understand me, and I'm not aware of the cruelty I've so often felt in the States. I've reached a point in my life where the most precious thing is compassion—and I get this here." In late winter she and Mickey settled in, renting a mews cottage on a quiet cul-de-sac in Chelsea. It was Judy's first permanent address since Rockingham Avenue, and it was there, at

At home in London with Mickey Deans, March 1969

4 Cadogan Lane, that Mr. and Mrs. Deans—or Gladys and George, as they liked to call themselves—set up housekeeping.

After their return from Scandinavia, they left that quiet cottage only to visit the even more tranquil house that Judy's publicists, Matthew West and Brian Southcombe, shared in West Sussex, an hour and a half from London. Built in the sixteenth century as the local lord's lookout against deer poachers, the Deer Tower—for that was its name—stood high atop a hill, and from her lofty bedroom Judy gazed out on a landscape of singularly English splendor. Below her window was a riot of color, a country garden abloom with daffodils, wisteria, rhododendrons and all the other flowers and flowering shrubs that proclaimed the arrival of spring. A little farther away, at the bottom of the hill, a squadron of swans glided across a lake, on the other side of which lay a Gothic ruin and an endless sweep of farms and fields. This was the vista, little changed from the days of Shakespeare, Spenser and Marlowe, that Judy looked on and loved, staying in her room for hours on end to read and relax.

Judy also loved the idea of being a wife again—that most proper title, in her view. "How do I love thee? Let me count the ways," Elizabeth Barrett Browning had written. But Judy could count only one way in which she expected to be loved. She wanted security, a man who would guard and protect her; and Mickey, the man who could fix anything, fitted the bill. "Mickey takes care of everything," she bragged, "of everything and of me." And Mickey was pleased to do it. "Judy was in love with love," said Mickey's friend Robert Jorgen, "and Mickey was in love with the idea of taking care of her." The salvation of Judy Garland had become Mickey's mission, too.

Yet no one could be with Judy every minute of every day, and Mickey, like his predecessors, searched for convenient excuses to go off on his own. Sometimes the dutiful Matthew West would sit with Judy in a restaurant, waiting for a husband who never appeared. Other times, West would take her to the Deer Tower, where they expected to be joined by Mickey, then receive a telephone call from him, saying that a business dinner in London would prevent him from coming. "Mickey was a bit of a scalawag, a party animal," said West. "I think he probably wanted to get away from her, to be free, just for a few hours, of her constant demand for attention."

His absences did not go unnoticed by Judy. By the end of May, when they visited New York, their relationship was showing such strain that she telephoned Tucker Fleming and Charles Williamson to ask for refuge in Los Angeles. "I've got to get away from Mickey," she said. After their polite rejection, Judy turned to John Carlyle, to whom she had proposed marriage the year before. But Carlyle, too, fended her off. "Look, Madame Gumm," he said, "you're a married lady now." Thus it was that Judy spent her forty-seventh birthday, June 10, in bed, with Mickey nowhere in sight and with only two callers, Charles Cochran, in whose East Side apartment she was staying, and one of Cochran's friends.

Her sentiments changed from day to day, however, and after an evening with Mickey's parents in nearby New Jersey—they lived in a modest red bungalow in the town of Garfield—Judy was all smiles again, touched by his mother's concern for her health and welfare. "If you'd only come out here for a few weeks, I'd make you well," asserted Mary DeVinko, alarmed by her daughter-in-law's frail appearance. Thrilled to have become part of her new husband's family, Judy exclaimed that Mickey's parents were really her parents, too. "If anything happened to Mickey, I could probably go to New Jersey and live with them forever!"

|||

After her ebullient performance in Copenhagen's Falkoner Center, one admiring reviewer declared that Judy Garland had eighteen lives. What that Danish critic did not know was that Judy had already used up seventeen of those—and was fast consuming the final one. What he also did not know was that her costume had hidden a wasted body, thin to the point of emaciation. A woman once possessed of a ravenous appetite, Judy now scarcely ate, doing little more than moving her food around her plate and erupting in annoyance when anyone nudged her to eat more. "I have a husband," she would shoot back, "and my husband tells me what to do!"

Body and mind are inseparable, and Judy's physical decline had been preceded by an emotional one. The life she had led had made her the oldest woman in the world, she had told John Meyer a few months earlier—by her own reckoning, she was four hundred and twelve. When Meyer had protested that she would, as always, bounce back, Judy had responded with a truth born of exhaustion. "No, darling, I've bounced back too often. The spring is shot." She had lost not only her resilience, but her spirit, her willingness to fight.

Even more, Judy had lost her reason for being. A creation of her audience, she had proudly pronounced herself, and she had clung to the sound of applause with religious zeal, fearful, perhaps, that if it disappeared, so would she. One witness to that chilling rite of devotion was Allan Davis, a London director, who visited her backstage at the Talk of the Town, where she was listening to a recorded playback of that evening's performance. "Oooh!" she cried when she heard the first burst of applause. Then, leaning into her makeup mirror, she kissed her own reflection. "You're a star!" she exclaimed. "You're a star! You're a star!"

By June all the cheers in the world would probably not have convinced her of that, however. Her public was slipping away, she believed, and she was slipping away with it. "I've lost my audience," she informed John Carlyle. But she was mistaken. She had not lost her audience. Her audience had lost her: she no longer had either the energy or the desire to stand on a stage and conjure up the magic, the phenomenon that had been Judy Garland.

|||

On June 17, a week after her bleak birthday in Manhattan, Bob Jorgen took Judy and Mickey to New York's Kennedy Airport for their return flight to London. Having recently watched his mother decline and die, Jorgen recognized the danger signals. After waving good-bye at the gate, he suddenly called Mickey back. "Take very good care of her," he said, "because she's dying." But not even Jorgen could have guessed how soon that ominous prediction would be realized, how very little time Judy had left.

Her mood had brightened somewhat after leaving New York, and the following Saturday, June 21, she and Mickey planned to have some fun, to see a show put on by Danny La Rue, a female impersonator. When they failed to appear, Matthew West called their house at intermission. Mickey had a cold, Judy told him, and they had decided to stay home. They still expected to join him the next morning—the first Sunday of summer—for an outing to the Deer Tower.

That was a trip not taken. At ten-forty on Sunday morning, Mickey was awakened by a call from Los Angeles. Partying late—it was the middle of the night in California—John Carlyle and Charlie Cochran wanted to talk to the lady of the house. But Judy was in the bathroom, the door to which she had, as always, bolted from the inside, and she did not respond to Mickey's knock. Alarmed, he climbed onto the roof, looked through the bathroom window and saw her apparently asleep on the toilet, her head slumped forward, her hands on her knees. Climbing inside, Mickey lifted her up and was reassured to hear what sounded like a moan. What he actually heard was the last bit of air escaping from her lungs. As he raised her farther, he saw that her skin was discolored and that blood was dribbling from her mouth and nose. She had been dead, the coroner later reported, for six to eight hours.

"Barbiturate Poisoning," the coroner, Gavin Thurston, wrote on her death certificate, and an autopsy showed that her blood contained an extremely high level of barbiturate, 4.9 percent—the equivalent of ten one-and-a-half-grain Seconal capsules. Thurston found no evidence of suicide, however; he attributed her death to a mistake, an "incautious self-overdosage." What had probably occurred, he said, was that she had taken several capsules, woken up and, forgetting how many she had already swallowed, gulped down a few more to put her back to sleep. "The circumstances of her death," he ruled, "are quite clearly accidental."

Judy had explained how easily such an accident could happen—she had, in effect, foretold the manner of her ending—two years earlier in a reflection on the death of Marilyn Monroe. "You take a couple of sleeping pills," she had explained, "and you wake up in twenty minutes and forget you've taken them. So you take a couple more, and the next thing you know you've taken too many."

Following the inquest on Wednesday, Judy's body was flown to New York, where it was driven to the Frank E. Campbell Funeral Home on Manhattan's East Side. After a brief delay while her makeup was redone—the London mortuary had made her look like a prim little Englishwoman, with soft curls, pink lipstick and almost no eye shadow—her body was placed on public view. Lining up eight abreast, mourners circled the block all day and through the night, an unbroken procession of young and old, rich and poor, men and women. By the time the coffin was closed late Friday morning, an estimated 22,000 people had paid their respects. Another two thousand, still waiting, had to be turned away.

Funeral services began at one o'clock Friday afternoon, with Mickey, Sid and all three of Judy's children in attendance. Peter Delaney, who had come from England to officiate, read from Corinthians, one of Judy's favorite Bible passages: "And now abideth faith, hope, charity, these three; but the greatest of these is charity." James Mason gave the eulogy, and the service ended with "The Battle Hymn of the Republic," the song Judy had sung after the death of John Kennedy—"Mine eyes have seen the glory of the coming of the Lord." Covered by a blanket of yellow roses, her coffin was then carried by car to a crypt in Hartsdale's Ferncliff Cemetery, a few miles north of New York.

In the days that followed, columnists and editorial writers ruminated over her life and death. Some drew moral lessons, wagging their fingers at Hollywood, drugs, the culture of fame, Judy herself. Her life had been a tragedy, they said. But that was a charge Judy would have rejected—indeed, she had rejected it. If she had a choice, an English reporter had asked in January, would she do it all over again? "Oh, come on," Judy had laughed. "Don't for heaven's sake give me that old sob stuff routine. Of course I'd do it all over again. With all the same mistakes." Saddened by the silence, many did feel sorrow, however. "Bonne Nuit, Judy Garland," was the headline in a Montreal paper—"Good night, Judy Garland."

Posterity does not remember entertainers, James Mason said in his eulogy, adding that in years to come those who had not known her would be puzzled by the passions she had evoked. But Mason's was not the last word, or the right word, or a prophetic word. Even as he spoke, Judy's voice issued, unstilled and unstoppable, from the portable phonographs and radios carried by those outside the funeral home.

Carnegie Hall. The Palace. The Palladium. M-G-M and a hundred opening nights. Like old friends at a reunion, those triumphs, and many more, crowded together on that narrow Manhattan sidewalk, on that muggy afternoon in June. From the pavement to the top of the tallest building her voice rose, and rose still higher, as if, like the breath of exaltation, it would serenade heaven itself. Forget your troubles and just get happy, it said. Get ready for the judgment day.

$\mathscr{Notes}$

Much of this book is based on hundreds of interviews conducted over several years. Almost all were tape-recorded and transcribed—several thousand pages in all. To avoid confusing the reader with a too-lengthy list of names and titles, I have not always identified my sources in my narrative. I have done so, however, in the notes that follow, naming, with very few exceptions, everyone who gave me anything but commonplace information.

I have, in addition, relied on the written word: newspaper and magazine stories, histories, biographies and autobiographies. I have also, as noted below, made extensive use of the various collections in university libraries, most notably the Freed and Warner Bros. collections at the University of Southern California, which provide a remarkably detailed account of Judy's movie career.

CHAPTER 1. ETHEL AND FRANK

p. 4   Far from his home   Maude Ayres (Holman) to GC.

p. 4   He took a job   *Superior Evening Telegram,* Jan. 24, 1914.

p. 4   This time Frank   Register of Deeds, Douglas County, Wisconsin.

p. 4   Standing before a newly ordained   *Superior Evening Telegram,* Jan. 23, 1914.

p. 4   After the bridal dinner   The weather data were provided by James Christenson, a meteorologist at the Duluth weather bureau.

p. 4   Topping the bill   *Superior Evening Telegram,* Jan. 23, 1914.

p. 4   Their romance   *Superior Evening Telegram,* Jan. 24, 1914.

p. 5   Born in Hamilton   John Milne's application for employment, dated Oct. 10, 1888, can be found at the Marquette County (Michigan) Historical Society.

p. 5   Ethel's mother   The records do not show where Eva Milne was born. She was baptized in the Holy Trinity Church in Cornwall, Ontario, and the likelihood is that she was also born in Ontario. In those days, however, there was no Episcopal church in Massena, New York, and some American Episcopalians regularly attended services in Canada. It is possible that Eva's parents were among them. (Register of Baptisms, 1845–1923, Holy Trinity Church, Cornwall, Ontario.)

p. 5   The Milnes lived   The movements of the Milnes have been traced through a combination of census records and Marquette County directories.

p. 6   Sanitation meant   *Daily Mining Journal,* Dec. 11, 1906.

p. 6   On Independence Day   *Daily Mining Journal,* June 30, 1905.

p. 6   Both John and Eva   James Milne to GC.

p. 6   Teaming up to play   *Michigamme Area Centennial.*

p. 7   Their bickering   Harry Glyer (his mother was Mary Milne) to GC.

p. 7   All in all   Maude Ayres (Holman) to GC.

p. 8   Built in the Federal style   The residents of the Baugh house are listed in the 1880 census.

p. 9   Conversation was   Howse, *Falling Stars,* pp. 82–83.

p. 9   With no home   Report to the Rutherford County Chancery Court, April 30, 1896, as part of a continuing case of *J.D. & J.L. Baugh, executors, vs. Mary B. Gum & others.*

p. 11   Darrow personally presented   Frank Gumm to Henry M. Gass, 1934. University of the South archives.

p. 11   "It is so beautiful"   Percy, *Lanterns on the Levee,* p. 96.

p. 11   Small and friendly   Ibid., p. 94.

p. 11   Writing of the Easter services   *Sewanee Purple,* April 17, 1900, vol. XV, no. 2.

p. 12   Will Gumm died   Frank Gumm listed his occupation as stenographer in the 1910 census.

p. 12   In 1909 he left   "Tullahoma: Episodes from Its Past," edited by Betty Anderson Bridgewater, *Coffee County Historical Society Quarterly,* vol. VI, nos. 3 and 4 (1975), p. 84.

p. 12   Ovoca, he named it   Marjorie S. Collier, "Ovoca: The Meeting of the Waters," *Tullahoma* (Tenn.) *Time-Table,* Historic Preservation Society of Tullahoma, vol. VII, no. 1 (April 1986).

p. 12   In this new setting   Betty Anderson Bridgewater, *St. Barnabas's Parish: The First Hundred Years* (Tullahoma, Tenn.: Coffee County Historical Society, May 1974).

p. 12   He sang   Letter from Floyd Mitchell to David Dahl and Barry Kehoe, March 3, 1972. In the author's possession.

p. 12 In the most unlikely *Cloquet* (Minn.) *Vidette,* May 3, 1967, and Sept. 13, 1967.

p. 12 "Mr. Gumm" *Cloquet* (Minn.) *Pine Knot,* Sept. 16, 1911.

p. 13 With no other company Holman to GC.

p. 13 By his own count *Cloquet* (Minn.) *Pine Knot,* Dec. 18, 1914.

p. 13 Eventually he landed *Polk's Portland City Directory,* 1913, p. 103.

p. 14 This new life *Itasca County* (Minn.) *Independent,* March 5, 1914.

p. 15 Barlow and Bentz *Grand Rapids* (Minn.) *Herald-Review,* Dec. 14, 1914.

p. 16 Kindred Avenue Grand Rapids renamed most of its streets in 1932. I am using the names the Gumms knew in an earlier era.

p. 17 "The public likes" *Grand Rapids* (Minn.) *Herald-Review,* March 17, 1915.

p. 17 "Just one" Eleanor Downing to GC.

p. 17 "We had a piano" Mabel MacAdam (Ronzheimer) to GC.

p. 18 "I always liked" Gerold Frank, *Judy,* p. 7.

p. 18 As far as Ethel was concerned Ibid., p. 11.

p. 18 "Marc, I'm" Marcella Rabwin to GC.

p. 18 "Frank, it can cost" Ibid.

p. 19 "The beginning" Judy Garland's tape-recorded reminiscences.

p. 19 "That's the only time" Ibid.

p. 19 A cheerful contraption Burt Geving to GC.

p. 20 Almost every night Ibid.

p. 20 Frank and Ethel *Itasca County* (Minn.) *Independent,* Sept. 19, 1925.

p. 20 "At night" Judy Garland, as told to Joe Hyams, "The Real Me," *McCall's,* April 1957.

p. 20 Ethel was in Duluth John Graham, "Baby, Take a Bow. . . . ," *Rainbow Review,* no. 37 (Oct. 1979).

p. 21 "Can I do that" Ibid.

p. 21 "Added attraction" *Itasca County* (Minn.) *Independent,* Dec. 20, 1924.

p. 21 There are several versions John Graham, "Baby, Take a Bow. . . . ," *Rainbow Review,* no. 37 (Oct. 1979).

p. 21 If she cried Ibid.

p. 22 "We referred" James Milne to GC.

p. 22 Frank did not complain Marcella Rabwin to GC.

p. 23 When two of the New Grand's ushers Katherine Doran Berkeland to GC.

p. 23 In no hurry *Itasca County* (Minn.) *Independent,* July 24, 1926.

p. 23 To get into Finch, *Rainbow,* p. 27.

p. 24 By the end *Grand Rapids* (Minn.) *Herald-Review,* Oct. 27, 1926.

p. 24   As luck had it   I am indebted to Ronald Carter, the son of the build-ing's owner, who gave me a copy of the lease.

p. 25   He signed his lease   *Antelope Valley Ledger-Gazette,* May 20, 1927.

p. 25   "Gumm Family"   Ibid., May 27, 1927.

p. 26   Three years later   Like Grand Rapids, Lancaster changed many street names in the 1930s. I have opted to use the older names, cur-rent at the time of which I am writing.

p. 27   Babe always seemed   Wilber Lundy to GC.

p. 27   "We didn't want"   Henry Ivan Dorsett to GC.

p. 27   Always careful   Ina Mary Ming (Miller) to GC. All quotations of Ming come from interviews with GC.

p. 28   "The girls and I"   Dorothy Walsh (Morrison) to GC.

p. 28   Learning that   Finch, *Rainbow,* p. 40.

p. 28   Months later   Frank, *Judy,* pp. 32–33.

p. 29   "A compact woman"   Black, *Child Star,* p. 5.

p. 29   "One Hundred"   Finch, *Rainbow,* p. 41.

p. 30   "I'll Get By"   Ann Rutherford to GC.

p. 30   At one tiny theater   Frank, *Judy,* pp. 38–39.

p. 30   "Without Babe"   Maurice Kusell to GC.

p. 31   "Baby Gumm"   *Antelope Valley Ledger-Gazette,* April 15, 1932.

p. 31   "Mary Jane and Jimmie"   Dorothy Walsh (Morrison) to GC.

CHAPTER 2. A MEAGER STREAM—AND A LOVE LIKE NIAGARA

p. 33   "When I was"   Judy Garland, as told to Joe Hyams, "The Real Me," *McCall's,* April 1957.

p. 33   "Boy, did he"   Glen Settle to GC.

p. 33   "She adored"   Dorothy Walsh (Morrison) to GC.

p. 34   "She was somehow"   Grace Pickus to GC.

p. 34   There are many stories   Wilber Lundy to GC.

p. 34   If they included   Irma Story, Jr., to GC.

p. 35   "Everybody wanted"   Ibid.

p. 36   What did she want   Ibid.

p. 36   "She hated going"   Ina Mary Ming (Miller) to GC. Miller provided much of my information concerning the trips from Lancaster to Los Angeles.

p. 37   "I've got to keep"   Dorothy Walsh (Morrison) to GC.

p. 37   And her mother   This early introduction to drugs has been con-firmed by Dorothy Walsh (Morrison) and Ann Miller, whose own mother was a good friend and confidante of Ethel Gumm.

p. 37   Babe herself thought   Garland's tape-recorded reminiscences.

p. 38   "Slow down!"   Dorothy Walsh (Morrison) to GC.

p. 38   These arguments   The account of her parents' late-night arguments and their aftermath is taken from Judy's unfinished, unpublished autobiography, "The Judy Garland Story," which is located in the Random House Collection in Columbia University's Butler Library, New York City.

p. 38   Ethel never physically abused Babe   Ibid.

p. 38   One year she had arranged   Ibid.

p. 39   Inside the house   Ina Mary Ming (Miller) to GC.

p. 39   Nothing in the world   Garland's tape-recorded reminiscences.

p. 40   On the hottest days   Walter Primmer to GC.

p. 40   "He was a sour"   Wilber Lundy to GC.

p. 40   "He was a peculiar"   Sam Ming, quoted in Dahl and Kehoe, *Young Judy.*

p. 40   "A terrifying man"   "The Judy Garland Story."

p. 41   "We thought"   Dorothy Walsh (Morrison) to GC.

p. 41   Searching for   Ina Mary Ming (Miller) to GC.

p. 42   "Boy, those look"   Henry Ivan Dorsett to GC.

p. 42   To fend off   Irma Story, Jr., to GC.

p. 42   In the high school   There are several sources for this anecdote.

p. 42   "I don't see"   Henry Ivan Dorsett to GC.

p. 43   Though Babe later   "The Judy Garland Story."

p. 43   She and her daughters   *Antelope Valley Ledger-Gazette,* March 1, 1929.

p. 43   Impressed as much   Maurice Kusell to GC.

p. 43   Ethel brought her   *Antelope Valley Ledger-Gazette,* Dec. 30, 1932.

p. 44   Twenty-four hours   *Antelope Valley Ledger-Gazette,* August 3, 1933.

p. 44   Providing an education   Rooney, *Life Is Too Short,* p. 37.

p. 44   Mary Jane and Jimmie   Anne Shirley (Lederer) to GC.

p. 44   A plain girl   Cary, *Hollywood's Children,* p. 229.

p. 45   When Mrs. Lawlor   Ibid.

p. 45   Admired and appreciated   Rooney, *Life Is Too Short,* p. 97.

p. 45   "Well, I met"   Frank, *Judy,* pp. 44–45.

p. 46   "Of course the house"   Anne Shirley (Lederer) to GC.

p. 46   "She was sure"   Dorothy Walsh (Morrison) to GC.

p. 46   Though New York   Frank, *Judy,* p. 46.

p. 46   He lost the argument   *Antelope Valley Ledger-Gazette,* June 21, 1934.

p. 46   Their first stop   *Antelope Valley Ledger-Gazette,* July 5, 1934.

p. 46   But the club   Finch, *Rainbow,* p. 47.

p. 47   Another, somewhat older   Maxene Andrews interview, SMU Oral History Collection. The episode with the Andrews Sisters is described in this interview.

p. 48   Rush over   Frank, *Judy*, p. 50.

p. 48   Jessel was unimpressed   Wagner, *You Must Remember This*, p. 91.

p. 48   "These kids"   *The Superior Evening Telegram*, November 8, 1937. There are many versions of how George Jessel changed the name Gumm to Garland. I believe that this version, which came from Ethel herself and which was the earliest I could find, is probably the most nearly accurate.

p. 48   Babe evoked   *Antelope Valley Ledger-Gazette*, Aug. 23, 1934.

p. 48   Finally heading home   *Antelope Valley Ledger-Gazette*, Oct. 25, 1934.

p. 48   When she jumped   Judy Garland, "I'm Judy Garland—and This Is My Story." *New York Journal-American*, Feb. 24, 1964.

p. 49   Although she did not   "A Garland for Judy," *Photoplay*, Sept. 1940.

p. 49   Writing about their appearance   Frank, *Judy*, pp. 53–54.

p. 49   Her singing   Quoted in the *Antelope Valley Ledger-Gazette*, Dec. 20, 1934.

p. 49   "Boy, those were"   Letter from Frank Gumm to Mr. and Mrs. John D. Perkins, Oct. 9, 1935. I am indebted to David Dahl and Barry Kehoe, who gave me a copy.

p. 49   He ate his meals   Gumm to Perkins, Oct. 9, 1935.

p. 50   "Frankie's lover boy"   Robert Settle to GC.

p. 50   "When the dominoes"   Ronald Carter to GC.

p. 51   "Frank would walk"   W. M. Redman to GC.

p. 51   Though they did not give   I am indebted to Ronald Carter, who gave me copies of his father's correspondence regarding the Valley Theater.

p. 51   "The New Year"   *Antelope Valley Ledger-Gazette*, Jan. 3, 1935.

p. 52   "I regret"   *Antelope Valley Ledger-Gazette*, March 28, 1935.

p. 52   When his old barber   Letter from Gumm to Perkins, Oct. 9, 1935.

p. 52   "Little Frances Garland"   Frank, *Judy*, p. 56.

p. 53   "What can we do"   Fricke, *Judy Garland*, pp. 22–23.

p. 53   "That's a rough"   Garland's tape-recorded reminiscences.

p. 53   Though the biggest   Ina Mary Ming went with her on one audition to M-G-M, Dorothy Walsh on another.

p. 53   In early September   Leonard Gershe to GC. Gershe was told this story by both Edens and Garland.

p. 55   "We have a girl"   Beery's words are taken from a recording of the show.

p. 55   On Mariposa   Dorothy Walsh (Morrison) to GC.

p. 56   "Awfully pitiful"   Letter from Gumm to Perkins, Oct. 9, 1935.

p. 57   "Judy's mother was"   Mary MacDonald to GC.

p. 57   Marc Rabwin was called   Rabwin consulted his records for David Dahl and Barry Kehoe, who gave me a copy of his statement.

p. 58   *Your eyes made*   She made a slight alteration in the lyrics, changing "repeating through again" to "repeating through and through."

p. 58   Indeed, that very night   Dorothy Walsh (Morrison) to GC.

p. 59   It was Judy's first   Ibid.

p. 59   Judy was later   Judy Garland, "I'm Judy Garland—and This Is My Story," *New York Journal-American,* Feb. 24, 1964.

p. 59   "Now," she thought   Frank, *Judy,* p. 80.

CHAPTER 3. A PRINCESS IN THE REALM OF MAKE-BELIEVE

p. 61   One resident   Cerra, *Culver City: The Heart of Screenland,* pp. 49–50.

p. 62   The entrance   The physical description of M-G-M is mostly taken from various issues of *Lion's Roar,* an elaborate magazine the studio sent to distributors and theater owners.

p. 62   On the five   George P. Erengis, "MGM's Backlot," *Films in Review,* Jan. 1963.

p. 63   As Mary Astor   Astor, *A Life on Film,* p. 185.

p. 65   When Judy   Schatz, *The Genius of the System,* pp. 174, 359.

p. 65   "It had the climate"   Davis, *The Glamour Factory,* p. 7.

p. 65   To those who agreed   William Saroyan, "Best Angel God Ever Saw," *Saturday Evening Post,* Nov. 16, 1963, p. 94.

p. 65   "There seemed to be"   Gil Perkins to GC.

p. 66   "Your problems"   Hepburn, *Me,* p. 225.

p. 66   District Attorney Buron Fitts   Marx and Vanderveen, *Deadly Illusions,* pp. 200–202.

p. 66   "It's not"   Rooney, *Life Is Too Short,* p. 186.

p. 67   Ava Gardner liked   Gardner, *Ava: My Story,* p. 46.

p. 67   Even the mother   Black, *Child Star,* p. 320. And see "The Judy Garland Story."

p. 67   "Don't think they"   My account of Judy's sexual encounters with M-G-M's executives is taken from the unpublished "The Judy Garland Story," as are the remarks attributed to her.

p. 67   "I often thought"   Ibid.

p. 68   "Yes or no"   Ibid.

p. 68   "Young girls"   Selznick, *A Private View,* p. 76.

p. 68   "Mr. Mayer had spies"   Ann Rutherford to GC.

p. 69   At the end   Marx, *Mayer and Thalberg,* pp. 128–29.

p. 69   "His relationship with God"   Behrman, *People in a Diary,* p. 158.

p. 69   "I hate disloyalty!"   Marion, *Off with Their Heads!,* p. 325.

p. 69   When Lena Horne   Lena Horne to GC.

p. 70   The list of those he assaulted   Crowther, *Hollywood Rajah,* p. 168.

p. 70   Sensing the menace   Powell, *A Life in Movies,* p. 530.

p. 70   Short in stature   Grady, *The Irish Peacock,* pp. 242–44. I am borrowing this observation from Grady, who was M-G-M's chief talent scout for many years.

p. 70   "When Dad died"   Judy Garland, "The Real Me," as told to Joe Hyams, *McCall's,* April 1957.

p. 70   "We have just signed"   "The New Pictures," *Time,* Dec. 27, 1943.

p. 71   On a lot crowded   James Stewart, as quoted in *Rainbow Review,* winter 1975.

p. 71   "Make no mistake"   Rita Maxwell to GC.

p. 71   Left with almost nothing   The figures are from papers submitted to the Los Angeles Superior Court.

p. 71   "It looked as though"   Dorothy Walsh (Morrison) to GC.

p. 72   "They didn't know"   Title unknown, *Redbook,* Nov. 1961.

p. 72   She was to play   "Schumann-Heink, Great Singer, Dead," *The New York Times,* Nov. 18, 1936. The *Times* obituary gives a detailed account of Schumann-Heink's life.

p. 72   Accompanied by her mother   " 'Baby Nora Bayes' Sings On WHN Awaiting Pix," *Variety,* June 17, 1936.

p. 73   "If they don't want Deanna"   "Juveniles—Judy Garland, Tom Kelly—Air Views on Life, Films," *New York Post,* Feb. 15, 1938.

p. 73   Her first suitor   Pasternak, *Easy the Hard Way,* pp. 165–69.

p. 74   She poured so much   The Directors Guild of American oral history project. Interview with David Butler, director of *Pigskin Parade,* p. 137. Directors Guild, Los Angeles.

p. 74   "The voice!"   June Levant to GC.

p. 74   "Daffy and delightful"   The New York newspaper reviews of *Pigskin Parade* are dated Nov. 14, 1936.

p. 75   A "fat little frightening pig"   Title unknown, *National Enquirer,* Oct. 23, 1960.

p. 75   "What I like to do"   James Reid, "Who Said 'The Terrible Teens'?" *Motion Picture,* May 1940.

p. 75   "The Boss"   Marion, *Off with Their Heads!,* p. 260.

p. 75   After her tearful exit   *Deanna's Diary: Fan Club Publication of Deanna Durbin Devotees,* vol. V, no. 1 (1941); Dunning, *Tune In Yesterday,* pp. 178–81.

p. 76   "When am I"   Frank, *Judy,* p. 93.

p. 76   "Mayer let Tiffany go"   Stanley Kramer to GC. Kramer was then an assistant film editor at M-G-M.

p. 76   On February 2, 1937   For a description of Ben Bernie, see Dunning, *Tune In Yesterday,* pp. 59–60.

p. 77   It was a song   As with so many other events in Judy Garland's early life, there are several different versions of how she arrived at an important point in her career, namely the day she sang "Dear Mr. Gable" at Clark Gable's birthday party. The most complete and, to my mind, the most plausible chronology was provided by John Graham in a chapter titled "Shall I Sing a Melody?" from his unpublished Garland biography. I have largely followed his outline of the days leading up to that moment.

p. 78   When she ended   Rooney's account of what happened that day on the set of *Parnell* can be found in his autobiography *Life Is Too Short,* pp. 102–105.

p. 78   Flustered as she was   *Life,* Feb. 14, 1937.

p. 78   Judy, wrote columnist Sidney Skolsky   John Graham, from his unpublished Garland biography.

p. 78   "I have never seen"   Ann Rutherford to GC.

p. 79   *Broadway Melody*   I am listing Judy's pictures, here and afterward, in the order of their release dates, not the dates of their actual production, which sometimes overlapped.

p. 79   As Metro had anticipated   *New York Herald Tribune,* Sept. 3, 1937.

p. 79   Many reviewers   *New York Daily Mirror,* Sept. 3, 1937.

p. 79   So visible had she become   Selznick, *Memo from David O. Selznick,* p. 153.

p. 80   She was that rarity   Pasternak, *Easy the Hard Way,* pp. 225–26.

p. 80   "There are moments"   Lillian Sidney to GC.

p. 81   Placed near the bottom   For the sake of consistency, I am, unless otherwise noted, using New York City release dates throughout this book.

p. 81   She was "a kid"   Astor, *A Life on Film,* p. 142.

p. 81   "Judy, none of your tricks"   *Movie Mirror,* March 1938.

p. 81   "There was always"   Ralph Blane to GC.

p. 81   Even after she had reached   Viertel, *The Kindness of Strangers,* p. 271.

p. 81   Small wonder   Judy Garland, "I'm Judy Garland—and This Is My Story," *New York Journal-American,* Feb. 25, 1964.

p. 82   Once she actually started   Fordin, *The World of Entertainment!,* p. 7.

p. 82   Trying to turn   Jackie Cooper, " 'This Was a Little Girl Who Was Used and Used and Used and Hardly Loved at All,' " *TV Guide,* Nov. 4, 1978.

p. 82   A movie star in the making   *New York Post,* Nov. 26, 1937.

p. 82   "From the time"   Judy Garland, as told to Joe Hyams, "The Real Me," *McCall's,* April 1957.

p. 82   Stood in front   Peter Wyden, "What Happened to Judy Garland?" *St. Louis Post-Dispatch,* July 2, 1950.

p. 83   "My idea of a good time"   Judy Garland, as told to Joe Hyams, "The Real Me," *McCall's,* April 1957.

p. 83   Metro was not playing games   Ann Rutherford to GC.

p. 83   Mayer's chicken soup   Tex McCrary and Jinx Falkenburg, "New York Close-up," *New York Herald Tribune,* Aug. 27, 1951. Joe Hyams, "A Star Is Born—and Raised," *New York Herald Tribune,* Sept. 20, 1956.

p. 84   The day after   Joe Mankiewicz to GC.

p. 85   Arranged with all the care   Epes W. Sargent, "Exploitation," *Variety,* Feb. 9, 1938.

p. 85   "M-G-M's Sensational Singing Star"   *New York Sun,* Feb. 10, 1938.

p. 85   Nonplussed   James Goode, "Judy," *Show Business Illustrated,* Oct. 31. 1961. Roger Edens described the scene for the magazine's writer.

p. 85   "Kid has"   *Variety,* Feb. 16, 1938.

p. 85   When she reached Pittsburgh   *Variety,* March 2, 1938.

p. 87   "It was the most incredible"   Saul Chaplin to GC.

p. 87   In Pittsburgh   "Judy Garland's Pittsb'g Record at Current Scale," *Variety,* March 9, 1938.

p. 87   Hoping to cash in   "Inside Stuff—Pictures," *Variety,* March 9, 1938.

p. 87   Declaring that she had   "Life Goes to a Party with Judy Garland, Who Becomes the Sweetheart of Sigma Chi," *Life,* March 28, 1938.

p. 87   "Local Girl Starred"   *Itasca County* (Minn.) *Independent,* Dec. 18, 1936.

p. 88   On the morning of March 31   Judy's trip to Grand Rapids is recounted in the *Grand Rapids* (Minn.) *Herald-Review* (March 30 and April 6, 1938) and the *Itasca County* (Minn.) *Independent* (April 1 and April 8, 1938).

p. 88   That week's issue   "Life Goes to a Party with Judy Garland, Who Becomes the Sweetheart of Sigma Chi," *Life,* March 28, 1938.

p. 88   After making an appearance   John L. Saxhaug to GC.

p. 88   Defying the blizzard   Bill Binet to GC.

p. 88   Summing up her stay   "Judy Posed for Grand Rapids Picture," *Itasca County* (Minn.) *Independent,* April 6, 1938.

p. 88   She believed   Judy Garland, "My Story," magazine unknown, Jan. 1951.

p. 89   In a scene   Ibid.

CHAPTER 4. PRODUCTION NO. 1060—*THE WIZARD OF OZ*

p. 91 "Metro has acquired" "LeRoy Will Produce 'Wizard of Oz'—," *Daily Variety,* Feb. 24, 1938.

p. 91 For the film announced that day I am measuring popularity in raw numbers. By all accounts, more people have seen *The Wizard of Oz,* in movie houses and in its many showings on television, than any other film.

p. 92 The star, the producer and the budget For my account of the making of *The Wizard of Oz,* I am indebted to two excellent, full-length histories, Aljean Harmetz's *The Making of The Wizard of Oz* and *The Wizard of Oz: The Official 50th Anniversary Pictorial History,* by John Fricke, Jay Scarfone and William Stillman. Michael Patrick Hearn also gives a concise but informative account in his introduction to the published version of the screenplay.

p. 92 But Temple Fordin, *The World of Entertainment!,* p. 9.

p. 93 Many of his old friends Wilk, *They're Playing Our Song,* p. 146.

p. 94 Looking toward Fricke, Scarfone and Stillman, *The Wizard of Oz,* p. 18.

p. 94 The difficulty, for the technical staff anyway Dooley, *From Scarface to Scarlett,* p. 611.

p. 94 It turned most yellows Harmetz, *The Making of The Wizard of Oz,* pp. 220–21.

p. 95 "LeRoy Starts" Fricke, Scarfone and Stillman, *The Wizard of Oz,* p. 62.

p. 95 "He just didn't quite understand" Hay, *MGM,* p. 284.

p. 95 "He just didn't have" Harmetz, *The Making of The Wizard of Oz,* p. 140.

p. 95 Even her acting Ibid., p. 143.

p. 96 "There was more of Fleming" John Gallagher, "Victor Fleming," *Films in Review,* March 1983.

p. 97 After one of the male midgets Dona Massin was present when the plight of the unfortunate midget was first reported: Dona Massin to GC.

p. 97 "We had a hell" Harmetz, *The Making of The Wizard of Oz,* p. 188.

p. 98 Her seemingly uncontrollable attacks Astor, *A Life on Film,* pp. 141–42.

p. 99 "We used to long" Lahr, *Notes on a Cowardly Lion,* p. 195.

p. 99 Rarely involving himself Joe Mankiewicz to GC. For an account of this meeting see also Paul Attanasio, "Joseph Mankiewicz, Master of the Movies," *The Washington Post,* June 1, 1986.

p. 100 "I wanted" Schickel, *The Men Who Made the Movies,* p. 154.

p. 101 Trimmed as well Fricke, Scarfone and Stillman, *The Wizard of Oz,* p. 122.

p. 101 In England Ibid., p. 195.

p. 101 Overlooking the fact Harmetz, *The Making of The Wizard of Oz,* p. 81.

p. 102 Nothing could have prepared them Inez Robb, "Rooney, Garland 'Mobbed' in N.Y.," *Los Angeles Examiner,* Aug. 14, 1939.

p. 103 Indulging in a rare moment "Leo on Diet," *Hollywood Reporter,* Aug. 18, 1939. Another Metro executive, J. Robert Rubin, joined Mayer and Schenck in sending the telegram to LeRoy.

p. 103 After interviewing her *New York Journal-American,* Oct. 24, 1939.

p. 105 "What a wonderful thing" Wiley and Bona, *Inside Oscar,* p. 99.

p. 105 The second time Ibid.

p. 105 Her old pal Fricke, *Judy Garland,* p. 53 (caption note).

p. 107 "Our sweetest songs" "To a Skylark," ll. 89–90.

p. 108 " 'Rainbow' has always been" James Bacon, "Judy Was Always Girl of Somewhere Over Rainbow," *Los Angeles Herald-Examiner,* June 23, 1969.

p. 108 Oz had given her Judy Garland, as told to Joe Hyams, "The Real Me," *McCall's,* April 1957.

p. 109 Audiences were still Freed Collection.

p. 109 Judy had made "Names and Credits of the Box Office 'Big Ten' of 1939," *Box Office Digest: 1940 Annual.*

p. 109 "For Mr. Grauman" Judy Garland, as told to Gladys Hall, "Judy Garland's Gay Life Story, Part II." Magazine unknown.

p. 109 A movie star needs Gerald Clarke, "Judy Garland, *The Wizard of Oz* Star in Bel-Air," *Architectural Digest,* April 1992.

p. 110 "We're going to move" Dorothy Walsh (Morrison) to GC.

p. 110 An idealized vision *Lion's Roar,* Feb. 1945, includes a photograph of Judy standing in front of the house and the picket fence.

p. 111 "Did I hear" Ethel M. Gumm, "Deep, Deep in My Heart," 1931.

p. 111 Although publicity photographs Lupton A. Wilkinson, "Fame Is Fun for Judy," newspaper unknown, Oct. 8, 1939.

p. 111 "Ethel didn't love" Dorothy Walsh (Morrison) to GC.

p. 112 "They were absolutely" Ibid.

p. 113 "That was the most awful" Watson and Chapman. *Judy: Portrait of an American Legend,* p. 26.

p. 113 "From here on in" Frank, *Judy,* p. 144.

p. 113 "He was a fast-talker" James Milne to GC.

p. 114   They finally confessed failure   California Superior Court, County of Los Angeles. Index No. D260983.

p. 114   Many years later   Ina Mary Ming (Miller) to GC.

CHAPTER 5. THE MEN OF HER DREAMS

p. 118   "Nobody thinks less"   James Reid, "Who Said 'The Terrible Teens'?" *Motion Picture,* May 1940.

p. 120   She probably got   Galen Reed to GC.

p. 120   When her mother   Judy Garland to Charles Murphy, February 1936. This letter was shown to me by its owners, Tucker Fleming and Charles Williamson.

p. 120   At thirteen or fourteen   Bartholomew quote from an interview with him in *When the Lion Roars,* a Turner Network Television (TNT) documentary about M-G-M broadcast in 1992. Cooper quote from Jackie Cooper, " 'This Was a Little Girl Who Was Used and Used and Used and Hardly Loved at All,' " *TV Guide,* Nov. 4, 1978.

p. 120   Judy, he rather fetchingly confessed   Irene Thirer, " 'Tough Guy' Billy Halop Would Relish Role of Film Comedian," *New York Post,* May 19, 1938.

p. 120   One who went to bed   Buddy Pepper to GC.

p. 120   No one would have been surprised   The "Kissing Bug" quote is from Morella and Epstein, *Lana,* p. 33. Mickey Rooney speaks of his relationship with Turner in his memoir *Life Is Too Short,* pp. 97–99. (In her own memoir, Turner puts her sexual initiation several years later than Rooney does and does not include Rooney among her partners.)

p. 120   Nor would anyone have been astonished   The story about Rooney in the car was told to GC by Gilbert Perkins, a stuntman who drove Rooney's car on such an occasion. Rooney's description of Turner is from *Life Is Too Short,* p. 98.

p. 122   "She laughed more"   Buddy Pepper to GC.

p. 122   Judy had a secret crush   Frank, *Judy,* pp. 88–89.

p. 122   "People like me"   Judy Garland, "My Story," magazine unknown, Jan. 1951.

p. 122   The years spent rushing   Rooney, *Life Is Too Short,* p. 290.

p. 122   When one boy arrived   David Jackson, the younger brother of Judy's date, told me this story.

p. 123   When a date upbraided him   Levant, *The Memoirs of an Amnesiac,* p. 117.

p. 123   a "demure Jean Harlow"   Ibid., p. 35.

p. 123   "What do you think"   Ibid., pp. 34–35.

p. 124   Despite the wide   Ibid., pp. 34.

p. 124   "If we had married"   Kashner and Schoenberger, *A Talent for Genius* (photo caption).

p. 124   "Oh, my God"   Gardner, *Ava*, p. 88.

p. 124   "an uncompromising searcher"   Schuller, *The Swing Era*, p. 693.

p. 125   From then on   Shaw, *The Trouble with Cinderella*, p. 37.

p. 125   "I got Ava Gardner"   Artie Shaw to GC.

p. 125   They had met when Shaw was playing   One Garland biographer, Gerold Frank, reckons the time as the summer of 1936. Shaw, however, had already heard her sing "Dear Mr. Gable" when they met, which places the date after the release of *Broadway Melody of 1938.*

p. 125   Excited by his innovative style   Except where noted, all Artie Shaw's comments are to GC.

p. 126   Supremely confident   Shaw, *The Trouble with Cinderella*, p. 91.

p. 127   "And zoom!"   Silvers, *This Laugh Is on Me*, p. 104.

p. 127   "It really was"   Morella and Epstein, *Lana*, p. 38.

p. 127   Like everybody else   The account of Judy's initial reaction to the news of Shaw's marriage is taken from Gerold Frank's *Judy*, pp. 145–49.

p. 127   "You've broken her heart!"   Artie Shaw to GC.

p. 127   Wrapped up   Ibid.

p. 127   When he later tried   Frank, *Judy*, p. 148.

p. 128   Walking into the dressing room   Margaret Whiting to GC. Whiting also tells this story in her memoir, *It Might as Well Be Spring.*

p. 128   Describing her marriage   Turner, *Lana*, p. 55.

p. 128   Judy's answer   Allyson, *June Allyson*, p. 14.

p. 128   "I liked the boys"   Morella and Epstein, *Lana*, p. 30.

p. 129   "Every boyfriend I get"   William Tuttle to GC.

p. 129   "dangerously near being glamorous"   *Modern Screen*, August 1940.

p. 129   After a summer preview   Freed Collection.

p. 129   Wearing a blue organdy dress   Mary Morris, "Judy Garland's Life and [illegible]," *PM*, June 10, 1945.

p. 130   Fortunately for Judy   *Los Angeles Examiner*, March 9, 1940.

p. 130   No less notable   Davidson, *Spencer Tracy: Tragic Idol*, p. 78; Swindell, *Spencer Tracy*, p. 167.

p. 130   Escorted by such a changing cast   Turner, *Lana*, p. 99.

p. 131   "It was kind of 'in' "   Rita Maxwell to GC.

p. 131   Glad to oblige   *Los Angeles Examiner*, July 23, 1940.

p. 132 Wowed by the glamour "The New Pictures," *Time,* May 5, 1941.

p. 133 Judy had been at Metro St. Johns, *Some Are Born Great,* p. 52.

p. 134 "Until M-G-M" Judy Garland, as told to Joe Hyams, "The Real Me," *McCall's,* April 1957.

p. 134 "Mr. Mayer calling her" Irene Sharaff to GC.

p. 135 "What is Judy so worried about?" Freed Collection.

p. 135 A hapless witness Lillian Sidney to GC.

p. 137 The proof of that simple proposition Morella and Epstein, *The Complete Films and Career of Judy Garland,* p. 205.

p. 137 One was Warner Bros.' "Cinema," *Time,* March 28, 1938.

p. 137 Another rise, to $2,500 "Judy Garland Given $1500 Weekly Raise," *Los Angeles Examiner,* Sept. 27, 1940.

p. 137 "The success of the little Garland girl" *Los Angeles Examiner,* May 29, 1941.

p. 137 From the spring of 1939 I am not including in my count a 1942 short, *We Must Have Music.*

p. 138 "After such a hit" Freed Collection.

p. 138 "You Asked for *another*" The quote is from a preview trailer for *Strike Up the Band.*

p. 139 "We performed magic" Rooney, *Life Is Too Short,* p. 143.

p. 139 At Metro, Mickey gave Judy Judy Garland, "My Story," magazine unknown, Jan. 1951.

p. 139 "Just before" Ibid.

p. 140 "With other actresses" Rooney, *Life Is Too Short,* p. 143.

p. 140 "Mickey understood me" Judy Garland, "I'm Judy Garland—and This Is My Story," *New York Journal-American,* Feb. 25, 1964.

p. 140 "I have always" Rooney, *i.e.: An Autobiography,* p. 102.

p. 140 "One of the hottest" " 'Girl Crazy.' " *Box Office Digest,* Aug. 9, 1943.

p. 140 What is surprising Freed Collection.

p. 141 He could do everything "Cinema," *Time,* Jan. 19, 1942.

p. 141 By 1939, Berkeley's reputation Hay, *MGM,* p. 215.

p. 141 "There was fun" Thomas and Terry, *The Busby Berkeley Book,* p. 27.

p. 142 On one picture Hay, *MGM,* p. 223.

p. 142 An alcoholic Rooney, *Life Is Too Short,* p. 139.

p. 142 "If you couldn't toe the line" Ibid.

p. 142 The effect Review of *Girl Crazy, Sunday Express,* Dec. 5, 1943.

p. 142 The cruelty Hopper and Brough, *The Whole Truth and Nothing But,* p. 122.

p. 142 Conjuring up the image Ibid.

p. 143   The torment   Esther Williams to GC.

p. 143   By the end   Memo from Fred Datig, August 2, 1940. Freed Collection.

p. 143   it was probably then   Several sources, including Dorothy Walsh (Morrison), confirm that for several months Ethel was denied entrance to M-G-M.

p. 143   The first scene   The account of Edens's dispute with Berkeley is taken from Hugh Fordin's *The World of Entertainment!*, pp. 83–86.

p. 144   "Don't try to make"   Crowther, *Hollywood Rajah*, p. 240.

p. 144   "If a story"   Marion, *Off with Their Heads!*, p. 99.

p. 145   Small wonder   Garland's tape-recorded reminiscences.

p. 145   "I won't marry"   Cal York, "The Marriage Dilemma of Judy Garland," *Photoplay*, May 1941. The writer makes it clear that Judy's comment was made some time before he wrote the article, which pushes the date back to 1940.

p. 146   That "bouncy butterball"   Carmichael, *Sometimes I Wonder*, p. 239.

p. 146   By April 1940   The Garland-Mercer recording of "Friendship" is on *Judy Garland: The Best of the Decca Years* (vol. 1), MCA Records, 1990.

p. 146   As besotted with Judy   Jean Bach to GC. She was a good friend of Mercer's.

p. 146   Quiet and "painfully shy"   "Radio," *Time*, June 3, 1946.

p. 146   At parties   "Will Judy *Be Happy* Married?" *Screen Guide*, 1941 (exact date unknown).

p. 146   "Little was thought"   May Mann, "Next—a Ring for Judy," King Features Syndicate, 1941. (The clipping I have does not show the name of the publication or the exact date.)

p. 147   "How did you know"   Frank, *Judy*, p. 149.

p. 147   "The most appreciative"   Sidney Fields, "The 'Rose' That Always Blooms—with Music," *New York Mirror*, Nov. 13, 1946.

p. 147   "I got my first engine"   "Composer Has Yard Full of Steam Engines," *Los Angeles Examiner*, April 27, 1959.

p. 148   "Dave Rose—Eccentric Genius"   "Will Judy *Be Happy* Married?" *Screen Guide*, 1941 (exact date unknown).

CHAPTER 6. A RIDE TO NOWHERE ON THE GAR-ROSE RAILWAY

p. 152   "That baby"   Fordin, *The World of Entertainment!*, p. 39.

p. 153   "I wish you girls"   Finch, *Rainbow*, p. 113.

p. 153   Rose, who had been   Frank, *Judy*, p. 162.

p. 153 "If you ask me" Louella Parsons column, *Los Angeles Examiner,* Aug. 3, 1940.

p. 153 "She seemed like such a baby" Arden, *Three Phases of Eve,* p. 52.

p. 154 "I am wondering" Louella Parsons column, *Los Angeles Examiner,* Feb. 19, 1941.

p. 154 "If Judy has only" Frank, *Judy,* p. 159.

p. 154 "that cold storage plant" Chandler, *Raymond Chandler Speaking,* p. 131; Louella Parsons story, *Los Angeles Examiner,* May 29, 1941.

p. 154 "I want a home wedding" Louella Parsons story, *Los Angeles Examiner,* May 29, 1941.

p. 155 But once having started Jimmie Fidler, "Judy Garland and Rose Fly Off to Be Married," *Los Angeles Times,* July 29, 1941. Also, "Judy Garland Becomes Mrs. Dave Rose," *Movie-Radio Guide,* date unknown.

p. 155 DEAR MR. FREED Fordin, *The World of Entertainment!,* p. 48.

p. 155 "Even if we don't get" "Judy Garland Forced to Forego Honeymoon," *Los Angeles Times,* July 29, 1941.

p. 156 "She was insanely" Sidney Miller to GC.

p. 156 Quickly making himself *Los Angeles Examiner,* Oct. 28, 1941.

p. 156 It was Ethel Mary Morris, "Judy Garland's Life and New Love," *PM,* June 10, 1945.

p. 156 "David was small" Ann Rutherford to GC.

p. 157 February 19, 1942 The dates are taken from M-G-M production notes in the Freed Collection.

p. 157 "It sounds so patriotic" Fordin, *The World of Entertainment!,* p. 31.

p. 157 "I guess you're right" Ibid., p. 32.

p. 158 One of the first stars "Throat Ill Ends Judy's Tour," *Los Angeles Examiner,* Feb. 3, 1942.

p. 158 After visiting *Los Angeles Examiner,* Feb. 6, 1942.

p. 158 Forced to halt Ibid.

p. 159 "Judy hasn't been well" Louella Parsons column, *Los Angeles Examiner,* April 23, 1942.

p. 159 Indeed, said Hedda Hopper Hopper and Brough, *The Whole Truth and Nothing But,* p. 124.

p. 159 Judy herself thought Judy Garland, "I'm Judy Garland—and This Is My Story," *New York Journal-American,* Feb. 25, 1964.

p. 159 "Love to" Hopper and Brough, *The Whole Truth and Nothing But,* p. 124.

p. 160 But Judy was The "mixed-up little girl" quotation is from Jane Ardmore, "Judy," *The American Weekly,* Oct. 1, 1961. Judy's comments about her sex life with Rose are from an interview with Harry Rubin, who came into her life many years later.

p. 160   "He acts"   Dorothy Walsh (Morrison) to GC.

p. 160   She loved to dance   "We're Sorry, Judy," *Photoplay,* date unknown.

p. 160   "Judy was outgoing"   Dorothy Raye to GC.

p. 160   "Always churned up"   Rose made his comment to a *Time* magazine reporter in May 1946. Rose's breakdown was the subject of a story in the *Los Angeles Examiner,* Nov. 23, 1944 ("Sgt. David D. Rose in Army Hospital").

p. 161   Judy came home   James Milne to GC. Milne, Judy's cousin, was visiting at the time.

p. 161   "Sullen" was the label   "One Wins Decree While Other Files Her Suit," *Los Angeles Examiner,* May 18, 1940.

p. 161   "Brooding" was the adjective   A. E. Hotchner, *Today's Woman,* Aug. 1952.

p. 161   But she had not spoken   Judy told Dorothy Ponedel, her makeup woman, of watching Rose ride his trains late at night. Ponedel described the conversation in her unpublished autobiography, a copy of which is in the possession of the author. The quotation about "little toy trains" is from Peter Coutros, "Living with Herself Was No Bed of Roses," New York *Daily News,* June 25, 1969.

p. 161   "I'm miserable"   Frank, *Judy,* p. 167.

p. 161   One of the most prominent   Ibid., p. 164.

p. 161   Dinner guests   Maxwell is quoted in Finch, *Rainbow,* pp. 181–82.

p. 162   Judy herself   Peter Coutros, "Living with Herself Was No Bed of Roses," New York *Daily News,* June 25, 1969.

p. 162   Acting as if   Mary Morris, "Judy Garland's Life and New Love," *PM,* June 10, 1945.

p. 162   "Sometimes I'd"   Ibid.

p. 162   "We simply can't"   Fordin, *The World of Entertainment!,* p. 39.

p. 162   What panic, then   *Los Angeles Examiner,* Nov. 27, 1942.

p. 163   "Now, Judy"   "The Judy Garland Story."

p. 163   When she married David   Judy Garland, as told to Joe Hyams, "The Real Me," *McCall's,* April 1957.

p. 163   After that   Allyson, *June Allyson,* p. 42.

p. 163   "We regret"   Louella Parsons story, *Los Angeles Examiner,* Jan. 26, 1943.

p. 164   "I do like to be"   Judy Garland, "I'm Judy Garland—and This Is My Story," *New York Journal-American,* Feb. 28, 1964.

p. 164   "The most beautiful man"   Anne Baxter is quoted in Guiles, *Tyrone Power: The Last Idol,* p. 9.

p. 164   Imagine, then   This meeting and many subsequent events in the Garland-Power affair are described in ibid., pp. 151–65.

p. 164   "There was an immediate attraction"   Watson Webb to GC.

p. 165   "Oh, he's wonderful!"   Anne Shirley (Lederer) to GC.

p. 165   It was as if a light came on   The admirer was Rosalind Russell. Guiles, *Tyrone Power,* p. 67. The woman who perceived an aura was Coleen Gray. Davis, *The Glamour Factory,* p. 103.

p. 165   "We've had them all"   Guiles, *Tyrone Power,* p. 58.

p. 165   A bisexual   Power's bisexuality is detailed in Hector Arce's *The Secret Life of Tyrone Power* and discussed more discreetly in Guiles's *Tyrone Power.* I have, in addition, interviewed one man who spoke convincingly of his own affair with Power and who told of other men who had also had sexual relations with Power.

p. 165   *That,* Judy did almost instantly   Watson Webb to GC.

p. 166   "Miss Garland has the faculty"   Harry Mines, "Picturized Review," *Los Angeles Daily News,* Nov. 26, 1942.

p. 166   He had, to quote from his favorite author   Cram, *Forever,* p. 13.

p. 166   It was a youthful   Among actors, birth dates are often suspect, and two or three dates have been given for Annabella's birth. I accept the calculation of Watson Webb, who was her close friend as well as Power's, that she was born in 1908.

p. 166   "This is forever"   Cram, *Forever,* p. 60.

p. 166   Few other women   Guiles, *Tyrone Power,* p. 152; Watson Webb to GC.

p. 166   Aware, for her part   Judy later told Harry Rubin that she was aware of Power's bisexuality, but hoped to change it into unambiguous heterosexuality. Harry Rubin to GC.

p. 167   Audiences liked   The "now-come-of-age" quote is from "Picture of the Month," *Lion's Roar,* Nov. 1942.

p. 167   *For Me and My Gal*   The overturning of the Astor Theater's house record is from Chester B. Bahn, "The Astor's Pet Picture," *Lion's Roar,* Nov. 1942.

p. 167   "To be involved"   Anne Shirley (Lederer) to GC.

p. 168   The "vice-president"   Rooney, *i.e.: An Autobiography,* p. 110.

p. 168   "She gave a report"   Judy Garland, as told to Joe Hyams, "The Real Me," *McCall's,* April 1957.

p. 168   She had grown up in Beverly Hills   For Betty Asher's background, I am indebted to her brother, William Asher. The dates of her attendance at UCLA were confirmed by the UCLA Registrar's Office.

p. 168   "The next thing I knew"   Artie Shaw to GC.

p. 169   On orders from Mayer   Al Jennings to GC. Jennings was the assistant director on several of Judy's pictures during the forties, and it was his responsibility to ensure that such edicts were obeyed.

p. 169 Asher's friendship   Judy Garland, as told to Joe Hyams, "The Real Me," *McCall's,* April 1957.

p. 169 That Judy and Asher   The fact that Judy had sexual relationships with women was confirmed by several people who knew her well, including one woman, Nancy Barr, with whom she later had sex. Asher's sexual history was provided by her brother.

p. 169 Much of her uneasiness   Guiles, *Tyrone Power,* p. 156.

p. 170 "It was hard for Tyrone"   Watson Webb to GC.

p. 170 Furious, she made   Guiles, *Tyrone Power,* p. 156.

p. 170 "Honey, don't worry"   Dona Massin to GC. Massin worked on *Girl Crazy.*

p. 170 her doctor   Memo from Fred Datig, January 29, 1943. Freed Collection.

p. 171 Over dinner at Perino's   Watson Webb to GC.

p. 171 "I'm just the luckiest"   Tyrone Power to Watson Webb, April 6, 1943. I am indebted to Webb for showing me this letter.

p. 171 Quick divorces   For the divorce laws of the forties I am relying on Bacal and Sloane, *ABC of Divorce.*

p. 172 Writing to Webb   Tyrone Power to Watson Webb, May 25, 1943.

p. 172 Whenever he brought up   Guiles, *Tyrone Power,* p. 160.

p. 173 The most damaging story   Frank, *Judy,* pp. 174–75.

p. 173 Retaliating, as she often did   Dorothy Walsh (Morrison) to GC.

p. 173 "We'll find each other"   Cram, *Forever,* p. 15.

p. 173 "land of lost content"   A. E. Housman, "A Shropshire Lad," l. 40.

p. 173 "It really was different"   Guiles, *Tyrone Power,* p. 161.

p. 173 "It was no small affair"   Ibid., p. 194.

p. 174 "My God"   Ibid., pp. 184–85.

CHAPTER 7. IN LOVE WITH HARVARD COLLEGE

p. 177 In a statement   Carey, *All the Stars in Heaven,* p. 255, quotes the high-level praise for *Mrs. Miniver.*

p. 178 Even films that, like most of Judy's   Hay, *MGM,* p. 193.

p. 178 Pleased to accept   Day, *This Was Hollywood,* p. 266.

p. 179 Harvard College generally went   Peter B. Flint, "Joseph L. Mankiewicz, Literate Skeptic of the Cinema, Dies at 83," *The New York Times,* Feb. 6, 1993.

p. 179 "Joe knows more"   Geist, *Pictures Will Talk,* p. 171.

p. 179 "Everyone," recalled one woman   Buckley, *The Hornes,* p. 184.

p. 180 "We made each other laugh" Unless otherwise noted, all quotations of Mankiewicz, and all descriptions of his thoughts about Judy, come from discussions with GC.

p. 181 "Oh, he's so brilliant" Frank, *Judy*, p. 179.

p. 182 Indeed, Freud himself Gay, *Freud*, p. 512.

p. 183 "I was a nut" Geist, *Pictures Will Talk*, pp. 129–30.

p. 183 "I wasn't too bright" Judy Garland, "There'll Always Be an Encore," *McCall's*, Jan. 1964.

p. 183 Joe probably advanced According to his datebooks, Menninger did not visit California in 1943; this would indicate that he met Judy in 1942. For this information, I am grateful to Connie Menninger at the Menninger Clinic.

p. 183 Although she was beginning Joe Mankiewicz to GC.

p. 184 A onetime president For discussions of Simmel's clinic, see Friedman, *Menninger*, pp. 63–64, and Gay, *Freud*, pp. 461–63.

p. 184 Fleeing the Nazis Meryman, *Mank*, pp. 198–99.

p. 184 At the outset Judy Garland, "There'll Always Be an Encore," *McCall's*, Jan. 1964.

p. 184 "I'll live" Frank, *Judy*, p. 187.

p. 185 "Mr. Mayer and I" Ibid., p. 186.

p. 185 The inevitable showdown For Santa Fe schedules, as well as other railroad information, I am indebted to Kevin V. Bunker, collections assistant at the library of the California State Railroad Museum in Sacramento.

p. 185 Mr. Mayer had heard Joe Mankiewicz to GC.

p. 187 Besides seeing Simmel Mary Morris, "Judy Garland's Life and [illegible]," *PM*, June 10, 1945.

p. 188 When Judy was finally through Judy Garland, "There'll Always Be an Encore," *McCall's*, Jan. 1964.

p. 188 Encapsulating those requirements Roazen, *Freud and His Followers*, p. 171.

p. 188 One should never expect Ibid.

p. 188 The other was an elderly German Farber and Green, *Hollywood on the Couch*, p. 30.

p. 188 "The Obermacher" The word *Obermacher* cannot be found in any German dictionary, but it is likely that Mankiewicz, who spoke German, meant something like "supervisor."

p. 188 "A big pack of lies" Ponedel's unpublished autobiography, in author's possession.

p. 189 "Will you tell Judy" Frank, *Judy*, p. 185.

p. 189   "I could never" Judy Garland, "There'll Always Be an Encore," *McCall's,* Jan. 1964.

p. 189   "Imagine whipping" Judy Garland, "I'm Judy Garland—and This Is My Story," *New York Journal-American,* Feb. 25, 1964.

p. 189   Why did she persist Finch, *Rainbow,* p. 121.

p. 190   To have said Max de Schauensee, "Judy Garland Discloses Amazing Sense of Rhythm at Dell," *Philadelphia Evening Bulletin,* July 2, 1943.

p. 192   "Perhaps M-G-M" *The New York Times,* April 30, 1943.

p. 192   The story line Joseph Laitin, "Meet Sally Benson of 'Meet Me in St. Louis,' " *St. Louis Post-Dispatch,* June 3, 1960.

p. 193   "I don't think" Irving Brecher to GC.

p. 193   "A flaming rocket" M-G-M's description of Lucille Bremer is in "Meet Lucille Bremer," *Lion's Roar,* Feb. 1945.

p. 193   He saw great things Minnelli, *I Remember It Well,* p. 130.

p. 193   For once he took her side Ibid.

p. 193   But Freed was not only Fordin, *The World of Entertainment!,* p. 31.

p. 194   Mispronouncing words Irene Sharaff to GC.

p. 194   "I have something" Black, *Child Star,* pp. 319–20.

p. 194   "If you want to shave" Irving Brecher to GC.

p. 195   "I felt a lot of the stuff" Kobal, *Gotta Sing Gotta Dance,* p. 201.

p. 195   With Mayer's approval Ibid.

p. 195   So slowly Hay, *MGM,* p. 218.

p. 197   Accepting the role All times are taken from the production notes in the Freed Collection.

p. 197   The last week *Los Angeles Examiner,* Dec. 28, 1943.

p. 197   "I've had a violent headache" Al Jennings to GC.

p. 197   "Miss Judy Garland" Freed Collection.

p. 198   "I always have to be" Minnelli, *I Remember It Well,* p. 139.

p. 198   After one such delay Astor, *A Life on Film,* pp. 175–76.

p. 198   "I just went out there" Judy Garland, "My Story," magazine unknown, Jan. 1951.

p. 198   Though he did not say so Minnelli, *I Remember It Well,* p. 132.

p. 199   "You wished" Irene Sharaff to GC.

p. 199   As the cameras Minnelli, *I Remember It Well,* p. 132–34.

p. 199   Baffled and "scared" Judy Garland, "My Story," magazine unknown, Jan. 1951.

p. 199   Quiet and restrained Irving Brecher to GC for the account of Minnelli's frustration. (Although Brecher and Fred Finklehoffe were both listed as scriptwriters, Finklehoffe left midway through shooting, and Brecher clearly deserves the greater credit.) Judy's imitation of Minnelli is recounted in Christopher Finch's *Rainbow,* pp. 134–35.

p. 199 She did not enjoy   Evie Johnson to GC. Judy told Johnson of her feelings about Bremer.

p. 199 To prepare Margaret   O'Brien denied that her mother aroused tears by telling her that her dog was to be killed. Minnelli, however, said her mother told him that that was indeed her method and that one day, when Margaret was not responding as she usually did, she asked him to take on the unpleasant chore (Minnelli, *I Remember It Well,* p. 133). I have accepted Minnelli's memory over that of O'Brien, who was only six at the time.

p. 200 "It's awful!"   Al Jennings to GC.

p. 200 Like her, she said   Dorothy Raye to GC. Raye was a member of the cast of *Meet Me in St. Louis.*

p. 200 "He's real"   Dorothy Walsh (Morrison) to GC.

p. 200 "She was mad"   Ralph Blane to GC.

p. 200 To Drake's embarrassment   Buddy Pepper to GC. Drake ruefully confessed his failure to Pepper.

p. 201 "There was never"   Al Jennings to GC.

p. 201 But on an illness-plagued set   Ibid. All absences are documented in the production notes.

p. 201 Late in the afternoon   Al Jennings to GC.

p. 201 "Judy, I've been watching"   Frank, *Judy,* p. 199.

p. 202 On the simplest level   Edwin Schallert, "Old St. Louis Glows with Rare Charm," *Los Angeles Times,* Jan. 1, 1945.

p. 202 "Make a bee-line"   Bosley Crowther, "The Screen," *The New York Times,* Nov. 29, 1944.

p. 202 "If a picture doesn't haunt you"   Joe Hyams, "How Minnelli Won His 'Gigi' Oscar," *New York Herald Tribune,* May 4, 1959.

p. 202 Audiences thought so   I am not counting *Gone With the Wind,* which the studio distributed but did not make, as an M-G-M picture.

p. 203 "Arthur," Judy said   *Movie Marketplace,* March/April 1992.

CHAPTER 8. A MARRIAGE MADE IN METRO-GOLDWYN-MAYER

p. 205 Judy was uncharacteristically silent   Ralph Blane to GC. "Tootsie wootsie" is a phrase from *Meet Me in St. Louis*'s title song, "Meet Me in St. Louis, Louis."

p. 206 As their relationship   Al Jennings to GC.

p. 206 So it continued   Minnelli, *I Remember It Well,* p. 138.

p. 207   Vincente's father   I am basing my account of Minnelli's early life in part on information kindly provided me by Marilyn M. Cryder of the Delaware County (Ohio) Historical Society. I have also referred to Minnelli's autobiography, *I Remember It Well,* and to Stephen Harvey's biography, *Directed by Vincente Minnelli.* Where primary sources, such as an interview with Minnelli's father, conflict with Minnelli's autobiography, as is sometimes the case, I have accepted the primary sources.

p. 207   In 1902   Jesse J. Currier, "A Delaware Saga Moves from Torchlit Tent Show to Broadway," *Birth of American Holidays* (New Haven: Yale University Press, 1935).

p. 207   "If there is anything"   Ruth Arell, "From a Tent Show to the Show Place of the Nation," *Plain Dealer* (Cleveland), Dec. 30, 1934.

p. 208   "Here was a man"   Minnelli, *I Remember It Well,* p. 50.

p. 208   If Whistler violated   The black room is described in "The Minnelli Motif," *Lion's Roar,* Nov. 1945.

p. 209   "To tell the truth"   Kathryn Grayson to GC.

p. 209   "There was an absolute silence"   Dorothy Raye to GC.

p. 209   In New York   James Loyd to GC. Loyd was a close friend of Gaba's.

p. 210   Though Gaba stayed   Artie Shaw to GC. Shaw was the recipient of such confidences.

p. 210   His colleagues at M-G-M   Dorothy Tuttle Nitch to GC. She was a dancer in the Freed Unit.

p. 210   "It's not that at all!"   Dorothy Walsh (Morrison) to GC.

p. 210   *Oh, see the little violins*   Betsy Blair to GC.

p. 211   If Vincente's model   Marie Torre, "Life Has Done Right by Kay Thompson," *New York World-Telegram,* Oct. 28, 1948.

p. 211   Thus it was   Harry Niemeyer, "New Lease on Life for Kay Thompson," *St. Louis Post-Dispatch,* Nov. 11, 1947. This article provides background on Thompson.

p. 212   "I guess I've had"   Joe Mankiewicz to GC.

p. 213   "I don't know"   Fordin, *The World of Entertainment!,* p. 147.

p. 213   As far as Judy was concerned   Minnelli, *I Remember It Well,* p. 145.

p. 214   Although *The Clock*   "The New Pictures," *Time,* May 14, 1995.

p. 214   It did exactly   Agee, *Agee on Film,* p. 165.

p. 215   "Whenever you look"   Minnelli, *I Remember It Well,* p. 150.

p. 215   Returning to the set   One of the extras told me this story, asking not to be identified.

p. 216   His proudest moment   Ruth Arell, "From a Tent Show to the Show Place of the Nation," *Plain Dealer* (Cleveland), Dec. 30, 1934.

p. 216   "Vincente loved"   Lena Horne to GC.

p. 217   "Vincente saw something"   Irene Sharaff to GC.

p. 217   The jealous and watchful Hayworth   Leaming, *If This Was Happiness,* pp. 118–19.

p. 217   A similar mix-up   Ponedel's unpublished autobiography, in the author's possession.

p. 218   She missed the sound   Louella Parsons, "The Mystery of Judy Garland," *Photoplay,* July 1944.

p. 218   A quiet and reliable husband   Lucille Ryman Carroll to GC.

p. 218   Everyone at M-G-M   *Los Angeles Examiner,* Dec. 5, 1944.

p. 218   "I want Mr. Mayer"   Cal York, "The Marriage Dilemma of Judy Garland," *Photoplay,* May 1941.

p. 219   "We were now"   Minnelli, *I Remember It Well,* p. 158.

p. 219   "These were our happiest times"   Ibid., p. 166.

p. 219   "More than halfway"   Roberta Ormiston, "Halfway to Heaven," *Photoplay,* Oct. 1945.

p. 219   "Right away"   Ibid.

p. 219   "There were no strangers"   Quoted in Sam Roberts, "New York: 1945," *The New York Times,* July 30, 1995.

p. 220   Then, with her other hand   Minnelli, *I Remember It Well,* p. 158.

p. 220   "Whenever I came"   Roberta Ormiston, "Halfway to Heaven," *Photoplay,* Oct. 1945.

p. 220   Joining in Metro's campaign   Ibid.

p. 220   "Vincente was the only"   James Loyd to GC.

p. 220   Amazed at how quickly   Minnelli, *I Remember It Well,* p. 162.

p. 221   When the visitors   Ibid., p. 160.

p. 221   Denying a newspaper report   Roberta Ormiston, "Halfway to Heaven," *Photoplay,* Oct. 1945.

p. 221   Phoning California   Frank, *Judy,* p. 218.

p. 221   But delicate it was   Ponedel's unpublished autobiography, in the author's possession.

p. 222   "I like it so much"   Roberta Ormiston, "Halfway to Heaven," *Photoplay,* Oct. 1945.

p. 222   "Her desire"   Minnelli, *I Remember It Well,* p. 168.

p. 222   "I just don't know"   Dorothy Walsh (Morrison) to GC.

p. 223   A couple of months   *Movie Life,* date unknown, and Hopper's autobiography, *The Whole Truth and Nothing But,* pp. 125–26.

p. 223   When the pregnancy   Dona Massin to GC.

p. 223   With dark hair   Minnelli, *I Remember It Well,* p. 174.

p. 223   While there was no reason   *Los Angeles Examiner,* April 13, 1946.

p. 223   Two weeks later   *Los Angeles Examiner,* April 29, 1946.

p. 224 "Actually," she asserted   Edwin Schallert, "Judy Garland Achieves New Level of Poignancy," *Los Angeles Times,* date unknown, but around June 1, 1946.

p. 224 "She really loves"   Lynn Bowers, "Judy's Pin-Up Problem," magazine and date unknown.

p. 224 The studio was so eager   Some of the details of her contract are in the production notes for *The Pirate.* Freed Collection.

p. 224 "She's always said"   *Los Angeles Examiner,* Dec. 5, 1946.

p. 225 "The tension"   Judy Garland, as told to Joe Hyams, "The Real Me," *McCall's,* April 1957.

p. 225 *The Pirate* sounded like such fun   Minnelli, *I Remember It Well,* p. 177.

p. 225 In all, Judy was   Fordin, *The World of Entertainment!,* p. 212.

p. 226 At least two or three times   Wallace Worsley to GC.

p. 226 After keeping   Ibid.

p. 226 Other times amphetamines   Brecher, *Licit and Illicit Drugs,* pp. 278–301.

p. 226 "I'm going to burn"   Fordin, *The World of Entertainment!,* p. 208.

p. 226 She suffered   Hopper and Brough, *The Whole Truth and Nothing But,* p. 126.

p. 226 To retaliate   Minnelli, *I Remember It Well,* pp. 187–88.

p. 226 "How," wondered   Ibid.

p. 227 "Vincente and I"   Hirschhorn, *Gene Kelly,* p. 138.

p. 227 "Would have fallen asleep"   Freed Collection.

CHAPTER 9. A HELL IN HEAVEN

p. 229 To Judy, Joe Mankiewicz observed   Joe Mankiewicz to GC.

p. 229 Things had become   Ponedel's unpublished autobiography, in the author's possession.

p. 230 "As director"   Minnelli, *I Remember It Well,* p. 187.

p. 230 Those were harrowing   Ibid.

p. 230 Wallace Worsley could   Wallace Worsley to GC.

p. 230 At least twice   Freed Collection.

p. 230 Vincente never used   Kenny DuMain to GC. DuMain was a dancer in *The Pirate.*

p. 230 Those two rooms became   Minnelli, *I Remember It Well,* p. 168.

p. 231 Late at night   Kathryn Grayson to GC.

p. 232 Simmel was still unable   For the background of Hacker, see Farber and Green, *Hollywood on the Couch,* p. 80.

p. 232 "The mind is its own place"   *Paradise Lost,* bk. 1, ll. 254–55.

p. 232   Her friend Lee Gershwin   Frank, *Judy*, pp. 228–29.

p. 233   "After all"   Minnelli, *I Remember It Well*, p. 187.

p. 233   By the beginning   *Los Angeles Examiner*, Feb. 5, 1947.

p. 233   Judy, for her part   Brynner, *Yul*, pp. 43–44.

p. 234   In any event   Parsons's column was in the *Los Angeles Examiner*, Jan. 22, 1947. Vincente's reference to Judy's infatuations is in *I Remember It Well*, p. 208.

p. 234   Feeling that she could not   The friend who told me the story has asked me not to reveal her name.

p. 234   Eventually it reached the ears   Susann, *Valley of the Dolls*, p. 256.

p. 235   "Mama went away"   Minnelli, *I Remember It Well*, p. 190.

p. 236   On the recommendation   The name has since been changed to the Austen Riggs Center.

p. 236   Unlike the German-accented analysts   Knight's time in Kansas is recounted in Lawrence J. Friedman's *Menninger*, p. 213. The assessment of Knight as an analyst comes from Dr. Margaret Gibson, who underwent training analysis with him. Dr. Margaret Gibson to GC.

p. 237   "I can't stand it"   Knight related Judy's comment and his own response to Dr. Gibson, who relayed them to me.

p. 237   "She has made"   *Los Angeles Examiner*, Aug. 15, 1947.

p. 237   Giving in to her demand   Minnelli, *I Remember It Well*, pp. 194–95.

p. 238   "Look, sweetie"   Fordin, *The World of Entertainment!*, p. 225.

p. 238   "Listen, buster"   Finch, *Rainbow*, p. 159.

p. 238   Kelly's unrestrained scene-stealing   Kathryn Grayson to GC.

p. 239   "My compliments"   "Jympson Harman at the pictures," *The Evening News* (London), March 24, 1949. Harman was, of course, wrong about his dates when he used the phrase "last year."

p. 239   "Did he give me confidence?"   Giles, *Fred Astaire*, p. 17.

p. 240   "What am I"   Sylvia Sidney to GC. At the time, Judy regarded Sidney as her best friend.

p. 240   The skies became   Fordin, *The World of Entertainment!*, p. 234.

p. 240   Summing up   Irving Hoffman, "N.Y. Reviewers Go to Town for MGM's 'Easter Parade,' " *Hollywood Reporter*, July 1948 (exact date unknown).

p. 240   Praising Walters   "Pretentious flourishes" is from Howard Barnes's review in the *New York Herald Tribune*, July 1, 1948. A similar slap at Minnelli came from the *Daily Mail* (London), March 25, 1949.

p. 241   "How's it going"   Minnelli, *I Remember It Well*, p. 196.

p. 241   In *Easter Parade*   *The Observer* (London), March 27, 1949.

p. 241   "Who in hell"   Marion, *Off with Their Heads!*, p. 320.

p. 241   The million television sets   Friedrich, *City of Nets*, p. 343.

p. 242 "There are no" Parsons, *Tell It to Louella,* p. 61.

p. 243 So widespread Rosenstein, *Hollywood Leg Man,* p. 204.

p. 243 Of all the actors and actresses Astaire, who was also responsible for the success of *Easter Parade,* was not a Metro employee, as Judy was.

p. 243 After listing Harold Heffernan, "More Troubles—Film Stars in Spat," *St. Louis Post-Dispatch,* Oct. 15, 1948.

p. 244 Her showmanship Astaire, *Steps in Time,* p. 292.

p. 244 "If we can only do" Frank, *Judy,* p. 239.

p. 245 By now, Judy believed Judy Garland, "I'm Judy Garland—and This Is My Story." *New York Journal-American,* Feb. 26, 1964.

p. 245 At last Freed Collection.

p. 246 On July 19 Frank, *Judy,* p. 238.

p. 246 There she was, Rogers coyly told Eileen Creelman, "After 10 Years Ginger Puts On Dancing Shoes to Team Up With Fred, Her Old Partner," *Milwaukee Journal,* May 10, 1949.

p. 246 "I'm missing" "Special: Louella's Inside Story of Judy's Troubles," *Modern Screen,* date unknown.

p. 246 "I've been asked" Harrison Carroll, "Fear Judy Garland, Ginger Rogers Feud After Incident on Set," publication unknown, Sept. 27, 1948. A more dramatic version of this incident has Judy being led from the set, screaming insults at Rogers. I believe that Carroll's more restrained version, which was printed in his column immediately afterward, is likelier to be accurate.

p. 246 "What," he asked June Levant to GC.

p. 247 "I was crazy" Sylvia Sidney to GC.

p. 247 "I felt just like" Article by Hedda Hopper (title unknown), *Nashville Tennessean Magazine,* July 10, 1949.

p. 247 The difference Harold Heffernan, "More Troubles—Film Stars in Spat," *St. Louis Post-Dispatch,* Oct. 15, 1948.

p. 247 If anything Minnelli, *I Remember It Well,* pp. 197–98.

p. 247 "There was no one" Judy Garland, "There'll Always Be an Encore," *McCall's,* Jan. 1964.

p. 248 "I don't believe" Minnelli, *I Remember It Well,* p. 199.

p. 248 "Now, goddamn it" Frank, *Judy,* p. 240.

p. 249 As a tangible symbol Pasternak, *Easy the Hard Way,* pp. 227–30.

p. 249 "What did you do" Watson and Chapman, *Judy,* p. 54.

p. 249 Those high spirits Review, *The New York Times,* date unknown.

p. 250 Further rounds " 'Summertime' Enchanting; 'Lining' Bright Musical," *Hollywood Reporter,* date unknown.

p. 250 The unsurprising result Al Jennings to GC.

p. 251 Her marriage to Vincente Minnelli, *I Remember It Well,* p. 200.

p. 251   Relations turned   Ibid., p. 210.

p. 251   She was also intimidated   Guilaroff, *Crowning Glory,* p. 225.

p. 252   "This monster"   Kobal, *Gotta Sing Gotta Dance,* p. 226.

p. 252   "How could you"   Guilaroff, *Crowning Glory,* p. 225.

p. 252   In an effort   Frank, *Judy,* pp. 248–49.

p. 252   Once again   Al Jennings to GC.

p. 253   "What's the matter"   Guilaroff, *Crowning Glory,* p. 227.

p. 253   "My God"   Fordin, *The World of Entertainment!,* p. 276.

p. 253   Trying to give her   Freed Collection.

p. 253   "It's too late"   Fordin, *The World of Entertainment!,* p. 276.

p. 253   "I couldn't learn"   Judy Garland, "There'll Always Be an Encore," *McCall's,* Jan. 1964.

p. 254   "This is a tough one"   Frank, *Judy,* pp. 251–52.

p. 254   "We desire"   Ibid., p. 249.

p. 254   When Jennings   One of the two men, Les Peterson, Mickey Rooney's former publicist, described her reaction in an office memo the following day, May 11.

p. 255   "Where's everybody going?"   Al Jennings to GC.

p. 255   "For your information"   Freed Collection.

p. 255   "I'd stand on my head"   "Judy Garland out of Films for Year," *Los Angeles Examiner,* May 21, 1949.

p. 255   "Judy Garland out"   Ibid.

p. 255   "Certainly," said the indignant Parsons   *Los Angeles Examiner,* May 13, 1949.

CHAPTER 10. "I AM AN ADDICT"

p. 257   A year earlier   Frank, *Judy,* p. 299, and Fricke, *Judy Garland,* p. 113.

p. 257   "We did everything"   Lucille Ryman Carroll to GC.

p. 258   Each evening   Sylvia Sidney to GC.

p. 258   "I rammed it"   Noël Coward, *The Noël Coward Diaries,* p. 333.

p. 258   What else can you do   Virginia Bohlin, "What Else Could I Do?" *Motion Picture,* 1949 (exact month unknown).

p. 259   The day after   Evie Johnson to GC.

p. 259   Mornings would sometimes find her   Betsy Blair to GC.

p. 259   Like a dog   William Tuttle to GC.

p. 259   "It was a terrible thing"   Garland's tape-recorded reminiscences.

p. 259   On one particularly bleak day   Sylvia Sidney to GC.

p. 259   Sidney was also present   Ibid.

p. 260   After the debacle   Kotsilibas-Davis and Loy, *Myrna Loy,* p. 117.

p. 260 A defeated   Hopper and Brough, *The Whole Truth and Nothing But,* p. 127; Hedda Hopper, "Money Need Spurs Judy Garland On," *Los Angeles Times,* May 1949 (exact date unknown).

p. 260 "She is in a terribly bad way"   Hepburn, *Me,* p. 221.

p. 260 "What do you think"   Minnelli, *I Remember It Well,* pp. 210–11.

p. 261 She was, in her own words   Judy Garland, as told to Joe Hyams, "The Real Me," *McCall's,* April 1957.

p. 261 "By all means"   Garland's tape-recorded reminiscences.

p. 261 "There's nothing the matter"   Hopper and Brough, *The Whole Truth and Nothing But,* p. 127.

p. 261 After a few days   *Los Angeles Examiner,* June 7, 1949.

p. 262 "If I was cured"   Judy Garland, "There'll Always Be an Encore," *McCall's,* Jan. 1964. The story of Judy in the children's hospital is taken from this article and various other Garland reminiscences.

p. 263 There had been other   Judy Garland, "There'll Always Be an Encore," *McCall's,* Jan. 1964.

p. 263 "I didn't give a goddamn"   Garland's tape-recorded reminiscences.

p. 263 "I'll never work"   Harrison Carroll, "Judy Garland Home . . ." paper and date unknown.

p. 263 "We're going to bring"   Al Jennings to GC.

p. 264 "Excess Baggage"   "Poundage Nearly Costs Judy Garland a Role," *Los Angeles Times,* Nov. 1, 1949.

p. 264 "Please, just knock"   Oral history project, Southern Methodist University.

p. 265 At another point   Hirschhorn, *Gene Kelly,* p. 164.

p. 265 "Everybody is against me"   Guilaroff, *Crowning Glory,* p. 228.

p. 265 Carpenter even attempted   Carleton Carpenter to GC.

p. 265 Parsons said   Louella Parsons, "Judy Is Given 1 More Chance," *Los Angeles Examiner,* Nov. 1, 1949.

p. 266 "That's all"   Joe Pasternak interview, SMU Oral History Collection.

p. 266 "If you stop"   Hirschhorn, *Gene Kelly,* p. 163.

p. 266 "How dare this look"   Davis, *The Glamour Factory,* p. 249.

p. 266 Drinking too much   Saul Chaplin to GC.

p. 267 As was so often the case   Chaplin, *The Golden Age of Movie Musicals and Me,* p. 128.

p. 267 "Put her up"   Al Jennings to GC.

p. 267 If she could get   Minnelli, *I Remember It Well,* p. 217.

p. 268 one besotted literary critic   Fadiman, *Party of One,* p. 286.

p. 268 At the conclusion   Schary, *Heyday,* p. 215.

p. 269   Indeed, Judy may well   Frank, *Judy,* pp. 279–80.

p. 269   In what she was later to term   Judy Garland, "There'll Always Be an Encore," *McCall's,* Jan. 1964.

p. 270   "I've got an ulcer"   Frank, *Judy,* p. 274.

p. 270   "Oh," exclaimed Saul Chaplin   Saul Chaplin to GC.

p. 270   "IMPORTANT!"   Memo to Arthur Freed from Walter Strohm, the production manager, and other supervisors, July 6, 1950. Freed Collection.

p. 271   "If she doesn't"   Silverman, *Dancing on the Ceiling,* p. 126. Donen told his biographer (p. 125) that Judy did not come in at all during the week ending June 17. His memory is inaccurate. Though she was late on two of the five days, she worked every day, according to the production notes.

p. 271   In baseball   Hedda Hopper, "Great Garland Talent in Critical Jeopardy," *Los Angeles Times,* June 22, 1950.

p. 271   As soon as it heard   "Judy Happy over NBC Offer," *Hollywood Citizen-News,* June 24, 1950.

p. 271   "Cheer up"   New York *Daily News,* June 24, 1950.

p. 272   Smashing a water glass   Florabel Muir, New York *Daily News,* June 21, 1950.

p. 272   "I wanted"   " 'I Couldn't Solve Anything Running Away,' Says Judy," *Los Angeles Examiner,* Dec. 29. 1950.

p. 272   "Judy Garland Cuts Throat"   *Los Angeles Mirror,* June 20, 1950.

p. 272   "Judy Garland Slashes Throat"   *Los Angeles Times,* June 21, 1950.

p. 272   "Hollywood Heartbreaks"   *Los Angeles Evening Herald & Express,* June 21, 1950.

p. 273   But she was probably   Ponedel's unpublished autobiography, in the author's possession.

p. 273   Florabel Muir   *Los Angeles Mirror,* June 20, 1950.

p. 273   Also in Judy's corner   Hedda Hopper, "Great Garland Talent in Critical Jeopardy," *Los Angeles Times,* June 22, 1950.

p. 273   "Judy, as everyone"   Louella Parsons, "No Intent to Injure Self, Physician Says," *Los Angeles Examiner,* June 21, 1950.

p. 274   "Goddamnit," Alsop bitterly complained   Frank, *Judy,* p. 282.

p. 274   "I tried to do"   Louella Parsons, "No Intent to Injure Self, Physician Says," *Los Angeles Examiner,* June 21, 1950.

p. 274   "Judy's the bouncy type"   Virginia MacPherson, "Judy Garland's Suicide Try," *Los Angeles Evening Herald & Express,* June 21, 1950.

p. 274   "She apparently"   *Hollywood Citizen-News,* June 23, 1950.

p. 274   After talking to her   Hepburn, *Me,* pp. 221–22.

p. 274   Thus it was   "Judy Garland Slashes Throat After Film Row," *Los Angeles Times,* June 21, 1950.

p. 275   "Oh, golly"   Judy Garland, "The Plot Against Judy Garland," *Ladies' Home Journal,* August 1967.

p. 275   "You have your job"   "Judy Garland Slashes Throat After Film Row," *Los Angeles Times,* June 21, 1950.

p. 275   One of Florabel Muir's readers   Florabel Muir, "Friends Cheer Judy Garland. . . ." *Los Angeles Mirror,* June 21, 1950.

p. 275   At one of Los Angeles's evangelical churches   Russell, *Jane Russell,* pp. 110–11.

p. 276   Assuming she would go   Ponedel's unpublished autobiography, in the author's possession.

p. 276   "We're all"   "Times Square Crowds Cheer Judy Garland," *Los Angeles Examiner,* Sept. 6, 1950.

p. 276   Another outpouring   "Judy Garland's Brave Triumph," *Los Angeles Examiner,* Nov. 12, 1950.

p. 276   What they said   *Los Angeles Examiner,* June 30, 1950.

p. 276   Fifteen years   Hedda Hopper, "Judy Garland Obtains Release from Studio," *Los Angeles Times,* Sept. 30, 1950.

p. 277   "In an oblique"   Billy Rose, "Pitching Horseshoes," New York *Daily News,* Sept. 1, 1950.

p. 277   Anslinger knew   Anslinger and Oursler, *The Murderers,* pp. 164–66. In his book, Anslinger mentions neither Judy nor Schenck by name. In 1969, however, he confirmed that Judy was indeed the anonymous star mentioned in his book. (Art Petacque, "Ex–Narcotics Chief Tried to Get Judy Off Drugs," *New York Post,* June 20, 1969.) The executive to whom he spoke, the "head of the studio" in New York, could therefore have been no one but Schenck.

p. 278   For her, she said   Judy Garland, as told to Joe Hyams, "The Real Me," *McCall's,* April 1957.

p. 278   Nor did she consider   Silverman, *Dancing on the Ceiling,* p. 126.

p. 278   About Schary   Marion, *Off with Their Heads!,* p. 321.

p. 278   Less than a year   Crowther, *Hollywood Rajah,* p. 287.

p. 278   "I know how you and Nick"   Schary, *Heyday,* pp. 235–36.

CHAPTER 11. RESURRECTION

p. 281   In Hollywood   Memo from David Kapp, of Decca Records, to Isabelle Marks, Nov. 15, 1950. USC film collection.

p. 281   "The slate"   Judy Garland, "an open letter from judy garland," *Modern Screen,* Nov. 1950.

p. 281 "What I want to do" "Judy Garland Plans Long Screen Absence," *The New York Times,* Oct. 2, 1950.

p. 281 "Freddie," Judy said Frank, *Judy,* p. 289.

p. 282 "Judy needed" Shirley Emerson, "Made for Fame," *Motion Picture,* date unknown.

p. 282 "I'd obviously failed" Minnelli, *I Remember It Well,* pp. 238–39.

p. 283 "So characteristic" *Los Angeles Examiner,* Dec. 25, 1950.

p. 283 Her new love's name Sid Luft to GC.

p. 283 "She thought" Ibid.

p. 283 "I don't want" Frank, *Judy,* p. 291.

p. 284 As surprised as her friends Norman Garrett, "The Unvarnished Facts About Judy Garland's Husband," *Top Secret,* Dec. 1955.

p. 284 On two occasions "Bari Husband in Club Fight," *Los Angeles Examiner,* May 11, 1950.

p. 284 Now, back in Los Angeles The fight with the manager of the New York bar is detailed in Frank's *Judy,* p. 295; the fight outside the Mocambo was reported by the *Los Angeles Examiner* ("Starr's Nose Broken in Luft Fight," Nov. 1, 1950).

p. 284 "Boy, 12" Frank, *Judy,* p. 309.

p. 285 "Hey, Jew" Sid Luft to GC. Most of the details of Luft's background come from GC's conversations with Luft himself.

p. 285 "And if you keep" Ibid.

p. 285 "A professional" Joe Mankiewicz to GC.

p. 286 Pleased with her acquisition "Take a Letter, Mr. He-Man," *Los Angeles Examiner,* Jan. 12, 1938.

p. 286 "A slicker" Eleanor Lambert to GC.

p. 287 "During our marriage" " 'I Was Only Breadwinner,' Lynn Bari's Reply to Luft," *Los Angeles Examiner,* Aug. 29, 1947.

p. 287 This time "Divorce Won by Lynn Bari," *Los Angeles Examiner,* Dec. 27, 1950.

p. 287 "Judy, don't mess" Frank, *Judy,* p. 296.

p. 287 "Judy was so crazy" Ponedel's unpublished autobiography, in the author's possession.

p. 287 "What is happening" Jimmie Tarantino, "Judy Garland Victim of Hollywood Turmoil," *Hollywood Life,* Jan. 6, 1951.

p. 288 "The history of my life" Introduction to her Palladium act, April 9, 1951.

p. 289 Reviewing the performance Minnelli, *I Remember It Well,* p. 249.

p. 290 "Good lord, girl" A. E. Hotchner, "Judy Garland's Comeback," *Today's Woman,* Aug. 1952.

p. 290 "Honestly, I've hit" Magazine unknown, March 1951.

p. 290 "Plump and jovial" "Judy Garland's Weight Intrigues British Press," *Los Angeles Times,* April 6, 1951.

p. 290 "I may be awfully fat" *Time,* April 16, 1951.

p. 291 She felt, she said Buddy Pepper, "No Sad Songs for Judy," *Photoplay,* July 1951.

p. 291 And what of a Judy Garland Unknown London newspaper, Oct. 13, 1957.

p. 292 "That's one of the most" "Judy Garland Falls on Stage but Gets London Ovation," *Los Angeles Times,* April 10, 1951.

p. 292 Even before she concluded "British Cheer Judy Garland Despite Fall," *Los Angeles Times,* April 10, 1951.

p. 292 Her eyes misting "Judy Garland Gets Ovation in London Stage Debut," *New York Herald Tribune,* April 10, 1951.

p. 292 "I doubt" Milton Shulman, *Evening Standard* (London), May 2, 1951.

p. 292 When she had finished Buddy Pepper, "No Sad Songs for Judy," *Photoplay,* July 1951.

p. 292 "Where do I go" Unknown London newspaper, April 15, 1951.

p. 293 Though Sid did not know it "Judy Can Net 15G. . . ." *Variety,* Aug. 29, 1951.

p. 293 "Sid," said the eager Schwartz Frank, *Judy,* p. 328.

p. 294 On October 4 Spitzer, *The Palace,* pp. 212–18.

p. 294 At the Palace Green and Laurie, *Show Biz,* pp. 275–76.

p. 294 "The Palladium experience" Dorothy Kilgallen, "Rainbow for Judy," *American Weekly,* Dec. 30, 1951.

p. 294 "She's going to be" Jean Bach to GC.

p. 295 Fortunately for her Figures from the National Climatic Data Center, Asheville, N.C.

p. 295 When she was through Bill Smith, "Palace Return to Two-a-Day Is Showman's Dream; Judy a Smash," *The Billboard,* Oct. 27, 1951.

p. 295 Vaudeville, dead Newspaper unknown.

p. 296 "Who can follow" Harrison Carroll, "Cornel Won't Raise Picture Price. . . ." paper and date unknown.

p. 296 At the end of that final show Phyllis Battelle, "Tears Flow, 3296 Sing N.Y. Tribute to Judy," *Los Angeles Examiner,* Feb. 25, 1952.

p. 296 "Shout; for the Lord" Joshua 6:16.

p. 296 "Where lay" Fadiman, *Party of One,* pp. 286–88.

p. 297 "I have a machine" Judy Garland, "I'm Judy Garland—and This Is My Story," *New York Journal-American,* Feb. 28, 1964.

p. 297 The sound that emerged Pleasants, *The Great American Popular Singers,* p. 286.

p. 297   She put the words   SMU Oral History Collection.

p. 298   "I really mean"   *Show Business Illustrated.* Nov. 14, 1961.

p. 298   "The whole premise"   Charles Petzold, "Judy Can't Sing Rock 'n' Roll," *Courier-Post* (Camden, N.J.), July 14, 1967.

p. 298   Nora Bayes   Stein, *American Vaudeville,* p. 268.

p. 298   Her second secret   Doug Kelly to GC. Kelly was a friend of Judy's in the late fifties and sixties.

p. 298   "It was like breathing"   Judy Garland, "There'll Always Be an Encore" (conclusion), *McCall's,* Feb. 1964.

p. 299   "A dominant aspect"   From *The Lives of a Cell.* Quoted in Marilyn Berger, "Lewis Thomas, Whose Essays Clarified . . ." *The New York Times,* Dec. 4, 1993.

p. 299   Stroke victims   For background on this subject, I recommend the following articles: Rick Weiss, "Music Therapy," *Washington Post,* July 5, 1994; Sandra Blakeslee, "The Mystery of Music: How It Works in the Brain," *The New York Times,* May 16, 1995; Joel L. Swerdlow, "Quiet Miracles of the Brain," *National Geographic,* June 1995.

p. 300   "I'm nervous"   John L. Scott, "Judy, Picture of Health . . ." *Los Angeles Times,* April 20, 1952.

p. 300   Hundreds waited   "Judy Garland Sets Record Ticket Call," *Los Angeles Times,* April 14, 1952.

p. 301   Most of Los Angeles   Cordell Hicks, "Vaudeville Fans Rub Elbows with Society Folk . . ." *Los Angeles Times,* April 22, 1952.

p. 301   The Garland show   Ibid.

p. 302   "If Judy had a dollar"   *Motion Picture,* July 1951.

p. 302   "So Sid Luft"   "Rainbow or Rain of Woes?" *Movie Stars Parade,* Sept. 1952.

p. 302   The first disquieting sign   Ponedel's unpublished autobiography, in the author's possession, and an interview by GC with Buddy Pepper.

p. 302   "I had a beer"   "Judy Garland Reported in Traffic Crash-Melee," *Los Angeles Times,* Oct. 2, 1951.

p. 303   Most of the charges   "Luft Fined on Drunk Charge," *Los Angeles Times,* Dec. 14, 1951.

p. 303   Still more ammunition   "Rainbow or Rain of Woes?" *Movie Stars Parade,* Sept. 1952.

p. 303   "You're bitter"   Ibid.

p. 303   In 1951   "Judy Garland Pays Heed to Warrant," *Los Angeles Times,* May 15, 1952.

p. 303   Sid handled her finances   "Lynn Bari, Judy Garland in Battle over Money, Love," *Los Angeles Herald Express,* May 15, 1952.

p. 303   Sid had been   "Judy Garland Marriage to Sid Luft Disclosed," *Los Angeles Times,* June 12, 1952.

p. 304   "None of this"   Joan King Flynn, "Someone to Watch Over Me," *Modern Screen,* April 1952.

p. 304   "I want to protect"   Ibid.

p. 304   "I know what's going on"   Ponedel's unpublished autobiography, in the author's possession.

CHAPTER 12. A GOLDEN DEAL AND A DEATH IN A PARKING LOT

p. 307   "Your artistry goes"   *Variety,* Oct. 9, 1952.

p. 308   "I used to be scared"   "Florabel Muir Reporting," *Los Angeles Mirror,* Sept. 8, 1952.

p. 308   With most of their money   *1997 CCH Index—Standard Federal Tax Reports,* p. 11,549.

p. 309   "I'm not beautiful"   Hugh Martin to GC. The hairdresser, Ernest Adler, told the story to Martin.

p. 309   Although she seemed   The account of her depression and attempted suicide is taken from Gerold Frank's *Judy,* pp. 359–62.

p. 309   Forest Lawn's Little Church   "Rites Conducted for Judy Garland's Mother," *Los Angeles Times,* Jan. 9, 1953.

p. 309   Their mother had always been   Johnny Thompson to GC. Thompson was Jimmie's husband; he attended the funeral.

p. 310   All Judy   Johnny Thompson to GC.

p. 310   Watching the two   Garland's tape-recorded reminiscences.

p. 310   So strained   Minnelli, *I Remember It Well,* p. 189.

p. 310   Eventually, silence gave way   Ibid.

p. 310   Most of her friends   Frank, *Judy,* p. 368.

p. 310   Before long   *Los Angeles Examiner,* June 26, 1950.

p. 311   "Judy didn't want"   Johnny Thompson to GC.

p. 311   "Poor Ethel!"   Dorothy Walsh (Morrison) to GC.

p. 311   "I'll tell you"   Finch, *Rainbow,* p. 190.

p. 311   Hurt and insulted   Paul V. Coates column, *Los Angeles Mirror,* May 2, 1952.

p. 311   "Garland's Maw"   *Los Angeles Mirror,* June 12, 1952.

p. 312   "Judy and I"   Sheilah Graham, "Just for Variety," *Variety,* June 16, 1952.

p. 312   "If you have a daughter"   Sheilah Graham, "Hollywood," *New York Daily Mirror,* July 20, 1952.

p. 312   "My mother's a fucking riveter"   Harry Rubin to GC. Judy made the remark to Rubin.

p. 312 "What have I done" Frank, *Judy,* p. 366.
p. 312 Americans have always idealized Theodore Roosevelt is quoted in Victoria Secunda's *When You and Your Mother Can't Be Friends,* p. 43.
p. 312 Apparently forgetting Lazar with Tapert, *Swifty,* pp. 151–52.
p. 313 "Maybe I fulfilled" Judy Garland, "There'll Always Be an Encore," *McCall's,* Jan. 1964.
p. 314 As she grew older Garland's tape-recorded reminiscences.
p. 314 "Nothing, ever" Simone de Beauvoir, *A Very Easy Death,* p. 34.
p. 314 "A career" The final script of *A Star Is Born* by Moss Hart, dated October 7, 1953.
p. 314 *A Star Is Born,* she told Sidney Skolsky column, *New York Post,* Oct. 31, 1954.
p. 315 Belying his cynical screen reputation Sperber and Lax, *Bogart,* p. 466.
p. 315 "Those two alley cats" Haver, *A Star Is Born,* p. 71. Haver's 300-page book offers the most exhaustive account of the making of the movie.
p. 315 "Understand Want Me" Telegram from Flynn to Steve Trilling, Aug. 8, 1953. Warner Bros. Collection, USC.
p. 315 "James Mason Set" Telegram from Steve Trilling to Flynn, Aug. 15, 1953. Warner Bros. Collection, USC.
p. 317 Cukor grumbled Haver, *A Star Is Born,* p. 133.
p. 317 "Don't worry" Gene Allen to GC.
p. 317 Hired to supervise Harry Rubin to GC. Rubin is the chief source for most of the episodes he witnessed or was involved in.
p. 318 "Miss Garland phoned" Memo from Eric Stacey to various Warner Bros. executives, Nov. 19, 1953. Warner Bros. Collection, USC.
p. 318 "It scared me" George Cukor interview, Columbia Oral History Collection.
p. 318 Judy would complain Haver, *A Star Is Born,* pp. 184–85.
p. 318 "Judy, you've given us" Gilbert Perkins to GC. Perkins was playing tennis with Warner and heard his end of the conversation. A column item of Dec. 29, 1953 (newspaper unknown), also mentioned their conversation.
p. 318 "A charming fellow" Warner, *My First Hundred Years in Hollywood,* pp. 316–19.
p. 319 *A Star Is Born* was a movie George Cukor to Moss Hart, March 30, 1954. Warner Bros. Collection, USC.
p. 319 "Big mistake" Haver, *A Star Is Born,* p. 190.
p. 320 "Don't let 'em" *Los Angeles Examiner,* Aug. 5, 1954.

p. 320 "Neither the human mind"   Haver, *A Star Is Born,* p. 196.

p. 320 "He snipped"   Haver, *A Star Is Born,* p. 197.

p. 320 "What you should do"   Frank, *Judy,* p. 383.

p. 321 What, Noël Coward was to ask   Coward, *The Noël Coward Diaries,* pp. 248–49.

p. 321 Extravagance also marked   Edwin Schallert, " 'Star Is Born' Hit at Lavish Premiere," *Los Angeles Times,* Sept. 30, 1954.

p. 322 "Brilliantly staged"   "New Day for Judy," *Life,* Sept. 13, 1954.

p. 322 "One of the grandest"   Bosley Crowther, *The New York Times,* Oct. 12, 1954.

p. 322 "A mighty long"   "The New Pictures," *Time,* Oct. 25, 1954.

p. 322 Though James Mason   Ibid.

p. 322 "It is a curious instinct"   Ed Sullivan, "Toast of the Town," *New York Mirror,* Oct. 13, 1954.

p. 322 Jack Warner   Although Warner Bros. claimed *A Star Is Born* cost $6 million to produce (not counting distribution and advertising expenses), Ronald Haver reckoned its cost at $5,019,770. Only *Duel in the Sun,* which cost $5,225,324, was more expensive. Haver, *A Star Is Born,* p. 203.

p. 324 "I'll kill you"   Sperling and Millner, *Hollywood Be Thy Name,* pp. 284–85.

p. 324 "*Marvelous* things"   George Cukor interview, SMU Oral History Collection.

p. 324 "It is our destiny"   Quoted in Phillip Lopate, "A Master Who Confounded the Categorizers," *The New York Times,* Nov. 16, 1997.

p. 325 "Congratulations!"   Letter to Jack Warner, Oct. 14, 1954. Warner Bros. Collection, USC.

p. 325 These remarks proved prophetic   Haver, *A Star Is Born,* p. 217.

p. 325 Judy, the Associated Press had said   Bob Thomas, Associated Press report, June 1954 (exact date unknown).

p. 326 "This is the biggest robbery"   Aline Mosby, "Judy Feels 'Grateful' Over Oscar Condolences," *New York World Telegram,* April 12, 1955.

p. 326 "There should have been"   Louella Parsons, " 'Little Joe' Judy's Joy," *Los Angeles Examiner,* April 1, 1955.

p. 326 "I admit"   "Judy vs. Grace—Could Be a Tie," *New York Journal-American,* March 20, 1955.

p. 326 "It confirmed her belief"   Bacall, *By Myself,* p. 220.

p. 327 "It's only the beginning"   "20,000 Hail Judy Garland at 'Star Is Born' Premiere," *New York Herald Tribune,* Sept. 30, 1954.

p. 327 "We did too much"   Sid Luft interview for a Garland television documentary, p. 34 of transcript. A copy is in the possession of the author.

p. 327 Hauled into court "Luft Wins Court Round in Lynn Bari Battle," *Los Angeles Herald-Examiner,* Jan. 27, 1955.

p. 328 To prevent Joe Hyams, "Judy Garland—Problem Girl," *New York Herald Tribune,* Sept. 21, 1956.

p. 328 All the love Zuma Palmer, "Radio-Television" *Hollywood Citizen-News,* Sept. 21, 1955.

p. 329 "I've never seen her" Mike Connolly, "Rambling Reporter," *Hollywood Reporter,* July 1956 (exact date unknown).

p. 329 She attracted Joe Hyams, "Judy Garland Star in Night Club, Too," *New York Herald Tribune,* Aug. 10, 1956.

p. 329 "New York is good" Associated Press report by William Glover, Nov. 10, 1956.

p. 330 "I'm sorry" "Protecting the Source," *Time,* Jan. 12, 1959.

p. 330 "I must say" Dorothy Kilgallen, "The Voice of Broadway," *New York Journal-American,* Jan. 14, 1959.

p. 330 In October *Variety,* Oct. 23, 1957.

p. 330 "Why don't you" Earl Wilson, "Screaming Dispute with Patron Leads to Canceled Contract," *Los Angeles Mirror News,* Jan. 2, 1958.

p. 330 "Judy Garland Quits" *Los Angeles Mirror News,* Jan. 2, 1958.

p. 331 "Judy Garland," wrote Earl Wilson, "Judy Walks Out in New Uproar," *Los Angeles Mirror News,* March 31, 1958.

p. 331 Moved by what it termed "Judy's Comeback," *Los Angeles Examiner,* July 26, 1958.

CHAPTER 13. THE HOLMBY HILLS RAT PACK

p. 333 "I've found" Helen Hover Weller, "Judy Garland's Untold Story," *Movie Stars,* January 1955.

p. 334 "Sid took a castle" Harry Rubin to GC.

p. 335 "If the light" Bacall, *By Myself,* p. 220.

p. 335 "Do you sing?" Lazar with Tapert, *Swifty,* p. 153.

p. 335 "And I can tell you" Joe Hyams, *Bogie,* p. 11.

p. 335 If the gibes Bogart, *Bogart,* p. 45.

p. 335 But talent, Bogart added Bacall, *By Myself,* p. 221.

p. 336 "What fun" Ibid., p. 222.

p. 337 Based on an actual case Johnson, *Flashback,* p. 261.

p. 337 After reading the script Nunnally Johnson interview, Columbia Oral History Collection.

p. 337 "Schizophrenic," he explained Cameron Shipp, "The Star Who Thinks Nobody Loves Her," *Saturday Evening Post,* April 2, 1955.

p. 337 "Wonderful in every way" Crane, *Detour,* p. 134.

p. 338　"Shh!"　Harry Rubin to GC.

p. 338　During shooting　Irene Sharaff to GC.

p. 338　Later, for the picture's premiere　Michael Woulfe to GC.

p. 338　"You're a gumshoe"　Frank, *Judy*, p. 398.

p. 338　"Where are they?"　Paul Sand to GC. Sand played opposite Judy in her famous tramp number. He heard her screams.

p. 339　"I think Sid"　Kendis Rochlen, "Candid Kendis," *Los Angeles Mirror-News,* Feb. 3, 1955.

p. 339　Theirs was more than a marriage　Joe Hyams, "Mr. and Mrs. Luft, Inc.," *New York Herald Tribune,* Sept. 18, 1956.

p. 339　In September 1956　Ibid.

p. 340　When Judy visited　C. Z. Guest to GC.

p. 340　Owed six times that　Warner, *My First Hundred Years in Hollywood,* pp. 316–20.

p. 340　So strained were the Lufts' finances　Frank, *Judy*, pp. 430–32.

p. 341　Unable to do either　"Judy Garland Goes to Court in Sack," *Rocky Mountain News* (Denver), April 5, 1958.

p. 341　"So I'm broke"　" 'Broke—But I'll Get Along,' Says Judy," *New York Journal-American,* April 1, 1958.

p. 341　The *Los Angeles Examiner*　Jack Lotto, "Judy Garland, Luft Row Over Money," *Los Angeles Examiner,* April 1, 1958.

p. 341　Much also went　Harry Rubin to GC.

p. 341　By contrast　Associated Press dispatch, June 26, 1953.

p. 342　"It's nouveau riche"　Sid Luft to GC.

p. 342　Before the Bogarts bought　Bacall, *By Myself,* p. 197.

p. 342　"Listen," he said　Harry Rubin to GC.

p. 342　Many of those greenbacks　Hopper and Brough, *The Whole Truth and Nothing But,* p. 128, and *Time,* Feb. 13, 1956.

p. 342　Indeed, one of Jack Warner's complaints　Warner, *My First Hundred Years in Hollywood,* pp. 316–19. All of Warner's remarks are quoted from his autobiography.

p. 342　How much money　*Time,* Feb. 13, 1956.

p. 342　"Nobody ever made money"　Florabel Muir, "Judy Sues Sid, Blames the Nags," New York *Daily News,* Feb. 4, 1956.

p. 342　"I love Sid"　Louella Parsons, "Judy, Luft Reconciled," *Los Angeles Examiner,* Feb. 7, 1956.

p. 342　"You could hear her"　Robert Street to GC.

p. 343　Years later　Sid Luft to GC.

p. 343　Despite a prenuptial property agreement　Though the agreement was dated October 10, 1953, more than a year after their marriage, it memorialized an oral agreement they said they had entered into before their marriage. It was filed with the Los Angeles County Clerk on August 11, 1958.

p. 343   Sid was both too proud   Sid Luft to GC.

p. 343   In a 1955 article   Judy Garland, "How *Not* to Love a Woman," *Coronet,* Feb. 1955.

p. 343   On a trip to Long Island   Anne Ford Johnson to GC.

p. 343   At a party at Chasen's   Mike Connolly, "Rambling Reporter," *Hollywood Reporter,* date unknown.

p. 343   Claiming that Sid had beaten her   Evie Johnson to GC.

p. 344   "Get that son-of-a-bitching pig"   Harry Rubin to GC.

p. 344   What Sid did   Sid denied that Judy had extramarital affairs during their marriage.

p. 344   Frank Sinatra   Harry Rubin to GC.

p. 344   And off   Ibid.

p. 345   Though no one   "Divorce Bug Again Bites Judy Garland," *Los Angeles Mirror-News,* Feb. 26, 1958.

p. 345   Alleging, for the first time in public   *Frances Gumm Luft vs. Michael Sidney Luft.* Los Angeles Superior Court, March 4, 1958.

p. 345   "You don't know"   Otash, *Investigation Hollywood!,* pp. 159–70. The head of the detective unit, Otash devotes a chapter in his memoirs to the Garland-Luft dispute.

p. 345   Still, no one was surprised   Louella Parsons, "Judy Garland, Luft in Reconciliation," *Los Angeles Examiner,* April 15, 1958.

p. 347   He must be the leader   Judy Garland, "How *Not* to Love a Woman," *Coronet,* Feb. 1955.

p. 347   Despite the bouquets   Shana Alexander, "Judy's New Rainbow," *Life,* June 2, 1961.

p. 347   "I don't think"   Frank, *Judy,* p. 451.

p. 347   For seven weeks   This was probably accomplished, medical experts tell me, by the use of intravenous diuretics, which caused the fluids to be excreted in her urine. It is also possible, though less likely, that the fluids were removed by the insertion of a needle directly into her abdomen.

p. 347   "You want to know"   Jane Ardmore, "Judy," *The American Weekly,* Oct. 1, 1961.

p. 348   "He's magnetic"   "She Will Tell the Troops—and Maybe Even the Marines," *Daily Mail* (London), Oct. 21, 1960.

p. 348   "I was liked"   Shana Alexander, "Judy's New Rainbow," *Life,* June 2, 1961.

p. 348   "I want to get off"   Frank, *Judy,* p. 455.

p. 349   She enjoyed weekends   William Hickey, "21 Years After the Wizard of Oz . . ." *Daily Express* (London), July 15, 1960.

p. 349   Indeed, Coward was   Coward's deference to Judy is noted in Philip Hoare's biography, *Noël Coward.*

p. 349   "You are probably"   "A Redbook Dialogue: Noël Coward and Judy Garland," *Redbook,* Nov. 1961.

p. 349   It was, rather   Judy Garland, "Show Page," *Sunday Guardian* (London), Sept. 11, 1960.

p. 349   "Now we know"   "Judy's a Hit in Gay Paree," *Los Angeles Mirror,* Oct. 12, 1960.

p. 350   "Greetings, Mr. President"   John Moynihan, *Evening Standard* (London), Nov. 9, 1960.

p. 351   At Sid's behest   Contract between Judy Garland and Freddie Fields Associates, December 1960; a copy is in the possession of the author.

p. 351   In exchange for handing Fields   *Michael Sidney Luft vs. Creative Management Associates, Ltd.* Los Angeles Superior Court, No. 832,645, July 22, 1964.

p. 351   He was not a job hunter   Jody Jacobs, "Fields' Day," *Women's Wear Daily,* June 1, 1970.

p. 351   His plan for Judy   " 'Revitalized' Judy Garland to Star in London Musical Prior to B'way," *Variety,* December 1960 or early January 1961.

p. 352   "With Freddie"   Shana Alexander, "Judy's New Rainbow," *Life,* June 2, 1961.

p. 352   "You two are the luckiest"   James Goode, "Judy," *Show Business Illustrated,* Nov. 14, 1961.

p. 352   "Leopold and Loeb"   James Goode, "Judy," *Show Business Illustrated,* Oct. 31, 1961.

p. 352   Nineteen sixty-one   Jane Ardmore, "Judy," *The American Weekly,* Oct. 1, 1961.

p. 352   The first critic   Virgil Miers, "Phenomenal Night with Judy as She Sings as Never Before," *Dallas Times Herald,* Feb. 22, 1961.

p. 353   "He treated me"   Sheilah Graham, "Everything Looks Good to Judy Garland Today," newspaper unknown, March 4, 1962.

p. 353   "Damn it"   Shana Alexander, "Judy's New Rainbow," *Life,* June 2, 1961.

p. 353   "she gave the impression"   Stanley Kramer to GC.

p. 353   "Judy Doesn't Fizzle"   General background on the Hollywood Bowl concert can be found in the *Hollywood Bowl* magazine, July

1993, which features an interview with Patton S. Moore, the Bowl's superintendent of operations for forty-two years.

p. 354   Two decades earlier   Sidney Skolsky, "Judy Smash Hit at Bowl," *Hollywood Citizen-News,* Sept. 18, 1961.

p. 354   After the twenty-fourth number   " 'Judy at Carnegie' Capacity $20,100; Star's Surcharged Gotham Comeback," *Variety,* April 1961 (exact date unknown).

p. 355   Carnegie Hall was validation   "Hollywood: The New New Garland," *Time,* Nov. 16, 1962.

p. 356   But the most   Rowland Barber, "The Eternal Magic of Judy Garland," *Good Housekeeping,* January 1962.

p. 356   The screenwriter   Mayo Simon to GC.

CHAPTER 14. A STANDOFF AT THE STANHOPE AND THE END OF SID

p. 360   As impressed as everyone else   "Hollywood: The New New Garland," *Time,* Nov. 16, 1962.

p. 360   It was they   Judy Garland, "I'm Judy Garland—and This Is My Story," *New York Journal-American,* Feb. 28, 1964.

p. 360   "I hated"   Ibid.

p. 360   "I'd never seen"   Ibid.

p. 360   She took a walk   Ibid.

p. 361   Showing up nonetheless   Frank, *Judy,* p. 485.

p. 361   "You know, Sid"   Ibid., pp. 484–86.

p. 361   "You just don't"   Sheilah Graham, "Judy Rolls with the Punches," *New York Mirror,* Feb. 25, 1962.

p. 362   "That boy"   Abby Mann to GC.

p. 362   "I'm going"   Ibid.

p. 363   The standoff   All the New York tabloids carried reports of the day's events.

p. 363   "Get in"   James C. Lischetti to GC.

p. 363   "My marriage"   "Judy's Next Step May Be Divorce," *New York Post,* May 1, 1962.

p. 363   Claiming that she had hired   Mike Pearl, "Judy Hired Goons—Luft," *New York Post,* May 1, 1962. Sid's claim that he was held down was stoutly denied by James C. Lischetti, one of the two detectives who helped Judy at the Stanhope Hotel. James C. Lischetti to GC.

p. 364   "Whatever happens"   Dorothy Kilgallen, "The Voice of Broadway" *New York Journal-American,* May 8, 1962.

p. 364   Neither the edict   "Judy Puts All-Night Guard On Hidden Children," *Daily Express* (London), May 1, 1962.

p. 364   As she started work   Bogarde, *Snakes and Ladders,* p. 252.

p. 364   Bogarde had been hearing   Unless otherwise noted, all Dirk Bogarde's comments were made to GC.

p. 364   Judy, he wrote   Bogarde, *Snakes and Ladders,* p. 235.

p. 365   But Judy saw nothing   Dirk Bogarde to GC.

p. 366   "The theory was"   Mayo Simon to GC.

p. 367   "I'm a goddamned star"   Bogarde, *Snakes and Ladders,* p. 255.

p. 367   "Who is smoking"   Ronald Neame reported this to GC.

p. 367   "Here's Dorothy Adorable"   Dirk Bogarde to GC.

p. 368   "You said the first take"   Ronald Neame to GC.

p. 368   Banging her head   Dirk Bogarde to GC.

p. 368   "How are things"   Mayo Simon to GC.

p. 369   Though few other actors   Bogarde, *Snakes and Ladders,* pp. 260–61.

p. 370   "Only if you"   Paar, *P.S. Jack Paar,* p. 159.

p. 371   "David Begelman told me"   Judy Garland, "I'm Judy Garland—and This Is My Story," *New York Journal-American,* Feb. 28, 1964.

p. 371   "The Great Garland Gamble"   Dwight Whitney, "The Great Garland Gamble," *TV Guide,* Oct. 19–25, 1963.

p. 371   "Thousands of dollars"   Richard Warren Lewis, "The TV Troubles of Judy Garland," *Saturday Evening Post,* Dec. 9, 1963. I have relied, for much of my discussion of *The Judy Garland Show,* on this long, comprehensive and thoughtful article.

p. 372   His mistake   Ibid.

p. 372   "Judy Garland will have to"   St. Johns, *Some Are Born Great,* p. 68.

p. 372   "I was stunned"   Richard Warren Lewis, "The TV Troubles of Judy Garland," *Saturday Evening Post,* Dec. 9, 1963.

p. 372   "In TV"   Dwight Whitney, "The Great Garland Gamble," *TV Guide,* Oct. 19–25, 1963.

p. 373   "It's pure"   "Question Mark," *Newsweek,* Nov. 4, 1963.

p. 373   "We're in trouble"   Richard Warren Lewis, "The TV Troubles of Judy Garland," *Saturday Evening Post,* Dec. 9, 1963.

p. 374   "It's like"   Frank, *Judy,* p. 528.

p. 374   "I won't have"   Sanders, *Rainbow's End,* p. 272.

p. 375   "You were just great"   Ibid., p. 363.

p. 375   In the obscure recesses   Judy Garland, "How *Not* to Love a Woman," *Coronet,* Feb. 1955.

p. 375   "I am not a man"   Alfred T. Hendricks, "Hollywood Nightclub Fight Wins the Consolation Prize," *New York Post,* Nov. 23, 1962.

p. 376   "Judy Garland and Sid Luft Reconciled"   *Los Angeles Times,* Feb. 14, 1963.

p. 376   "Her orchestra"   Mort Lindsey to GC.

p. 376   Thrilled merely   Mayo Simon to GC. Simon was present at a couple of these rehearsals.

p. 377   "David's the boss"   Tom Cooper to GC.

p. 377   "I just want"   Alma Cousteline to GC.

p. 377   Begelman had, for example   Jeanie Kasindorf, "The Incredible Past of David Begelman," *New West,* Feb. 13, 1978. Kasindorf's article provides a summary of Steinberg's report.

p. 378   After his friends   McClintick, *Indecent Exposure,* p. 42. McClintick's book is an excellent study of Begelman and his sordid dealings.

p. 378   "Look," she told Sid   Jeanie Kasindorf, "The Incredible Past of David Begelman," *New West,* Feb. 13, 1978.

p. 379   Milton must   *Paradise Lost,* bk. 2, ll. 109–111, 112; compare bk. 1, ll. 490–92.

CHAPTER 15. A NEED TO BE NEEDED AND A DISASTER IN MELBOURNE

p. 381   "I need"   Garland's tape-recorded reminiscences. The lover was Mark Herron.

p. 381   One ugly-minded lover   The lover made that boast to a source who requested anonymity.

p. 382   "A marriage of sounds"   Jim Gregory, "Andre Phillipe: 'My Dates with Judy Garland,' " *Movieland & TV Times,* July 1964.

p. 382   On a photograph   *People,* Aug. 21, 1978.

p. 382   At the very beginning   Ray Aghayan to GC.

p. 382   Tall, slim and good-looking   Ron Saw, "Judy Slogs the Rainbow Trail," *Sydney Mirror,* May 12, 1964.

p. 382   After graduation   Lanchester, *Elsa Lanchester Herself,* p. 178.

p. 383   Judy, said Harry M. Miller   Miller's comment comes from a 1992 Australian television documentary, *Judy in a Land Called Oz,* produced and directed by Ian Stahlhut.

p. 383   All three   "Judy Is over the Rainbow," *Sydney Mirror,* May 11, 1964. I am grateful to Francis Gallagher for loaning me hundreds of clippings from Australian newspapers and magazines regarding Judy's tour.

p. 383   "A Knockout"   "Judy Garland a Knockout at Stadium," *Sydney Morning Herald,* May 14, 1964.

p. 383   "More, more"   Margaret Jones, "10,000 Fans Cheer Judy Garland," *Sydney Sunday Herald,* May 17, 1964.

p. 384   Nor did Judy sweeten the mood   Charles Higham to GC. Higham also described the scene for an Australian magazine: "Just Like the Good Old Days," *The Bulletin* (Sydney), May 23, 1964.

p. 384   "Look this way"   Ron Saw, "Judy Slogs the Rainbow Trail," *Sydney Mirror,* May 12, 1964.

p. 384   "Oh, my God"   Charles Higham to GC.

p. 384   "Listen, they're going crazy"   Miller himself has offered two widely different versions of what he said. In view of Judy's response, I believe that Herron's version, which he gave in a BBC television documentary, is almost certainly the accurate one.

p. 384   She took too many   *Judy in a Land Called Oz,* produced and directed by Ian Stahlhut.

p. 385   Her bizarre behavior   "Is Judy Mentally Ill?" *Melbourne Truth,* May 30, 1964.

p. 386   "We can't go"   Frank, *Judy,* p. 540.

p. 386   "She's getting mean"   Mark Herron to John Carlyle, June 3, 1964.

p. 386   "I've been told"   "Judy Garland in London for Vacation," *Los Angeles Times,* July 1, 1964.

p. 387   Like them, she was expected   My description of this episode is taken from newspaper accounts in both Britain and the United States.

p. 387   "Beautiful" was the word   Mark Herron to John Carlyle, Sept. 4, 1964.

p. 387   "They say"   Ibid.

p. 387   "Judy Begins"   Morris Duff, *Toronto Star,* Feb. 15, 1965.

p. 388   "My, I'm a loud lady"   "Show Business," *Time,* Aug. 18, 1967.

p. 389   "The boys in the tight trousers"   Ibid.

p. 389   Turned down for several movie roles   Herman, *Showtune,* pp. 143–46.

p. 389   But her second appearance   John Carlyle to GC.

p. 390   Angry because ABC had forced her   Rick Sommers to GC. Sommers, who was acting as Judy's go-between, also witnessed the near destruction of the dressing room.

p. 390   "I don't want to be"   Judy Garland, "The Plot Against Judy Garland," *Ladies' Home Journal,* Aug. 1967.

p. 391   The morning   Abby Mann to GC.

p. 391   "Oh, Bill"   William O. Harbach to GC.

p. 391   That she could not get it   Ibid. The watchman described the scene to Harbach.

p. 391   "I think I've got"   Garland's tape-recorded reminiscences.

p. 392   "When you have lived"   Ivor Davis, "When You've Lived the Life I've Lived . . ." *Daily Express* (London), March 11, 1967.

p. 392   That may have been true   *Hollywood Citizen-News,* Dec. 2, 1966.

p. 393   "Mr. Herron"   Alma Cousteline to GC.

p. 393   In addition to all her other pills   Ibid.

p. 393   "They took me"   Garland's tape-recorded reminiscences.

p. 394   "I'm goddamned mad!"   Ibid.

p. 394   Too timid   Alma Cousteline and Rick Sommers to GC.

p. 394   Responding to a frantic   Tom Green to GC.

p. 395   Only later   Ibid.

p. 395   On another occasion   Alma Cousteline to GC.

p. 395   "It hadn't been"   Judy Garland, "The Plot Against Judy Garland," *Ladies' Home Journal,* Aug. 1967.

p. 395   "I used to hear"   Ibid.

p. 395   When Steve McQueen   Luft, *Me and My Shadows,* pp. 147–52.

p. 395   The cottage survived   "Judy Fights Fire with Tumbler," *Honolulu Advertiser,* April 15, 1965.

p. 396   Her second arson   My account of the Rockingham Avenue fire draws on interviews with Alma Cousteline, Rick Sommers and Esteban Matison, all of whom were there at the time.

p. 396   Picking up the nearest weapon   Alma Cousteline to GC.

p. 396   Is it any surprise   Nancy Barr to GC. Barr spent many hours with Judy and her children, particularly in New York.

p. 396   "It will stop"   Luft, *Me and My Shadows,* p. 157.

p. 397   "Daddy, I've got Mama"   Doug Kelly to GC.

p. 397   "That bitch!"   Alma Cousteline to GC.

p. 397   "Biblical looking"   Jane Ardmore, "Judy," *The American Weekly,* Oct. 1, 1961.

p. 397   "Take care"   Scottie Singer to GC. Singer was a young woman whom David Begelman recruited to look after Judy in the summer of 1963.

p. 397   "Judy Garland Is Broke,"   Walter Benson, "I'm Broke, Admits Judy Garland," *National Enquirer,* Dec. 18, 1966.

p. 398   "Everybody was dropping her"   Tom Green to GC. Unless otherwise noted, Green's comments, and anecdotes concerning him, come from interviews with GC.

p. 398   "She's just like"   Ibid.

p. 398   His Garland collection   Hazel Flynn, "Museum May Get Garland Collection," *Hollywood Citizen-News,* Dec. 5, 1962.

p. 399   "I have the unfortunate habit"   Judy Garland, "There'll Always Be an Encore," *McCall's,* Feb. 1964.

p. 400   "How long"   Walter Benson, "I'm Broke, Admits Judy Garland," *National Enquirer,* Dec. 18, 1966.

p. 400   During her absence   Alma Cousteline to GC.

p. 400   "Lionel, go get"   Ibid.

p. 400   Others did what they could   Nancy Barr to GC. Barr was one of those who helped out.

p. 400   "Where did all my money go?"   Tom Green to GC.

p. 400   Judy kept a scrapbook   Doug Kelly to GC.

p. 400   "Every time she'd get"   Ibid.

p. 400   But when she was alone   Garland's tape-recorded reminiscences.

p. 401   "Ole Man Sorrow's come"   The song was "My Man's Gone Now," with lyrics by DuBose Heyward and music by George Gershwin. Before beginning, Judy herself noted that she had never sung it before.

CHAPTER 16. LIZA—RIDING A WHIRLWIND

p. 403   "Liza's a girl"   Frank Meyer, "Liza's a Girl Riding a Whirlwind . . . and Loving It," *Miami Beach Daily Sun,* June 12, 1966. "Eel de France," New York *Daily News,* Nov. 13, 1966.

p. 404   Years later   Robert Street to GC. Street was present on several such occasions.

p. 404   "Can you believe"   Donald Brooks to GC.

p. 404   Judy liked to brag   Judy Garland, "There'll Always Be an Encore" (conclusion), *McCall's,* Feb. 1964.

p. 404   "It was as though"   Mike Selsman to GC.

p. 405   "It's just so terrible"   Eleanor Lambert to GC.

p. 405   The child most like her   "A Redbook Dialogue: Noël Coward and Judy Garland," *Redbook,* Nov. 1961.

p. 405   Liza, too   Liza Minnelli to GC. I interviewed Liza Minnelli extensively for a cover story I wrote for *Time* magazine in 1972: "The New Miss Show Biz: Liza Minnelli," *Time,* Feb. 28, 1972.

p. 406   Sitting at a piano   *Time* file for ibid.

p. 406   Just as Judy   Judy Wieder, "Liza Minnelli," *The Advocate,* Sept. 3, 1996.

p. 406   Unbeknownst to either   Stephen MacLean to GC. MacLean is the author of *Peter Allen,* a definitive biography.

p. 407   A huge betrayal   Judy Wieder, "Liza Minnelli," *The Advocate,* Sept. 3, 1996.

p. 407   Not only did she   "Show Business," *Time,* March 9, 1970.

p. 407   She decided   "The New Miss Show Biz: Liza Minnelli," *Time,* Feb. 28, 1972.

p. 407   Peter answered   Nancy Barr to GC.

p. 407   "Miss Minnelli"   Alma Cousteline to GC.

p. 407   When Judy was able   John Carlyle to GC.

p. 407   "She doesn't want"   Alma Cousteline to GC.

p. 407   After hearing Lorna   Doug Kelly to GC.

p. 407   "Liza has a lot"   John Carlyle to GC.

p. 408   With no one else   Frank, *Judy,* p. 584.

p. 408   Anybody but Sid   *U.S. v. Raymond R. Filiberti,* No. 63 CR 295, District Court for the Southern District of New York, March 27, 1963, and subsequently.

p. 408   She undertook   Vincent Canby, "Judy Garland Sets the Palace Alight," *The New York Times,* Aug. 1, 1967.

p. 408   "It was as if"   Ernie Santosuosso, "Familiar Blockbuster Magic," *The Boston Globe,* Sept. 1, 1967.

p. 408   "We have taken"   Min S. Yee, "100,408 Hear Judy on Common," *The Boston Globe,* Sept. 1, 1967.

p. 408   Though Judy initiated   Thomas Pugh and Paul Meskil, "Judy Flies to London, Steals Home," New York *Daily News,* Oct. 12, 1967; Frank, *Judy,* p. 595.

p. 409   "Almost a classic"   Rowland Posey to John Carlyle, Feb. 22, 1968. I am indebted to Carlyle for a copy of this letter.

p. 409   Unless her bill   Tom Green to GC.

p. 409   Hauled off   Tom Green, "Judy Garland Put Me in Jail," *Photoplay,* April 1969.

p. 409   Once unleashed   Nancy Barr to GC.

p. 410   "I loved Judy"   Ibid.

p. 410   Probably not knowing   Luft, *Me and My Shadows,* p. 210.

p. 410   The result   Ibid., pp. 198–99.

p. 410   That was followed   Ibid., pp. 211–13.

p. 410   "I'm a great star"   Nancy Barr to GC.

p. 411   The woman who had always   John Carlyle to GC.

p. 411   John Carlyle put her up   Tucker Fleming and Charles Williamson to GC.

p. 411   New candidates   Meyer, *Heartbreaker.* My account of Judy's affair with Meyer is largely based on his memoir, which details their weeks together day by day and often hour by hour.

p. 412   Within days   Ibid., p. 156.

p. 412   "She can be greater"   Ibid., p. 50.

p. 412   Jackie Scott   Jackie Scott to GC.

p. 412   For Meyer, the exaltation   John Meyer to GC.

p. 412   "I finally got"   Earl Wilson, "It Happened Last Night," *New York Post,* Dec. 17, 1968.

CHAPTER 17. MINE EYES HAVE SEEN THE GLORY

p. 415   "A cool cat"   John Springer to GC.

p. 415   "If I was dead broke"   Unless otherwise noted, Mickey Deans's statements were made to GC.

p. 416   Given to blunt talk   Mickey Deans to GC.

p. 416   With a new man   James Green, "Judy Wows 'Em with Songs to Remember," *Evening News* (London), Dec. 31, 1968.

p. 416   "If you can't"   "Jeers Rout Judy Garland on Hostile London Stage," *Hollywood Citizen-News,* Jan. 24, 1969.

p. 417   "God is"   Mickey Deans to GC.

p. 417   "I can't understand it"   Clive Hirschhorn, "Judy Weds but Stars Stay Away," *Sunday Express* (London), March 16, 1969.

p. 417   "Of course"   *Expressen* (Stockholm), exact date unknown. I am grateful to Francis Gallagher for providing me with Judy's Scandinavian reviews and their English translations.

p. 417   "She was almost broke"   David Wigg, "Judy Garland Gets 500 Theaters as Wedding Gift," *Memphis* (Tenn.) *Press-Scimitar,* March 15, 1969.

p. 417   To reap   Ibid.

p. 418   "I don't know"   Clive Hirschhorn, "Judy Weds but Stars Stay Away," *Sunday Express* (London), March 16, 1969.

p. 419   That was the vista   Matthew West to GC.

p. 419   "Mickey takes care"   Arthur Helliwell, "Happy at Last!" *The People* (London), Jan. 5, 1969.

p. 419   "Judy was in love"   Robert Jorgen to GC. Jorgen also made the trip to Garfield, N.J.

p. 419   Other times, West   Matthew West to GC.

p. 420   "I've got to get away"   Tucker Fleming and Charles Williamson to GC.

p. 420   "Look, Madame Gumm"   John Carlyle to GC.

p. 420   Thus it was   Charles Cochran to GC.

p. 420   "If you'd only come"   Deans and Pinchot, *Weep No More, My Lady,* p. 217.

p. 420   Thrilled to have become   Robert Jorgen to GC.

p. 420   After her ebullient performance   Review by Sven Borre, *Ekstrabladet* (Copenhagen), March 26, 1969.

p. 420   "I have a husband"   Matthew West to GC.

p. 420   The life she had led   Meyer, *Heartbreaker,* p. 204.

p. 421   One witness   Allan Davis to GC.

p. 421 "I've lost" John Carlyle to GC.

p. 421 "Take very good care" Robert Jorgen to GC.

p. 422 "You take a couple" Judy Garland, "The Plot Against Judy Garland," *Ladies' Home Journal,* Aug. 1967.

p. 422 Following the inquest My account of Judy's funeral is taken from the numerous stories in the New York newspapers.

p. 423 "And now abideth" I Cor. 13.

p. 423 If she had a choice Arthur Helliwell, "Happy at Last!" *The People* (London), Jan. 5, 1969.

p. 423 "Bonne Nuit" Pierre Luc, "Bonne Nuit, Judy Garland," *Montreal-Matin,* June 25, 1969.

Bibliography

Adams, Edie, and Robert Windeler. *Sing a Pretty Song: The "Offbeat" Life of Edie Adams, Including the Ernie Kovacs Years.* New York: William Morrow, 1990.

Agee, James. *Agee on Film: Reviews and Comments by James Agee.* New York: McDowell, Obolensky Inc., 1958.

Allyson, June, with Frances Spatz Leighton. *June Allyson.* New York: G. P. Putnam's Sons, 1982.

Anslinger, Harry J., and Will Oursler. *The Murderers.* New York: Avon Books, 1961.

Antelope Valley Press. *Remember When . . . 75th Anniversary Edition.* Palmdale, Calif.: April 22, 1990.

Arce, Hector. *The Secret Life of Tyrone Power.* New York: William Morrow, 1979.

Arden, Eve. *Three Phases of Eve.* New York: St. Martin's Press, 1985.

Astaire, Fred. *Steps in Time.* New York: Harper & Brothers, 1959.

Astor, Mary. *A Life on Film.* New York: Delacorte, 1971.

Bacal, Jacques, and Louise Sloane. *ABC of Divorce.* New York: E. P. Dutton, 1947.

Bacall, Lauren. *By Myself.* New York: Knopf, 1979.

Bach, Bob, and Ginger Mercer, eds. *Our Huckleberry Friend: The Life, Times and Lyrics of Johnny Mercer.* Secaucus, N.J.: Lyle Stuart, 1982.

Baxter, Anne. *Intermission: A True Story.* New York: G. P. Putnam's Sons, 1976.

Beauchamp, Cari. *Without Lying Down: Frances Marion and the Powerful Women of Early Hollywood.* New York: Scribner, 1997.

Behrman, S. N. *People in a Diary.* Boston: Little, Brown, 1972.

Benchley, Nathaniel. *Humphrey Bogart.* Boston: Little, Brown, 1975.

Benson, Sally. *Meet Me in St. Louis.* New York: Random House, 1942.

Bergreen, Laurence. *As Thousands Cheer: The Life of Irving Berlin.* New York: Viking, 1990.

Bernhardt, Sarah. *Memories of My Life.* 1908. Reprint, New York: Benjamin Blom, 1968.

Black, Shirley Temple. *Child Star: An Autobiography*. New York: McGraw-Hill, 1988.

Boese, Donald L. and Richard R. Cain. *Grand Rapids Companion*. Grand Rapids, Minn.: Grand Rapids Centennial Committee, Itasca County Historical Society, 1991.

Bogarde, Dirk. *Snakes and Ladders*. London: Grafton Books, 1979.

Bogart, Stephen Humphrey. *Bogart: In Search of My Father*. New York: Dutton, 1995.

Bordman, Gerald. *Jerome Kern: His Life and Music*. New York: Oxford University Press, 1980.

Braudy, Leo. *The World in a Frame: What We See in Films*. New York: Doubleday, 1976.

———. *The Frenzy of Renown: Fame and Its History*. New York: Oxford University Press, 1986.

Brecher, Edward M., and the Editors of *Consumer Reports*. *Licit and Illicit Drugs*. Boston: Little, Brown, 1972.

Brochu, Jim. *Lucy in the Afternoon: An Intimate Memoir of Lucille Ball*. New York: William Morrow, 1990.

Brynner, Rock. *Yul: The Man Who Would Be King*. New York: Simon & Schuster, 1989.

Buckley, Gail Lumet. *The Hornes*. New York: Knopf, 1986.

Burk, Margaret Tante. *Are the Stars out Tonight? The Story of the Famous Ambassador and Cocoanut Grove*. Los Angeles: Round Table West, 1980.

Cahn, Sammy. *I Should Care: The Sammy Cahn Story*. New York: Arbor House, 1974.

Callow, Simon. *Charles Laughton: A Difficult Actor*. New York: Grove Press, 1987.

Carey, Gary. *All the Stars in Heaven: Louis B. Mayer's M-G-M*. New York: E. P. Dutton, 1981.

———, with Joseph L. Mankiewicz. *More About All About Eve: A Colloquy*. New York: Random House, 1972.

Carmichael, Hoagy, with Longstreet, Stephen. *Sometimes I Wonder: The Story of Hoagy Carmichael*. New York: Farrar, Straus and Giroux, 1965.

Cary, Diana Serra. *Hollywood's Children: An Inside Account of the Child Star Era*. Boston: Houghton Mifflin, 1979.

Cerra, Julie Lugo. *Culver City: The Heart of Screenland*. Chatsworth, Calif.: Windsor Publications, in cooperation with the Culver City Chamber of Commerce, 1992.

Chandler, Raymond. *Raymond Chandler Speaking*. Edited by Dorothy Gardiner and Kathrine Sorley Walker. Boston: Houghton Mifflin, 1962.

Chaplin, Saul. *The Golden Age of Movie Musicals and Me.* Norman, Okla.: University of Oklahoma Press, 1994.

Clark, Tom, with Dick Kleiner. *Rock Hudson: Friend of Mine.* New York: Pharos Books, 1989.

Coleman, Emily R. *The Complete Judy Garland: The Ultimate Guide to Her Career in Films, Records, Concerts, Radio, and Television, 1935–1969.* New York: Harper & Row, 1990.

Considine, Shaun. *Bette & Joan: The Divine Feud.* New York: E. P. Dutton, 1989.

Cooper, Jackie, with Dick Kleiner. *Please Don't Shoot My Dog: The Autobiography of Jackie Cooper.* New York: William Morrow, 1981.

Coward, Noël. *The Noël Coward Diaries.* Edited by Graham Payn and Sheridan Morley. Boston: Little, Brown, 1982.

Cram, Mildred. *Forever.* New York: Knopf, 1935.

Crane, Cheryl, with Cliff Jahr. *Detour: A Hollywood Story.* New York: Arbor House, 1988.

Cronyn, Hume. *A Terrible Liar: A Memoir.* Toronto: Key Porter Books, 1991.

Crowther, Bosley. *The Lion's Share: The Story of an Entertainment Empire.* New York: E. P. Dutton, 1957.

———. *Hollywood Rajah: The Life and Times of Louis B. Mayer.* New York: Holt, Rinehart and Winston, 1960.

Dahl, David, and Barry Kehoe. *Young Judy.* New York: Mason/Charter, 1975.

Davidson, Bill. *Spencer Tracy: Tragic Idol.* New York: E. P. Dutton, 1987.

Davis, Ronald L. *The Glamour Factory: Inside Hollywood's Big Studio System.* Dallas: Southern Methodist University Press, 1993.

Day, Beth. *This Was Hollywood: An Affectionate History of Filmland's Golden Years.* New York: Doubleday, 1960.

De Beauvoir, Simone. *A Very Easy Death.* New York: G. P. Putnam's Sons, 1966.

Dewey, Donald. *James Stewart: A Biography.* Atlanta: Turner Publishing, 1996.

DeWitt, William H., ed. *Antelope Valley History: The Journal of the West Antelope Valley Historical Society* 1 (1988).

Dietz, Howard. *Dancing in the Dark.* New York: Quadrangle, 1974.

Dody, Sandford. *Giving Up the Ghost: A Writer's Life Among the Stars.* New York: M. Evans and Co., 1980.

Dooley, Roger. *From Scarface to Scarlett: American Films in the 1930s.* New York: Harcourt Brace Jovanovich, 1981.

Drutman, Irving. *Good Company: A Memoir, Mostly Theatrical.* Boston: Little, Brown, 1976.

Duke, Vernon. *Passport to Paris.* Boston: Little, Brown, 1955.

Dunning, John. *Tune In Yesterday: The Ultimate Encyclopedia of Old-Time Radio, 1925–1976.* Englewood Cliffs, N.J.: Prentice-Hall, 1976.

Edwards, Anne. *Judy Garland: A Biography.* New York: Simon & Schuster, 1975.

Eells, George. *The Life That Late He Led: A Biography of Cole Porter.* New York: G. P. Putnam's Sons, 1967.

Engstead, John. *Star Shots: Fifty Years of Pictures and Stories by One of Hollywood's Greatest Photographers.* New York: E. P. Dutton, 1978.

Eyman, Scott. *Ernst Lubitsch: Laughter in Paradise.* New York: Simon & Schuster, 1993.

Fadiman, Clifton. *Party of One.* New York: World, 1955.

Farber, Stephen, and Marc Green. *Hollywood on the Couch: A Candid Look at the Overheated Love Affair Between Psychiatrists and Moviemakers.* New York: William Morrow, 1993.

Finch, Christopher. *Rainbow: The Stormy Life of Judy Garland.* New York: Grosset & Dunlap, 1975.

Firestone, Ross. *Swing, Swing, Swing: The Life and Times of Benny Goodman.* New York: Norton, 1993.

Fishgall, Gary. *Against Type: The Biography of Burt Lancaster.* New York: Scribners, 1995.

Fordin, Hugh. *The World of Entertainment!: Hollywood's Greatest Musicals.* New York: Doubleday, 1975.

Frank, Gerold. *Judy.* New York: Harper & Row, 1975.

Fricke, John. *Judy Garland: World's Greatest Entertainer.* New York: Holt, 1992.

———, Jay Scarfone, and William Stillman. *The Wizard of Oz: The Official 50th Anniversary Pictorial History.* New York: Warner Books, 1989.

Friedman, Lawrence J. *Menninger: The Family and the Clinic.* New York: Knopf, 1990.

Friedrich, Otto. *City of Nets: A Portrait of Hollywood in the 1940's.* New York: Harper & Row, 1986.

Furia, Philip. *Ira Gershwin: The Art of the Lyricist.* New York: Oxford University Press, 1996.

Gabler, Neal. *An Empire of Their Own: How the Jews Invented Hollywood.* New York: Crown, 1988.

Gardner, Ava. *Ava: My Story.* New York: Bantam Books, 1990.

Gay, Peter. *Freud: A Life for Our Time.* New York: Norton, 1988.

Geist, Kenneth L. *Pictures Will Talk: The Life and Films of Joseph L. Mankiewicz.* New York: Scribners, 1978.

Giles, Sarah. *Fred Astaire: His Friends Talk.* New York: Doubleday, 1988.

Grady, Billy. *The Irish Peacock: The Confessions of a Legendary Talent Agent.* New Rochelle, N.Y.: Arlington House, 1972.

Graham, Sheilah. *Hollywood Revisited.* New York: St. Martin's Press, 1985.

Granger, Stewart. *Sparks Fly Upward.* New York: G. P. Putnam's Sons, 1981.

Green, Abel, and Joe Laurie, Jr. *Show Biz from Vaudeville to Video.* New York: Holt, 1951.

Green, Stanley. *Encyclopaedia of the Musical Film.* New York: Oxford University Press, 1981.

Greenberg, Harvey R., M.D. *The Movies on Your Mind: Film Classics on the Couch, from Fellini to Frankenstein.* New York: Saturday Review Press/E. P. Dutton, 1975.

Grenfell, Joyce. *In Pleasant Places.* London: Macmillan London, 1979.

Guerry, Moultrie, with additional chapters by Arthur Ben Chitty and Elizabeth N. Chitty. *Men Who Made Sewanee.* Sewanee, Tenn.: The University of the South Press, 1981.

Guilaroff, Sydney, as told to Cathy Griffin. *Crowning Glory: Reflections of Hollywood's Favorite Confidant.* Los Angeles: General Publishing, 1996.

Guiles, Fred Lawrence. *Tyrone Power: The Last Idol.* New York: Doubleday, 1979.

Gussow, Mel. *Darryl F. Zanuck: Don't Say Yes Until I Finish Talking.* New York: Da Capo Press, 1971.

Hadleigh, Boze. *Conversations with My Elders.* New York: St. Martin's Press, 1986.

———. *Hollywood Lesbians.* New York: Barricade Books, 1994.

Harmetz, Aljean. *The Making of the Wizard of Oz.* New York: Knopf, 1977; reprint, Limelight Editions, 1987.

Harnne, Howard, ed. *The Judy Garland Souvenir Songbook.* New York: Chappel & Co., 1975.

Harris, Warren G. *Gable and Lombard.* New York: Simon & Schuster, 1974.

Harvey, Stephen. *Directed by Vincente Minnelli.* New York: The Museum of Modern Art and Harper & Row, 1989.

Haver, Ronald. *A Star Is Born: The Making of the 1954 Movie and Its 1983 Restoration.* New York: Knopf, 1988.

Hay, Peter. *MGM: When the Lion Roars.* Atlanta: Turner Publishing, 1991.

Heimann, Jim. *Out With the Stars: Hollywood Nightlife in the Golden Era.* New York: Abbeville Press, 1985.

Henstell, Bruce. *Sunshine and Wealth: Los Angeles in the Twenties and Thirties.* San Francisco: Chronicle Books, n.d.

Hepburn, Katharine. *Me: Stories of My Life.* New York: Knopf, 1991.

Herman, Jan. *A Talent for Trouble: The Life of Hollywood's Most Acclaimed Director.* New York: G. P. Putnam's Sons, 1995.

Herman, Jerry, with Marilyn Stasio. *Showtune: A Memoir by Jerry Herman.* New York: Donald I. Fine, 1996.

Higham, Charles. *Charles Laughton: An Intimate Biography.* New York: Doubleday, 1976.

———. *Merchant of Dreams: Louis B. Mayer, M.G.M. and the Secret Hollywood.* New York: Donald I. Fine, 1993.

Hirschhorn, Clive. *Gene Kelly: A Biography.* New York: St. Martin's Press, 1984.

Hoare, Philip. *Noël Coward: A Biography.* New York: Simon & Schuster, 1995.

Hoffman, Muriel Martens. *Leaves from the Gum Tree: A History of the Gum Family in America.* Fairbury, Ill.: Cornbelt Press, 1984.

Hoopes, Roy. *When the Stars Went to War: Hollywood and World War II.* New York: Random House, 1994.

Hopper, Hedda, and James Brough. *The Whole Truth and Nothing But.* New York: Doubleday, 1963.

Housman, A. E. *The Collected Poems of A. E. Housman.* New York: Holt, 1940.

Howse, Elisabeth O. *Falling Stars.* Apparently privately printed, n.d.; © 1960 by Mrs. G. S. Ridley, Jr.

Hughes, Mary B. *Hearthstones: The Story of Historic Rutherford County Homes.* Murfreesboro, Tenn.: Mid-South Publishing Co., 1942.

Huston, John. *An Open Book.* New York: Knopf, 1980.

Hyams, Joe. *Bogie: The Biography of Humphrey Bogart.* New York: New American Library, 1966.

Isherwood, Christopher. *Diaries, Volume One: 1939–1960.* New York: HarperCollins, 1996.

Jablonski, Edward. *Harold Arlen: Happy with the Blues.* Garden City, N.Y.: Doubleday, 1961.

———. *Gershwin.* New York: Doubleday, 1987.

Jasen, David A. *Tin Pan Alley.* New York: Donald I. Fine, 1988.

Johnson, Nora. *Flashback: Nora Johnson on Nunnally Johnson.* New York: Doubleday, 1979.

Johnson, Nunnally. *The Letters of Nunnally Johnson.* Dorris Johnson and Ellen Leventhal, eds. New York: Knopf, 1981.

Kashner, Sam and Nancy Schoenberger. *A Talent for Genius: The Life and Times of Oscar Levant.* New York: Villard, 1994.

Kaufman, Gerald. *Meet Me in St. Louis.* London: British Film Institute, 1994.

Keyes, Evelyn. *Scarlett O'Hara's Younger Sister: My Lively Life in and out of Hollywood.* Secaucus, N.J.: Lyle Stuart, 1977.

King, Alan, with Chris Chase. *Name-dropping: The Life and Lies of Alan King.* New York: Scribners, 1996.

Kobal, John. *Gotta Sing Gotta Dance: A History of Movie Musicals.* New York: Exeter Books, 1983.

———. *People Will Talk.* New York: Knopf, 1985.

Koestenbaum, Wayne. *The Queen's Throat: Opera, Homosexuality, and the Mystery of Desire.* New York: Poseidon Press, 1993.

Kotsilibas-Davis, James, and Myrna Loy. *Myrna Loy: Being and Becoming.* New York: Knopf, 1987.

Lacey, Robert. *Grace.* New York: G. P. Putnam's Sons, 1994.

Lahr, John. *Notes on a Cowardly Lion: The Biography of Bert Lahr.* New York: Knopf, 1969.

Lake, Veronica, with Donald Bain. *Veronica.* New York: Citadel Press, 1971.

Lamarr, Hedy. *Ecstasy and Me: My Life as a Woman.* New York: Fawcett, 1967.

Lambert, Gavin. *On Cukor.* New York: G. P. Putnam's Sons, 1972.

———. *Norma Shearer.* New York: Knopf, 1990.

Lamour, Dorothy, with Dick McInnes. *My Side of the Road.* Englewood Cliffs, N.J.: Prentice-Hall, 1980.

Lanchester, Elsa. *Elsa Lanchester Herself.* New York: St. Martin's Press, 1983.

Langley, Noel, Florence Ryerson, and Edgar Allan Woolf. *The Wizard of Oz: The Screenplay.* Michael Patrick Hearn, ed. New York: Delta Books, 1989.

Lasky, Jesse L., with Don Weldon. *I Blow My Own Horn.* New York: Doubleday, 1957.

Laurie, Joe, Jr. *Vaudeville: From the Honky-Tonks to the Palace.* New York: Holt, 1953.

Lawford, Patricia Seaton, with Ted Schwarz. *The Peter Lawford Story: Life with the Kennedys, Monroe and the Rat Pack.* New York: Carroll & Graf, 1988.

Lazar, Irving, with Annette Tapert. *Swifty: My Life and Good Times.* New York: Simon & Schuster, 1995.

Leaming, Barbara. *Orson Welles: A Biography.* New York: Viking, 1985.

———. *If This Was Happiness: A Biography of Rita Hayworth.* New York: Viking, 1989.

Lees, Gene. *Inventing Champagne: The Worlds of Lerner and Loewe.* New York: St. Martin's Press, 1990.

Leigh, Janet. *There Really Was a Hollywood.* New York: Doubleday, 1984.

Leigh, Wendy. *Liza: Born a Star.* New York: Dutton, 1993.

Lerner, Alan Jay. *The Street Where I Live.* New York: Norton, 1978.

LeRoy, Mervyn, as told to Dick Kleiner. *Mervyn LeRoy: Take One.* New York: Hawthorn Books, 1974.

Levant, Oscar. *The Memoirs of an Amnesiac.* New York: G. P. Putnam's Sons, 1965.

Levy, Emanuel. *George Cukor, Master of Elegance: Hollywood's Legendary Director and His Stars.* New York: William Morrow, 1994.

Levy, Shawn. *King of Comedy: The Life and Art of Jerry Lewis.* New York: St. Martin's Press, 1996.

Luft, Lorna. *Me and My Shadows: A Family Memoir.* New York: Pocket Books, 1998.

MacLean, Stephen. *Peter Allen: The Boy from Oz.* Sydney: Random House, 1996.

Madsen, Axel. *Stanwyck.* New York: HarperCollins, 1994.

————. *The Sewing Circle: Hollywood's Greatest Secret, Female Stars Who Loved Other Women.* New York: Birch Lane Press, 1995.

Marion, Frances. *Off with Their Heads!: A Serio-Comic Tale of Hollywood.* New York: Macmillan, 1972.

Marshall, James. *Santa Fe: The Railroad That Built an Empire.* New York: Random House, 1945.

Marx, Samuel. *Mayer and Thalberg: The Make-Believe Saints.* New York: Random House, 1975.

———— and Joyce Vanderveen. *Deadly Illusions: Jean Harlow and the Murder of Paul Bern.* New York: Random House, 1990.

Mast, Gerald. *Can't Help Singin': The American Musical on Stage and Screen.* Woodstock, N.Y.: Overlook Press, 1987.

Maxwell, Elsa. *R.S.V.P.: Elsa Maxwell's Own Story.* Boston: Little, Brown, 1954.

McClintick, David. *Indecent Exposure: A True Story of Hollywood and Wall Street.* New York: William Morrow, 1982.

McGilligan, Pat, ed. *Backstory 2: Interviews with Screenwriters of the 1940s and 1950s.* Berkeley, Calif.: University of California Press, 1991.

McGilligan, Patrick. *George Cukor: A Double Life.* New York: St. Martin's Press, 1991.

Meryman, Richard. *Mank: The Wit, World and Life of Herman Mankiewicz.* New York: William Morrow, 1978.

Minnelli, Vincente, with Hector Arce. *I Remember It Well.* New York: Doubleday, 1974.

Mordden, Ethan. *The Hollywood Musical.* New York: St. Martin's Press, 1981.

————. *Movie Star: A Look at the Women Who Made Hollywood.* New York: St. Martin's Press, 1983.

————. *The Hollywood Studios: House Style in the Golden Age of the Movies.* New York: Knopf, 1988.

Morella, Joe and Edward Z. Epstein. *The Complete Films and Career of Judy Garland.* Secaucus, N.J.: Citadel Press, 1969.

Morris, Jan. *Sydney.* New York: Random House, 1992.

Murphy, George, with Victor Lasky. *"Say . . . Didn't You Used to Be George Murphy?"* City of publication unknown: Bartholomew House, 1970.

Otash, Fred. *Investigation Hollywood!* Chicago: Henry Regnery, 1976.

Paar, Jack. *P.S. Jack Paar.* New York: Doubleday, 1983.

Parsons, Louella O. *Tell It to Louella.* New York: G. P. Putnam's Sons, 1961.

Pasternak, Joe, as told to David Chandler. *Easy the Hard Way.* New York: G. P. Putnam's Sons, 1956.

Percy, William Alexander. *Lanterns on the Levee: Recollections of a Planter's Son.* New York: Knopf, 1941.

Pickus, Grace Graham. *In Love with Life in Lancaster: Hard Times, 1927–1932.* Rosamond, Calif.: Kern-Antelope Historical Society, 1983.

———. *A Page in the History of Antelope Valley: The Arthur F. Pickus Story.* Rosamond, Calif.: Kern-Antelope Historical Society, 1989.

Pittard, Mabel. *Rutherford County.* Edited by Robert E. Corlew III. Memphis: Memphis State University Press, 1984.

Pleasants, Henry. *The Great American Popular Singers.* New York: Simon & Schuster, 1974.

Powdermaker, Hortense. *Hollywood, The Dream Factory: An Anthropologist Looks at the Movie-makers.* Boston: Little Brown, 1950.

Powell, Michael. *A Life in Movies: An Autobiography.* New York: Knopf, 1987.

Prideaux, Tom, and the Editors of Time-Life Books. *The World of Whistler: 1834–1903.* New York: Time-Life Books, 1970.

Reed, Rex. *People Are Crazy Here.* New York: Dell, 1974.

Reeves, Thomas C. *The Life and Times of Joe McCarthy.* New York: Stein & Day, 1982.

Riva, Maria. *Marlene Dietrich by Her Daughter.* New York: Knopf, 1993.

Roazen, Paul. *Freud and His Followers.* New York: New American Library, 1976.

Robbins, Jhan. *Yul Brynner: The Inscrutable King.* New York: Dodd, Mead, 1987.

Rooney, Mickey. *i.e.: An Autobiography.* New York: G. P. Putnam's Sons, 1965.

———. *Life Is Too Short.* New York: Villard Books, 1991.

Rosenstein, Jaik. *Hollywood Leg Man.* Los Angeles: Madison Press, 1950.

Rosten, Leo C. *Hollywood: The Movie Colony, The Movie Makers.* New York: Harcourt, Brace and Co., 1941.

Rottsolk, James E. *Pines, Mines, and Lakes: The Story of Itasca County, Minnesota.* Grand Rapids, Minn.: Itasca County Historical Society, 1960.

Russell, Jane. *Jane Russell: My Path and My Detours.* New York: Franklin Watts, 1985.

St. Johns, Adela Rogers. *Some Are Born Great.* New York: Doubleday, 1974.

Sanders, Coyne Steven. *Rainbow's End: The Judy Garland Show.* New York: William Morrow, 1990.

Schary, Dore. *Heyday.* Boston: Little, Brown, 1979.

Schatz, Thomas. *Hollywood Genres: Formulas, Filmmaking, and the Studio System.* Philadelphia: Temple University Press, 1981.

————. *The Genius of the System: Hollywood Filmmaking in the Studio Era*. New York: Pantheon Books, 1988.

Schickel, Richard. *The Men Who Made the Movies*. New York: Atheneum, 1975.

Schuller, Gunther. *The Swing Era: The Development of Jazz, 1930–1945*. New York: Oxford University Press, 1989.

Seaman, Barbara. *Lovely Me: The Life of Jacqueline Susann*. New York: William Morrow, 1987.

Secunda, Victoria. *When You and Your Mother Can't Be Friends*. New York: Delacorte Press, 1990.

Selznick, David O. *Memo from David O. Selznick*. Rudy Behlmer, ed. New York: Viking Press, 1972.

Selznick, Irene Mayer. *A Private View*. New York: Knopf, 1983.

Sennett, Ted. *Hollywood Musicals*. New York: Harry N. Abrams, 1981.

Settle, Glen Allen. *The Antelopes Left and the Settle-ers [sic] Came*. Rosamond, Calif.: Kern-Antelope Historical Society, 1975.

————, ed. *Here Roamed the Antelope*. Rosamond, Calif.: Kern-Antelope Historical Society, 1963.

————, ed. *Along the Rails from Lancaster to Mojave*. Rosamond, Calif.: Kern-Antelope Historical Society, 1967.

————, ed. *Lancaster Celebrates a Century*. Lancaster, Calif.: City of Lancaster, 1983.

———— and Dorene B. Settle, eds. *Antelope Valley Pioneers*. Rosamond, Calif.: Kern-Antelope Historical Society, 1984.

Sharaff, Irene. *Broadway & Hollywood: Costumes Designed by Irene Sharaff*. New York: Van Nostrand Reinhold, 1976.

Shaw, Artie. *The Trouble with Cinderella: An Outline of Identity*. New York: Farrar, Straus and Young, 1952.

Shirer, William L. *20th Century Journey: A Memoir of a Life and the Times*. Boston: Little, Brown, 1990.

Silverman, Stephen M. *Dancing on the Ceiling: Stanley Donen and His Movies*. New York: Knopf, 1996.

Silvers, Phil, with Robert Saffron. *This Laugh Is on Me: The Phil Silvers Story*. Englewood Cliffs, N.J.: Prentice-Hall, 1973.

Skolsky, Sidney. *Don't Get Me Wrong—I Love Hollywood*. New York: Putnam, 1975.

Smith, Reid. *Majestic Middle Tennessee*. Prattville, Ala.: Paddle Wheel Publications, 1975.

Spada, James. *Peter Lawford: The Man Who Kept the Secrets*. New York: Bantam Books, 1991.

———— with Karen Swenson. *Judy and Liza*. New York: Doubleday, 1983.

Sperber, A. M., and Eric Lax. *Bogart.* New York: William Morrow, 1997.

Sperling, Cass Warner, and Cork Millner, with Jack Warner, Jr. *Hollywood Be Thy Name: The Warner Brothers Story.* Rocklin, Calif.: Prima Publishing, 1994.

Spitzer, Marian. *The Palace.* New York: Atheneum, 1969.

Stack, Robert, with Mark Evans. *Straight Shooting.* New York: Macmillan, 1980.

Starr, Kevin. *Material Dreams: Southern California Through the 1920s.* New York: Oxford University Press, 1990.

Steen, Mike. *Hollywood Speaks! An Oral History.* New York: G. P. Putnam's Sons, 1974.

Stein, Charles W., ed. *American Vaudeville: As Seen by Its Contemporaries.* New York: Knopf, 1984.

Susann, Jacqueline. *Valley of the Dolls.* New York: Bernard Geis Associates, 1966.

Swindell, Larry. *Spencer Tracy . . . A Biography.* New York: World Publishing, 1969.

Taylor, John Russell, and Arthur Jackson. *The Hollywood Musical.* New York: McGraw-Hill, 1971.

Thomas, Bob. *Astaire: The Man, the Dancer.* New York: St. Martin's Press, 1984.

Thomas, Tony, and Jim Terry, with Busby Berkeley. *The Busby Berkeley Book.* Greenwich, Conn.: New York Graphic Society, 1973.

Thomson, David. *Showman: The Life of David O. Selznick.* New York: Knopf, 1992.

Todd, Ann. *The Eighth Veil.* New York: G. P. Putnam's Sons, 1981.

Tormé, Mel. *The Other Side of the Rainbow: with Judy Garland on the Dawn Patrol.* New York: William Morrow, 1970.

————. *It Wasn't All Velvet.* New York: Viking, 1988.

Tornabene, Lyn. *Long Live the King: A Biography of Clark Gable.* New York: G. P. Putnam's Sons, 1976.

Turner, Lana. *Lana: The Lady, the Legend, the Truth.* New York: E. P. Dutton, 1982.

Valentino, Lou. *The Films of Lana Turner.* Secaucus, N.J.: Citadel Press, 1976.

Vermilye, Jerry. *The Films of the Thirties.* Secaucus, N.J.: Citadel Press, 1982.

Vidor, King. *King Vidor.* (Interview by Nancy Dowd and David Shepard; a Directors Guild of America Oral History.) Metuchen, N.J.: The Directors Guild of America and the Scarecrow Press, 1988.

Viertel, Peter. *Dangerous Friends: At Large with Hemingway and Huston in the Fifties.* New York: Doubleday, 1992.

Viertel, Salka. *The Kindness of Strangers.* New York: Holt, Rinehart and Winston, 1969.

Wagner, Walter. *You Must Remember This.* New York: G. P. Putnam's Sons, 1975.

Warner, Jack L., with Dean Jennings. *My First Hundred Years in Hollywood.* New York: Random House, 1965.

Watson, Thomas J. and Bill Chapman. *Judy: Portrait of an American Legend.* New York: McGraw-Hill, 1986.

Wayne, Jane Ellen. *Gable's Women.* New York: Prentice-Hall Press, 1987.

Whiting, Margaret, and Will Holt. *It Might as Well Be Spring: A Musical Autobiography.* New York: William Morrow, 1987.

Wiley, Mason and Damien Bona, Gail MacColl, ed. *Inside Oscar: The Unofficial History of the Academy Awards.* New York: Ballantine Books, 1986.

Wilk, Max. *They're Playing Our Song.* New York: Zoetrope, 1986.

Wilkerson, Tichi, and Marcia Borie. *The Hollywood Reporter: The Golden Years.* New York: Coward-McCann, 1984.

Woll, Allen L. *The Hollywood Musical Goes to War.* Chicago: Nelson-Hall, 1983.

Wood, L. H. *Geography of Michigan.* Kalamazoo, Mich.: Horton-Beimer Press, 1914.

Writers' Program, Work Projects Administration in the State of Minnesota. *The WPA Guide to the Minnesota Arrowhead Country.* 1941. Reprint, St. Paul: Minnesota Historical Society Press, 1988.

Zimmerman, Karl. *Santa Fe Streamliners.* New York: Quadrant Press, 1987.

Acknowledgments

Biography, like the making of movies that has occupied so many of the preceding chapters, is a collaborative art, and many people contributed to my life of Judy Garland. So many, indeed, contributed so much that it is hard to know with whom to begin. But perhaps it would be most appropriate if I expressed my gratitude first to Francis Gallagher, to whom I owe an immense debt. A Garland fan of many years, Gallagher, who died just as I was writing finis to my long project, was an astute student of Judy and her works, and he opened the door to the larger world of Garlandiana. Once inside, I found many welcoming hands. Charlotte Stevenson gave me scrapbooks that chronicled, in loving detail, several decades of Judy's life. Ron Marcellin volunteered clippings from the New York newspapers. Ruth Ginther sent me tape recordings of just about every song Judy ever sang, as well as interviews and other talks. Ron O'Brien also provided valuable information, and so did Roslyn Portnoy and Rick Sommers. In England, Ken Sephton pointed to important sources, and Philip Hoare took time from writing his own biographies to research the London newspapers.

Other writers also gave me generous assistance. Barry Kehoe, who, with David Dahl, wrote *Young Judy,* an account of Judy's early life, copied his notes and interviews for me; James Spada, the co-author of *Judy and Liza*, handed me several important leads; Fred Lawrence Guiles, the author of *Tyrone Power,* offered me information about Judy's romance with Power that he did not use in his own book; Charles Higham, the author of many biographies, told me of Judy's travails in Australia; and Roy Moseley led me to sources in both London and Los Angeles.

Librarians also extended me the courtesies so common in their admirable profession. Ned Comstock and his associates at the Department of Special Collections of the University of Southern California allowed me many days with the Freed and Warner Bros. collections. Sam Gill and his colleagues at the Margaret Herrick Library of the Academy of Motion Picture Arts and Sciences gave me access to their priceless resources. In Dallas, Ronald L. Davis opened up the oral history collection of Southern Methodist University. In New York, I relied on the libraries of Columbia University and the Lincoln Center Library of the Performing Arts. In Bridgehampton, where I live, I received more than a little help from the staff of the Hampton Library, which uncomplainingly sent to other libraries for many of the specialized books I needed.

Barbara Shalvey transcribed dozens of hours of tape-recorded interviews, as she had done with my previous biography of Truman Capote, and patrolled the New York libraries for me. Steven Varni also provided valuable assistance in New York, as did Paul Scheifer in Los Angeles. In Murfreesboro, Tennessee, I relied on Virginia Wilkinson, and in Superior, Wisconsin, Barry Singer was greatly helpful. In Grand Rapids, Minnesota, John Kelsch, the head of the Judy Garland Children's Museum, gave me many hours, and so did his wife, Elizabeth, who photocopied hundreds of pages of the two local newspapers for me. In Lancaster, California, Grace Pickus performed the same onerous task and also provided me with the wisdom of her own long experience in that desert community.

Tom Green, who had not talked publicly about Judy since her death, candidly filled many gaps in my narrative. Mickey Deans, Judy's last husband, generously gave me days of his time, as well as his hospitality. Although they were writing their own stories of life with Judy, Sid Luft and Mark Herron, Judy's third and fourth husbands, did consent to see me, and I am grateful for their courtesy. John Carlyle gave me many hours and many leads, and Leonard Gershe, a man of many talents, gave me not only valuable insight but the title of my book.

My agent, Helen Brann, patiently steered me through shark-filled waters and brought me at last to that most excellent of editors, Robert Loomis. The entire Random House team, indeed, has reminded me that excellence still exists in publishing, and I want to thank Benjamin Dreyer, who saw my book through production; Jolanta Benal, who copyread my manuscript and whose keen eye saved me from some embarrassing infelicities; James Lambert, who gave my book its elegant design; Robbin Schiff, who came up with such a beguiling cover; and Bob Loomis's able assistant, Barbé Hammer. Sarah Longacre, an independent picture researcher, also worked tirelessly to find just the right illustrations.

I regret that space allows me to no more than mention the many others who so kindly helped me, often for many tiring hours: Tempe Adams, Briley Adcock, Ray Aghayan, Gene Allen, June Allyson, Patty Andrews, Steven M. L. Aronson, Annie Armour, William Asher, Erving Austin, Frank Avent, Jean Bach, Jim Bacon, Jim Bailey, Janet Bank, Paul Barnes, Nancy Barr, Helen Barrow, Lionel Bart, Michael Benson, Vera Bentz, Carl Bergman, Katherine Berkeland, Mary Jo Beyerstedt, Jeanne Biggers, Bill Binet, Betsy

Blair, Ralph Blane, Dirk Bogarde, Henri Bollinger, Norman Borine, Eddie Bracken, Irving Brecher, Betty Bridgewater, Donald Brooks, Rand Brooks, Rock Brynner, Randall F. Buckley, Chuck Bullidow, Joey Bushkin, Carleton Carpenter, Lucille Ryman Carroll, Ronald Carter, John Cebalo, Betty Chaplin, Saul Chaplin, Frank Chapman, Elizabeth N. Chitty, Jim Christenson, Larry Chrysler, Charles Cinnamon, Shirley Hadfield Clitherow, Charles Cochran, Joseph J. Cohn, Claudette Colbert, Lester Coleman, Marjorie Collier, David Patrick Columbia, Betty Comden, Ned Comstock, Mrs. John Connor, Tom Cooper, Alma Cousteline, Mart Crowley, Hume Cronyn, Marilyn Cryder, David Dahl, Ida Dahl, Allan Davis, Edward N. DeBaer, Catherine Deeney, Gloria DeHaven, Anne Boyce Denslow, Armand Deutsch, Jackie Dingmann, Henry Ivan Dorsett, Eleanor Downing, Kenny DuMain, Dominick Dunne, Milt Ebbins, Buddy Ebsen, Allan Eichler, Cecil Elmgreen, Carol Erickson, Margaret Erickson, Michael Feinstein, Dorothy Feist, George Feltonstein, Dick Fisher, Tucker Fleming, John Fricke, Gilbert Galla, John Gass, Ed Geller, Burt Geving, Cecil Gibb, Margaret Gibson, Harry D. Glyer, Milton Goldman, Gilbert Golla, Ethel Gorence, Derek Granger, Kathryn Grayson, Jack Grinnage, Howard Gronquist, C. Z. Guest, Fred Guiles, Frances Gumm, Norma Gurba, Flo Haley, William Harbach, Lee Ann Harry, Stephen Harvey, Peter Lind Hayes, Steve Henderson, Katharine Hepburn, Peggy Hessevick, C. David Heymann, Darryl Hickman, George Hoare, Maude Holman, Leonora Hornblow, Lena Horne, Jean Howard, James K. Huhta, Florence Huntley, Bob Irvine, David Jackson, Phoebe Jacobs, Al (James) Jennings, Evie Johnson, Jimmy Jones, Bob Jorgen, Stefan Kanfer, Lawrence Kaufman, Doug Kelly, Hilary Knight, Stanley Kramer, Nita Krebs, Miles Kreuger, Maurice L. Kusell, John Lahr, Eleanor Lambert, Gavin Lambert, Richard Lamparski, Burton Lane, Omer Lavallée, Anne (Shirley) Lederer, Harriet Lee, Peggy Lee, Janet Leigh, Wendy Leigh, June Levant, Peter Levinson, Mort Lindsey, Eileen Linton, Marguerite Lloyd, Archie Lofberg, Gene Loyd, Wilber Lundy, Andrew Lytle, Tom MacLeod, Mary MacDonald, Thomas Macfie, Stephen MacLean, George Maharis, Joe Mankiewicz, Rosemary Mankiewicz, Abby Mann, Dorothy Manners, Ronald Marcellin, Jerry Maren, Joe G. Marino, Frank Martin, Hugh Martin, Leslie Martinson, Samuel Marx, Dona Massin, Esteban Matison, Carol Matthau, Rita Maxwell, Ada Brown McLean, Ruth Mechaneck, Kay Meehan, Connie Menninger, Ken Merrill, John Meyer, Ann Miller, Ina Mary Miller, Sidney Miller, James Milne, John Milne, Jr., Robert Milne, Joe Mitchenson, William Moran III, Dorothy Walsh Morrison, Ronald Neame, Robert Nesbitt, Christopher Nickens, Dorothy Tuttle Nitch, Dorothy Oakes, Sheila O'Bannon, Margaret O'Brien, Virginia O'Brien, Irma Ootes, Janis Paige, Linton Parker, Ken Partridge, William Patterson, Richard Paxton,

Margaret Pellegrini, Buddy Pepper, LeRoy Percy, Gilbert Perkins, Woolf Phillips, Ben Piazza, Arthur Pickus, Grace Pickus, Mrs. Homer Pittard, Roslyn Portnoy, Elva Price, Carole Prietto, Walter Primmer, Marcella Rabwin, Alice Ratcliffe, Harry Raybould, Dorothy Raye, Christopher Reardon, W. M. Redman, Galen Reed, Jr., Burt Rhodes, Annie Roberts, Gloria Romanoff, Mabel Ronzheimer, Mickey Rooney, Glen Rose, Annie Ross, Edith Roth, Harry Rubin, Ann Rutherford, Paul Sand, John L. Saxhaug, Janet Schebendach, Scott Schechter, Jackie Scott, Mike Selsman, Ken Sephton, Glen A. Settle, Robert Settle, Nick Sevano, Irene Sharaff, Artie Shaw, James Shade, William L. Shirer, George Sidney, Lillian Sidney, Sylvia Sidney, Mayo Simon, Scottie Singer, Ralph Spielman, John Springer, Robert Stack, Harry H. Stein, David Stenn, Marti Stevens, Paula Stone, Irma Story, Ann Straus, Robert Street, Elaine Stritch, Jessica Tandy, Dace Taube, Bill Thomas, Brenda Thomas, Connie Thompson, Johnny Thompson, Martha Todd, Charles Triplett, William Tuttle, Billy C. F. Tweedie, Arthur Unger, Robert Vogel, Watson Webb, Matthew West, Edward A. White, Margaret Whiting, Lucy Whitesell, Esther Williams, Charles Williamson, Francis Willis, Alberta Gum Wilson, Lois Wakefield Wirta, Lana Wood, Thelma Wood, Wallace Worsley, Michael Woulfe, Michael Wright, Pam Wulk, Ned Wynn.

Index

Photo Credits

Aquarius, Hastings, U.K.: Frank and Ethel Gumm (p. 2); collection of the author: Gumm sisters (p. 29), Judy with Jack Haley, Ray Bolger and Bert Lahr in *The Wizard of Oz* (p. 90), Judy and Mickey Rooney in *Babes on Broadway* (p. 176), Judy, Jack Warner and Sid Luft at the *Star Is Born* premiere (p. 323), Judy with Mark Herron (p. 380); Minnesota Historical Society, St. Paul, Minn.: Judy and Ethel on a visit to Grand Rapids (p. 32); Photofest, New York: Judy and Deanna Durbin (p. 60), Judy, Hedy Lamarr and Lana Turner (p. 136), Judy, Mickey Rooney, Busby Berkeley and Louis B. Mayer (p. 143), Judy and David Rose (p. 150), Joe Mankiewicz (p. 180), Judy and Vincente Minnelli on the set of *The Pirate* (p. 228), Judy and Fred Astaire in *Easter Parade* (p. 239), four *Annie Get Your Gun* costume shots (p. 256), "Get Happy" (p. 268), Judy and James Mason on the *Star Is Born* set (p. 306), Judy with Frank Sinatra and Liza Minnelli (p. 346), Judy and Liza Minnelli at the opening of *Flora, the Red Menace* (p. 402); Archive Photos, New York: "Trembling lips . . ." (p. 116), Liza Minnelli and Peter Allen (p. 405); Corbis, New York: Judy, Mickey Rooney and Ann Rutherford (p. 119); Camera Press/ Retna, New York: Judy and Vincente Minnelli wedding (p. 204); Cornell Capa/ *Life* Magazine/© Time Inc.: Judy falls at the Palladium (p. 280); Buddy Pepper: Judy en route to England (p. 289); Evie Johnson: Judy, Clifton Webb, Merle Oberon, Van Johnson and Noël Coward (p. 332), Judy with Janet Gaynor (p. 336); photo no. 5T-505-7-62 in the John F. Kennedy Library, 28 Nov. 1962: Judy in the Oval Office (p. 350); Bob Willoughby, Vence, France: Judy and Sid Luft in a London recording studio (p. 358), Judy with Dirk Bogarde and Lorna and Joey Luft (p. 366); Burton Berinsky, New York: Judy at the Palace (p. 414); *The Evening Standard* 3/14/69: Judy with Mickey Deans (p. 418)

ABOUT THE AUTHOR

GERALD CLARKE is the author of *Capote,* the much-acclaimed, bestselling biography of Truman Capote. He has also written for many magazines, including *Esquire, Architectural Digest,* and *Time,* where for many years he was a senior writer. A native of Los Angeles and a graduate of Yale, he now lives in Bridgehampton, in eastern Long Island, New York.